Economic Performance in the Americas

Economic Performance in the Americas

The Role of the Service Sector in Brazil, Mexico and the USA

Nanno Mulder

CEPII, Centre for International Economics, Paris, France

Edward Elgar

Cheltenham, UK • Northampton, MA, USA

Published by
Edward Elgar Publishing Limited
Glensanda House
Montpellier Parade
Cheltenham
Glos GL50 1UA
UK

Edward Elgar Publishing, Inc.
136 West Street
Suite 202
Northampton
Massachusetts 01060
USA

A catalogue record for this book is available from the British Library

Library of Congress Cataloguing in Publication Data
Mulder, Nanno, 1967–
Economic performance in the Americas: the role of the service sector in Brazil, Mexico and the USA/ Nanno Mulder.
p. cm.
Includes index.
1. Service industries—Brazil. 2. Service industries—Mexico. 3. Service industries—United States. 4. Brazil—Economic conditions—1945– 5. Mexico—Economic conditions—1918– 6. United States—Economic conditions—1945– I. Title.

HD9985.B72 M85 2002
338.4'097—dc21

2002021388

ISBN 1 84064 547 4

Printed and bound in Great Britain by Biddles Ltd
www.biddles.co.uk

Contents

List of Figures *vii*
List of Tables *ix*
Acknowledgements *xiii*

1. **Introduction** 1

2. **Structural Change and the Shift to Services** 7
   Introduction 7
   Changes in Sectoral Composition and the Process of Development 11
   The Larger Share of Services in Final and Intermediate Demand 14
   Why the Service Share Grew Faster in Employment than in GDP? 22
   Overall Trends and Compositional Changes 27

3. **Measurement of Real Service Output** 31
   Measurement of Service Output 31
   Research on Real Output Measurement 33
   Real Output Measures by Category of Service 35

4. **Transport and Communications** 43
   Transport and Communications in the last two Centuries 43
   Comparison of Output and Productivity Levels in 1975 58
   Reconciliation of Census and National Accounts Data 75
   Labour Productivity 77
   Conclusion 77

5. **Wholesale and Retail Trade** 83
   Long-term trends 83
   Determinants of Demand for Distributive Services 92
   Measurement of Output and Productivity in Distributive Services 103
   Value Added and Employment in 1975/77 107
   Comparative Output and Productivity Levels 108

6. **Financial Services** 123
   Long-term Development 123
   Determinants of Long-term Development 128
   Output and Productivity Levels 143

7. **Health Care** 155
Introduction 155
Long-term Development 157
Determinants of Long-term Development 166
Output and Productivity Levels 176

8. **Education** 187
Introduction 187
Long-term Development 188
Determinants of Long-term Development 192
Output and Productivity Levels 203

9. **Commodity-producing Sectors** 213
Agriculture 213
Mining 214
Manufacturing 215
Construction 236

10. **Comparative Performances of the Service and Commodity Sectors** 241
Introduction 241
The Impact of Sectoral Change on Labour Productivity 242
The Contribution of Labour Reallocation to Overall Economic Growth 247
Unit Value Ratios 248
Labour Productivity Levels, 1975 251
Comparative Labour Productivity Performance, 1950–96 254
Impact of Differences in Production Structure on Productivity 258
Conclusion 259

Appendix A: Population and Employment 263

Appendix B: GDP Indices and Levels of GDP 267

Appendix C: Exchange Rates and Prices 271

Appendix D: The Service Sector 273

Appendix E: Reconciling Census and National Accounts Data 277

References 283

Statistical References 301

Index 307

Figures

2.1	Share of Goods and Services in Final Demand, 1970–96	15
2.2	Share of Goods and Services in Intermediate Demand, 1970–96	20
4.1	Rail Passenger Traffic (passenger km) per Capita, 1873–1993 (Semi-logarithmic Scale)	48
4.2	Rail Freight Traffic (ton km) per Capita, 1873–93	48
4.3	Labour Productivity in Transport and Communications, 1950–96 (US = 100)	78
5.1	Distribution's Share of Total Employment, 1950–96	84
5.2	Labour Productivity in Distributive Services, 1950–96 (USA = 100)	118
6.1	Share of Financial Services in GDP at Current Prices, 1950–96	126
6.2	Employment in Financial Services as Percentage of the Total, 1950–96	127
6.3	Trends in Price Level, Brazil and Mexico, 1880–1996	137
6.4	Investment as Percentage of GDP in Current Prices, 1950–94	142
6.5	Labour Productivity in Banking and Insurance, 1950–96 (USA = 100)	151
7.1	Labour Productivity in Health Care, 1950–96 (USA = 100)	184
8.1	Labour Productivity in Education, 1950–96 (USA = 100)	209
9.1	Indices of Value Added, Employment and Labour Productivity (1970 = 100)	217
9.2	Trends in Brazilian and Mexican Relative Price Levels in Manufacturing	231
9.3	Labour Productivity Levels in Manufacturing, 1970–98 (USA = 100)	232
10.1	Labour Productivity Levels by Sector, 1975	242
10.2	Comparative Price Levels, Brazil/USA and Mexico/USA, 1950–96	250
10.3	Value Added per Person Engaged, Brazil/USA, 1950–96 (USA = 100)	255
10.4	Value Added per Person Engaged, Mexico/USA, 1950–96 (USA = 100)	256

Tables

2.1 Structure of Employment by Sector of the Economy, 1900–96 8
2.2 Structure of GDP at Current Prices by Sector of the Economy, 1900–96 9
2.3 Income Distribution: Gini Coefficients and Quintile Ratios, 1950–91 17
2.4 Population Structure, 1950–90 (Percentage of Total Population) 18
2.5 Labour Productivity Growth by Sector, 1950–96 23
3.1 Real Output Measures by Category of Service 36
4.1 Length of Railway Line and Line per Head of Population, 1873–1993 44
4.2 Transport Cost Savings as a Percentage of GDP due to Railways, 1890–1913 46
4.3 Stock of Registered Vehicles and Vehicles Relative to Population, 1929–93 51
4.4 Civil Aviation, 1927–93 54
4.5 Number of Post Offices, Pieces of Mail and Telegraph Messages per 100,000 population, 1880–1993 55
4.6 Number of Telephones (000s) and Telephones per Capita, 1907–93 56
4.7 Value Added and Employment in Transport and Communications, 1975 65
4.8 Length of Average Passenger Trips in km, Freight Hauls in km and Population Density, 1975 66
4.9 Adjustment for Terminal Services after Correction for Population Density, 1975 68
4.10 Quantity Relatives Before and After Adjustments for Terminal Services and Quality Differences, 1975 69
4.11 Quality Indicators for Transport and Communications, 1975 71
4.12 Unit Value Ratios for Transport and Communications, 1975 75
4.13 Reconciliation of Census and National Accounts Data, 1975 76
4.14 Labour Productivity in Transport and Communications, 1975 78
5.1 Wholesale and Retail Trade Establishments, 1929–93 85

5.2	Number of Establishments in Wholesale and Retail Trade per Capita and Average Size, 1975/77	106
5.3	Ratios of Purchased Goods to Sales, Other Inputs to Sales and Value Added to Sales in Brazilian, Mexican and US Distribution, 1975/77	106
5.4	Value Added and Employment in Wholesale and Retail Trade, Brazil, Mexico and the USA, 1975/77	108
5.5	ICP Reweighted Fisher PPPs for Gross Value Added, Distribution	110
5.6	ICP Fisher PPPs for Sales, ICOP Fisher UVRs for Purchases and Other Inputs and Implicit Fisher UVRs for Value Added, Distribution, 1975 prices	111
5.7	Reconciliation of Census and National Accounts Data, 1975/77	115
5.8	Labour Productivity in Distribution, Double and Single Deflation Fisher Results, 1975/77	117
6.1	Banking Establishments, 1950–92	128
6.2	Average Annual Growth of Prices (Per Cent), 1880–1996	136
6.3	Nominal and Real Interest Rates, 1950–96	138
6.4	Output in Banking and Insurance, 1975	147
6.5	Unit Value Ratios for Banking and Insurance, 1975	149
6.6	Labour Productivity in Financial Services, as a Percentage of the USA, 1975	150
7.1	Health Outcomes, 1960 and 1990	156
7.2	Infant Mortality and Inputs, 1903–50	164
7.3	Public Expenditure on Health Care as a Percentage of GDP, 1955–94	164
7.4	Value Added and Employment as a Percentage of Total GDP and Employment, Health Care, 1950–96	165
7.5	Inputs in Health Care, 1965–92	166
7.6	Population Characteristics, Socio-economic Development, 1950–90	168
7.7	Value Added and Employment in Health Care, 1980, 1987/88	177
7.8	Quality of Health Care	181
7.9	Unit Value Ratios for Health Care, 1980, 1987/88	182
7.10	Labour Productivity in Health Care, 1980, 1987/88	183
8.1	Number of Students by Level of Education, Percentage of the Age Group and Number of Pupils per Teacher, 1900–90	189
8.2	Indicators of the Quality of Education, 1980, 1987/88	191
8.3	Share of Illiterates in Total Population (Per Cent), 1890–1950	192
8.4	Educational Attainment of Working Population (Percentage Distribution), 1970–90	193
8.5	Public Expenditure on Education as a Percentage of Total GDP, 1950–90	193

8.6 Value Added and Employment as a Percentage of Total GDP and Employment, Education, 1950–96 194
8.7 Value Added and Employment in Education, 1980, 1987/88 204
8.8 Unit Value Ratios for Education, 1980, 1987/88 207
8.9 Labour Productivity in Education, 1980, 1987/88 208
9.1 Gross Value of Output, Inputs, Value Added, Employment and Labour Productivity in Agriculture, 1975 214
9.2 1975 Benchmark Results for Mining: Wieringa and Maddison (1985) and Houben (1990) 215
9.3 Number of Product Matches, Unit Value Ratios and Percentage of Matched Sales, 1975 221
9.4 Number of Product Matches, Unit Value Ratios, Coefficients of Variation and Percentage of Matched Sales, 1985 and 1988 226
9.5 Comparison of Census and National Accounts Estimates of Value Added and Employment, 1975/80/85/87/88 227
9.6 Relative Levels of Labour Productivity, Value Added, Employment and Prices, Brazil/USA and Mexico/USA, 1975, 1985 and 1988 (USA = 100) 229
9.7 Extrapolation of Relative Productivity Levels from 1985/88 to 1975 and Comparison with Results of van Ark and Maddison (USA = 100) 235
9.8 Relative Levels of Unit Labour Costs, 1985 and 1988 (USA = 100) 235
9.9 Value Added, PPPs, Employment and Comparative Productivity Levels by Major Branch of Construction, 1975, 1975/77 (1975 prices) 237
10.1 Relative Levels of Labour Productivity for each Sector Compared to the Total Economy (Current Prices), 1900–96 243
10.2 Decomposition of Labour Productivity Growth: Intrasectoral Effect, Static and Dynamic Shift Effects, 1950–96 245
10.3 Sectoral Contributions to Labour Productivity Growth, 1950–96 245
10.4 Sources of GDP Growth, 1950–94 247
10.5 Unit Value Ratios by Sector and the Laspeyres Paasche Spread, 1975 249
10.6 UVRs, Productivity Levels and Relative Prices, 1975 252
10.7 Decomposition of Labour Productivity Differences, 1950–96 259
E.1 Labour Productivity in Small Establishments as a Percentage of that in large Establishments, Brazil and Mexico, 1975 279
E.2 Imputation of Value Added in Activity Omitted in Censuses and Adjusted Estimate of Total Value Added, Brazil, 1975 280
E.3 Imputation of Value Added in Activity Omitted in Censuses and Adjusted Estimate of Total Value Added, Mexico, 1975 281

Acknowledgements

My research has benefited enormously from the help of various academics and statisticians. I am particularly grateful to Eduardo Pereira Nunes and Regis Bonelli in Brazil, Victor Urquidi, Enrique Hernandez Laos and Ruud Buitelaar in Mexico, and Al Madansky and Micheal Ward in the USA.

I thank the members of the Groningen Growth and Development Centre, Bart van Ark, André Hofman, Remco Kouwenhoven, Dirk Pilat, Marcel Timmer and Adam Szirmai, whose comments and suggestions have been very useful. I acknowledge in particular Bart van Ark's advice on the adaptation of the ICOP approach to services and his suggestions on Chapters 2 and 3. I also very much appreciate the comments from Ronald Albers, Bernard Chane Kune, Niels Hermes, Nina Kousnetzoff, Sarah Pressman, Isabelle Rabaud, Jan Pieter Smits, Daan van Soest, Cor van Stralen and Albert de Vaal. I am grateful for comments received at seminars at the Brazilian Institute for Economic Research (IPEA), Institute of Social Studies, Inter-American Development Bank, University of Chicago, Latin America University for Social Sciences (FLACSO), University of Illinois at Urbana-Champaign; the NBER conference 'International and Interarea Comparisons of Prices, Income and Output' and at meetings of the International Association for Research in Income and Wealth. I thank Edwin Evers for his editorial help, and Laure Boivin for her excellent help in the layout of the text. Thanks to Sylvie Montout and Luis Peres Lopes for letting me use the fruits of our research.

I owe thanks to the CEPII and in particular to Michel Fouquin and Colette Herzog, for having provided me with the opportunity to finish this work.

My wife Maritza and my son Sebastian made life around the writing of this book very pleasant! I also very much appreciate the support from my parents, Lambert and Iet Mulder, and other family members – Helma, Niels, Roos and Joop.

I am most grateful to Angus Maddison for his guidance throughout all the stages of this research. His challenges and ideas have been my main source of inspiration and satisfaction. I value his extensive and timely comments on many drafts.

Finally, I thank the Dutch Foundation for Scientific Research (NWO) for the funding of this research.

1. Introduction

This study presents a detailed analysis of the development and performance of the economies of Brazil, Mexico and the USA from 1950 to 1996. Particular attention is paid to the service sectors, for which a longer historical perspective is provided stretching back well into the nineteenth century. It begins with an analysis of the increased orientation of the three economies towards the service sector. This common process hides large differences between the two Latin American countries and the USA in terms of the *types* of service activities that gained importance, as well as the *forces* that have made them the dominant sector in all three countries. The study continues with an overview of the measurement of real output in services necessary to compare the performances between the three countries. Most of the remaining part deals with a number of service branches in detail, showing their development and performance over the long run, and the underlying causes of success or failure. The performance in the commodity sectors is also assessed, in particular in manufacturing. The study concludes by confronting the service and commodity sector performances to evaluate the benefits and costs of structural change.

This study was undertaken as part of the research programme of the International Comparison of Output and Productivity (ICOP) project of the University of Groningen. Most ICOP studies focus on agriculture, mining and manufacturing. As the service sector has been the biggest sector in high- and most middle-income economies for several decades, there was clearly an important gap to be filled, even though in this area measurement problems are more severe than in the commodity sectors.

Pilat (1994) was the first ICOP author to include some rough comparisons of output and productivity in services for Korea/USA and Japan/USA. The study is the first to apply the ICOP approach to a large range of service sectors. The methodology for international comparisons in transport and communications and wholesale and retail trade was further developed by van Ark *et al.* (1999), who compared five member countries of the Organisation for Economic Cooperation and Development (OECD). Van Ark and Monnikhof (2000) extended these comparisons to 24 countries for transport and communications and 19 countries for trade.[1]

This study covers the three biggest economies in the Western hemisphere. The USA was selected because it is the world's largest economy, has the highest productivity levels and is the major locus of innovation in services. Brazil and Mexico are the largest countries in Latin America, ranking tenth and twelfth among the world's two hundred or more economies in 1997. As for population, Brazil was the sixth largest country and Mexico the eleventh in that year. The three countries combined represented 25 per cent of world output and 9 per cent of world population in 1997. They are also countries for which there have already been major ICOP studies on relative levels of performance in the commodity sector.[2]

From 1950 to 1982 Brazil and Mexico experienced rapid growth of gross domestic product (GDP) per capita and a major change in the sectoral composition of their economies. During this period the share of service employment increased from 26 to about 45 per cent, mostly at the expense of agriculture. In the relatively depressed period that followed, service shares grew another 12 points.

To evaluate the performance of these economies, a focus is made on productivity growth, which is the most reliable measure for assessing potential changes in economic welfare. The focus is on labour productivity and leaves aside capital and total factor productivity. Labour productivity is measured by value added per person engaged. The emphasis on this partial indicator was inevitable due to lack of data on capital inputs by sector in Brazil and Mexico, but in most services labour is in any case the main production factor.

International productivity comparisons require a conversion factor to translate value added in different currencies into a common unit. The exchange rate reflects at best the relative price of goods and services entering international trade and is generally a poor proxy for measuring prices of non-tradables. Even for traded goods and services, exchange rates are often not representative of relative values due to exchange controls, international capital flows and trade barriers.

Purchasing power parities (PPPs) are an alternative conversion factor. Expenditure PPPs are based on private consumption, investment and government expenditure. These have been used by several authors to compare output and productivity (Hernandez Laos, 1994; and others, see Maddison and van Ark, 1994 for a longer list).

The first major international comparison of final expenditure was done by Clark (1940), comparing 29 countries. The pioneering study by Gilbert and Kravis (1954) stimulated international comparisons by supplying more sophisticated purchasing power converters. Kravis, Heston and Summers developed the expenditure approach further within the International Comparisons Project (ICP) from the 1960s onwards. Their 1975 edition, in which they covered 34 countries, was the *magnum opus* of ICP (Kravis *et al.*, 1982). The ICP work was taken up by mainly Eurostat and the OECD who currently compare prices every three years. Other recent ICP comparisons are carried out by economic commissions of the United Nations for Asia, the Middle East and Latin America. The most comprehensive round is 1993 which covers almost one hundred countries.

Expenditure PPPs can be used for total economy comparisons of per capita income and labour productivity (van Ark and McGuckin, 1999). However, their application in the sectoral approach raises several problems. As expenditure values do not only include the production value of the industry in question but also the added values of industries further down the chain, the PPP needs to be adjusted for transport and distribution margins and taxes; see Jorgenson and Kuroda (1990) for Japan *vis-à-vis* USA, and Lee and Tang (1999) for Canada *vis-à-vis* USA. The PPPs also need to be corrected to exclude the relative prices of imported goods and include the prices of exported goods. Hooper (1996) adjusted expenditure PPPs for margins and import and export prices, but he recognises that the latter adjustments require strong assumptions. Finally, expenditure PPPs exclude intermediate sectors like mining, freight transport, trade and business services, which are 'disguised' and embodied in final expenditure. Another difference is in the basic source material: ICP uses special surveys whereas ICOP draws on information from production censuses and national accounts permitting cross-checks which are not possible with ICP (van Ark, 1993). Hence the use of these 'proxy' PPPs is not unambiguous.

The method preferred here is the industry of origin approach, as pioneered by Rostas (1948) and Paige and Bombach (1959). This approach proposes two ways to compare real production across countries: (a) direct comparisons of real quantities (litres, tons, units), and (b) conversion of industry output in a common currency with a factor that reflects across country differences in producer prices. The two methods yield the same results if all output is covered. In practice, however, the methods provide often different results because of differences in sampling, weighting and coverage of output. With incomplete coverage, method (a) assumes the quantity relative of matched output and method (b) the price relative of matched output representative for the quantity and price relatives of non-matched output, respectively. For four decades most studies used the currency conversion method, as this method allows a larger part of output to be covered than using quantity ratios. Physical quantities are still used for comparisons in agriculture, mining and some service industries such as transport and communications (van Ark and Timmer, 2001).

This study contains a number of novelties. It surveys the literature on the increased service orientation of high- and middle-income economies and the driving forces. For Brazil, Mexico and the USA a comprehensive overview is given of the developments of major parts of the service sector in the nineteenth and twentieth centuries, as well as the causes of its delayed development in Latin American countries. It reviews previously used measures of output and productivity in services, and presents new yardsticks. Indicators are developed to account for quality differences between countries. Value added in the unregistered sector in the benchmark year is estimated and confronted with official figures. Finally, the comparative results for services are compared with those of the commodity-producing sectors to provide a comprehensive assessment of productivity differences between countries, and to identify areas where catch-up was quickest.

The subsequent chapters are organised as follows. Chapter 2 shows that since 1950 different service activities were responsible for the growing weights of the service sector in the three economies. In Brazil and Mexico distribution, transport and non-market services (education, health care and government services) grew most rapidly compared to business services in the USA. Moreover, different forces shaped the increased service orientation. In Brazil and Mexico the increased demand for education and health care and lagging productivity growth were the main drivers. The latter originated from the rapid pace of urbanisation and the related accumulation of informal labour in service activities such as street-vending and personal services. In the USA the expansion resulted from the rise in the intermediate demand for services as well as the 'cost disease', that is the rising relative unit labour costs and lagging productivity growth in services relative to the goods sector.

To assess the productivity performance, the industry of origin approach is used which requires producer prices at the most detailed level possible. In general these prices are obtained implicitly by dividing gross revenues by the quantity of produced services. Quantity information is readily available for most commodity sectors, but for only few service industries. Moreover, in services it is often unclear what exactly is being produced. Chapter 3 reviews for each service category the guidelines of the System of National Accounts 1993, the practices of national accounts in OECD countries, yardsticks proposed by other studies and finally the measures adopted here.

Several service branches are analysed in more detail in Chapters 4 to 8: transport, communications, wholesale and retail trade, banking, insurance and real estate, health care and education. These branches were chosen on the basis of their relative importance in terms of employment and GDP and the availability of data to measure output. The other service industries were regrouped in a residual 'other services', and include entertainment and recreation services, other business services, hotels and restaurants, legal services, personal services, repair services, social and miscellaneous services.

The relatively backward position of services in Brazil and Mexico in 1950 is explained by their sluggish development in the preceding century. In the nineteenth century, for example, the USA experienced major improvements in transport, first by extending its road network, followed by the expansion of canals, and, most important, by the construction of a huge network of railways from the 1840s onwards. In Brazil and Mexico, transport conditions did not improve until the arrival of railways in these countries several decades later than in the USA. High transport costs constrained their economic development. Railways introduced enormous savings, ranging from 6 to 39 per cent of GDP.[3] Other service branches also developed slowly in the Latin American countries.

Since 1950 rising per capita incomes, industrialisation and urbanisation has accelerated the development of the service sector in Brazil and Mexico. From 1950 to 1982 Brazil's labour productivity performance relative to that of the USA somewhat improved in finance, transport and communications, but stagnated in other services. In Mexico, distribution, finance and other services showed some catch-up with US productivity levels in the same period. Since 1982 relative productivity has fallen in almost all service industries in Brazil and Mexico.

Chapters 4 to 8 give a number of reasons which explain the relatively slow catch-up or stagnation of Brazilian and Mexican services in the post-war period. These include excessive regulation in transport and distribution, and the lack of incentives for productivity improvements in health care and education, and in public enterprises in transport and communications. High inflation constrained the development of the financial sector in Mexico, while it had the opposite effect in Brazil. Poverty substantially deprived the productivity performance of the service sector, as most informal and underemployed workers are concentrated in this sector.

To put the performances of the service sectors into perspective, Chapter 9 presents the achievements of the commodity sector in the three countries. For agriculture, mining and manufacturing, relative levels of output and labour productivity are presented for 1975. For manufacturing, benchmark comparisons for 1985 and 1988 are also introduced. In 1975, labour productivities in agriculture, mining and manufacturing were 6, 45 and 46 per cent of the US level. In Mexico, the relative levels in the same branches were 10, 39 and 25 per cent. The extrapolated results for 1950–96 show that the performances of Brazilian and Mexican agriculture stagnated relative to that of the USA. In the Latin American countries mining showed fast catch-up, in particular in the 1970s; this trend was reversed from the mid-1980s onwards. Brazilian manufacturing productivity relative to its US counterpart improved from 1950–77, after which its relative performance fell until the

1990s when it stabilised. In contrast, Mexico's relative manufacturing performance was stable from 1950–82, after which it fell.

The concluding chapter confronts the productivity performances of the commodity and the service sectors. Until 1982 the two Latin countries showed a modest catch-up with US productivity levels in the service sector, but their relative performance worsened later. In Brazil and Mexico, the relative performance in the service sectors after 1950 was slightly better than that in their secondary sectors, but much better than in their primary sectors. In Brazil, productivity levels in the secondary and tertiary sectors rose approximately 10 percentage points from 1950 to 1982. In Mexico, the comparative performance in both sectors remained stable. From 1982 to 1996 the secondary sectors experienced a larger fall in productivity than services in both countries, despite the faster rate of employment growth in services. Hence the growing weights of the service sector in GDP and in particular employment, and the corresponding drop in the share of agriculture, had a positive impact on Brazil and Mexico's comparative labour productivity performance.

This overall finding hides large differences in the relative performances between and within service industries. The increased service orientation was accompanied by an increase in relative productivity levels in some parts of services, which increased productivity levels of the economy as a whole. However, the large increase in the service share in employment also reflects the hoarding of informal labour in sectors like retailing and personal services. In general this pool of informal labour contributes little to growth and development as its labour productivity is low due to little schooling and capital.

NOTES

1. For an overview of the ICOP project and its roots, see Maddison and van Ark (1988), van Ark (1993), Maddison and van Ark (1994) and van Ark and Timmer (2001).
2. Maddison and van Ooststroom (1993) for agriculture; Maddison and van Ark (1989) and Mulder *et al.* (2002) for manufacturing; and Houben (1990) for mining.
3. The cost savings were estimated between 5 and 9 per cent for the USA in 1890 (Fogel, 1964), between 6 and 22 per cent of GDP for Brazil in 1913 (Summerhill, 1997) and between 8 and 39 per cent for Mexico in 1910 (Coatsworth, 1981).

2. Structural Change and the Shift to Services

INTRODUCTION

In the twentieth century Brazil, Mexico and the USA experienced a large transformation of the sectoral composition of their economies, as illustrated by the composition of employment and GDP (see Tables 2.1 and 2.2). The service shares increased, whereas those of the primary sector fell. In the USA this process was already well under way at the beginning of this century, whereas in Brazil and Mexico these shifts only started in the 1930s. Between 1950 and 1996 the share of services in employment doubled from one quarter to almost 60 per cent in the two Latin American countries and increased from 57 to 79 per cent in the USA. In the same period the share of the primary sector in employment fell from approximately 60 to less than 25 per cent in Brazil and Mexico, compared to a drop from 12 to 3 per cent in the USA. Trends in the employment shares of the secondary sector moved in the opposite direction over the post-war period: they increased by 6 and 9 percentage points, respectively, in Brazil and Mexico, while the share fell from 30 to 19 per cent in the USA.

In the first half of twentieth century, the service sector represented a much higher share of nominal GDP than of employment in all three countries. After 1950, its share further increased. However, due to the lower rate of labour productivity growth in services compared to the rest of the economy, the growth of the service sector share of GDP was much smaller than in employment. From 1950 to 1996, the largest increase of the service sector share was in the USA (57 to 76 per cent), followed by an increase of 10 percentage points to 66 per cent in Mexico and a rise of 8 percentage points to 61 per cent in Brazil. In the Latin American countries, the share of the primary sector in total GDP dropped from over 20 per cent in 1950 to approximately 8 per cent in 1996, whereas the USA experienced a fall from 10 to 3 per cent. Opposite trends were observed for the secondary sector shares in the post-war period, which increased in both Brazil and Mexico, but fell in the USA.[1] The long-term development of these three countries may therefore be summarised by rising shares of the service sector in GDP and a sharp fall in the relative importance of the primary sector.

Table 2.1 *Structure of Employment by Sector of the Economy, Brazil, Mexico and the USA, 1900–96*

	1900	1920	1940	1950	1973	1989	1996
				Brazil			
Agriculture & mining	69.8	72.3	72.6	60.9	51.0	27.3	23.6
Manufacturing & construction	2.0	12.4	8.1	13.0	15.6	22.2	19.1
Services, of which:	28.3	15.3	19.3	26.1	33.4	50.6	57.3
Transport & communications	0.7	2.6	2.9	4.1	3.4	3.8	4.1
Wholesale & retail trade	3.2	5.0	4.1	5.6	6.7	12.6	14.9
Finance & real estate	n.a.	0.2	0.3	0.7	1.4	2.3	1.8
Government & social services	n.a.	0.7	1.2	2.5	4.2	7.2	8.1
Other services	24.3	6.8	10.9	13.2	17.7	24.7	28.5
Total	100.0	100.0	100.0	100.0	100.0	100.0	100.0
				Mexico			
Agriculture & mining	71.5	72.0	67.2	57.2	36.1	22.3	20.1
Manufacturing & construction	14.6	12.8	13.2	13.9	21.5	22.4	22.1
Services, of which:	13.9	15.2	19.5	28.9	42.4	55.3	57.8
Transport & communications	1.4	1.5	2.5	2.4	3.2	3.8	4.2
Wholesale & retail trade	5.1	5.5	7.7	8.0	11.1	14.1	15.2
Finance & real estate				1.0	1.5	1.8	1.9
Government & social services	7.4	8.1	9.3	2.3	5.5	10.2	11.0
Other services				15.2	21.2	25.4	25.6
Total	100.0	100.0	100.0	100.0	100.0	100.0	100.0
				USA			
Agriculture & mining	39.1	27.8	19.4	12.4	4.4	3.1	2.9
Manufacturing & construction	25.1	28.8	26.5	30.3	27.2	20.7	18.5
Services, of which:	35.8	43.4	54.1	57.4	68.4	76.1	78.5
Transport & communications	6.1	9.0	5.1	5.9	4.4	3.9	4.2
Wholesale & retail trade	12.0	14.1	18.4	18.5	20.0	22.1	21.7
Finance & real estate	n.a.	n.a.	3.3	3.3	4.7	5.9	5.8
Government & social services	4.2	6.2	12.6	16.1	23.1	23.5	23.5
Other services	13.5	14.1	14.8	13.6	16.2	20.8	23.3
Total	100.0	100.0	100.0	100.0	100.0	100.0	100.0

Sources: See Appendix A.

Table 2.2 *Structure of GDP at Current Prices by Sector of the Economy, Brazil, Mexico and the USA, 1900–96*

	1900	1920	1940	1950	1973	1989	1996
				Brazil			
Agriculture & mining	46.1	38.2	9.5	24.7	13.1	8.5	8.9
Manufacturing & construction	10.1	13.6	6.2	22.8	34.4	31.2	31.8
Services, of which:	43.8	48.2	54.3	52.6	52.6	60.4	59.3
Transport & communications	n.a.	3.2	3.9	3.4	4.1	4.4	4.9
Wholesale & retail trade	14.1	15.9	15.8	15.6	16.7	12.5	13.3
Finance & real estate	n.a.	n.a.	n.a.	15.1	13.3	13.6	10.4
Government & social services	n.a.	n.a.	n.a.	6.6	8.1	12.0	16.0
Other services	n.a.	n.a.	n.a.	11.8	10.3	17.8	14.8
Total	100.0	100.0	100.0	100.0	100.0	100.0	100.0
				Mexico			
Agriculture & mining	35.4	31.5	21.2	22.1	11.9	10.3	8.2
Manufacturing & construction	12.7	10.6	17.3	22.6	26.7	28.1	26.3
Services, of which:	51.9	57.9	61.4	55.3	61.4	61.5	65.5
Transport & communications	4.1	4.9	7.4	7.9	4.6	7.2	8.2
Wholesale & retail trade	n.a.	n.a.	n.a.	20.2	20.5	16.6	13.7
Finance & real estate	n.a.	n.a.	n.a.	8.5	9.8	8.7	10.7
Government & social services	n.a.	n.a.	n.a.	3.8	8.1	9.2	11.3
Other services	n.a.	n.a.	n.a.	14.8	18.3	19.8	21.5
Total	100.0	100.0	100.0	100.0	100.0	100.0	100.0
				USA			
Agriculture & mining	32.3	18.3	13.8	10.2	5.7	3.8	3.3
Manufacturing & construction	21.3	26.0	29.5	32.8	28.5	23.5	20.9
Services, of which:	46.4	55.7	56.7	57.0	65.9	72.8	75.8
Transport & communications	3.0	4.6	3.8	6.2	6.3	5.7	5.8
Wholesale & retail trade	18.0	16.9	18.3	17.9	16.6	15.6	15.3
Finance & real estate	n.a.	n.a.	10.6	11.1	14.0	17.7	19.0
Government & social services	8.0	9.3	14.5	12.6	18.7	19.4	19.5
Other services	n.a.	n.a.	9.5	9.2	10.3	14.4	16.2
Total	100.0	100.0	100.0	100.0	100.0	100.0	100.0

Sources: The 1900–40 structures were based on GDP in constant prices (Appendix B), and the 1950–96 shares on GDP in current prices (Appendix C).

In other Latin American countries, services also have become the major sector in the second half of the twentieth century. In 1998 the service sector represented more than 60 per cent of GDP of all countries in the region except for Bolivia and Ecuador where services accounted between 50 and 60 per cent of GDP. Services represent a somewhat smaller share of employment in Latin America, though its share is always above 50 per cent (World Bank, *World Development Indicators 2001*).

The service sector is relatively less important in developing countries in other parts in the world. In the largest Asian economies such as China, Indonesia, India and the Philippines, which have a much lower income per capita, the service sector represents between 35 and 45 per cent of GDP and employment. In developing countries with similar income levels as Brazil and Mexico, such as Thailand, Turkey and several transition countries, the service shares are almost as high.

There is no unique relationship between GDP per capita and the sectoral structures of GDP and employment, as the experiences of Brazil and Mexico on the one hand and that of the USA on the other show. Per capita income levels in Brazil and Mexico in 1996 were similar to those in the USA in 1915. A comparison of the sectoral compositions shows that in the two Latin American countries the share of the primary sector in employment and GDP was much lower, and that of services much higher compared to the USA.[2] Other studies on Brazil (Rocha, 1997; Pereira de Melo *et al.,* 1999) also found that the evolution of the sectoral composition of GDP and employment today is very different from that of developed countries in the past.

Berry (1978) confronted the economic structures of a larger sample of Latin American countries in 1970 with that of developed countries in the nineteenth century, and found that in particular the service sector share was much higher in the Latin American countries. He explains this by technological progress, which allowed manufacturing firms in Latin America to operate with a much smaller workforce than firms in Europe and the USA a century ago, the higher rate of outsourcing, the more urbanised society and the more unequal income distribution in Latin America. Another study on India (Mazumdar, 1995) also observed the dominance of services today and the dissimilarity between the economy's sectoral structure and that of developed countries in the past.

Tables 2.1 and 2.2 also show the differences between the two Latin American countries and the USA in terms of the type of service activities that gained importance over time. In the twentieth century transport and communications increased its employment share in the former two countries, whereas the opposite occurred in the USA. Wholesale and retail trade increased their share in all three countries, although in the USA its share levelled off in the 1990s. Finance and real estate, government and social services increased their share in all countries, but represented a much higher share of employment in the USA compared to the Latin American countries. In Brazil, the share of financial services reached almost 3 per cent in the early 1990s thanks to hyperinflation, after which the share fell again by 0.5 percentage points. The 'other services' category, which included business services, hotels and restaurants and personal services, increased its share in all countries to one quarter of total employment in 1996. In Brazil and Mexico personal services is the largest component of 'other services', whereas in the USA business services is by far the largest category.

Similar differences can be noted for the GDP structures. In Brazil and Mexico the share of transport and communications increased until 1996, whereas in the USA this share fell after 1973. Surprisingly, the share of distribution decreased in all three countries, in particular in Brazil and Mexico. Finance and real estate represented almost the same share of GDP in Brazil and the USA, whereas in Mexico this share was much lower.

CHANGES IN SECTORAL COMPOSITION AND THE PROCESS OF DEVELOPMENT

Analyses of changes in the sectoral composition of output and employment along with increases in per capita income are not confined to Brazil, Mexico and the USA alone, as documented by many studies starting with Sir William Petty in 1691.[3] Fisher (1935, 1939) and Clark (1940) were among the pioneers to study and provide explanations of the changes in composition of the labour force for a larger set of countries (six European countries, Australia, Japan, New Zealand and the USA) during the nineteenth and early twentieth centuries. They found a systematic relationship between economic growth and a move of labour from agriculture to manufacturing and, increasingly, to services.

In the late 1950s Rostow developed a theory of five stages of economic growth: traditional society, preconditions, take-off, drive to technological maturity and age of high mass consumption. He viewed economic development as a linear process. His theory was based on the long-run experience of developed countries which had all reached the stage of mass consumption. In Rostow's analysis the relevant sectoral breakdown is not into agricultural, manufacturing and services but into some modern manufacturing sectors and the rest of the economy. Economic progress totally depends on the development of the modern relative to the traditional sectors. During the take-off stages the modern sector reaches a critical level and produces changes which lead to a massive and progressive structural transformation of the economy and society (Rostow, 1990).[4]

Kuznets studied processes of economic growth and structural change at the same time as Rostow. His aim was not to develop a growth theory, but to identify typical patterns of economic development based on longitudinal data in his early studies (see, for example, Kuznets, 1957), and cross-section analysis later on (Kuznets, 1966, 1971). He criticised Rostow's simplified linear theory of five stages. In Rostow's view economic development only required the development of some modern manufacturing sectors. In contrast, Kuznets had a much more structuralist approach as he stressed the role and division of production among all three sectors of the economy.

Moreover, Kuznets also strongly rejected the existence of a linear development path as described by Rostow. Kuznet's rejection was in particular based on his comparison between the findings of longitudinal and cross-section analyses which made him increasingly sceptical of the strong correlation between income levels and sectoral structures. His 1971 book deals almost entirely with this subject. On the basis of a longitudinal study of 14 developed[5] and 3 developing countries,[6] he draws the following conclusions. With regard to the structure of GDP, the share of agriculture decreased from 40 per cent in the early nineteenth century to 10 per cent around 1967. The share of industry – including construction, utilities, transport and communications – rose from between 22 and 25 per cent to between 40 and 50 per cent. The share of services did not show a clear trend, that is it increased in some countries but not in others.

However, his cross-section analysis of 57 countries for 1958 yielded quite different results. The observed decline of agriculture in a time series analysis exceeded the differential estimated from the cross-section. Similarly, the actual increase in the share of manufacturing and services exceeded the predicted share.

Kuznets found the same inconsistency between intertemporal and interarea series with regard to employment shares: the long-term trends from 1800 to 1965 showed that the share of agriculture in employment decreased from between 50 to 60 per cent to between 10 to 20 per cent. Services absorbed most of the outflow out of agriculture, as the share of manufacturing rose only slightly.[7] Kuznets concludes that the structure of GDP was 'industrialised', while that of employment was 'servicised'. Again cross-section analysis for 1950 and 1960 showed quite different trends: for less developed countries, the share of agriculture was higher, whereas for developed countries it was lower than predicted by the study of time series.

Chenery and Taylor (1968), Chenery and Syrquin (1975) and Syrquin (1986, 1988) also studied patterns of sectoral change using mostly cross-section analysis. Compared to Kuznets, Chenery's work was more disaggregated. Moreover, he included data on many more developing countries (more than 100) in the period 1950–70. In contrast to Kuznets,

Chenery made extensive use of statistical analysis to discern average patterns of economic development and structural change.

In contrast to Kuznets, they found a strong correlation between economic structure and per capita income. This uniform relationship was obtained only after they controlled for factors that affect structural change but which are unrelated to per capita income. These include, firstly, the relative abundance in natural resources. Countries rich in natural resources industrialise relatively late as the cost of increasing export earnings is lower through primary exports than manufactures. Secondly, the size of countries also matters as the transformation of GDP and employment tends to occur faster in large countries as they benefit from scale economies. Other forces include technological change, trade policy and urbanisation.

In addition to Chenery, other authors also found consistent patterns of change in the sectoral compositions of employment and GDP. Maddison (1980) compared changes in the structure of employment in 16 OECD countries from 1870 to 1976, and found a declining share of agriculture and a rising share of services. The share of industry followed a bell-shape pattern: it rises first, then flattens out and finally declines. Other studies confirming uniform patterns include Gregory and Griffin (1974),[8] Batchelor *et al.* (1980),[9] Gemmell[10] (1982) and Döhrn and Heilemann (1996).[11]

Several conclusions can be drawn on the average patterns of economic development and changes in sectoral compositions, if account is taken of factors that affect structural change but which are unrelated to per capita income. Firstly, the share of agriculture in GDP and employment falls in the process of income growth, and the service sector share rises. Secondly, the share of industry rises and then falls. Thirdly, the shares of manufacturing and agriculture are smaller and that of services larger today in developing countries than the corresponding shares in developed countries when they had similar income levels. Fourthly, the common trends of the service expansion sector in Brazil, Mexico and the USA hide large differences in the *types* of service activities that developed most rapidly in each country.

Among the various trends in sectoral transformation, a focus is made below on the increasing importance of the service sector as this is the main tendency in Brazil, Mexico and the USA, as well as in most other countries, in the post-war period. The main determinants of its growing share are reviewed and their importance is evaluated in the context of the three countries studied here.

THE LARGER SHARE OF SERVICES IN FINAL AND INTERMEDIATE DEMAND

The speed at which the share of services in employment and GDP increases depends on the rate of growth of income per head, changes in the structure of final and intermediate demand, differential rates of labour productivity growth by sector, employment opportunities per sector and miscellaneous factors. Changes in the composition of final and intermediate demand could be estimated only from 1970 onwards,[12] whereas productivity growth rates could be compared across sectors from 1950 onwards. The types of forces behind the service sector expansion differ greatly between Brazil and Mexico on the one hand and the USA on the other.

Rising Incomes and Demand Elasticity

The increase in the share of services in output and employment is partly driven by the substitution of primary and manufactured goods for services when per capita income rises, also referred to as Engel's law. Changes in the composition of final demand play a key role in the analysis of Chenery and Taylor (1968), Clark (1940), Fisher (1935, 1939), Kuznets (1966, 1971) and Maddison (1980). The hierarchy of consumer preferences explains the dominant position of agricultural products in the consumption of people with low incomes. As per capita income increases, the need for basic commodities becomes saturated and demand shifts to manufactured products, which accelerates the growth of manufacturing. After a certain income level has been reached, consumers acquire a stock of durable goods, such as televisions and washing machines, and will spend a smaller fraction of their income on these products for replacement purposes. In turn, they will increase the share of their budgets spent on services. Changes in demand structure can be measured by income elasticities: the demand for a product is elastic when its share in spending increases with income, and inelastic when its share decreases.

Nominal expenditure data for our three countries confirm Engel's law. From the 1970s to the mid-1990s the shares of services in final demand rose from 28 to 43 per cent in Brazil and from 57 to 62 per cent in the USA, whereas in Mexico it only rose from 32 to 34 per cent during the same period (see Figure 2.1). Education and health care were the fastest growing categories of final demand in Brazil and Mexico, corresponding to the large increase in the supply of these services for the poor (see Chapters 7 and 8). In the USA, health care and transport are the services that showed the highest increase in final demand. In the USA, services account for the major share of final expenditure.

Figure 2.1 *Share of Goods and Services in Final Demand, Brazil, Mexico and the USA, 1970–96*

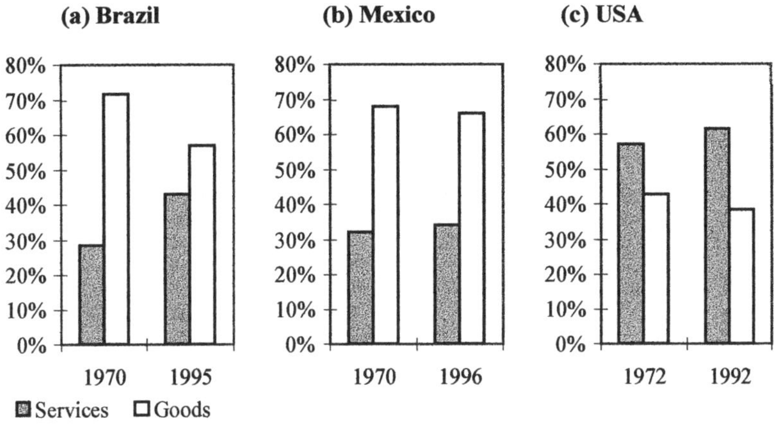

Sources: Brazil: IBGE, *Matriz de Insumo-Produto* (various issues). Mexico: INEGI, *Cuentas Nacionales de México* (various issues). USA: 1972 from Department of Commerce, Bureau of the Economic Analysis (1979); 1992 from Department of Commerce, Bureau of Economic Analysis (1997).

Kravis *et al.* (1982, 1983), Summers (1985) and Falvey and Gemmell (1996) criticised the studies confirming Engel's law as they are based on comparisons of *nominal* instead of *real* expenditure on services across countries and over time. The comparison of the *real* final consumption of services – that is, in terms of the actual physical flows – across countries yields very different results. This is shown when purchasing power parities (PPPs) instead of exchange rates are used to convert expenditures to a common currency. It turns out that, in real terms, people in low-income countries spend the same proportion of their income on services as those in high income countries. Kravis *et al.* (1983) also show, on the basis of the experiences of France, the UK and the USA from 1950 to 1977, that the real income share spent on services remained constant. Gutierrez (1993), using final consumption data at constant prices of six OECD countries in 1972–84, contradicted these results as he found that income elasticities for services are above those for goods.

For Brazil, Mexico and the USA, differences between the service share in expenditure almost disappear when real instead of nominal expenditure are used. Expenditure data for 1975 show that the service share in expenditure in national prices was 27, 26 and 44 per cent. However, in real (PPP) terms the share of services in expenditure expands to 31 and 29 per cent in Brazil and Mexico, respectively, whereas the US share contracts to 32 per cent (Kravis *et al.*, 1982). These changes result from the increase in the relative price of services and the decrease in the relative price of goods with rises in per capita income. Real expenditure data for 1993 also show that the shares of services in final expenditure are similar in the three countries (World Bank, 2001).

Real expenditure data for 1975 and 1993 show that, although the shares of services in final expenditure were almost the same, the types of services consumed varied greatly across countries. In Brazil and Mexico, people consumed relatively much more domestic services, transport services and education, whereas Americans spent proportionally more on communication, health care, housing, hotel and restaurants and recreation.

This finding points to another critique on Engel's law, as it does not differentiate between types of services, as the share of only some services in spending increases, while the share of others falls when income rises. In this respect, three types of services are distinguished. New services – education, health care and recreation – have a high income elasticity. The development of complementary services (also referred to as intermediary or producer services) such as finance, transportation, wholesale and retail trade depend on the growth of production in the goods-producing sector. The demand for the third category, old services (for example domestic servants) falls as per capita income rises. This threefold breakdown was confirmed by empirical studies such as Katouzian (1970) who studied ten industrialised countries over a period of 50 years. Sabolo (1975) found the same trends in 25 countries using data for the 1950–71 period. In Brazil, Mexico and the USA, the rising share of complementary and new services is confirmed by the intertemporal data on expenditure. Due to the lack of detailed data on the three countries, the drop of share of old services could not be confirmed.

The final demand for services depends not only on per capita income, but also on the distribution of income, age composition of the population, the participation rate of women in the labour market, urbanisation and on the role of governments. These will be discussed in more detail below.

(a) Per capita incomes and income distribution

From 1950 to 1982 per capita incomes in Brazil and Mexico converged somewhat to US levels, after which they diverged. Aggregate per capita income data need to be supplemented by evidence on the distribution of income, as low-income groups have different spending patterns from high-income groups. The Gini coefficients in Table 2.3 illustrate that from 1950 to 1989 the income distributions in Brazil and Mexico were more unequal than that in the USA. In the course of time, the distribution of income has become more unequal in Brazil, while in Mexico it has become slightly more equal. However, after the 1970s this distribution became more unequal in the USA, a pattern that was followed by Mexico in the 1980s.

Table 2.3 *Income Distribution: Gini Coefficients and Quintile Ratios, Brazil, Mexico and USA, 1950–91*

	Gini Coefficient			Ratio of Fifth to First Quintile		
	Brazil	Mexico	USA	Brazil	Mexico	USA
1950	n.a.	0.60	0.36	n.a.	35.4	9.5
1960	0.53	0.56 [b]	0.35	17.8	17.8 [b]	8.6
1975	0.60 [a]	0.58	0.34	23.7 [a]	25.4	7.5
1985	0.62	0.51	0.37	22.2	13.6	9.3
1989	0.60	0.55	0.38	26.3	18.5	9.7
1991	n.a.	n.a.	0.38	n.a.	n.a.	9.8

Notes:
[a] Refers to 1976.
[b] Refers to 1963.
Source: Squire and Deininger (1996).

Gini coefficients do not indicate the shares of income earned by particular groups of households. This is illustrated by the ratio of the income share earned by the quintile of richest households to that of the quintile of poorest ones (see Table 2.3). The higher the ratio, the larger the share of income earned by the wealthiest. Although the Gini coefficient in 1950 in Mexico was the same as the 1976 and 1989 coefficients in Brazil, the share of income earned by the richest as compared to the poorest was much larger in Mexico than in Brazil.

Gini coefficients and income distribution by quintiles do not show what proportion of the population lives below the poverty line. International comparisons are very difficult as each country adopts its own definition of poverty.[13] An alternative, internationally comparable, poverty indicator is the number of children per 1,000 new-born that die before age of five: 69 in Brazil, 38 in Mexico and 11 in the USA in 1990 (see Chapter 7). The information on per capita revenues, income distribution and infant mortality suggests that in 1990 more people lived in poverty in Brazil than in Mexico.

High-income inequality increases the consumption of luxury services, such as domestic servants and expensive leisure activities. However, the demand for more basic types of services such as education, health care and telecommunications was constrained, as the middle- and low-income groups received smaller fractions of income. Brazil and Mexico had similar income levels, but services accounted for a larger share of final spending in Brazil than Mexico in 1970 and 1995–96. The larger income inequality in Brazil compared to Mexico may explain the higher proportionate share of services.

(b) Changes in demographics and labour-force participation

Population growth and age structure have important consequences for the relative demand for certain types of services, in particular education and health care. The necessity for schooling largely depends on the share of the young in the total population, which is determined by birth and infant mortality rates. The demand for health care is to a large degree affected by the share of the elderly in the total population. The need for other services, such as proximity shopping, specialised transport and tourism, also depends on the age structure of the population. The high share of the young as shown in Table 2.4 in combination with an increased public commitment to schooling explains the boom in expenditure on education from 0.5 and 0.6 per cent of GDP in 1955 to 3.7 and 3.5 per cent in 1990 in Brazil and Mexico respectively. Since the 1970s the proportion of people under 15 has been falling in both countries.[14] Nevertheless, the relative expenditure has continued to rise, due to rising enrolment levels in the different types of education. In the USA, the ageing of the population is a major cause of the rapid growth of health care spending from 4 to 14 per cent of GDP over the 1950–94 period.

Table 2.4 Population Structure, Brazil, Mexico and the USA, 1950–90 (Percentage of Total Population)

	14 years and below			60 years and over		
	Brazil	Mexico	USA	Brazil	Mexico	USA
1950	42	43	31	4	4	10
1975	40	46	25	6	3	11
1990	34	38	22	8	4	17

Source: See Table 7.6.

The volume of housing and retail services grew in line with the number of households, which, in the post-war period, lay above the growth of the population due to higher divorce rates, fewer children per family and a growing proportion of one-person homes. Another socio-economic development that caused the demand for services to rise faster than population was the increasing participation of women in the labour market. This boosted the necessity of laundry services, nursery schools, prepared food and restaurant services, which were previously produced at home. Home provision is not considered as a market activity. From 1950 to 1990 the proportion of women in the work-force doubled from 15 to 30 per cent in

Brazil, and increased from 13 per cent to 23 per cent in Mexico (Hofman, 1998). US female participation rates were much higher throughout the whole period.[15] The higher share of working women boosted the demand for these formerly domestic services.

Another labour market trend is the shortening of working hours and as a result an increase in leisure time. Since 1950 working hours have been cut in Brazil, Mexico and the USA,. In the USA this process had already started in 1860. In the early 1990s Americans worked roughly 20 per cent less than Brazilians and Mexicans.[16] In addition to the higher incomes of the Americans, the extra leisure time explains why US citizens spent relatively more on hotels and restaurants, recreational services and tourism.

(c) Urbanisation

The final demand for services also strongly depends on whether people live in rural areas or cities. City dwellers buy relatively more products in stores, while rural citizens grow part of their own food consumption themselves. Rural people also engage more in barter trade. Urban households have a higher demand for communication and recreational services (Falvey and Gemmell, 1996). Even though per capita incomes in Brazil and Mexico were much lower than in the USA in 1990, the share of the population living in cities of more than 100,000 inhabitants was about the same: 42 per cent in Brazil, 43 per cent in Mexico and 41 per cent in the USA (World Bank, *World Development Indicators 2001*). Since the 1970s Mexico City and São Paulo have been among the largest cities in the world.

The impact of urbanisation on the development of the service sector strongly depends on the development level of countries (Pandit, 1990). In developed countries, cities offer the possibility to achieve scale and scope economies which are particularly important for producer services. This means that among countries with similar income levels, the more urban ones tend to have a higher share of business services. In contrast, in less developed countries urbanisation increases the demand for mostly traditional and informal services, such as local transport, personal services and street-vending.

(d) The expanding role of government

Since 1950 public education and health care have belonged to the fastest growing categories of final demand. In Brazil and Mexico government expenditure as a share of GDP increased from 1 per cent in 1950 to 7 per cent in 1990. In the USA it rose from 5 to 11 per cent. The increased expenditure share largely stems from the public commitment to provide these services for the largest possible range of the population, including the poor. In these countries the increase of educational and health standards is considered indispensable for improving people's well-being and productivity, and as such forms a precondition for economic development (see Chapters 7 and 8).

In the 1950–96 period the demand for other government services (including the armed forces) also rose strongly in Brazil and Mexico. The implementation of import substitution policies in these countries required a large government, controlling extensive parts of the economy. From 1950 to 1996 the share of government (excluding education and health care) in total employment rose from 3 to 10.2 per cent in Brazil and from 4.5 to 16.9 per cent in Mexico. In contrast, in the USA, the role attributed to the government first increased, but later contracted, as is illustrated by the rising share of employment from 11.5 per cent in 1950 to 14.3 per cent in 1967, after which it fell to 9.7 per cent in 1996.

Growing Share of Services in Intermediate Demand

When per capita income rises, the share of services in intermediate demand increases, which, in turn, raises the proportion of the service sector in employment. Figure 2.2 shows that from the 1970s until the early 1990s in all three countries the share of services in intermediate demand increased at the expense of goods. The largest increase of services in intermediate demand occurred in the USA: from 39 to 52 per cent of intermediate demand. Smaller increases occurred in Brazil (from 21 to 25 per cent) and in Mexico (from 18 to 25 per cent).

Figure 2.2 Share of Goods and Services in Intermediate Demand, Brazil, Mexico and the USA, 1970–96

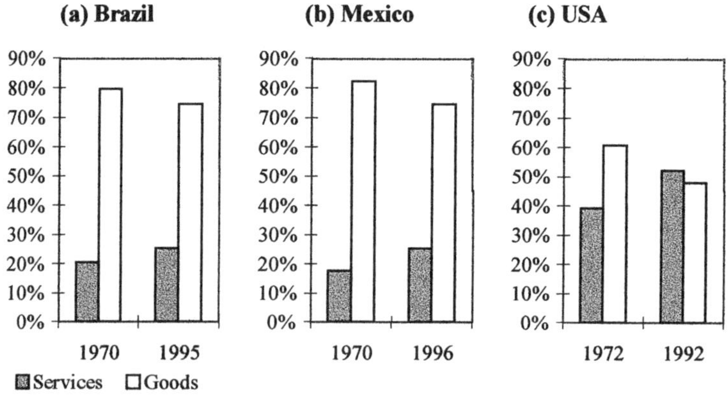

Source: See Figure 2.1.

The changes in the shares of individual services in intermediate demand differed from country to country (not shown in Figure 2.2). In Brazil the share of transport in total intermediate demand fell from 1970 to 1995. In contrast, the demand for financial services and business services increased. In Mexico the intermediate demand for transport rose most rapidly, while demand for distributive services and real estate decreased from 1970 to 1996. In the USA, the intermediate demand for transport fell, while the demand for distributive and financial services increased in 1972–92.

The growing share of services in intermediate demand is explained by two simultaneous processes: outsourcing and innovation. The former refers to purchases of service inputs from outside firms, which were previously produced internally. In recent decades rapid improvements in information and communication technologies have made outsourcing much more feasible, as these permit the rapid exchange of information between the contractor and the service producer. As such, firms tend to focus on their core business and contract other firms for catering, cleaning, financial services, marketing and other services.

Innovation relates to the increased complexity of production and the corresponding increased use of intermediate services. The output of firms has become more differentiated and the life-cycle of their products has shortened, in order to respond to rapidly changing consumer preferences ('customising'). Manufacturing and services have become more integrated, and especially the latter represent a growing share of the sales value of products. In high-income countries, innovation has been a far more important source of the growth of intermediate services than outsourcing (Klodt *et al.*, 1997).

Inflation

In Brazil high inflation in the early 1960s, 1980s and 1990s sharply reduced real incomes, especially of the poor, whose earnings were not protected against inflation. Spending on durables and most services fell and concentrated increasingly on food. Nevertheless, some services benefited from high inflation, such as hypermarkets, where consumers immediately spent their income after having received their salaries. Banks also benefited from hyperinflation, as financial intermediation became an increasingly profitable activity, on account of the large spread between the real debit and credit interest rates. Moreover, a variety of profitable monetary and non-monetary assets were introduced to protect depositors and banks against inflation. In Brazil the share of the financial sector in GDP reached 12 per cent in 1993, but after the stabilisation of prices this share dropped to 6 per cent in 1996. The share of finance in employment reached 2 per cent in the late 1980s, but dropped later to 1.4 per cent. Mexico also experienced substantial inflation in the 1980s, which, in contrast to Brazil, had a negative impact on the share of finance in GDP and employment. This was because deposits were not indexed, which induced many people to transfer their money holdings abroad.

WHY THE SERVICE SHARE GREW FASTER IN EMPLOYMENT THAN IN GDP?

The service sector share increased much faster in employment than in nominal GDP in all three countries over the 1950–96 period. Moreover, in the USA the service sector share grew faster in nominal than in real GDP.[17] The first trend is mainly explained by lagging productivity growth, while the second trend originates mainly from the so-called 'cost disease'.

Lagging Productivity Growth

In all three countries labour productivity in services grew slower than in the other sectors from 1950 to 1996, which caused the share of services in employment to rise faster than its share in GDP (see Table 2.5). In Brazil and the USA, labour productivity in the primary sector grew three times, and productivity in the secondary sector twice as fast as productivity in services. In Mexico the differences between sectors are even larger; for example productivity in agriculture increased four times, and the secondary sector twice as fast as in services. Within the service sector, public utilities and transport and communications performed better relative to distribution and 'other services' in all three countries.

The impact of lagging labour productivity growth in services on the tertiary sector employment share is estimated by the growth of the service employment share minus the increase in the service share of GDP at constant prices. When the proportionate increase in the service share of employment equals that of GDP, productivity growth in the tertiary sector is the same as the advances in the rest of the economy. However, in Brazil and Mexico, and to a much lesser extent in the USA, the percentage point increase in the service share of GDP was smaller than that of employment during the 1950–96 period. For example, in Brazil the service employment share increased 32 points while the service share of GDP grew only 9 points. The difference, 23 points, may be attributed to lagging productivity growth. As such, sluggish productivity growth 'explains' about three-quarters of the increase of the service employment share during the 1950–96 period in Brazil, 60 per cent in Mexico and only 11 per cent in the USA.

Table 2.5 *Labour Productivity Growth by Sector, Brazil, Mexico and the USA, 1950–96 (Average Annual Compound Growth Rates)*

	Brazil	Mexico	USA	Brazil Minus USA	Mexico Minus USA
Primary sector	3.2	2.7	2.8	0.4	–0.1
Secondary sector	2.4	1.4	2.2	0.2	–0.8
Tertiary sector, of which:	1.2	1.0	1.0	0.2	0.0
Public utilities	4.4	4.5	3.7	0.7	0.8
Transport & communications	4.5	1.9	2.6	1.9	–0.7
Wholesale & retail trade	–0.1	0.9	1.6	–1.7	–0.7
Finance	1.5	2.4	0.6	0.9	1.8
Real estate	1.5	–0.1	1.4	0.1	–1.5
Health care		0.1	–0.4		0.5
Education	0.8 }	–0.3	–0.3	0.8 }	0.0
Government		0.5	0.9		–0.4
Other services		0.1	0.6		–0.5
Total (all branches)	2.6	2.2	1.3	1.3	0.9

Sources: Appendices A, B and C.

Several reasons may explain the sluggish productivity growth in services. Baumol (1967) refers to the limited options for technological innovations in services, as they are labour intensive, require little capital and cannot be produced on a large scale. Gordon (1996) emphasised that some services may have reached their technological frontier and have exhausted the sources of productivity growth.[18]

The view that services have little potential for labour productivity growth is too pessimistic and simplistic, as productivity gains have been achieved in several service industries. For example, in public utilities, transport and communications, and finance, direct interaction between producer and consumer is not absolutely necessary. Although many of these so-called disembodied services are still produced during direct contact with the client, the progress in telecommunications and information technology allows for their distribution over large distances. This offers many possibilities for realising economies of scale and productivity improvements.

Productivity gains were more limited in embodied services, which require a direct interaction between producer and consumer. In cultural activities, education, health care, and wholesale and retail trade, there are fewer options to automate activities, as labour is indispensable for the production of the service itself. The possibilities for productivity increases in the service sector depend on the relative importance of embodied and disembodied services in the total (Bhagwati, 1984). In Brazil and Mexico the low rates of labour productivity growth in services originate mainly from the expansion of embodied services, such as distribution, education, health care and personal services.

The Service Sector as a Refuge for Labour

In Brazil and Mexico productivity in services also grew slowly because this sector absorbed millions of workers which had no job opportunities in the other sectors, in particular agriculture. This process was strongly linked to the rapid pace of urbanisation of the two countries. Due to a lack of dynamism of the modern industrial sector, only a few workers could be absorbed. Migrants from rural to urban areas were forced into service activities requiring low qualifications such as informal retailing and personal services.

The large expansion of informal activity was accelerated by the economic depression of the 1980s. As there were few benefit schemes for the unemployed in these countries, working in the informal sector was their only alternative source of income. Most informal activity is concentrated in services, as it requires little human and physical capital.

In Brazil and Mexico, the informal work-force represented about 60 per cent of the total in 1993. In Brazil 41 per cent of this informal work-force were employed in retailing, followed by food stands (19 per cent), and other services (13 per cent) in 1985 (IBGE, 1989). From 1985 to 1995, street-vending was the most rapidly growing part of retailing. In the service sector as a whole, informal employment increased the most in this period (Pereira de Melo *et al.*, 1999). In Mexico retailing accounted for 46 per cent of informal employment, followed by repair services (12 per cent) and food stands (11 per cent) in 1988 (INEGI, 1990).

Other Factors Constraining Productivity Growth in Brazil and Mexico

(a) Regulatory environment

In the two Latin American countries, many services, such as public utilities, transport and communications, were provided almost exclusively by public enterprises until the mid-1990s. In general, public service providers were very inefficient, as is demonstrated by their low productivity levels. Although in other branches most companies were private, they were strongly regulated. In the wholesale and retail trade, the government imposed opening hours, regulated the location of stores and requested high social contributions from formal employees. Furthermore, store owners required an operation permit which often took up to a year to obtain. The long and costly procedures incited many distributors to operate on an informal basis. Informal distributors had no access to credit or other facilities, and therefore most of them were not able to increase the size of their business, nor were they able to operate from a fixed location (see Chapter 5).

In banking, the governments in all three countries imposed interest rate ceilings, which were intended to control the cost of credit and reserve requirements. In Brazil and Mexico reserve requirements were increasingly used to finance the growing budget deficit in the 1970s and 1980s. As a result banks intermediated fewer funds to the private sector. In all countries the sphere of operations of each type of financial institution was limited until the late 1980s and 1990s. In Brazil and Mexico universal banks – offering banking, insurance, and stock exchange services – were forbidden until the 1980s. In the USA, the government prohibited the opening of bank branches in other states, and as a result the banking sector remained highly fragmented, with thousands of small banks. The US government also forced banks and other financial institutions to insure their deposits. This arrangement induced moral hazard behaviour by fund managers and contributed to the Savings and Loans Crisis in the second half of the 1980s (see Chapter 6).

(b) Limited international trade and foreign direct investment

In Brazil and Mexico most service industries were protected against foreign competition until the late 1980s, or in some cases (banking, telecommunications) even until the mid-1990s. This delayed technological progress and productivity improvement, as many firms had few incentives to increase the efficiency and quality of their products. This was especially the case in communications, finance and transport.

In Brazil and Mexico some transfer of technology, however, occurred through foreign direct investment, especially in the wholesale and retail trade. Foreigners set up stores in Mexico in the 1970s and in Brazil in the 1980s. They introduced new store formats, such as hypermarkets, and new forms of inventory management. Foreign retailers offered a larger choice of goods at often lower prices, and demanded a wider range of products of better quality and in larger quantities from domestic manufacturers. In Brazil the largest wholesale and retail chains were foreign-owned in the early 1990s. Since the 1980s the efficiency gains of the larger stores have been more than compensated by low or negative productivity growth of the small stores and street vendors, which dominated employment in distribution in both Brazil and Mexico.

The Cost Disease

Another trend observed in the USA is the faster increase of the service sector in nominal compared to real GDP. The most frequently cited explanation for this trend is the 'cost disease', first formulated by Baumol (1967). Owing to lower productivity growth and the faster rise of costs and prices in the service relative to the goods-producing sector, the service sector increases its shares in nominal GDP and employment faster than in real GDP. Baumol's thesis was based on four hypotheses: labour productivity in services stagnates whereas that in the goods sectors grows at positive rates, productivity growth is translated into wage increase, wages are equalised across sectors meaning that the wage increase in services is the same as that in the goods sector and, finally, the demand for services is inelastic with respect to prices.

Under these circumstances output and wages grow at the same rate in the goods sector and the unit cost of its output remains constant. In contrast, the unit cost of output in services rises as productivity stagnates but wages increase at the same rate as in the rest of the economy. As the demand for services is inelastic to prices, the composition of real output between goods and services remains constant. In nominal terms, however, the share of services rises relative to goods. Moreover, the share of services in the labour-force will also increase at a faster rate than in real GDP.

Baumol *et al.* (1991) showed that in the USA per capita income is positively linked to the share of the service sector in GDP at current prices and employment. In contrast, it is negatively, though not significantly, related to the service sector share in real GDP. The cost disease hypothesis has also been confirmed for other developed countries such as France and Japan (Petit, 1993).

For Brazil and Mexico the cost disease is not confirmed, as the service share in nominal and real GDP grew by the same amount, that is from around 50 to 60 per cent in the 1950–96 period. For Brazil Baumol's hypothesis also was rejected by Pereira de Melo *et al.* (1999), who found that between 1970 and 1995 the share of services grew at the same rate in GDP at constant and GDP at current prices.

The rejection of Baumol's hypothesis mainly originates from the fact that wages are not equalised between the service and goods-producing sector. This is mainly because the share of informal employment is much higher in the service sector. As informal employees have little or no bargaining power, they are unable to equalise their earnings to those in the (mostly formal) secondary sector (Pereira de Melo *et al.*,1999)

OVERALL TRENDS AND COMPOSITIONAL CHANGES

In Brazil, Mexico and the USA, services became the dominant sector in the second half of the twentieth century. In Brazil and Mexico this was mostly at the expense of agriculture while in the USA the industrial sector also contracted. These common trends hide large differences in the types of services that gained importance. Large differences also exist with regard to the forces driving service sector growth. In Brazil and Mexico the dominant forces are the rise in final demand for education and health care, and lagging productivity growth. The latter is for a large part explained by the rapid pace of urbanisation and the related accumulation of informal labour in service activities such as street vending and personal services. In the USA the main factors are the rise in the intermediate demand for services as well as the 'cost disease' (rising relative unit labour costs and lagging productivity growth in services relative to the goods sector).

NOTES

1 In the USA the secondary sector had already reached its highest share in GDP in 1953. In Brazil and Mexico the highest shares were observed in the mid-1980s.

2 The shares of primary, secondary and tertiary sectors in GDP were 9, 30 and 61 per cent in Brazil and 8, 26 and 66 in Mexico in 1996, and 23, 24 and 53 per cent, respectively, in the USA in 1915 (see Appendices B and C). Shares in employment were 24, 18 and 56 per cent in Brazil and 24, 26 and 50 per cent in Mexico in 1996, and 24, 26 and 50 per cent, respectively, in the USA in 1915 (see Appendix A). The higher service shares of GDP and employment in Brazil and Mexico in 1996, compared to the USA in 1915, was due to several causes. Firstly, levels of labour productivity in manufacturing in Brazil and Mexico in 1996 were higher than those in the USA in 1915. Fewer workers were required to produce a certain level of output and hence they represented a smaller share of employment than manufacturing employees in the USA in 1915. Secondly, the demand for services in the Latin American countries in 1996 was relatively higher as they were more urbanised and their governments had assumed a greater commitment to provide education and health care than the USA did in 1915.

3 He explained the higher income per capita of the Netherlands relative to France and the UK by the relatively higher shares of employment engaged in manufacturing and distribution in the former relative to the two latter countries.

4. The take-off stage could only be reached if three criteria were satisfied. Firstly, the country had to increase its investment rate, with investment amounting to no less than 10 per cent of the national income. This requirement could be satisfied either through investment of the country's own savings or through foreign aid or

foreign investment. Secondly, the country had to develop one or more substantial manufacturing sectors with a high rate of growth. Thirdly, a political, social and institutional framework had to exist or be created to promote the expansion of the new modern sector. Under this theory economic growth was measured by increases in per capita income.

5. Argentina, Australia, Belgium, Canada, Denmark, France, Germany, Italy, Japan, Netherlands, Norway, Sweden, UK and the USA. For most countries, time series start around 1830.
6. Egypt, Honduras and the Philippines.
7. In the Middle Ages agriculture probably accounted for between 70 and 80 per cent of employment in Europe. The transformation of shares must have been much slower before the nineteenth century (Kuznets, 1971, p. 310).
8. On the basis of the growth experiences of ten countries from 1910 to 1970, they concluded that economies experience a common pattern of change. They reached this conclusion after pooling the cross-sections instead of looking at differences in one year. They also allowed for differences in the initial structure of the economy between countries.
9. His approach resembles that of Chenery, as he also allows for country specifics. On the basis of seven economic and demographic determinants, he identifies seven country groups. These subgroups are justified as he recognises that although no universal growth pattern exists that can be applied to every country, there are still groups of countries for which generalisations can be formulated (Gemert, 1985).
10. Gemmell's study covered 30 countries and two benchmarks (1960 and 1970). He omitted other explanatory variables in his analysis, although he removed small and resource-abundant countries from his sample. He also found uniform relationships, which are different from those of Chenery and Syrquin (1975), between the relative shares of sectors and per capita income.
11. This study was based on a cross-section of 31 middle-income countries in the 1978–88 period. They excluded atypical countries from their sample, such as city states and high-inflation countries in Latin America, and controlled for population size and natural resource endowments.
12. The impact of increased final and intermediate demand for services on the service share in employment and GDP is evaluated on the basis of input output tables. The first year for which these are available for both Brazil and Mexico is 1970. For the USA the 1972 input output table was used, which is closest to 1970. The most recent tables were for 1995 in Brazil, 1996 in Mexico and 1992 in the USA. Imported goods and services were excluded. The intertemporal analysis of the I/O tables shows that the share of the service sector in total production increased from 29 to 36 per cent in Brazil in 1970–95, from 24 to 30 per cent in Mexico in 1970–96, and from 49 to 60 per cent in the USA in 1972–92.

13. In Brazil, it is defined as the level of family income necessary to provide a basic level of food and shelter. It was estimated that about 40 per cent of the population lived under this level in the early 1990s (Euromonitor, 1995). In the USA, the percentage of the population living below the poverty line – the cost of a minimum adequate diet multiplied by three to allow for other expenses – decreased from 22 per cent in the late 1950s to 15 per cent in 1994 (Department of Commerce, *Statistical Abstract of the United States*, 1996). No estimates were available for Mexico.
14. In 1970 the share of people under 15 in the total population was 42, 46 and 28 per cent in Brazil, Mexico and the USA, respectively. In 1995 the share had fallen to 32, 36 and 22 per cent (World Bank, *World Development Indicators 2001*).
15. It increased from 34 per cent in 1950 to 58 per cent in 1990 (Department of Commerce, Historical Statistics of the USA, 1975, and *Statistical Abstract of the United States*, 1995).
16. From 1950 to 1994 the average number of annual hours worked per person decreased from 2,042 to 1,860 hours in Brazil, from 2,154 to 2,032 in Mexico (Hofman, 1998) and from 1,867 hours in 1950 to 1,589 hours in 1992 in the USA (Maddison, 1995b).
17. Services increased their share in nominal GDP by 18 per cent and in real GDP by only 8 per cent from 1950 to 1996.
18. Moreover, he questions the validity of the (US) national accounts labour productivity growth rates, as the consumer price index (CPI) suffers from an upward bias, as it does not sufficiently take into account quality improvements in services. This led to an understatement of productivity growth, especially in the wholesale and retail trade.

3. Measurement of Real Service Output

MEASUREMENT OF SERVICE OUTPUT

Output is harder to define in services than in the commodity sector as a service is 'some change is the condition of one economic unit produced by the activity of another unit. Most services consist of material changes in the persons or the property of the consumers' (Hill, 1999). Services should be distinguished from (im)material goods, as only the latter can be stocked. Therefore no ownership rights can be established over a service and ownership cannot be transferred from one to another economic unit. In contrast to goods, services cannot be traded independently from their production and consumption.

Den Hartog and Bilderbeek (1999) stress that in addition to their intangible characteristics, services also need to be characterised by two other dimensions: the way service suppliers and clients communicate (the interface), for example electronic data interchange; and the service delivery system/organisation, which refers to internal organisational arrangements that need to be managed to allow service workers to carry out their job properly and to develop and offer services.

In the context of their multidimensionality, there a four major difficulties to define the basic unit of output in services (Sherwood, 1994). Firstly, the specification of a complex bundle. For many services the transaction unit represents not just one but a bundle of services which are interdependent. It is often difficult to specify all parts of a bundle and to keep them separate so that price changes of the entire bundle can be matched with changes occurring in the individual components. For example, the price of a supermarket is the mark-up added to the wholesale food price. Its output is a complex bundle of displaying and providing information on goods, making goods available to customers at times and places convenient to consumers and the provision of supplementary services such as credit and packaging.

The service-mix is different for each country. For example, in road passenger transport, the average bus speed may be higher in one country, while in the other, buses run with greater frequency. In their international comparisons Gilbert and Kravis (1954, p. 79) distinguished three types of services: identical, common and unique services. The first type refers to services that are identical among countries, the second to services with common names but different characteristics between countries and the third type to services that exist only in one country. Most services belong to the second and third category. The price of a service should capture all its characteristics. A bus ticket is taken to represent the total price of the transport from one place to another, the comfort of the bus, its speed, the frequency of service and safety.

Secondly, for many services not all aspects of the bundle can be described or measured. For example in banking, the lack of a single transaction unit led researchers to make different assumptions as to the way underlying services are attached to the activities or products. Output refers either to the activities (number of loans issued, money transfers and so on) or to the products (values of loans, savings). There is no consensus on what representation is the best.

Thirdly, the involvement of customers in production raises difficult issues. One must distinguish the services from outcomes to specify what is exactly being transacted. For example in health care, the transaction is the visit to a doctor's office and the outcome relates to the change in the health condition of the patient resulting from this visit. As a patient's health is affected by many other factors, it is difficult to single out the physician's contribution. Collective services, that is services provided by a single unit resulting in a change of many customers or their goods, pose additional problems. As the number of recipients goes up, one should account for congestion. For example, as the number of students per teacher rises, the quality of teaching falls. Moreover, changes in the number of recipients may sometimes be beyond the control of the provider and should not affect the measured volume of services. For example, a drop in the number of students per class may result from changing demographics and not from the poor quality of teaching.

A fourth problem, which also exists for goods, is the accurate measurement of changes in quality over time or between countries. Taking account of the quality dimension of services when defining real output is as important as defining the basic units. However, even the most detailed 'service-mix' specification will not fully capture the quality of the product or 'product content'.[1] Van Ark (1993, pp. 36–37) distinguished two approaches to deal with the quality problem: either products of similar quality are matched, or the hedonic pricing technique is used. The latter treats goods or services as a bundle of quality characteristics, each of which affects the price. Their relative contribution is determined by regression analysis. Kravis *et al.* (1982, pp. 50–59) used this technique to compare prices of cars and dwellings[2] across countries. Hedonics have also been used to measure real output in retailing (Department of Labor, Bureau of Labor Statistics, 2001). Although the hedonic approach is not without problems (Gordon, 1990, pp. 92–100),[3] it is one of the few alternatives to account for changes in the characteristics of services between countries or points of time.

Economists have claimed that quality differences are more difficult to measure in services than in goods, because the unit of output tends to be vaguer. This makes it more difficult to distinguish price and quality changes. However, the indicator chosen to reflect quality changes is a subjective choice from a range of alternatives for both goods and services (Elfring, 1988, pp. 44–45).

RESEARCH ON REAL OUTPUT MEASUREMENT

Despite the dominance of the service sector in almost all economies of the world, relatively little research has been done on what service industries exactly produce. Fortunately this situation has changed somewhat in the 1980s and 1990s with the multiplication of research projects undertaken by both statisticians and academics. The measures described here are taken from the ICOP project of the Groningen Growth and Development Centre as well as various other sources. The ICOP work on services started with Pilat (1994), who developed output measures for transport and communications, banking and education. The most comprehensive study in terms of sectoral coverage was Mulder (1999), on which this book is based, who refined ICOP procedures for transport and communication, banking and education and developed new measures for wholesale and retail trade, insurance, real estate and health care. For transport, communication and distribution, van Ark *et al.* (1999) and van Ark and Monnikhof (2000) further developed the methodologies and extended the geographical coverage to some 20 countries.

Other academic studies carried out by some key institutions and individuals greatly contributed to output measurement in services. Firstly, since 1980 the National Bureau of Economic Research has sponsored research in this area and has devoted two major conferences on the topic (Kendrick and Vacarra, 1980 and Griliches, 1992). Secondly, the *Scandinavian Journal of Economics* devoted an issue to volume measurement in services in 1992. Thirdly, the Centre for the Study of the Living Standards brought together several researchers at a conference in 1997 on 'Service Sector Productivity and the Productivity Paradox', of which several papers were published in a special issue of the *Canadian Journal of Economics* (No. 2, 1999).

Fourthly, from 1992 to 1998, the McKinsey Global Institute (MGI) carried out various case studies on banking, health care, retail trade, telecommunications and transport (MGI, 1992, 1996) or analysed service sector productivity as part of country studies (MGI, 1993, 1995, 1997). MGI followed mostly a case-study approach.[4] Fifthly, since 1997 Triplett and Bosworth have directed a project entitled 'Service Sector Output and Productivity', at the Brookings Institution. They conduct research on the hard-to-measure sectors such as health care (Triplett, 1999). Moreover, they organised several workshops on output measurement in banking, education, health care, insurance and retail trade (see Triplett and Bosworth, 2000).

Another line of research on volume measurement is carried out by the national accounts departments of various statistical institutes as well as coordinating agencies such as Eurostat, OECD and United Nations. Two main documents were produced providing some guidelines of real output measurement in services: the System of National Accounts 1993 (SNA) – a joint publication of the various international organisations – and the European System of Accounts – 1995 (ESA) published by Eurostat. In the second half of the 1990s, Eurostat established Task Forces to further develop guidelines for output measurement in comparison-resistant sectors such as business services, education, finance, government and health care. Their reports present three types of measures: (1) the ideal measures ('A measures'); (2) measures which are less demanding in terms of data ('B measures'); and (3) measures which poorly reflect service output ('C measures'). The latter are mostly input measures such as hours worked or labour costs.

Similar work is carried out by OECD as part of the national accounts expert meetings. These meetings resulted in two publications (OECD, 1987, 1996) surveying methods of output measurement in services in the member countries. In contrast to the Eurostat Task Forces, it provides few recommendations on the best measures. Finally, the UN created a working group on service statistics in 1986 (the Voorburg Group). This group meets every year and discusses on-going research in the statistical offices on real output measurement in services.

In the next section the measurement of real output is discussed for the service categories analysed in detail in the book.[5] Each following chapter on particular service categories provides a more complete review, with the recommendations of the System of National Accounts 1993, the common practice of the national accounts of OECD countries and other methods used in previous comparisons in time and space. The chapters present in detail the approach used in this study, as well as the applicability of other reviewed methods to international comparisons.

REAL OUTPUT MEASURES BY CATEGORY OF SERVICE

Transport and Communications

SNA 1993, the national accounts of most countries and most productivity studies, usually measure real output by passengers kilometres (km) or ton km. These measures combine both the quantity of goods or number of persons and the distances over which they are transported. Transport is, however, not limited to the movement of freight and passengers, but also includes loading and unloading services at airports, ports, stations and terminals. Using the passenger km and ton km measures, it is assumed implicitly that the volume of terminal services is proportional to that of movement services. For example, the output of air transport is often estimated by ton km and passenger km and it is assumed that the volume of airport handling services is proportional to that of the pure flying activity. However, the assumption of a fixed relationship between the movement and terminal activities is highly questionable.

Another drawback of passenger km and ton km measures is that they fail to adjust for the changes in the composition of transported goods or passengers over time or between countries. A ton km of bulk represents less transport services than a ton km of jewellery. The classical measures also ignore other aspects, such as comfort of passenger transport, frequency, on-time performance, speed and so on.

In this study the passenger km and ton km measures are adjusted to account for different proportions of terminal services in total output across countries (see Table 3.1). This is done by taking a weighted average of the movement activity (in terms of passenger or ton km) and terminal activity (in terms of passengers or tons). The latter activity is weighted by the ratio of the average distances over which goods or passengers are transported between two countries and the former by one minus the share for terminal services. The output measures are also adjusted for international quality differences, using proxies such as passenger and road congestion.

Communications includes postal services and telecommunications. Output of postal companies is mostly measured by the number of letters and packages delivered, either unweighted or weighted by their postal rates. Although postal companies also often provide financial and miscellaneous services (car rental, sale of stationery and travel packages), they are rarely included in the measure of real output. Moreover, the number of mail items handled reflects the terminal activity but not the movement of mail. However, the bias of omitting this part of output seems limited. Differences in distances between origin and destination are often accounted for in postal

Table 3.1 *Real Output Measures by Category of Service*

ISIC	Sector	Output Indicator	Quality Adjustment
1	Agriculture	Products	No
2	Mining	Products	No
3	Manufacturing	Products	No
4	Public Utilities		
	Electricity	KWhour	No
	Water	M3 water	No
	Gas	M3 gas	No
5	Construction	Reweighted ICP proxies	No
6	Distribution		
61	Wholesale trade	Double deflation: deflation of sales using expenditure	No
62	Retail trade	PPPs and deflation of purchases for resale and inputs using ICOP UVRs	No
71	Transport:		
	Rail goods	Weighted index of ton-km (transport services) and tons (terminal services)	No
	Rail passenger	Weighted index of pass.-km and passengers	Yes
	Road goods	Weighted index of ton-km and tons	Yes
	Road passenger	Passengers	Yes
	Maritime goods	Tons	No
	Air goods	Weighted index of ton-km and tons	No
	Air passenger	Weighted index of pass.-km and passengers	Yes
72	Communications:		
	Postal services	Pieces of mail sent	Yes
	Telecommunications	Weighted index of network and calls	Yes
8	Finance & real estate:		
81	Banking	Weighted index of transactions, deposits and savings accounts, loans	No
82	Insurance	Health insurance and life insurance policies	No
83	Real estate	Number of houses, adjusted for size	Yes
9	Services & government:		
931	Education	Student numbers adjusted for level of education	Yes
933	Hospitals	Patients-days, adjusted for case-mix differences	Yes
933	Physicians	Patient visits	Yes
91	Government	ICP PPP for government services	No
*	Other services	Reweighted ICOP UVRs for services	No

Note: * Business services, hotels and miscellaneous services.

Sources: Chapters 3–8.

rates. Other aspects of the bundle of postal services, such as weight, delivery speed and safety, are also taken into account by these rates. In this study, real output is measured by the unweighted number of pieces of mail handled. To account for the better quality of US postal services, Brazilian and Mexican quantities were adjusted downwards, using the number of postal offices per 100,000 inhabitants as a proxy of access to postal services.

Telecom output includes installation and maintenance of the network and customer relations and output related to traffic (that is directory services and operation of switchboards). In national accounts, real output is most often measured by traffic-related measures only, such as the number or minutes of calls. Here output is estimated by a weighted average of traffic (number of calls) and network-related services (number of access lines), using employment in each function as weights.

Wholesale and Retail Trade

Wholesalers transmit goods from manufacturers to retailers and subsequently retailers sell to consumers. They sell goods and provide a large range of services such as credit, shopping convenience in terms of location, opening hours, product information and so on. Output equals the goods sold plus additional services delivered by stores. In absence of physical measures, output has to be estimated by monetary aggregates. Most national accounts and productivity studies estimate output by the value of trade margins. Another frequently used measure is sales.

In intertemporal comparisons, an appropriate price index is needed to deflate sales or gross margins. For this purpose, most national accounts use the producer or wholesale price index (PPI) for wholesale trade and the consumer price index (CPI) for retail trade (OECD, 1996). Several authors criticised the use of the CPI, as it often fails to take account of changes in the volume of retail services.

Comparisons in space require conversion factors to express sales, margins and value added to a common set of prices. Exchange rates are the most simple but little representative for distributive services. More appropriate are final expenditure purchasing power parities (PPPs). These were also adopted at first in this study in a single deflation procedure. However, expenditure PPPs are unsuitable converters for the gross margin and value added, mostly because they apply only to sales that equal consumer expenditure. ICP PPPs do not represent relative prices of goods purchased by distributors for resale, nor do they represent relative prices of intermediate inputs. In addition to single deflation, a double deflation procedure was also followed using two sets of converters: expenditure PPPs for the sales and industry-of-origin

UVRs for goods purchased to resale and intermediate inputs. On the basis of this procedure implicit UVRs are derived for value added.

Finance, Insurance and Real Estate

Banks provide services to borrowers in terms of loans, to savers in terms of checking and saving accounts and the facilitation of payments and a range of other services such as advice on investment and taxation, currency exchange, equity and bond management, insurance services and so on. Banks do not price many of these services directly; instead they charge in an indirect way, by retaining some of the payable interest to depositors or by charging a higher interest rate to lenders relative to a reference rate of interest. The latter rate excludes intermediation costs and the risk premium; for example the inter-bank or central bank lending rates. According to SNA 1993 and several productivity studies, the output of banks equals gross revenues from services for which clients are explicitly charged plus the value of the financial services indirectly measured (FISIM) for the services for which banks do not charge explicitly.

To deflate FISIM, most OECD countries use the number of workers or working hours, or labour compensation deflated by the CPI. Others simply deflate banking revenue by a consumer or producer price index from another sector (OECD, 1996). A better index is a weighted volume index that covers all loan and deposit activities that generate FISIM, using the share of each activity in profits as weights. Output indicators should be adjusted for quality changes, such as the use of the internet, extended opening hours of banks and so on.

Other possible output indicators are either *value* measures, such as the ratio of cash currency, demand deposits and time and savings deposits (for example M2) to total wealth (using GDP as a proxy), the value of loans, the value of deposits times average bank earnings per deposit, or *volume* measures of credit services, deposit and saving accounts services and transaction services.

In this study, quantity relatives are a weighted average of activities on the liability side (handling of transactions and facilitating demand and time deposits) and the asset side (issuing of loans) of the bank's balance sheet. Output of these services is measured respectively by the number of demand deposits in the Mexico/USA comparison and the number of cheques cashed in the Brazil/USA comparison, the number of time deposits and the number of loans issued.

Output in insurance equals total premiums earned minus total claims due plus income from investments into actuarial reserves. This definition of SNA has been criticised as clients contract insurance companies for covering a certain amount of risk and not for performing administrative tasks. Under this *risk-assumption* model, output equals the amount of premiums paid for risk protection. The premium reflects not only the efficiency of administrating premiums and claims, but also the efficiency of administrating risks. Real output measures are mostly based on the number of policies, the number of persons covered weighted by base year premiums (in health insurance), premiums paid deflated by the consumer price index for insurance or input indicators. In this study insurance output is measured by the number of life and health insurance policies. These were used to derive a quantity relative.

Real estate output includes establishments engaged in renting or leasing real estate to others; managing real estate for others; selling, buying or renting real estate for others; and providing other real estate-related services, such as appraisal services. Another major part of output is the services rendered by residential housing to their owners. SNA and ESA do not provide nominal and real output measures for this sector. For agents that sell, buy or rent real estate for others, several OECD countries measure nominal output by gross revenues and real output by the number of transactions. For agents that rent or lease real estate to others, as well as owner-occupied housing, nominal output is estimated by rents or imputed rents for rented or owner-occupied dwellings respectively. Rents are deflated by the overall CPI, rental price indices for new and older dwellings or (quality-adjusted) measures of the housing stock (OECD, 1996).

In this study only the services of owners and lenders of residential housing are included. Other real estate services were assumed to be proportional to those for dwellings. Real output is measured by the residential housing stock as published by the population censuses in Brazil, Mexico and the USA. These show the number of rooms per house and their connection to electricity, sewerage and water. In 1980 US dwellings were on average much larger and a much higher percentage had access to basic facilities. The quantity relative based on the number of housing units was adjusted correspondingly using the number of rooms as a proxy of size and access to sewerage or a septic tank as an indicator of access to basic facilities.

Health Care

Most OECD countries measure real output using input or throughput indicators. Some deflate expenditure using inputs, others extrapolate inputs in a base year using quantitative information. Others argue that output should be measured using health (outcome) measures instead of the input or 'throughput' measures. Outcome measures include the incidence of infant mortality, life expectancy, quality-adjusted life years (QUALYs) and satisfaction with care. Only a few micro studies have been done using these measures, as it is difficult to separate the contribution of health care from other factors affecting health outcomes.

In this study real output is measured by 'throughput' measures: inpatient days for hospital services and patient visits for services of dentists and physicians. The throughput data were adjusted for 'case-mix' differences between countries. The case-mix refers to the different compositions of patient groups in terms of types and severity of illness between countries as well as changes over time within a country. Each case-mix requires different amounts of health care inputs. Suppose an inpatient day in surgery requires twice as many services as one in internal medicine. Output measured by inpatient days would underestimate the volume of health services for countries with a relatively high share of treatments in surgery and overestimate services in countries with a concentration in internal medicine. The throughput measures were also adjusted for quality differences between countries, using patient satisfaction, the percentage of births attended by health staff, the number of doctors per 100,000 population, capital input per doctor and test scores of doctors as proxies.

Education

Output of education can be defined by its contribution to human capital formation. SNA views educational services as teaching provided schools, colleges and universities. Real output measures are constructed using quantity relatives of each service weighted by their share in costs or revenues. Quality depends on the number of pupils per teacher or the amount of capital equipment in forms of laboratories, libraries, computers and so on.

Few studies used outcome indicators. Some view education as an investment in human capital and define output as the '*opportunity costs*' of remaining in school instead of working, which equals the increase the average wage a person will earn over his or her working life thanks to the additional education. Another output indicator is test scores, carried out within and across countries. International comparisons used mostly input indicators such as the number of teachers or a combination of input and 'throughput' measures, such as the number of pupils taught.

In this study output is estimated by pupils enrolled in primary, secondary and tertiary education. Enrolment figures were adjusted for the opportunity cost and quality of education. The former is measured by the additional income a person is likely to earn over his working live thanks to completing the secondary or tertiary educational cycle. The numbers of pupils in primary and secondary education in Brazil and Mexico were adjusted twice to account for the lower quality of education relative to the USA. Firstly, dropout ratios were used to account for the lower percentage of pupils completing an educational cycle in the Latin American countries. Secondly, scores on international comparable tests were used to account for the overall lower quality of the teaching and learning environment.

NOTES

1. van Ark (1993, pp. 34–35) specifies an automobile according to its cylinder capacity, number of doors, number of gears and so on, which however fails to describe the durability of its parts and the car's safety. These latter aspects represent the quality of the product, or product content.
2. House rents were related to observable characteristics like floor area, year of construction and facilities (electricity, piped water, a flush toilet and a bathroom). Location was considered a factor increasing price rather than quantity. Regression analysis related these physical characteristics to rents, the former being the independent variables and the latter the dependent. Prices are subsequently estimated from each country's regression equation and then compared between countries.
3. Its result are sensitive to the choice of quality characteristics which are specified. In cases where a 'changed ratio of performance to physical characteristics has occurred', performance characteristics should be included as independent variables, although this may be difficult to measure. It may be also very difficult to compare quality when services acquire new characteristics which did not exist before.
4. In their case-study approach, it specified a set of outputs' and inputs' characteristics for the product and production process of a particular industry. Such case studies used benchmarking techniques to compare the efficiency of individual functions within the production process (in banking, for example, the performance of issuing loan activities, handling transactions and administrating deposits). MGI relied heavily on data obtained from individual firms, so that they can be compared to the 'best practice'.
5. This study does not analyse in detail business services, hotels and restaurants, household services and government, which are part of a residual category 'other services'.

4. Transport and Communications

TRANSPORT AND COMMUNICATIONS IN THE LAST TWO CENTURIES

The transport systems of Brazil, Mexico and the USA have improved enormously in the last two centuries. As the cost of freight and passenger transport dropped, geographical concentration of production and consumption became less necessary, which favoured the development of new regions. In addition to declining costs, the speed of transport increased rapidly, safety increased, as did the comfort of passenger travel.

Before the construction of railways in the late nineteenth century, improvements in transport in Brazil and Mexico were limited to minor road construction. In the USA, on the contrary, massive building of roads and canals from the late-eighteenth to the mid-nineteenth century decreased transport costs and favoured trade among urban centres. The major developments in rail, road, water and air transport are discussed below, and their impact on transport costs is also analysed. Developments in communications are also analysed.

Transport

Railways

Railway construction started in the USA about half a century earlier than in Brazil and Mexico, with the inauguration of a track connecting Baltimore and Ohio in 1830. Most US construction was financed by private capital, attracted by high profit margins. The US government encouraged railway expansion by lavish grants of public lands to the private companies. In Brazil most railway building was done by British investors, who received subsidies and fixed profit payments from the government. The Mexican government favoured railway construction by granting concessions to state governments who passed these on to mostly US investment companies. These attracted large sums of foreign capital and received large subsidies.

The US rail network increased at a relatively slow pace in the 1840s, from 4,827 km to 12,068 km, but 35,400 km were built in the 1850s (Davis *et al.*, 1972, p. 492). Most of the growth was in the Western states. The rail network continued to increase rapidly in the following decades to 225,000 km in 1890, 402,000 km in 1916 and peaked at 692,000 km in 1929 (see Table 4.1). In 1870–1930 most construction was in the south-west and north-west. The profit rate varied strongly from one line to another, depending on freight rates, links with other transport systems, management style and the pattern of regional economic development (Hughes, 1987, p. 258).

Table 4.1 Length of Railway Line and Line per Head of Population, Brazil, Mexico and the USA, 1873–1993

	Railway Line (km)			Railway Line per capita (m)		
	Brazil	Mexico	USA	Brazil	Mexico	USA
1873	1,129	539	85,851	0.1	0.1	2.0
1910	21,326	19,748	351,767	1.0	1.3	3.8
1938	34,207	23,331	411,324	0.9	1.1	3.2
1950	36,681	23,332	396,380	0.7	0.9	2.6
1973	30,429	24,670	354,000	0.3	0.4	1.7
1982	29,164	25,476	297,818	0.2	0.3	1.3
1993	30,379	26,434	212,789	0.2	0.3	0.8

Sources: Brazil: 1873–1985 from IBGE (1990); 1985–93 from IBGE, *Anuario Estatístico do Brasil* (various issues). Mexico: 1873–1982 from INEGI (1994b); 1993 from INEGI, *Anuario Estadístico de los Estados Unidos Mexicanos* (various issues). USA: 1873–1970 from Department of Commerce, Bureau of the Census (1975), 1970–93 from Association of American Railroads (various issues). Population from Maddison (1995b).

In Brazil railways arrived late. The Imperial government made its first concession in 1835, but failed to attract sufficient funds as potential investors expected low or negative profits. In the early 1850s the terms were improved: the government guaranteed minimum dividends to overcome investor risk aversion. The change of terms was successful, as the first line, the *Visconde de Mauá*, was inaugurated in 1854. It ran between Guanabara Bay and Petropolis (16 km). However, the rail network expanded by only 64 km per year until 1874. Construction accelerated after the adoption of a law in 1873 providing dividend guarantees on the first line constructed in each province.[1] All the railways ran from the interior to ports, instead of connecting different areas of the Empire. Regions developed independently, and ties among them remained weak (Bethell, 1985).

The first railway in Mexico was inaugurated in 1873, four decades later than in the USA and two decades later than in Brazil. It ran between Mexico City and Veracruz. During the Porfiriato railway construction boomed. The network grew from 640 km in 1877 to 19,205 in 1910. Most lines were constructed in 1881–84, 1887, 1890 and 1900–3.

The impact of railways on transport costs and economic growth has been discussed by many economic historians. They assumed that railways required less capital and labour than pre-railway modes to produce a given volume of transport services, and that therefore their shipment costs were lower. Reduced transport prices shorten the economic distance between geographically separated markets. Regions can trade at lower transaction costs. Exchange favours specialisation of each region in those goods and services for which it has a comparative advantage, raising its income and production levels. In addition to savings on transport costs, railways increase the speed and the reliability of transport, which in turn lowers the cost of holding inventories (Summerhill, 1995, p. 64).

Rostow (1960) also considered backward linkages indispensable in the growth process of the USA, as railways consumed iron, steel and fuel, induced innovations, reduced transport cost and marked the founding of large companies with large resources. In his *Stages of Economic Growth* (1960), he outlined a general scheme of economic development, in which the take-off plays a central role. This is the point at which a country can sustain a sufficient ratio of investment to GDP to propel itself into the next phase of steady economic progress. Innovation from leading sectors, railways in the case of the USA, play a key role in this process.

Fogel (1964) and Fishlow (1965) argued that the role of railways in US economic growth was much smaller than suggested by Rostow. Fogel estimated that the direct contribution of railways to GDP was only 4 per cent in 1890. He estimated the 'social saving' from lower costs of freight transport to be between 5 and 9 per cent of GDP in 1890 (see Table 4.2). Social saving was calculated by the difference between the actual cost of goods transported by rail, and the hypothetical transport cost of the same volume of traffic by canals and road. The magnitude of social saving depends on the elasticity of demand for freight services. Unit elasticity (equal 0) provides an upper boundary, whereas a low demand elasticity (equal minus 1) determines the lower boundary. Another major determinant of cost saving concerns the specification of the alternative mode of shipment in the absence of railways. For the upper boundary it was assumed that all freight would be moved by the technological second-best mode of shipment, whereas for the lower boundary a mix of relevant modes was taken. He estimated the hypothetical social savings of using railways instead of canals and roads by the cost of time lost due to the lower speed of transport, the cost of being unable to use waterways in the winter, the cost of road transport of goods from waterways to cities without access to waterways, the cost of higher losses of goods during transport, the higher cost of loading and unloading, and the capital cost of building and maintenance of canals excluded from water transport freight charges. Williamson (1974) argued that the gains from the expansion of agricultural production in the west thanks to railway construction in that area should also be included in the social savings. He thus arrived at a much higher estimate, that is 21 per cent of GDP in 1890.

Table 4.2 Transport Cost Savings as a Percentage of GDP due to Railways, Brazil, Mexico and the USA, 1890–1913

	Brazil 1913 (%)	Mexico 1910 (%)	USA 1890 (%)
Freight Transport			
Lower boundary	6	8	5
Upper boundary	22	39	9
Passenger Transport			
Lower boundary	2	0.8	3
Upper boundary	4	1.4	5

Notes: The social savings of freight transport increased over time from 2 per cent in 1869 to 22 in 1913 in Brazil, and from 15 per cent in 1889 to 39 in 1910 in Mexico (Summerhill, 1997). Savings grew over time as unit costs per ton km decreased and freight volumes increased.

Sources: Brazil from Summerhill (1995, pp. 90–92), 136; Mexico from Coatsworth (1981, pp. 71–72, 102–04); USA: freight transport savings from Fogel (1964); passenger transport savings from Boyd and Walton (1972, pp. 249–50).

To estimate the social savings from railway transport in Mexico in 1910, Coatsworth (1981) used the same counterfactual analysis as Fogel. He found it to be between 0.8 and 1.4 per cent of GDP for passenger transport,[2] and between 8 and 39 per cent for freight. He gave railways a larger role in Mexican development than Fogel did for the USA, as he estimated that half of the increase in per capita GDP in the 1880–1910 period was attributable to railway construction. Though railways contributed much more to economic growth in Mexico than in the USA, they provided little stimulus for industrialisation. The reduction in the transport costs of mining products was the main benefit and this was appropriated for a large part by foreign owners. In 1910 more than half of the profits of the railway companies went abroad.

Summerhill (1995) argues that railways, despite the absence of an integrated network, played a key role in the transition to rapid economic growth in Brazil. The extensive river system did not provide a cheap substitute for railways, as was the case in the USA, as most rivers were useless for transport purposes. This was either because rivers ran through regions that were unattractive for commercial purposes, or because they were only partly navigable. Road transport was the only major, but much more expensive, substititute for railways. His counterfactual analysis, along the same lines as Fogel, shows that the social savings in rail transport was between 6 and 22 per cent of GDP in 1913. The cost savings for passenger transport were about three times those in Mexico. In contrast to the strong forward linkages, there were few backward linkages in Brazil and Mexico as both countries relied almost entirely on foreigners for the supply of inputs, engineering and other labour.[3]

Brazil and Mexico differed markedly in the distribution of direct gains from rail transport. Mexico's transport savings accrued to the export sector and foreigners. In Brazil native and immigrant farmers, and domestic industry were the main beneficiaries. This difference was due to government action, which in Brazil ensured low rates for movement of agricultural goods produced and consumed domestically. The Brazilian policy resulted in a declining share of exports in railway freight from 60 per cent in 1887 to 30 in 1913 (Summerhill, 1995).

The US volume of passenger transport by rail per head of population surpassed that of Brazil and Mexico until the 1950s (see Figure 4.1). This was after two periods of high growth: 1900–20 and 1940–46. The subsequent decreased role of US railways was due to the rapid growth of private automobile ownership, bus lines and the emergence of airlines. It was reinforced by a declining quality of rail transport in the post-war period. Passenger traffic per capita in Brazil and Mexico decreased only slightly until 1993, though its relative importance in overall passenger transport declined.

The US volume of rail freight transported per head of population fluctuated widely, showing fast growth from 1873 to the early 1920s, and again in 1940–46 (see Figure 4.1). The Great Depression of the 1930s and the rapidly growing stock of trucks in the 1950s caused a large fall in the transport volume per capita. Though Brazil and Mexico showed much higher annual growth rates of freight traffic than the USA in the 1950–93 period (16 per cent and 8 per cent per annum in Brazil and Mexico, respectively, and only 1 per cent in the USA), they did not catch up with the US level, as is shown in Figure 4.2.

Figure 4.1 *Rail Passenger Traffic (passenger km) per Capita, Brazil, Mexico and the USA, 1873–1993 (Semi-logarithmic Scale)*

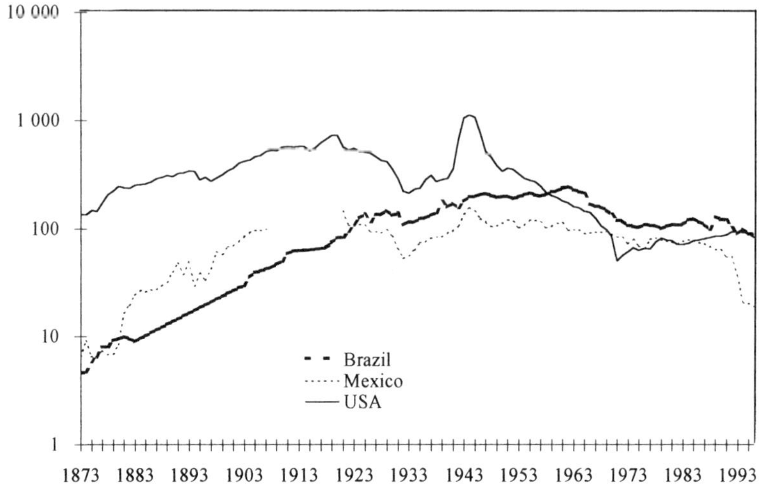

Source: See Table 4.1.

Figure 4.2 *Rail Freight Traffic (ton km) per Capita, Brazil, Mexico and the USA, 1873–93 (Semi-logarithmic Scale)*

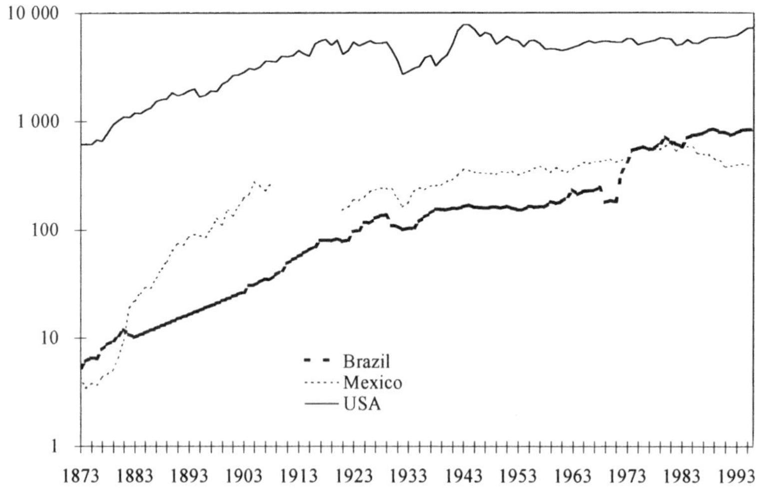

Source: See Table 4.1.

Railway rates in the USA became subject to regulation by the Interstate Commerce Commission founded in 1887. The quest for regulation originated from the railways and the shippers, as both had an interest in stabilising freight rates. Freight rates were based on equity motives and not on economic efficiency. Regulation was modified in 1903, 1906, 1910, 1920 and 1933 to overcome deficiencies of the original 1887 Act. Minimum and maximum rates, and limitations on changes in tariff rates were introduced in the course of time.

The relative importance of railways decreased drastically in the USA. Their share of freight transport decreased from 77 per cent in 1929 to 37 per cent in 1988, and the passenger share dropped from 15 to 0.7 per cent in the same period. The quality of transport also worsened. Most railway companies were facing huge losses by the end of the 1970s, due to legal restrictions on line closures and freight rates (Winston, 1993). Public policy changed in 1980 when the government deregulated railway transport, allowing companies to close unprofitable lines, and set their own rates. Deregulation contributed to declining freight rates in current and constant terms in the 1980s and 1990s, improved profitability and led to a fall in accident rates (Thomson, 1993).

Railways remained in public hands in Brazil and Mexico until the early 1990s. As in the USA their share in freight and passenger transport decreased over time, and so did the quality of transport. Trucking was the major beneficiary of the railway decline in both countries, as it was able to provide transport services of higher quality. Its development was also stimulated by the massive construction of roads.

Road Transport

Major improvements in the road network provided the first step towards decreasing transport costs in the nineteenth century. These investments were undertaken from 1790 to 1830 in the USA, and from the 1840s to the 1870s in Brazil and Mexico. Road improvement stagnated during the period of massive railway construction, but started again with the emergence of significant motor vehicle transport in the 1920s. Brazilian and Mexican efforts to improve roads in the nineteenth century were small compared to those in the USA. Road improvements were regionally concentrated: in Mexico in the area surrounding Mexico City, and the mining regions; in Brazil in the Rio de Janeiro and the coffee and sugar plantation areas. Only small regions benefited from this, though the aggregate saving of costs was minor.

Though the USA already had a road network of 32,180 km around 1790, the network was very poor due to dispersed responsibility between independent local authorities and individuals. The 44,730 km of private turnpikes constructed in the period 1790–1830 provided longer stretches of good quality roads. Most were built in the north and connected populated areas. They were mostly financed with private capital concentrated in small local companies. Longer stretches were served by several companies, each charging a toll in their own section. Profits were disappointing, as most traffic was over small distances where common free roads were available as well. Though larger wagons, increased speed and competition decreased road transport costs even further, it remained unprofitable to carry low-value commodities over long distances. In the 1830s road turnpikes were rapidly overtaken by canals as the main mode of long-distance freight transport. Freight rates per ton km on turnpikes were between ten to fifteen times of those on canals and rivers in 1853 (Taylor, 1951).

In Brazil the primitive road network, mostly of Indian origin, improved little during the colonial period. Paths and trails only served as transport by animals. After the discovery of gold at the end of the seventeenth century, some road improvement occurred in Minas Gerais. Flourishing colonial trade via the ports of Porto Alegre, Recife, Rio do Janeiro, Salvador and Santos stimulated road construction to the interior, though most new roads were of poor quality. Pack mules were the most inexpensive form of road transport, as they were organised in trains of six to over forty animals; they were cheap to feed and had great endurance. The number of mules increased rapidly over time, though they were often in short supply throughout the nineteenth century. Land transport was hindered by frequent robberies, especially in the region of Rio de Janeiro (Summerhill, 1995).

In the nineteenth century road construction remained very limited. In 1834 the central government transferred the responsibility for road construction and other public works to provincial administrations, which had little funding. Public efforts remained limited to the building of a few roads and minor subsidies to the construction of bridges by private firms (Bethell, 1985). The first road for wheeled vehicles, connecting Rio and Petropolis, was opened in the 1830s. In the 1850s this road was extended by a private stagecoach company further into regions with coffee plantations. The government constructed three other highways in Minas Gerais, Paraná and Santa Catarina in the 1860s. Average speed of coaches on these roads was about 30 km per hour (Burns, 1993). Private firms, especially coffee planters in Paraiba, were also actively engaged in road construction. The muleteers expanded muletrain routes to the interior. From the 1870s onwards road construction dropped off sharply as attention shifted to railways.

A limited number of roads, a shortage of pack animals, robberies and slow speed led to high transport costs, which hindered the distribution of agricultural and other products. Limited storage options were an additional problem. High transport charges separated producers and consumers, and limited the gains from trade and regional specialisation. Product markets remained fragmented and autarkic.

Mexico inherited an extensive road and trail network from colonial times. The Spanish administration widened Indian routes and built bridges financed by taxes on the mining industry. It also introduced wheeled vehicular transport between the mining centres in the north to Veracruz via Mexico City. Small road improvements, financed by tolls, were realised during the first decades of the independent Mexico. The first Juarez administration (1856–62), and the French occupation initiated major highway construction projects in the Valley of Mexico. Road construction and improvement slowed down after the French occupation had ended in 1867. From the mid-1880s to the mid–1920s road development halted altogether, as all attention was focused on the development of railways.

Table 4.3 presents the growth of the stock of vehicles in the 1927–93 period in Brazil, Mexico and the USA. The stock of cars rose rapidly in the USA from 4,000 in 1900 to 181,000 in 1910, and 1,906,000 in 1920 (Davis *et al.*, 1972); the number doubled from 1927 to 1950, and almost quadrupled from 1950 to 1973.

Table 4.3 *Stock of Registered Vehicles and Vehicles Relative to Population, Brazil, Mexico and the USA, 1929–93*

	Cars			Buses			Trucks		
	Brazil	Mexico	USA	Brazil	Mexico	USA	Brazil	Mexico	USA
	Panel A: Number of Registered Vehicles (000s)								
1929	167	62	23,121	105	6	34	3	16	3,550
1950	409	173	40,339	201	18	224	26	111	8,599
1975	3,395	2,401	106,712	658	51	2,822	2,523	888	24,790
1993	10,598	7,497	146,314	n.a.	106	654	2,473	3,501	65,300
	Panel B: Number of Registered Vehicles per 1,000 Population								
1929	5.1	3.7	189.1	3.2	0.4	0.3	0.1	0.9	29.0
1950	7.9	6.3	264.9	3.9	0.7	1.5	0.5	4.1	56.5
1975	32.4	39.9	494.1	6.3	0.8	13.1	24.1	14.8	114.8
1993	70.5	83.7	565.9		1.2	2.5	16.4	39.1	252.5

Sources: Brazil: IBGE (1990), p. 466; 1975 from Ministerio dos Transportes (1982); 1993 from United Nations (1993, p. 666). Mexico: INEGI (1994b, pp. 85–86); 1993 from INEGI (various issues). USA: Department of Commerce, Bureau of the Census (1975, p. 716); 1975 and 1993 from Department of Commerce, *Statistical Abstract of the United States* 1977 and 1995. Population from Maddison (1995b).

Though Brazil and Mexico started from much lower levels than the USA, the growth of their stock of vehicles was much faster over the whole twentieth century. Panel B shows that Brazil and Mexico lagged far behind the USA in terms of cars per capita. The Latin American countries narrowed the gap with the USA as the stock of vehicles grew 53 times in Brazil, 43 times in Mexico and only 4 times in the USA from 1950 to 1993. Nevertheless, the number of cars per capita in Brazil and Mexico remained far less than in the USA. The stock of trucks and buses also increased more rapidly in Brazil and Mexico compared to the USA. Until the 1940s Brazil had more buses than the USA in absolute terms.

The US trucking industry grew rapidly just after World War I. Most operations were conducted by working proprietors rather than commercial carriers. Road freight transport was used by a wide range of industries at some point in their production process (Barger, 1951). Before 1914 more than half of the trucks hired transported farm products. Trucking became subject to the Motor Carrier Act (MCA) of 1935, a regulatory framework aimed at reducing competition and stabilising rates. The MCA regulated entry, rates and services, and divided carriers into three classes: common carriers, who served fixed routes between terminals on a regular schedule with published rates; contract carriers, who transported goods for customers at rates arranged by written or oral contracts; and carriers exempted from regulation. In 1940 trucking traffic was small relative to railways: 43 million ton km compared to 603 billion ton km, respectively.

In Brazil and Mexico trucks became the predominant mode of freight transport in the 1950s. In the USA railways continued to dominate freight transport until the early 1980s. Though the cost per ton km of trucking was higher and rose faster than that of railways, trucking displaced railway transport as the main mode of transport, because it offered more flexibility and higher quality. Deregulation of the trucking industry in the USA, which started in 1980, contributed to this process. Entry into the common and contract carrier market became free and rates were deregulated. In the 1980s the number of carriers, especially the small ones, doubled and employment increased by one-third, shipping rates decreased and the quality of service improved (Thomson, 1993).

In Brazil the number of transport firms increased from 1,045 in 1968 to 10,542 in 1983, the number of employees grew from 30,000 to 216,000 and revenues from 0.6 per cent of GDP to 2.3 per cent of GDP over the same period (Castro, 1988). The number of firms and employees decreased in the remainder of the 1980s. The trucking industry is dominated by few large firms, and thousands of small ones. Large firms operate high-density routes, mostly interstate. Small firms provide intrastate transport services on low-density routes. The lack of competition on the interstate routes induced high transport rates.

The Mexican government introduced tight trucking regulations in 1945. As a result the industry provided costly, poor quality, unreliable and uncompetitive service (Fernandez, 1993). In the 1980s it was identified by the government as a major bottleneck to economic growth. To promote development and efficiency, the government deregulated most of the industry in 1990. Though the new policy increased the quality and lowered the cost of transport, inefficient private monopolies continue to exist at the state and local level.

Air Transport[4]

The development and diffusion of air transport technology has been relatively rapid. Aviation in the USA started in the late 1910s; in Brazil and Mexico in the 1920s. When airlines came into existence, Brazil and Mexico had a very meagre road infrastructure, a poor railway network, and only a small number of waterways. Freight and passenger transport often went directly from mule to plane. This was not the case in the USA, where a large rail, road and canal network had already been developed in the nineteenth century. Brazil and Mexico stimulated foreign investment and foreign participation in their airlines, whereas in the USA airline development was mostly a national affair. In all three countries the government allocated air routes between carriers and regulated fares. In the 1970s it became clear that regulation had led to inefficiency and high operating costs. The USA deregulated its airlines in 1978; Brazil and Mexico did not follow until the early 1990s. Competition lowered fares and boosted traffic. In the USA many companies went bankrupt or merged as a result of the increased competition.

Table 4.4 summarises the growth of civil aviation from 1927 to 1993. Between 1929 and 1950 the number of passengers transported grew about 25 per cent per year in all three countries. In Brazil the volume of freight transported increased 35 per cent per year between 1929 and 1945, and almost 50 per cent annually in the years until 1950. Growth rates in Mexico and the USA were substantially lower. From 1950 to 1975 passenger volume grew faster in the USA than in Brazil and Mexico, whereas in the 1975–93 period Mexico showed the highest growth rate.

Communications

The number of post offices and the volume of mail distributed, both stimulated by improved means of transport, grew rapidly in the nineteenth century. Traditional mail distribution by horse and mule was gradually replaced by stagecoaches in the course of the nineteenth century. In the

USA, steamboats and trains replaced stagecoaches in settled areas in the 1850s and 1860s, as they reduced transport costs even further. The US government maintained high postal rates until the second half of the nineteenth century (Taylor, 1951, p. 150).

Table 4.4 Civil Aviation in Brazil, Mexico and the USA, 1927–93

	Aircraft km (000s)			Passengers (000s)			Freight (1000 ton)		
	Brazil	Mexico	USA	Brazil	Mexico	USA	Brazil	Mexico	USA
1927	120	236	5 870	1	1	9	6	n.a.	19
1929	1,140	3,052	25,142	4	11	173	62	n.a.	102
1938	5,083	6,489	75,653	57	76	1,788	1,144	3,087	14,055
1945	19,652	27,084	241,578	263	413	7,052	8,638	11,177	127,370
1950	82,246	41,940	464,452	1,715	1,033	19,020	62,405	45,531	291,819
1975	170,200	93,100	3,605,769	7,773	6,523	205,000	460,500	76,200	6,999,105
1993	333,100	237,200	6,436,000	16,599	16,485	487,200	1,285,900	150,900	17,388,018

Notes: In Brazil and Mexico freight transport is measured by million ton km in 1975 & 1993.

Sources: Brazil: IBGE (1990, p. 471). Mexico: INEGI (1994b). Brazil and Mexico: 1993 aircraft km and passengers from ECLAC (various issues). USA: Department of Commerce, Bureau of the Census (1975, pp. 769–70); 1993 from Department of Commerce, *Statistical Abstract of the United States* (various issues).

Many post offices had a mobile character and were driven by horses or trains in the nineteenth century. Until 1929 Brazil and Mexico had roughly the same number of post offices per capita; later, however, Mexico maintained a relatively higher level. Americans were much better served than Brazilians and Mexicans, though the number of US post offices per 100,000 inhabitants dropped from 100 in 1900 to 27 in 1950 (see Table 4.5). In addition to letters, mail also included postcards, samples, newspapers, books and other printed material. From 1900 to 1950 the volume of mail per capita increased rapidly in all three countries. In this period Brazil managed to catch up with the USA, whereas Mexico lagged behind. In Brazil mail distributed per capita increased little from 1950 to 1975, but more than doubled from 1975 to 1993. In Mexico, on the contrary, the volume of mail per inhabitant declined after 1975. Brazil surpassed Mexico and the USA in terms of post offices per head of population in 1993. In the USA the number of post offices per 100,000 population decreased from 27 in 1950 to 11 in 1993. The volume of mail handled more than doubled during this period.

Table 4.5 *Number of Post Offices, Pieces of mail, and Telegraph Messages per 100,000 Population, Brazil, Mexico and the USA, 1880–1993*

	Post Offices			Pieces of Mail (000s)			Messages sent (000s)		
	Brazil	Mexico	USA	Brazil	Mexico	USA	Brazil	Mexico	USA
1880	n.a.	n.a.	85	10	59	n.a.	2	2	58
1896	14	13	99	36	233	8,001	10	11	83
1900	15	14	100	86	1,088	9,334	8	19	83
1910	15	19	64	136	1,344	16,008	13	32	81
1929	14	17	40	356	1,186	22,865	18	37	203
1938	12	17	34	423	1,601	19,959	28	42	156
1950	9	15	27	1,039	2,061	29,594	54	130	132
1975	6	6	14	1,189	1,706	40,900	16	48	31
1993	19	5	11	2,637	953	68,493	12	7	n.a.

Sources: Brazil: 1880–1975 from IBGE (1990, p. 473–78) and 1993 from IBGE (1994, pp. 5, 44–47), *Anuario Estatístico do Brasil*. Mexico: 1880–1975 from INEGI (1994b) and 1993 from INEGI, *Anuario Estadístico de los Estados Unidos Mexicanos 1994*. USA: 1880–1975 from Department of Commerce, Bureau of the Census (1975, pp. 789–91) and 1993 from Department of Commerce, *Statistical Abstract of the United States 1995*. Population from Maddison (1995b); 1880 and 1896 population figures for Brazil and Mexico were estimated using annual compound growth rates of the 1870–90 and 1890–1900 period, respectively.

The installation of telegraph lines in the 1840s and 1850s meant that, for the first time, communication was no longer tied to the speed of human messengers, as messages could be transmitted almost instantaneously over long distances. The first telegraph line was installed in the USA in 1844 and in Brazil in 1852. The US network expanded rapidly to more than 80,450 km of wire by 1860. New York was connected to San Francisco in 1861, and to Europe in 1866. Around that time most small telegraph companies merged into the Western Union Telegraph Company. In Brazil the construction of lines was accelerated during the Paraguayan war. A connection with the northern city of Belém was established in 1886, and with Europe in 1874 (Burns, 1993).

Telegraph traffic grew more rapidly in the USA than in Brazil and Mexico (see Table 4.5). The volume of messages transmitted per capita reached its peak in the USA in 1929. Thereafter the relative volume declined due to the rapid spread of telephones. The number of messages per head continued to grow in Brazil and Mexico until the 1960s. In 1950 more messages per capita were transmitted in Mexico than in the USA and Brazil. Probably because of the poor quality of the Brazilian telephone service, the volume of messages transmitted decreased only slightly from 1975 to 1993 in Brazil, though it dropped 80 per cent in Mexico.

In the 1880s telephone communication had successfully been developed. The American Telephone and Telegraph (AT&T) company installed more than half a million telephones in the USA in the 1890s (Brinkley *et al.*, 1991). Compared to the USA the number of telephones grew more rapidly in Brazil and Mexico from 1907 to 1950, though it developed from much lower levels (see Table 4.6). In per capita terms Brazil and Mexico also started to catch up with the USA, though the gap still remained large in 1950: one in four people had a telephone in the USA compared to only one in 100 in Brazil and Mexico. Brazil's and Mexico's backwardness was due to their lower average incomes and the higher share of the population in rural areas.

Table 4.6 Number of Telephones (000s) and Telephones per Capita, Brazil, Mexico and the USA, 1907–93

	Number of Telephones (000s)			Telephones per 1,000 Population		
	Brazil	Mexico	USA	Brazil	Mexico	USA
1907	15	n.a.	6,119	0.7	n.a.	70.1
1915	46	14	10,524	1.9	1.0	104.3
1920	59	29	13,273	2.2	1.9	124.2
1930	163	96	20,103	4.9	5.6	162.6
1940	273	180	21,928	6.6	8.7	165.3
1945	426	216	27,867	9.2	9.1	198.4
1950	550	285	43,004	10.6	10.4	282.4
1975	3,458	2,915	130,000	33.0	48.5	601.9
1993	12,809	11,891	147,000	85.2	132.8	568.5

Sources: Brazil: IBGE (1990, p. 477–78); Mitchell (1998). Mexico: INEGI (1994b). USA: Department of Commerce, Bureau of the Census (1975, p. 783). 1975 and 1993, see Table 5.6.

In the period 1950–93 telecommunications developed most rapidly in Mexico as 133 people out of 1,000 had an access line in 1993 compared to 85 in Brazil (see Table 4.6). The gap between Brazil and Mexico on the one hand, and the USA on the other, continued to narrow from 1950 to 1993, though in 1993 the USA still had seven times as many telephones per head as Brazil, and four as many as in Mexico.

Until the 1980s telecommunications were heavily regulated in all three countries. In the USA the Communications Act of 1934 granted the Federal Communications Commission (FCC) regulatory power over all interstate and foreign communication by wire, radio, television, satellite and cable. The

1934 Act authorised states to regulate intrastate traffic. The FCC granted companies, of which AT&T was the largest, regional monopolies on local traffic. AT&T also provided all long distance connections.

In the USA a series of court decisions deregulated the telecommunications industry in the course of time, though large parts remained government-controlled. In 1982 a federal decree forced the break-up of AT&T into seven regional holding companies and one long-distance company. The FCC forbade AT&T to participate in local telephone markets, and prohibited the regional Bells to enter the long-distance interstate market. Interstate rates have become more flexible over time, as has entry to this market. Before 1982 interstate rates were set by the FCC and were above marginal costs to cross-subsidise local rates which were kept below marginal costs. Deregulation reduced the long-distance rates, accelerated technological progress and increased the range of services (Winston, 1993).

In Brazil and Mexico telephone companies are owned by the state. In 1990, *Teléfonos de México* (Telmex) was privatised, though the long-distance and international service monopoly ended in 1997. Since 1990 other suppliers have been allowed on local markets. Telecommunications remained in public hands in Brazil, except for mobile services.

Conclusion on Long-term Trends

The USA developed all transport modes much earlier than Brazil and Mexico, starting with the large road networks in the late eighteenth and early nineteenth century. Road construction in the Latin American countries remained small until the second half of the twentieth century. The USA built an extensive canal network and developed steamboat services, so that water transport replaced road turnpikes as the predominant transport mode in the nineteenth century. Water permitted the transport of larger quantities of freight at a much lower cost than road transport. In Brazil inland waterways played a minor role and in Mexico they were virtually absent. Ocean transport also became cheaper, quicker and more reliable over time. The USA developed its own merchant fleet. Brazil and Mexico outsourced most of their maritime transport to British carriers because they offered lower transport tariffs.

Railways were a key sector in transport in all three countries. The USA developed its network about half a century earlier than Brazil and Mexico. Railways reduced transport costs to levels below those of ships, stimulated the development of large enterprises, capital markets, new forms of management, and made it possible to spread (stages of) production and consumption geographically. Brazilian railways connected the interior with the coast, but in general did little for interregional trade. The savings from cheaper transport seem to have been somewhat larger in Brazil and Mexico than in the USA, though a large share of these gains in the two Latin American countries went to foreign owners and operators.

In the second half of the twentieth century trucks gradually overtook railways as the principal mode of freight transport. This happened in the 1950s in Brazil and Mexico, and in the 1980s in the USA. Though freight transport by road was more expensive than by rail, the quality was much better. Trucking was stimulated by large-scale road construction, and a deteriorating rail service. Rail also lost most of its share in passenger transport, which was increasingly overtaken by private cars in all countries, air transport in the USA and bus services in Brazil and Mexico.

The governments of all three countries stimulated transport development by financing the infrastructure of airports, ports and roads. In the 1970s it became evident that government regulation had a negative impact on the efficiency, price and quality of transport services. To reverse this trend the US government deregulated the airlines, railways and trucking in the late 1970s and 1980s, followed by Mexico in the early 1990s. Brazil's liberalisation remained limited to airlines.

COMPARISON OF OUTPUT AND PRODUCTIVITY LEVELS IN 1975

Measurement of Real Output

Following the recommendations of SNA 1993, the national accounts of most countries measure real output by passengers kilometres (km) or ton km.[5] These measures combine both the quantity of goods or number of persons and the distances over which they are transported. Most productivity studies rely on the same measures.[6] Other yardsticks used to measure real output relate to the movement of transport equipment, such as vehicle km in road goods and passenger transport (Italian national accounts, see OECD, 1996), fuel consumption or hours flown in air transport (McKinsey, 1998).

Transport services are, however, not limited to the movement of freight and passengers, but also include loading and unloading services at airports, ports, stations and terminals. The use of passenger or ton km as real output measures assumes implicitly that the volume of terminal services is proportional to that of movement services. For example, the output of air transport is often estimated by ton km and passenger km and it is assumed that the volume of airport handling services is proportional to that of the pure flying activity. Various authors have criticised the assumption of a fixed relationship between the movement and terminal activities. Meyer and Gómez-Ibáñez (1980) found that Kendrick (1973), who used ton km as the output measure, overstated US intercity trucking output (and productivity) growth in 1948–70 because the average distance increased over time and the relative importance of terminal work declined.

The measures presented so far have also been criticised as they fail to adjust for the changes in the composition of transported goods or passengers over time or between countries. A ton km of bulk represents less transport services than a ton km of jewellery. Meyer and Morton (1975) made this point, criticising conventional measures of trends in US railways in 1947–70, because they failed to account for shifts in the composition of goods transported. Most authors neglect this point probably due to difficulties of measurement. Some exceptions include Tretheway *et al.* (1994) and Briard (2001), who accounted for changes in railway output in Canada and France, respectively.

Finally, the passenger and ton km measures fail to take into account other aspects of the bundle of services offered by transport firms, such as comfort of passenger transport, frequency, on-time performance, speed and so on. The SNA 1993 and some studies explicitly recommend the adjustment of real output measures for these aspects. Meyer and Gómez-Ibáñez (1980) analysed long-term trends of the quality of the US mass transit. On the one hand, quality improved in the course of time, because of the introduction of air-conditioning, the increase in the speed of the vehicle and a fall in crowded conditions (measured by passengers per vehicle mile). On the other hand offsetting declines in quality took also place, especially in terms of the frequency of service. Chakraborty and Kazarosian (1999) stress that road goods transport should be disaggregated according to the 'marketing objective' of firms as each objective results in a different bundle of transport services. These objectives include the lowest freight rate, on-time performance, safety, transport of hazardous materials and transport of heavy machinery.

Ideally, transport output should thus distinguish modes of transport and within each mode between movement and terminal services. These two activities should be broken down further by the types of goods transported or the types of services offered to passengers. Subsequently, the movement and terminal activities of each type of good or passenger transport is weighted by its unit movement or handling costs. Finally, other aspects of the transport services bundle should be considered, such as safety, speed and so on.

Various improvements adopted in the intertemporal real output measures could also be applied to international comparisons. Estimating deflators in intertemporal or international comparisons is essentially the same: in the former they are used to transform a current to a constant price series, while in the latter they allow values expressed in different currencies to be converted into a common one. As exchange rates and purchasing power parities based on final expenditure are unsuitable deflators, ratios of producer prices or unit values are used instead. These unit values are derived by dividing gross revenues, or cost in the case of subsidised services, (o) by produced quantities (q) for each service i in each country:

$$UV_i = \frac{o_i}{q_i} \tag{4.1}$$

The unit value is the average price at which a similar type of service is sold by all transport providers in a given year. In each bilateral comparison, services are matched according to more or less detailed descriptions, for example interurban railway passenger transport, road freight transport, airport passenger handling and so on.

For each matched service, the ratio of the unit values between two countries is calculated:

$$UVR_i^{xu} = \frac{UV_i^x}{UV_i^u} \tag{4.2}$$

with x being Brazil or Mexico and u the base country, the USA. The UVR indicates the relative producer price of the matched service in both countries. UVRs of individual services are used to estimate UVRs at more aggregate levels: branches and total transport. These levels correspond to those distinguished in the International Standard Industrial Classification (ISIC).

The UVR for a transport branch is the weighted mean of the individual transport services UVRs, using output values of the base country (USA) or the other country (Brazil or Mexico) as weights. The UVR for a branch using US weights is estimated as follows:

$$UVR_k^{xu(u)} = \sum_{i=1}^{I_k} UVR_{ik}^{xu} \times w_{ik}^{u(u)}$$

with

$$w_{ik}^{u(u)} = \frac{o_{ik}^{u(u)}}{\sum_{i=1}^{I_K} o_{ik}^{u(u)}} \tag{4.3}$$

with i=1,…,I_K the matched services in branch k, w_{ik} the output share of the ith service in branch k. $UVR_k^{xu(u)}$ indicates the unit value ratio between country x and the base country (USA) weighted at base country quantities indicated by the u in brackets. This equation can be rewritten to show that the use of base country value weights leads to the Laspeyres index:

$$UVR_k^{xu(u)} = \frac{\sum_{i=1}^{I_K} q_{ik}^u * UV_{ik}^x}{\sum_{i=1}^{I_K} q_{ik}^u * UV_{ik}^u} \tag{4.4}$$

Instead of US weights, weights of the other country quantities valued at base country prices can be used in equation (4.3):

$$UVR_k^{xu(x)} = \sum_{i=1}^{I_K} UVR_{ik}^{xu} \times w_{ik}^{u(x)}$$

with

$$w_{ik}^{u(x)} = \frac{o_{ik}^{u(x)}}{\sum_{i=1}^{I_K} o_{ik}^{u(x)}} \tag{4.5}$$

This index can be easily rewritten to show that it is a Paasche index:

$$UVR_k^{xu(x)} = \frac{\sum_{i=1}^{I_K} q_{ik}^x * UV_{ik}^x}{\sum_{i=1}^{I_K} q_{ik}^x * UV_{ik}^u} \tag{4.6}$$

This approach, also referred to as the unit value approach, is not feasible for all transport services due to data limitations. In some bilateral comparisons, that is not those in this study, basic transportation statistics do not provide quantities *and* values and secondary sources need to be consulted. These other sources may have different output coverage and sometimes differ in the treatment of taxes and subsidies. The UVR approach is also not applicable when the proportionate importance of terminal services is substantially different between countries and the statistics do not allow the separate measurement of UVRs for movement and terminal services.

The physical quantity approach was used for those transport services where the UVR approach cannot be applied. Both approaches yield the same results when all output is covered. For each matched service, the ratio of the quantities (q) in both countries is taken:

$$QR_i^{xu} = \frac{q_i^x}{q_i^u} \tag{4.7}$$

The QR of a branch is the weighted mean of the QR of the matched transport services, using gross revenues of country u as weights. This yields a Laspeyres quantity index:

$$QR_k^{xu(u)} = \sum_{i=1}^{I_K} QR_{ik} \times w_{ik}^{u(u)}$$

with $$w_{ik}^{u(u)} = \frac{o_{ik}^{u(u)}}{\sum_{i=1}^{I_K} o_{ik}^{u(u)}} \tag{4.8}$$

We can also use the weights of the other country x, which leads to a Paasche quantity index:

$$QR_k^{xu(x)} = \sum_{i=1}^{I_K} QR_{ik} \times w_{ik}^{x(x)}$$

with $$w_{ik}^{u(x)} = \frac{o_{ik}^{x(x)}}{\sum_{i=1}^{I_K} o_{ik}^{x(x)}} \tag{4.9}$$

The UVR for the branch k can now be derived implicitly by relating the branch QR to the gross revenues in the branch. A Laspeyres UVR is derived by the ratio of the gross revenues in country x to the Paasche quantity ratio divided by the gross revenues in country u:

$$UVR_k^{xu(u)} = \frac{(o_k^{x(x)} / QR_{ik}^{xu(x)})}{o_k^{u(u)}} \tag{4.10}$$

A Paasche UVR is derived by dividing the gross revenues in country x by the Laspeyres quantity ratio multiplied by the gross revenues in country u:

$$UVR_k^{xu(k)} = \frac{o_k^{x(x)}}{(QR_{ik}^{xu(u)} * o_k^{u(u)})} \tag{4.11}$$

Finally, the UVR for total transport is the weighted mean of the branch UVRs. The total transport UVR reflects better the composition of the branches it is composed of when the gross revenue weights of branches are replaced by value added (VA) weights in (4.3) and (4.5). The UVR using US weights is estimated as follows:

$$UVR^{xu(u)} = \sum_{k=1} UVR_k^{xu(u)} \times w_k^{u(u)}$$

with
$$w_k^{u(u)} = \frac{va_k^{u(u)}}{\sum_{k=1} va_k^{u(u)}} \tag{4.12}$$

Instead of US weights, weights of the other country value added at base country prices can be used:

$$UVR^{xu(x)} = \sum_{k=1} UVR_k^{xu(x)} \times w_k^{u(x)}$$

with
$$w_k^{u(x)} = \frac{va_k^{u(x)}}{\sum_{k=1} va_k^{u(x)}} \tag{4.13}$$

Van Ark and Monnikhof (2000) used gross revenues instead of value added weights to aggregate branch UVRs to total transport UVRs. Although gross revenue weights do not necessarily reflect the best relative importance of each mode in total transport, they have the advantage of being consistent with the aggregation steps at more detailed levels. Moreover, in a double deflation procedure, they are more appropriate than the value-added weights.

Output and Productivity Levels in 1975

Table 4.7 shows value added and employment in transport and communications in Brazil, Mexico and the USA. The contribution of a sector to overall GDP is best measured by value added.[7] Where possible census data are used. Although the coverage of economic activity of the national accounts is broader and more comparable, census data are often more reliable in Brazil and Mexico. The national accounts were used for US transport and for communications in all three countries.

The data on transport in Brazil and Mexico in Table 4.7 give an inadequate picture of the relative importance of each branch in total GDP and/or in employment, because of the large variance in census coverage of transport activities. Information on the relative importance of the various transport branches was derived from national accounts (see Table 4.13). Road freight transport was the predominant branch in all countries. The second most important item in Brazil and Mexico was road passenger transport, but the proportion was much smaller (6.1 per cent) in the USA. Private passenger car transport is much important in the USA, as is shown by the higher expenditure share on private transport at the bottom of Table 4.7, and the number of cars per head. Private passenger transport is not treated here as a market activity. It does not enter the national accounts and is therefore excluded from the sectoral totals. The USA also showed five times as many buses, and fifteen times as many trucks. The large discrepancy in the number of km of paved roads also reflects the large gap between the three countries. US railways and air transport accounted for a much larger share of transport GDP than their Brazilian and Mexican counterparts.

Most employees were engaged in road freight transport in Mexico and the USA, whereas in Brazil road passenger transport was the primary employment source. The second most important branch of transport in Brazil, Mexico and the USA was trucking, road passenger transport and railways, respectively. No breakdown existed of GDP and employment in communications. Telecommunications form a main part of the communications sector in all countries.

The estimation of physical output will be explained below for each mode of transport, using the Mexico USA comparison as an example. A difficult issue is the correct measurement of the quantity of transport services produced due to the mix of pure movement and loading and unloading activities. In domestic transport the share of terminal activity in total transport services increases with a fall in the average distance over which freight and passengers are carried.

Table 4.7 *Value Added and Employment in Transport and Communications, Brazil, Mexico and the USA, 1975*

Panel A: Value Added and Employment

	Value Added (Million US$)*			Persons Engaged (000s)		
	Brazil	Mexico	USA	Brazil	Mexico	USA
Transport						
Railways	73	300	12,737	28	99	548
Road passenger transport	709	939	3,476	221	167	307
Road freight transport	631	305	25,051	329	62	1,317
Water transport	65	72	3,969	13	6	198
Air transport	262	279	8,978	24	18	371
Transportation services	711	257	2,884	62	27	146
Transport (total)	2,451	2,153	57,095	456	379	2,887
Communications	917	246	34,664	153	22	1,180

Panel B: Infrastructures and Vehicle Stock

		Total			Per 1,000 Inhabitants		
	Unit	Brazil	Mexico	USA	Brazil	Mexico	USA
Infrastructure							
Railway track	km	30,809	24,912	351,665	0.3	0.4	1.6
Paved roads	km	64,744	60,643	5,022,837	0.6	1.0	23.3
Vehicle stock							
Private automobiles	000	3,395	2,401	106,712	32.4	39.9	494.1
Buses	000	2,523	888	24,790	24.1	14.8	114.8
Trucks	000	84	51	2 822	0.8	0.8	13.1

Notes: * Brazilian and Mexican value added were converted to US$ by the 1975 exchange rates. In 1975 per capita expenditure on (public and private) passenger transport was 690 cruzeiros in Brazil, 1,027 pesos in Mexico and 600 dollars in the USA. Private (mainly car) transport expenditure accounted for 74.9 per cent of the total in Brazil, 66.5 per cent in Mexico and 93.3 per cent in the USA. The imputed value of private passenger transport was 55,562 million cruzeiros in Brazil, 41,081 million pesos in Mexico and 120,901 million dollars in the USA (see Kravis *et al.*, 1982, p. 272). Transport GDP was 36,759 million cruzeiros, 55,158 million pesos and 57,095 million dollars, respectively.

Sources: Value added and employment: IBGE (1981b); communications IBGE (1987); Mexico: SPP (1979); USA: Department of Commerce (1986). Infrastructure: Sources: Brazil: IBGE (1990, pp. 457; 465); Mexico: INEGI (1994b); USA: Department. of Commerce (various issues), *Statistical Abstract of the United States*. Population: Maddison (1995b). Vehicle stock: Table 4.3.

Rail transport

Freight transport was the predominant railway activity: gross revenues from freight accounted for 98 per cent of railway revenue in the USA in 1975, 94 per cent in Mexico and 89 per cent in Brazil (see Appendix D).

To get an impression of the amount of terminal work in Mexico and the USA, average freight and passengers hauls are compared in Table 4.8. In domestic transport the share of terminal activity in total transport services increases with a fall in the average distance over which freight and passengers are carried. For example, the average distances of domestic freight transport by train were 469, 532 and 870 km in Brazil, Mexico and the USA, respectively, in 1975. If ton km were to be used as the output measure, the resulting UVR would be biased upwards in the countries with the shorter hauls, that is Brazil and Mexico, and labour productivity underestimated. Hence freight ton km and passenger km are acceptable proxies for transport output only if average transport distances are similar across countries.

Table 4.8 Length of Average Passenger Trips in km, Freight Hauls in km and Population Density, Brazil, Mexico and USA, 1975

	Brazil	Mexico	USA
Passenger transport (km)			
Commuter rail	36	n.a.	37
Intercity rail	n.a.	168	375
Domestic air	831	999	1,121
Freight transport (km)			
Rail	469	532	870
Road	343	323	523
Population density (people/sq. km)	12.8	30.8	23.6

Sources: Average distances estimated by ratio of passenger km to passengers or by ratio of ton km to tons (see Appendix D). Population density from World Bank (1997).

There are at least three methods to account for differences in the proportionate importance of terminal services between countries:

(a) separate total transport revenues (costs) and quantities produced into movement and loading and unloading services; for example air transport into flight and airport handling services. Subsequently, estimate separate UVRs for each;

(b) when revenues (costs) cannot be separated into movement and terminal services, it is sometimes possible to derive the share of terminal services in the total implicitly. Higher relative prices often reflect the proportionally higher costs of transporting goods over shorter distances.[8] This method requires the availability of charges for different lengths of transport hauls;

(c) adjust the quantity relatives of terminal and transport services.

As no data are available to carry out options (a) or (b), option (c) was used: total transport services are estimated by a weighted average of the movement activity (in terms of passenger or ton km) and turnover activity (in terms of passengers or tons). The new quantity relative (Q^{x*}/Q^{u*}) equals the measure of freight and passenger km in country x relative to the USA (Q^x/Q^u), adjusted for the share of turnover activity in total output by combining it with an estimate of the number of passengers or tons of freight handled (T^x/T^u):

$$\frac{Q^{x^*}}{Q^{u^*}} = \left[(1-S)\frac{Q^x}{Q^u} + S\frac{T^x}{T^u} \right] \tag{4.14}$$

The weights, (1–S) for movement services (that is Q^x/Q^u) and S for terminal services (that is T^x/T^u), are derived by the ratio of the freight hauls in country x and the USA. Clearly shorter travel distances and greater presence of terminals are often related to the greater population density in one country in comparison to another. However, after allowing for differences in population density, the *quality* of the transport service increases when there are more possibilities to load and unload:

$$S = (1 - \frac{H^x}{H^u}) * \frac{D^u}{D^x} \tag{4.15}$$

This method was used in this study and in van Ark *et al.* (1999). While terminal work in freight transport had relatively more importance in Mexico compared to the USA, the contrary was true for passenger travel. Output estimates, which made no allowance for terminal services, would underestimate Mexican freight transport activity and would overstate the same in passenger transport. An adjustment was made to the physical output measure to take account of terminal work, as shown in equations (4.12) and (4.13).[9] The adjustment factor is the highest for Brazil relative to the USA, given its relatively low population density, it offers more points of access to its transport infrastructure (see Table 4.9).

Table 4.9 Adjustment for Terminal Services after Correction for Population Density, Brazil and Mexico Relative to the USA, 1975

	Brazil/USA	Mexico/USA
Passenger transport		
Commuter rail	0.03	n.a.
Intercity rail	n.a.	0.42
Domestic air	0.26	0.19
Freight transport		
Rail	0.46	0.30
Road	0.34	0.29

Source: Table 4.8; method: see text.

Table 4.10 shows that the impact of the terminal adjustment on the quantity relatives (Q^X/Q^{USA}) was the largest in rail passenger transport in the Mexico/USA comparison where relative output increased about 50 per cent, followed by a 20 per cent rise of the relative output in Mexican trucking. Brazilian relative output increased almost 10 per cent in domestic air passenger transport and rail freight transport. The terminal adjustment had almost no impact on the relative volume of rail passenger transport in Brazil, as the average distance travelled on commuter trains was almost the same in the two countries.

When van Ark and Monnikhof (2000) applied it to 24 countries, they found that this adjustment gave too much weight to the terminal element and changed the equation. They multiplied the ratio of movement services (that is Q^x/Q^u), unadjusted for the terminal element, by a factor based on the relative average distances travelled $(Q/T)^u/(Q/T)^x$:

$$\frac{Q^{x^*}}{Q^{u^*}} = \frac{Q^x}{Q^u} * \left[\frac{(Q/T)^u}{(Q/T)^x}\right]^{\left[\frac{1}{(Q/T)^u/(Q/T)^x}\right]} \tag{4.16}$$

Table 4.10 Quantity Relatives Before and After Adjusting for Terminal Services and Quality Differences, Brazil/USA and Mexico/USA, 1975

	Brazil/USA			Mexico/USA		
	Traditional Measure	Adjusted for: Terminal Services	Adjusted for: Terminal Services and Quality	Traditional Measure	Adjusted for: Terminal Services	Adjusted for: Terminal Services and Quality
			Passenger transport			
Rail*	146.3	146.4	88.7	65.5	99.9	47.1
Urban transport						
City bus	n.a.	n.a.	n.a.	120.9	120.9	60.9
Subway	n.a.	n.a.	n.a.	33.0	33.0	19.0
Tramway/trolley	n.a.	n.a.	n.a.	105.4	105.4	51.9
Bus transport	210.8	210.8	144.2	145.8	145.8	83.9
Air				2.8	2.9	2.0
Domestic	2.4	2.6	1.8	n.a.	n.a.	n.a.
International	10.5	10.5	7.4	n.a.	n.a.	n.a.
			Freight transport			
Rail	5.4	5.9	5.9	3.0	3.6	3.6
Road	6.4	7.6	5.8	8.0	9.3	7.1
Water						
Rivers & lakes	0.4	0.4	0.4	0.5	0.5	0.5
Ocean & coast	1.9	1.9	1.9	1.1	1.1	1.1
Air				3.8	3.8	2.7
Domestic	10.4	10.4	7.3	n.a.	n.a.	n.a
International	23.5	23.5	16.4	n.a.	n.a.	n.a

Notes: * Rail refers to commuter rail in the Brazil/USA comparison and to intercity rail in the Mexico/USA comparison.
An adjustment for terminal services was made in rail and air passenger transport and in rail and road freight transport. The quantity relatives have been adjusted for quality differences in rail, urban, interurban and air passenger transport; and in road and air freight transport, as explained in Table 4.11 and in the text.

Sources: Basic data from Appendix D; quality adjustment from Table 5.13. Output was measured in ton km and passenger km or tons and passengers. For the USA short tons were converted to metric tons by a factor 0.907.

This adjusted equation for relative output has the advantage of being is asymptotic with increases in the terminal element. This means that when the differences between the distances travelled in the two countries are not too large, the adjustment for the terminal effect has the right direction and magnitude.

Studies reveal the inferior quality of Mexican rail passenger transport: trains were more crowded than US trains, they had less comfort, more delays, more accidents and travelled at lower speed. The number of passengers per train km demonstrates how crowded trains were (see Table 4.11). On average US trains carried less than half the number of passengers transported by Mexican trains, supposing that the size of Mexican and US trains were similar. As this was the only indicator of quality available, it was assumed to be a general proxy for the quality of the service, and adjusted Mexican output accordingly. A similar type of adjustment was made for the Brazil/USA comparison of rail passenger transport.

Road passenger transport

This branch consists of passenger transport by bus (urban and suburban, and long-distance), tramway and subway. School and sightseeing bus transport was excluded due to data limitations. Brazilians and Mexicans relied more heavily on bus transport than Americans (52 per cent and 35 per cent of transport GDP, respectively, compared with only 6 per cent).

The number of passenger journeys is a first approximation to measuring output if average distances travelled are similar in different countries. While the average trip in urban and suburban areas is probably very similar, it may differ greatly for intercity travel (see Smith *et al.*, 1982). Therefore, the output measure is biased only in the case of intercity bus passenger transport.

Important differences in quality exist. Mexican buses had less seat availability than their US counterparts, because they were smaller and on average more crowded. Data on the number of passengers per vehicle km (Meyer and Gómez-Ibáñez, 1980, p. 315) illustrate this (see Table 4.11). On average Mexican buses carried almost twice the number of passengers per vehicle km as their US counterparts. Other indicators of quality are frequency of service, number of accidents, respect of announced schedules and speed. The measures used here should reflect these quality differences. For lack of detailed information, it is assumed that differences in passenger density is a proxy for all quality differentials. The average number of people transported by bus also provided the quality indicator for the Brazil/USA comparison.

Road freight transport

Road freight was the most important branch in all three countries (see Table 4.13). However, the Mexican census only covered vehicles operating with special licences, transport goods over a fixed route or special kinds of product without a fixed route (see Islas Rivera, 1992). Transporters with such licences accounted for only 20 per cent of the total trucking industry. Due to the very low coverage, other sources[10] were used to compare Mexican road freight transport with the USA.

Table 4.11 Quality Indicators for Transport and Communications, Brazil/USA and Mexico/USA, 1975

	Brazil	Mexico	USA	Brazil/ USA	Mexico/ USA
Panel A: Rail Passenger Transport					
Passengers per train km, 1975	60.3	77.5	36.5	1.7	2.1
Panel B: Road Passenger Transport					
Passengers per bus km, 1975	n.a.	2.3	1.3	n.a.	1.7
Urban and suburban buses	n.a.	4.1	2.1	n.a.	2.0
Intercity buses	n.a.	0.3	0.2	n.a.	1.7
Tramway and trolley services	n.a.	7.3	3.6	n.a.	2.0
Passengers per bus, 1975	146,259	n.a.	100,057	1.5	n.a.
Panel C: Road Freight Transport					
Vehicle km (million), 1975	n.a.	56,275	2,136,913		
Automobiles and motorcycles	n.a.	39,674	1,673,360		
Trucks	n.a.	16,245	453,738		
Buses	n.a.	356	9,815		
Paved and unpaved roads in km	1,428,707	124,745	6,175,664		
Congestion (vehicle km per km of road)	n.a.	451,120	346,022	n.a.	1.3
Panel D: Telecommunications and Postal Services					
Local calls completed, 1989 (%)	39	92	99	0.4	0.9
Lines out of order, 1989 (%)	5	10	1	1.0	0.9
Average repair time, 1989 (days)	2	4	1	0.5	0.3
Degree of digitalisation, 1992 (%)	65	48	95	0.7	0.5
Average				0.6	0.6
Post offices per 100,000 population, 1975	8	6	14	0.5	0.4

Sources: Passengers per train km: Mexico and Brazil from transport censuses as described in Table 5.9; USA from Association of American Railroads (1978). Quality of road passenger and road freight transport: Brazil from Ministerio do Transportes (1982). Mexico from transport census as described in Table 5.9; USA from Department of Transportation (1977). Telecommunication quality indicators: ECLAC/UNIDO (1994). Number of post offices: Brazil: IBGE (1990); Mexico: INEGI (1994b); USA: Department of Commerce, *Statistical Abstract of the United States 1977*.

Table 4.11 shows that congestion on US roads was only three-quarters of that in Mexico. Congestion decreases the quality of road transport leading to a lower average vehicle speed, more traffic jams and more accidents. Mexican output was adjusted by this ratio, taking it as a proxy measure for all quality differences. No information on vehicle km was available for Brazil.

It was assumed that the congestion differential between Mexico and the USA was also representative for Brazil and the USA.

Air transport

Passenger transport is the main element in air activity. In 1975 the average passenger flight was 831 km in Brazil, 999 in Mexico and 1,121 in the USA. Compared to the USA the proportionate importance of terminal services was higher in Brazil and lower in Mexico. The quantity ratio of passenger km was adjusted in the case of domestic services[11] in order to account for differences in the relative importance of terminal services (see equation 4.14).

The quality of Mexican air passenger transport was inferior to that in the USA, because of more frequent delays, poorer service, lower frequency, more accidents and airlines served relatively fewer cities. It was assumed that the quality of the service was 70 per cent of that in the USA, and output was adjusted correspondingly. The same terminal services and quality adjustments were made as in the Brazil/USA comparison. Output of air freight transport was estimated by ton km.

Water transport

Two matches for freight transport over water were made in the Brazil/USA and Mexico/USA comparisons: one for sea transport, coastal transport and port activities, and another for freight on lakes and rivers. The output of water freight transport was measured in tons because data on ton km were not available, and it was assumed that average freight hauls were similar in Brazil and Mexico on the one hand and the USA on the other.

General transport services

These consist of a variety of services (including warehousing) to all modes of transport. No data were available on physical output produced in any of the three countries.

Communications

A breakdown of communications GDP was only available for Mexico and the USA and showed that telephone and telegraph services accounted for 90 per cent of the total value added. Americans used 130 million telephones in 1975, which is 38 times the Brazilian number of telephones and 45 times the Mexican figure. This represents 18 and 12 times as many telephones per capita in the USA as in Brazil and Mexico, respectively. On average each American made 17 times and 31 times as many phone calls as their Brazilian and Mexican counterparts, respectively.

Communications include postal services and telecommunications. In many countries postal companies do not only handle mail and telegraph services, but also provide financial and miscellaneous services (car rental, sale of stationery and travel packages). SNA-1993 and ESA-1995 do not provide guidelines on the real output measures to be used. The OECD (1996) survey shows that the national accounts measures of most member countries are restricted to the mail activity: the number of letters and packages delivered, either unweighted (as in New Zealand and Portugal) or weighted by their postal rates (Germany).

In contrast to the standard output measures in transport (passenger km and ton km), the number of mail items handled reflect the terminal activity in postal services but not the movement of mail. In most countries no data are available on the latter activity. The bias of omitting this part of output seems limited, as the movement of mail accounts for less than 10 per cent of total costs in for example the UK and the USA (Smith *et al.*, 1982). Moreover, differences in distances between origin and destination is often accounted for in postal rates. Other aspects of the bundle of postal services, such as weight, delivery speed and safety, are also taken into account in postal rates (Adie, 1990).

International comparisons are more difficult than intertemporal ones due to differences in the composition of postal services' output in terms of shares of mail handling, financial and miscellaneous services. As statistics are mostly limited to the mail-handling activity, output will be underestimated in countries where financial and miscellaneous services are proportionally more important. Another difficulty is the large differences in degree of subsidisation across countries, which make postal rates an inadequate measure of the bundle of services offered.

In this study real output is measured by the unweighted number of pieces of mail handled. To account for the better quality of US postal services, the Brazilian and Mexican quantities were adjusted downwards, using the number of postal offices per 100,000 inhabitants as a proxy of access to postal services. In combination with gross output at factor costs, UVRs are estimated as shown in equations (4.10) and (4.11).

Telecom service output may be divided into installation and maintenance of the network and customer relations, and output related to traffic (that is directory services and operation of switchboards). In the national accounts of OECD countries, real output is most often measured by traffic-related measures, such as the number or minutes of calls (OECD, 1996). In their international comparisons, McKinsey (1992) and Paige and Bombach (1959) also included network-related services, measured by the number of telephones or access lines. They estimated total output by a weighted average of traffic and network-related services, using employment in each function as weights. McKinsey's five-country comparison showed that about 85 per cent of telecom personnel were engaged in network and 15 per cent in traffic-related services. Physical output in telegraph services is commonly measured by the number of messages transmitted. Telecom firms also provide other services such as mobile telephones, whose output can be estimated in the same way as for fixed lines.

In this study it would ideally have been preferable to derive UVRs for network and traffic-related services separately. Although physical output data exist for both parts, gross revenues and costs were available only for the total. As McKinsey, telecom output was estimated as a weighted average of network and traffic-related services:

$$\frac{Q^{x^*}}{Q^{u^*}} = \left[(1-E)\frac{Q^x}{Q^u} + E\frac{N^x}{N^u}\right] \tag{4.17}$$

where Q^{x^*}/Q^{u^*} is the adjusted quantity relative, Q^x/Q^u the 'traditional' (national accounts) quantity relative in terms of number of calls, N^x/N^u the network quantity relative in terms of the number of access lines and E the share of telecom employment working in network-related services. In absence of information on employment shares, this study used those of McKinsey (1992). To account for quality differences between the Latin countries and the USA, the quantity relatives were adjusted using an average of four indicators: percentage of local calls completed, percentage of lines out of order, average repair time and degree of digitalisation. In combination with gross output at factor costs, UVRs are estimated as shown in equations (3.10) and (3.11).

Except for the quality adjustments, the same procedures for postal companies and telecommunications were adopted by van Ark *et al.* (1999) and van Ark and Monnikhof (2000).

Unit Value Ratios

Table 4.12 shows the Fisher UVRs for the three binary comparisons. UVRs obtained by the 'traditional' method, using passenger km or freight km as measures for outputs are presented first, followed by measures adjusted for terminal services, and finally with adjustments for both terminal service and quality of service. In most cases the terminal services adjustment increased output of Brazil and Mexico relative to that of the USA, and thus yielded a lower UVR.

Table 4.12 Unit Value Ratios for Transport and Communications, Fisher Results, Brazil/USA and Mexico/USA, 1975

	Brazil/USA (Cruzeiros/US$)			Mexico/USA (Pesos/US$)		
	Traditional Measure	Adjusted for: Terminal Services	Adjusted for: Terminal Services and Quality	Traditional Measure	Adjusted for: Terminal Services	Adjusted for: Terminal Services and Quality
Railways	3.67	3.38	3.56	8.63	7.00	7.68
Bus transport	2.10	2.10	3.07	3.45	3.45	6.40
Road freight	4.47	3.79	4.94	8.91	7.72	10.07
Air transport	11.14	11.14	11.14	18.49	18.49	18.49
Transport services	9.87	9.35	13.36	10.90	10.40	14.85
Transport (total)	4.59	4.25	5.53	7.37	6.78	9.42
Communications	10.32	10.32	17.23	10.64	10.64	16.59
Transport and Communications	5.52	5.25	7.52	7.81	7.37	10.83
Exchange rate	8.13	8.13	8.13	12.50	12.50	12.50

Sources: Volume indicators and value of output from Appendix D; terminal services' adjustment using shares of Table 4.9. The quality adjustment was based on Table 4.11. Column 1 refers to simple passenger km and freight km output measures, or passengers and freight tonnage if passenger km or ton km measures were not available. Column 2: see above text for railways, road freight transport, and air passenger transport; for the quality adjustment see Table 4.11, applied to rail and road passenger transport, road freight transport, air transport and communications.

In Brazil and Mexico the quality adjustment reduced the volume of services produced, and raised the price per unit of output. This increased the UVRs in the Brazil/USA and Mexico/USA comparisons. The impact of the quality adjustment was substantial as the Fisher UVR of air transport rose 43 per cent, and that of communications 67 per cent in the Brazil/US comparison. The largest increments of Mexico/US Fisher UVRs occurred in the same branches.

RECONCILIATION OF CENSUS AND NATIONAL ACCOUNTS DATA

To assess the coverage of the Brazilian and Mexican censuses, they are confronted with the respective national accounts in Table 4.13.[12] The Brazilian census covered only a minor part of railway and water transport value added and employment, but represented a larger share of air and road transport. The Mexican census seems to have overestimated air and railway transport value added and employment, and have included only a minor share of road freight transport.

Table 4.13 Reconciliation of Census and National Accounts Data. Value Added and Employment, Brazil and Mexico, 1975

	Value Added (Million National Currency Units)			Employment (000s)		
	Census	National Accounts	(1)/(2)	Census	National Accounts	(4)/(5)
Branch	(1)	(2)	(3)	(4)	(5)	(6)
Brazil						
Railways	595	2,332	0.26	28	136	0.21
Road transport	10,889	26,405	0.41	329	1,019	0.32
Water transport	530	4,574	0.12	13	40	0.33
Air transport	2,133	3,448	0.62	24	28	0.84
Transport services	5,777	n.a.		62	n.a.	
Transport (total)	19,923	36,759	0.54	456	1,224	0.37
Communications	11,358	9,544	1.19	153	153	1.00
Mexico						
Railways	3,752	3,395	1.11	99	89	1.11
Road passenger	11,734	19,455	0.60	167	278	0.60
Road freight	3,817	23,951	0.16	62	389	0.16
Water transport	896	1,466	0.61	6	9	0.61
Air transport	3,489	2,571	1.36	18	13	1.36
Transport services	3,218	4,320	0.75	27	36	0.74
Transport (total)	26,906	55,158	0.49	379	815	0.46
Communications	3,076	7,454	0.41	22	65	0.34

Notes: Employment in Mexico correspond to the number of paid jobs.

Sources: Census estimates of GDP and employment as described in Table 4.9. National accounts: see Appendix E.

The calculations of unregistered activity[13] value added confirm that the Brazilian national accounts underestimated value added in transport and communications (Appendix E). Mexican national accounts overestimated value added in transport, but underestimated value added in communications. The value-added figures have been adjusted to take account of unregistered activity.

LABOUR PRODUCTIVITY

The UVRs of Table 4.12 were used to convert value added to a common set of prices, which after dividing by employment yield relative productivity levels, as presented in Table 4.14. After accounting for differences in terminal services and for intercountry variations in quality of transport, Brazilian labour productivity was found to be 40 per cent of the US level in 1975. Relative levels varied widely between branches: 18 per cent of US levels in water transport to 85 per cent in transport services. Brazil's relative performance in communications was only 10 per cent of that in the USA. Productivity in Mexican transport was 38 per cent of the US level, and in communications 29 per cent in 1975. The highest relative productivity in Mexico was in road passenger transport, and lowest for railways.

Labour productivity was also calculated for the total of the formal and the unregistered sector. This is shown in Panel B of Table 4.14. When the informal sector is included, relative productivity of Brazilian transport thus falls from 40 per cent to 37 per cent of the US level in 1975, and that of communications rises from 9 to 14 per cent. Relative productivity of Mexican transport rises from 38 per cent to 43 per cent of the US level, and the relative performance in communications remains unchanged after including the unregistered sector.

Table 4.14 also shows that the traditional measure, which ignores loading and unloading services, yields lower productivity ratios for Brazil and Mexico relative to the USA. If output had not been adjusted for quality differences, Brazilian and Mexican productivity would have been 8 percentage points and 11 percentage points higher, respectively. These results refer to registered establishments covered by the production censuses.

Time series of GDP at constant prices and employment were used to extrapolate the results to cover the whole period 1950 to 1993 (see Figure 4.3). Until 1980 Brazilian transport and communication was catching up with US productivity levels. Mexican performance remained stable relative to the USA until the late 1970s. Between 1980 and 1993 relative productivity fell in both Latin American countries. Productivity of Brazilian transport and communications was half of that in Mexico in 1950, but surpassed Mexican levels by 1981.

CONCLUSION

US productivity grew a fairly constant rate. In the USA, deregulation of airlines and trucking in the late 1970s and 1980s does not seem to have accelerated productivity growth. Brazil's productivity level lay well below

Table 4.14 Labour Productivity in Transport and Communications, Fisher Results, Brazil/USA and Mexico/USA, 1975

	Brazil/USA			Mexico/USA		
	Traditional Measure	Adjusted for: Terminal Services	Adjusted for: Terminal Services and Quality	Traditional Measure	Adjusted for: Terminal Services	Adjusted for: Terminal Services and Quality
	Panel A: Results Based on Censuses Only					
Transport	48.2	52.0	40.0	48.7	53.0	38.1
Railways	24.6	26.7	25.3	18.9	23.3	21.3
Bus transport	109.9	109.9	75.2	179.3	179.3	96.7
Road freight	55.9	65.9	50.6	36.3	41.9	32.1
Water transport	17.8	17.8	17.8	43.1	43.1	43.1
Air transport	37.6	39.7	27.8	72.6	76.1	53.3
Related services	103.1	111.4	85.6	83.0	90.2	64.9
Communications	16.0	16.0	9.6	44.7	44.7	28.7
	Panel B: Results Based on Censuses and Activity Omitted in Censuses					
Transport	44.3	47.8	36.7	55.0	59.8	43.0
Communications	24.5	24.5	14.7	44.7	44.7	28.7

Sources: Results in Panel A from Appendix D; those from Panel B from Appendix E.

Figure 4.3 Labour Productivity in Transport and Communications: Brazil and Mexico as Per Cent of the USA, 1950–96 (US = 100)

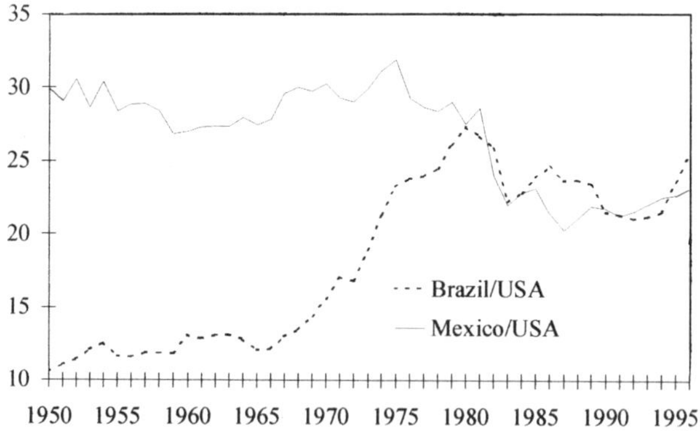

Sources: 1975 benchmark results from Table 4.14, time series of sectoral GDP at constant prices from Appendix B and employment from Appendix A.

that of Mexico in 1950. This was partly due to the larger share of inefficient, expensive railways of transport in the former country. In the course of time Brazil's transport sector was rationalised, thus replacing expensive rail transport by cheaper, more flexible and productive road transport of freight and passengers. In addition to its low level of labour productivity in 1950, the transport sector in Brazil was much less developed than that of Mexico interms of railway infrastructure (railway line per capita), transport equipment (number of aircraft and trucks per capita), post offices and mail distributed per capita. Around 1975 Brazil reached similar levels of development as Mexico according to these indicators, and also in terms of labour productivity. Brazilian and Mexican productivity levels fell during most of the debt crisis of the 1980s. Economic recovery and deregulation of the transport sector contributed to the modest recovery of productivity in the early 1990s in Brazil and Mexico (see Figure 4.3).

In Brazil and Mexico buses remained the predominant providers of public transport throughout the entire period. The expansion of the road network, the large number of towns connected, frequent services and low prices largely contributed to the popularity of buses. The popularity was reinforced by the fact that most people could not afford a private car or air transport. Ships were not a viable option, as few inland places had access to waterways. This left rail transport as the only serious alternative to buses. In 1950 railways still accounted for 40 per cent of passenger movement in Brazil and for 10 per cent in Mexico. However, the quality of rail passenger transport improved very little, or worse, it even deteriorated in terms of destinations served, frequency, prices, safety, and speed. This caused a sharp fall of the share of railway transport in passenger travel. In the USA air transport replaced long-distance transport by bus, car and train. Since 1978 this process has been stimulated by a gradual fall in air fares following deregulations. Surprisingly, the share of air transport in passenger travel decreased over time in Brazil as it remained highly regulated and expensive. Its share increased somewhat in Mexico.

In the USA railways are the major mode of freight transport, in contrast to Brazil and Mexico where trucks are the dominant means of transport. In Mexico and the USA the share of trucks in freight transport increased at the expense of railways. In Brazil the share of transport by truck increased until the early 1970s, then declined. The share of railway and water transport fell until the early 1970s, but this trend was reversed afterwards. In all three countries airlines accounted for a negligible share of freight transport throughout the post-war period.

In Brazil the relative decline in the use of ships, planes and trains for passenger travel and goods transport resulted in low labour productivity *vis-à-vis* the USA, while the growing use of buses contributed to a high relative performance in 1975 (see Table 4.14). The high relative productivity of goods transport by road in 1975, second after bus transport, can partly be attributed to the increased share of goods transported by trucks. In Mexico a similar relationship – between the trend in the share of each mode in passenger movement and freight transport and labour productivity levels in 1975 – can be observed, especially in railways and air transport.

NOTES

1. Between 1875 and 1879, 1,646 km were constructed, 3,540 km from 1880 to 1884 and 4,023 km during the final years of the Empire (1885–89). In 1889 the network totalled 9,654 km.
2. The social saving in passenger transport was estimated by the cost savings on travel fares and travel time, and was calculated using the same hypotheses for Brazil and Mexico. For first-class travel, it was assumed that the stagecoach was the second-best mode of transport, while for second-class travel walking was the only alternative means. The upper boundary assumed zero demand elasticity, whereas the lower bound estimate assumed a demand elasticity of minus 1 (Summerhill, 1997).
3. In 1910 Mexico spent 60 per cent of its rail revenues abroad, compared to 89 per cent in Brazil in 1908 (Summerhill, 1997).
4. This section draws heavily on Davies (1972, 1984, 1987), who gives a very detailed account of airline development in Brazil, Mexico and the USA.
5. See for example Barger (1951), Deakin and Seward (1969), Kendrick (1973) and Pilat (1994).
6. See Hariton and Roy (1979), Meyer and Gómez Ibáñez (1980) and Scheppach and Woehlke (1975).
7. Use of gross value of output rather than value added involves double-counting because production of other industries is included in the inputs.
8. Smith *et al.* (1982) cite data from British sample surveys of road freight transport in the mid-1960s to estimate transport charges broken down in a terminal charge and a charge per km of haul: $Y = a + b*X$, in which Y represents transport charges per ton, X the length of haul, a the intercept representing the terminal charge for a specific commodity and b the increment in cost for each km of haul. Coefficients for different commodity groups were used with data on tons carried and lengths of haul in order to derive a price ratio for the USA/UK. This price ratio was used to convert US output.
9. The adjustment for population density was not made in the case of Brazil, as the distribution of the rail, road and inland water network across the country is very uneven, so that this adjustment method would lead to implausible results.

10. Islas Rivera (1992, p. 66) gives an estimate of the total movement services of Mexican trucking. The gross value of output was derived from the Mexican national accounts. The average freight haul for Mexico and the USA was derived from the Department of Transportation (1994), *North American Transportation*, pp. 48–50. These estimates represented 1987, but assumed they were also valid for 1975. The number of tons transported was estimated using the data and ton km and average freight hauls for both countries.
11. For Mexico it was not possible to separate domestic and international air transport. However, the share of international flights in the total is relatively small and, therefore, the bias is minor.
12. For the USA value added and employment were directly taken from the national accounts, as the production censuses did not cover transport and communications.
13. Value added in the unregistered sector was imputed by multiplying unregistered employment by the labour productivity in small establishments. Employment in the unregistered sector, estimated by the difference between the census and national accounts, is shown in column 3. The sum of census value added and imputed value added of the unregistered sector yields the revised estimate of GDP (see column 7). The employment figures for Mexico are different from those listed in Table 4.13, as the former correspond to the number of persons engaged and the latter to the number of jobs (*puestos renumerados*).

5. Wholesale and Retail Trade

LONG-TERM TRENDS

(i) Employment and GDP

In the USA the share of distributive services in total employment increased from 6.1 per cent in 1870 (the first year for which this information is available) to 16.4 per cent in 1950. There was a rising proportion of female employment (Barger, 1955). In Brazil and Mexico, where information has been available since 1900, there have been similar trends. The share of distribution in the labour force increased from 3.2 per cent in 1900 to 5.6 per cent in 1950 in Brazil, and from 5.1 to 8.3 per cent in Mexico.[1]

Since 1950 the distributive share of employment in Brazil and Mexico has converged towards the level of the USA (see Figure 5.1). In 1996 the shares were 15 per cent for Brazil, 18 per cent for Mexico and 22 per cent for the USA. (Informal) distribution often provides a haven for those who cannot find work in other sectors. As a result distribution employment increases even in times of recession. This happened in Brazil and Mexico during the 'lost decade' of the 1980s.

The distributive share of GDP has shown an opposite trend to that of employment. In the USA it decreased from 18 per cent in 1950[2] to 15 per cent in 1996, in Brazil from about 15 to 8 per cent and in Mexico from about 25 to 17 per cent. A similar trend has been found in Europe (Fitzgerald and Knipper, 1993).

(ii) Establishments

The earliest year for which comparative evidence is available on outlets is 1945: Brazil and Mexico had about 500 stores per 100,000 inhabitants in 1949 and 1945, respectively, which was roughly one-third of the US level in 1948 (see Table 5.1). In the USA, the number of shops per person decreased from 1948 to 1977, after which the relative number of speciality shops increased again until 1992. The density of shops in Brazil increased until 1975, after which it declined. In Mexico the number of shops per

100,000 population rose even faster in the 1975–93 period compared to the three prior decades.[3] The share of stores selling food, drinks and tobacco products has fallen over the years in Brazil and Mexico,[4] whereas in the USA the share remained constant around 20 per cent.

Figure 5.1 Distribution's Share of Total Employment, Brazil, Mexico and the USA, 1950–96

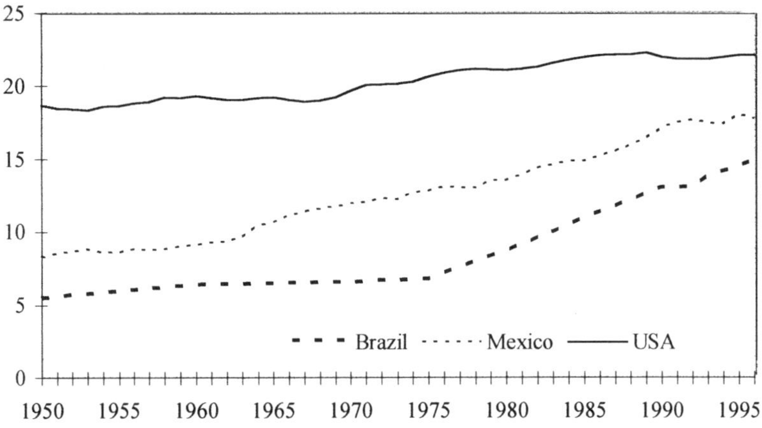

Source: Appendix A.

Shop density, presented in terms of outlets per inhabitant (Table 5.1), appears very low in Brazil and Mexico. However, these data underestimate the volume of retail services as they exclude unregistered establishments and street vendors. If informal traders were included, retail density would increase substantially. No information is available on the number of unregistered stores. In Mexico about 300,000 street vendors operated as informal traders in the early 1990s (Euromonitor, 1995).

(iii) Store Types

The data presented in Table 5.1 do not reflect the large variety of stores – in terms of size and lines of merchandise sold – between countries, and the changing character of stores within a country over time. McKinsey (1995) distinguished three stages in the evolution of store types. In the first stage shops are small, supply a small choice of a wide range of goods and are operated by family members ('mum-and-dad corner stores'). The main convenience is closeness to customers. Merchandise is sold directly by the store operator. Stage one stores depend entirely on wholesalers. They adopt few new technologies. The second stage is characterised by bigger stores offering an untargeted range of goods on a larger scale. Greater size generates scale economies in operation and increases the bargaining power of stores in the purchase of goods for resale from wholesalers. The quality of merchandise sold improves and prices are lower. Stores innovate in inventory management and check-out facilities.

Table 5.1 *Wholesale and Retail Trade Establishments in Brazil, Mexico and the USA, 1929–93*

	Outlets (000s)			Outlets per 100,000 Population		
	Retail Trade	Wholesale Trade	Total	Retail Trade	Wholesale Trade	Total
			Brazil			
1939	161	11	172	399	27	427
1949	248	29	277	489	57	546
1975	636	53	689	599	47	646
1985	675	45	720	504	34	537
1992	760	n.a.	n.a.	487	n.a.	n.a.
			Mexico			
1940	n.a.	n.a.	41	n.a.	n.a.	197
1945	n.a.	n.a.	126	n.a.	n.a.	531
1975	443	11	454	737	18	755
1993	1,144	75	1,219	1,254	82	1,336
			USA			
1929	1 476	164	1 640	1 208	134	1 342
1935	1 588	177	1 764	1 258	140	1 398
1939	1 770	190	1 961	1 346	145	1 491
1948	1 790	243	2 033	1 216	165	1 381
1977	1 855	383	2 238	842	174	1 016
1992	2 672	496	3 168	1 045	194	1 239

Sources: IBGE, *Censo Comercial* (various issues); 1992 from Euromonitor (1995). Mexico: SPP/INEGI, *Censo Comercial* (various issues); USA: Department of Commerce, Bureau of the Census (1975, pp. 843–850) and *Census of Wholesale Trade/Census of Retail Trade* (various issues). Population from Maddison (1995b).

In the final stage there are both small and large stores that supply a targeted range of goods, and focus on particular consumer groups. Stores are increasingly concentrated in shopping malls. Stage three covers three types of stores: specialised individual stores, speciality chains and discounters. Mail order is also a stage three format. Specialised individual stores and speciality chains earn high margins as they sell exactly the merchandise desired by a small target group. Discounters provide low prices and high efficiency. Stage two stores have a higher labour productivity in terms of sales per employee than stage one or three stores. In terms of value added (which include profits) per employee, stage three stores are more productive than stage one and two.

Until 1850 the retail sector was in the first stage in all three countries. The USA entered the second stage after the rapid spread of railways and the telegraph. Three new types of retailers emerged – chain stores, department stores and mail-order houses – which sold a larger volume of goods and more varieties than traditional retailers (see below). By 1950 most traditional stores were replaced by these new outlet types (Barger, 1955). Since 1950 chains have increasingly dominated retailing. They operate large outlets selling food and other convenience items as well as smaller stores carrying only a few lines of goods.

In the 1950s shopping centres[5] were introduced in the USA to service growing populations in suburbs and an increasing number of consumers with cars. The number of shopping centres increased from 3,700 in 1960 to 40,000 in the early 1990s. In 1985 40 per cent of all retail sales were generated in such centres. Shopping centres favoured the development of retail chains, as mall owners sought tenants whose ability to attract customers was known. By 1985 chains occupied between 70 and 95 per cent of shops in malls and generated 90 per cent of the sales (OECD, 1992a).

In Brazil the transition of the retail sector to the second stage did not occur until the early twentieth century, when department stores emerged in Rio and São Paulo. Self-service department stores were introduced in the 1950s by the retail chain *Pão de Açúcar*. In 1974 the French company *Carrefour* set up hypermarkets in Brazil. These turned out to be very profitable as they offered, in addition to a variety of cheap basic foodstuffs, a large range of non-food products on which profit margins were higher. Over the years hypermarkets and supermarkets replaced traditional stores: by 1995 they accounted for 85 per cent of total sales. However, in terms of outlets, traditional stores remained predominant in retailing as they still represented 85 per cent of the total in the same year (BNDES, 1996a). The first shopping centre was opened in São Paulo in 1966. Only seven malls were added in the 1970s, compared to 47 in the 1980s and 57 from 1990 to 1995. Brazil ranked fifth in the world in terms of number of shopping centres in 1995 (BNDES, 1996b).

In Mexico the first department stores opened around 1900 in Mexico City and Guadalajara. They were operated by French immigrants who had acquired experience in retailing and the textile industry abroad. These stores provided outlets for the textile factories. The development of the retail sector halted during the Revolution and its aftermath until the 1930s. The Great Depression and World War II also slowed down the development. The spread of department stores continued in the late 1950s, when the growth of cities accelerated. Part of the new department stores were operated by US chains, which played a key role in spreading new technologies (see below) (Gras and Fraschetto, 1993).

Discount stores spread in the 1960s. The first ones were outlets of apparel factories. Their founders, like those who opened department stores half a century earlier, had prior experience in the textile industry. Each discount chain had a different growth strategy. *Gigante*, a chain owned by the Angel Lozada family, expanded rapidly in the 1980s by buying regional or local discount stores. *Aurrera* and *Comercial Mexicana*, both also family-owned, spread by opening stores in cities outside Mexico City in the 1970s. In addition to nation-wide chains, regional discount chains developed in the north and the south-east (Gras and Fraschetto, 1993). The first shopping malls were not opened until the 1980s and it is only since the early 1990s that they have spread rapidly. Most were built by department store chains such as *Liverpool* and *El Palacio de Hierro*. Shopping centres mostly targeted the middle- and upper-income groups.

In Mexico traditional stores remained predominant, as the proportion of food items sold through supermarkets was only 21 per cent in 1992.[6] Since the early 1990s the modernisation of the retail sector was accelerated by the NAFTA agreement covering legal changes that facilitated foreign direct investment (Euromonitor, 1995).

In all countries the transition from traditional stores to department stores, supermarkets and hypermarkets led to a growth in the average size of firms and establishments. Firms achieved scale and scope economies in their operation, purchase of goods for resale and logistics (see below). Technological progress in transport and inventory management also facilitated the operation of larger units (Pilat, 1997). In Brazil and Mexico new methods were often introduced by foreign retail companies.

In Brazil and Mexico large retail firms increased their market share. In the former country, the largest retailer (*Carrefour*) generated 10 per cent of all food sales, while in Mexico the largest, CIFRA, accounted for 24 per cent in 1993. In the USA, on the contrary, concentration ratios remained low, for example the largest retailer (Kroger) accounted for only 2 per cent of food sales (Euromonitor, 1995).

Independent stores have formed buyers, combines and chains to achieve the same types of cost savings as larger stores. They jointly undertake buying from manufacturers and wholesalers, inventory management, logistics and marketing. These forms of cooperation have well advanced in the USA, but are rather novel in Brazil and Mexico.

In the early 1990s US retailing was in its third development stage, as characterised by McKinsey (see above). Brazilian and Mexican retailing are in the three development stages at the same time, for example composed of both a modern and traditional retail sector. This is partly due to the very unequal distribution of income. Traditional retailers accounted for the largest share of employment and establishments, but a smaller proportion of sales.[7]

(iv) Vertical Integration

Two-way vertical integration had already started in the second half of the nineteenth century in the USA, and in the early twentieth century in Brazil and Mexico. Manufacturers internalised the wholesale function as the distribution of their products became too complex and too costly to contract out. At the same time retailers integrated backwards, acquiring the wholesale function, to increase their bargaining power towards manufacturers. This process was guided by growing economies of scale and scope in the course of time (see below).

After 1950 vertical integration consisted mainly of retailers who absorbed the wholesale function. The retail sector became demand-driven instead of supply-driven (Dawson, 1995). Until the 1950s the main aim of distribution was to transmit mass-produced goods rapidly from manufacturer to consumer. This changed over the years due to the 'sophistication' of consumer demand. The demand for mass-produced goods was replaced by demand for specialised products and services. Nowadays retail trade plays a central role in identifying the wishes of different target groups, which are subsequently translated into what manufacturers produce. In the 1950s distributive services added 25 per cent to the value of consumer goods, or compared to manufacturing that added 40 per cent, transport 15 per cent and remaining functions such as overheads 20 per cent. In the 1990s the composition changed to 20 per cent manufacturing, 20 per cent transport, 40 per cent distribution and 20 per cent overheads (estimates by Dawson, 1995). No information on changes of these weights is available for the countries studied.

(v) Internationalisation

In Brazil and Mexico foreign direct investment played an important role in the spread of new technologies and management techniques. Foreign retailers provided forward linkages (offering a larger choice of goods at often lower prices), and backward linkages (the demand for a wider range of products, at better quality and in larger quantities, from domestic manufacturers). Moreover, foreign retailers and wholesalers often participated in financing new investments of manufacturers, and assisted in the management of inventories and deliveries. The change in economic policy – from import substitution to export orientation – in the late 1980s accelerated the opening of the distribution sector for foreign investors and foreign consumer goods.

In Brazil the first foreign-operated food retailer (*Carrefour*) started in 1975. It introduced hypermarkets, which at the time was a new retailing concept. During the 1980s and early 1990s, these stores spread rapidly. Profit margins were high, as food prices rose faster than the general rate of inflation. By 1990 it had become the largest food retailer in Brazil. In 1994 it operated over 40 stores. In that same year *Makro* (a Dutch company) became the main wholesaler in Brazil.

In Mexico Sears and Roebuck was the first foreign retailer, which opened its first store in 1947. In an evaluation of its presence after six years, Wood and Keyser (1953) concluded that Sears' presence had a large impact on domestic producers. In 1953 80 per cent of the merchandise sold by Sears originated from domestic manufacturers who had succeeded in improving the quality of their products and on-time delivery. They also became major suppliers of other retailers. Sears revolutionised retailing by offering credit on all purchases, including inexpensive items. In 1995 Sears operated 40 department stores. Another US chain, Woolworth, opened its first store in the 1960s, and expanded to 46 stores in 1993.

In the early 1990s, foreign – mostly US – retailers mostly established strategic alliances with Mexican companies. They provided capital and up-to-date retail technology in exchange for a distribution network. Wal-Mart and Price Club opened discount warehouses, in alliance with *Aurrera* and *Comercial Mexicana*, respectively, which sell a limited selection of brand name products packaged in large quantities. Discount stores destroyed many small shops, which were unable to compete with the low prices and extended ranges of goods. K-Mart and Liverpool established a joint venture to build new warehouses in 1993 (Euromonitor, 1995).

In Brazil and Mexico, franchising – know-how exchanged for royalties on sales of the franchise owner's products – has also grown very popular as a means of foreign penetration as it involves less risk than foreign direct investment. In Mexico franchise operators employed 45,000 people in fashion stores and fast-food restaurants in 1992 (Euromonitor, 1995).

(vi) Informal Retailing

The trends outlined above largely omit the role of the informal traders,[8] who form a major part of retailing in Brazil and Mexico. Most are small businesses operated by self-employed people and their families. Their informal character often results from the complex and costly legal environment in terms of permits and taxes (see below). They are close to their customers and mostly serve the poor whose mobility as well as their ability to store food is rather limited. Informal traders supply small, customised quantities of food, and often provide credit to customers (Musgrove and Galindo, 1988). Small traders are constrained by a lack of security and stability. Though such businesses have always existed, their relative importance has increased enormously since the 1960s, when large masses migrated from the countryside to the cities where job opportunities in the formal sector turned out to be disappointing.

By the 1980s the majority of outlets in Mexico, mostly selling food, beverages and other basic goods, operated on an informal basis. This is confirmed by a survey in Mexico City, showing that approximately 80 per cent of all establishments were illegal in 1985. Most of these had less than five employees, of whom 67 per cent only attended secondary school or less. These stores accounted for only 25 per cent of sales (Cross, 1998). No comparable data on this are available for Brazil.

As small informal stores have no bargaining power and often face more intermediaries than supermarkets, prices charged are expected to be higher in the small stores. From a comparison of retail prices between different types of outlet in the north-east of Brazil in 1985, Musgrove and Galindo (1988) conclude that this was not the case. The lower prices of informal traders compared to formal traders may result from lower costs of capital and labour, and lower mark-ups of the latter. Musgrove and Galindo (1988) show no evidence on this.

In addition to the increasing importance of informal retailers at a fixed location, the number of street vendors also rose in the course of time, especially in the 1980s (Maddison, 1992, p. 211). They differ from fixed location retailers in several respects. The control of the stock tends to be more labour-intensive, as the merchandise has to be watched to avoid theft, and moved to a safe location at the end of the day for storage overnight. As inventories are low, vendors can adapt quickly to changes in consumer demand. Street vendors also spend relatively less on overheads and labour as they work mostly with family members.

Cross (1998) estimated that in the Federal District of Mexico, which covers half (of) the agglomeration of Mexico City, there were roughly 200,000 street vendors in the early 1990s. Over the years the municipality of Mexico City changed its policy towards street-vending: from 1957 to 1966 it built over 100 markets for 50,000 vendors, while at the same time it repressed – relatively successfully – those who refused to move to the markets, or those who left markets due to problems. After the mayor left office in 1966, this policy was relaxed. This led to increasing numbers of street vendors in the 1970s and 1980s. They supported local high officials of the PRI in exchange for protection from removal and relocation.

(vii) Other Forms of Retailing

Consumption abroad: in Brazil and Mexico the underdeveloped nature of the retail sector, in terms of the limited range of goods and lack of convenient shopping outlets, induced many middle- and upper-class people to shop abroad, mostly in the USA. In the early 1990s three-quarters of the higher-income groups of Mexico City frequently travelled 15 hours by car in order to purchase clothes, consumer electronics and other high-value goods across the border in the USA (Euromonitor, 1995). Miami and New York were favourite shopping destinations for upper-class Brazilians. In both countries shopping abroad became less important as the range of goods and quality of shopping outlets at home improved.

The consortium system was introduced for lower middle-income groups in Brazil and Mexico in the 1980s, providing an alternative to inadequate bank credit facilities. Consortia enrolled buyers who participated in a 'no losers lottery'. Members made regular payments for a fixed amount of time. The money collected was subsequently used to buy wanted items, which were then allocated to members by a lottery. This system was popular for cars and consumer durables (Euromonitor, 1995).

Home shopping through mail orders has developed into an important part of retailing in the USA. Its success stems from the higher share of working women, the development of niche markets and improved home delivery. By 1990 mail order sales represented 2 per cent of total retail sales. The popularity of home shopping decreased somewhat in the early 1990s. This was probably due to new types of stores (see below) and technological improvements that shortened waiting times in shops and increased payment options. In Brazil, since the 1980s, retail sales by catalogues have been gaining popularity, especially for purchases of home appliances. In 1995 some catalogues were jointly issued with credit cards.[9] In Mexico, on the contrary, mail orders remained an insignificant part of retailing (Gras and Fraschetto, 1993). This may be explained by the higher prices charged compared to retail stores and the unreliability of the postal services.

For several decades the marketing of products on television, which can be directly ordered by telephone, has become an important distribution channel in the USA. In Brazil, two department stores – *Television Casa Centro* and *TV Mappin* – operate separate channels for telesales. Television shopping was also introduced in Mexico in 1993 (Euromonitor, 1995).

Warehouses offering a wide range of merchandise at low prices and a large surface were introduced in the USA in the 1980s, and have become very popular since. Most carry groceries and non-food items. In the early 1990s some chains, like Wal-Mart, exported this concept to Brazil and Mexico. In addition to those carrying a wide range of products, warehouses were developed to sell a special range of products such as health care products or toys. Warehouses made large investments in information technology, which enabled them to match their products closer to customer needs. It has also allowed close links with manufacturers especially in inventory management. In many cases warehouses buy their goods directly from manufacturers, which enable them to charge low prices to customers.

DETERMINANTS OF DEMAND FOR DISTRIBUTIVE SERVICES

The development of the distribution sector depends on demographic changes, urbanisation, increased expenditure per inhabitant, changes in the distribution of income, increased mobility of consumers, the legal environment, technological developments and inflation. Each factor is discussed below.

(i) Demographic and Socio-economic Changes

Population growth increases consumer demand. From 1820 to 1900 population grew fastest in the USA – about eightfold – compared to a fourfold increase in Brazil and a twofold growth in Mexico (see Appendix A). From 1900 to 1950 the Brazilian population tripled, whereas that of Mexico and the USA doubled. From 1950 to 1994 the population of Brazil and Mexico tripled and that of the latter rose 1.6 times.

The age structure of the population should also be taken into account, as youngsters have less to spend than people of working age and older. In Brazil and Mexico the proportion of people under 15 has been falling since the 1970s.[10] The ageing of the population has been particularly important in the USA,[11] and has a major impact on retail methods and shop locations. People of 60 years and older spend more on certain categories such as pharmaceuticals, demand more in-store service and easily accessible stores (Burt and Dawson, 1990).

An important socio-economic development is the rising participation of women in the labour market. From 1950 to 1990 the proportion of women in the work-force doubled from 15 to 30 per cent in Brazil, and increased from 13 per cent to 23 per cent in Mexico (Hofman, 1998). Female participation rates in the USA were much higher throughout the whole period.[12] Increased female participation raised family income but also raised the opportunity cost of shopping. As such it probably caused a drop in the demand for small shops but an increase for larger shops selling a wide variety of goods (Pilat, 1997). Moreover, the demand for convenience goods (microwaves, washing machines, dryers and prepared foods) surged.

Over the years the number of households grew faster than the population, as the number of children per family decreased and the number of one-parent families rose as a result of higher divorce rates. One-person households also became more common in the course of time. As each household required a minimum of appliances, furniture and other commodities, the demand for these products probably grew faster then the population. Smaller households also affect retail methods because they purchase groceries in smaller quantities.

(ii) Rising Income Levels

The development of the retail sector is closely linked to the level of per capita income. In poor agrarian countries retailing is relatively unimportant as most food is not traded through shops because it is produced by people for self-consumption. Purchases of other non-food items are small. Paradoxically food represents a small share of sales, a characteristic also found in modern retailing. As per capita income rises, the size of the retail sector increases, as does the proportion of food in total sales. Retail sales account for about 80 per cent of consumer spending. As income increases further, consumers spend proportionally less on food and more on other (luxury) goods (Engel's law), which is translated into a declining share of food in retail sales. In rich countries the proportion of retail sales in total spending falls below 50 per cent as consumers buy more services such as education, entertainment and health care. The proportion of food drops to below 20 per cent (Euromonitor, 1995).

From 1820 to 1900 income per head tripled in the USA, increased by half in Brazil and rose only 5 per cent in Mexico. Between 1900 and 1950 Mexican income tripled, compared to a doubling in the USA and a 50 per cent increase in Brazil. From 1950 to 1994 Brazilian income tripled, whereas that of Mexico and the USA grew 2.3 times (see Chapter 2). The per capita income gap between Brazil and Mexico on the one hand and the USA on the other narrowed from 1950 to 1982, but widened after 1982.

As per capita income rose little in the nineteenth century in Brazil and Mexico, grocery stores, and stores selling other basic goods, remained predominant. In the USA, on the contrary, diversification had already made significant headway in the nineteenth century. After 1950 per capita income rose fast in Brazil and Mexico, inducing important changes in the structure of the distribution.[13] In 1993 Brazilians spent 47 per cent of their income on retail purchases, compared to 63 per cent in Mexico and 33 per cent in the

USA. Food accounted for 69 per cent of retail sales in Brazil, 60 per cent in Mexico and 39 per cent in the USA in 1993 (Euromonitor, 1995).

Average per capita income does not take into account the distribution of income. As lower-income groups have a very different spending pattern than higher-income groups, the distribution of income (or income and wealth) has important consequences for the retail sector.[14] High-income inequality accentuates the predominance of small food stores in distribution.

From 1950 to 1989 income distribution in Brazil and Mexico remained more unequal than that in the USA, as indicated by the Gini coefficient of each country. This coefficient indicates income spread between households, but provides little information on shares of income earned by particular groups of households. Compared with the USA the high-income group (fifth quintile) in Brazil and Mexico earned a much larger share of income, while the lowest income group procured a much lower share. The second, third and fourth quintiles represented much lower shares in Brazil and Mexico compared to the USA (see Chapter 2).

Gini coefficients and income distribution by quintiles do not show what proportion of the population lives below the poverty line. As each country adopts its own definition of poverty, international comparisons are very difficult.[15] An alternative, internationally comparable, poverty indicator is the infant mortality rate (the number of children per 1,000 new-born that die before age 5) which is 69 in Brazil, 38 in Mexico and 11 in the USA in 1990 (see Chapter 7).

On the basis of the information on per capita income, income distribution and infant mortality, one may conclude that in 1990 more people lived in poverty in Brazil than in Mexico. This is in line with the characteristics of the retail sector, that is the larger share of food stores in retailing in Brazil compared to Mexico.

(iii) Consumer Mobility

Mobility of consumers increased rapidly over the years as car ownership became more common. In 1929 one in every five Americans had a car, in 1950 one in every four and in 1993 one in almost every two citizens. Brazilians and Mexicans were much less mobile, as in these countries the ratio was only one car in about every 200 people in 1929. Over time the large gap narrowed, though in 1993 the USA still had seven times as many cars per capita than the two Latin American countries (see Table 4.2).

In the USA consumer mobility has also been stimulated by keeping the variable cost of operating cars, mostly gasoline, relatively low, and by issuing driving licences at the age of 16. The massive expansion of the road network also facilitated automobile usage. Improved storage facilities of households, such as freezers and refrigerators, allowed for less frequent shopping. Part of the transport cost has thus been shifted from the retailer to the consumer.

Competition among stores increased due to higher consumer mobility, leading to larger stores, wider assortments and more chains. Many small food and other convenience goods stores were replaced by supermarkets and hypermarkets. The negative impact on the number of (food) stores was only partly counterbalanced by the expansion of the number of outlets selling cars and gasoline stations. In the USA, however, on the whole, the number of stores per head of population decreased between 1948 and 1977. New stores were more and more concentrated in shopping malls in suburban areas, often with free parking facilities. Since 1975 the relative number of stores also has fallen in Brazil. As the mobility of the poorest segment of the population has remained limited, many small food stores have continued to exist in poor neighbourhoods in Brazil and Mexico.

(iv) Urbanisation

Urbanisation proceeded faster in the USA than in Brazil and Mexico. This is illustrated by the higher share of population living in communities with more than 2,500 inhabitants in 1950: 64 per cent of the US population, compared to only 36 per cent in Brazil and 43 per cent in Mexico, respectively (see Chapter 2). By 1993, however, the latter two caught up with the USA, and in all the three countries the 'urban' population was three-quarters of the total.[16]

Expanding urban markets favoured economies of scale and technical progress in retailing in several ways. Growing markets attracted capital from other areas, and increasing sales led to a more efficient utilisation of existing capacity (Hall *et al.*, 1961, p. 137). New sites in expanding communities favoured the growth of modern stores, of which most had a larger surface, better equipment, and a higher sales per employee ratio. The age of settlement also determines the speed of innovation, as older areas have smaller buildings, fewer construction sites and are characterised by traditional attitudes as opposed to introducing new techniques. Earlier urban settlement in the USA, as compared to Brazil and Mexico, did not prevent the building of larger and modern stores in the USA, when many citizens migrated from the centre to the suburbs where space was relatively abundant.

Urbanisation also changes the composition of demand. This is because high-income groups concentrate in cities, which increases the demand for more specialised type of products of higher quality.

(v) The Legal Environment

Governments played an important role in shaping distributive services by different types of regulation throughout the late nineteenth and twentieth century. In the USA the Sherman Antitrust Act of 1890 eliminated entry barriers to competition. It increased business opportunities for owner-operated stores. Authorisation was no longer required for opening a store. Moreover, the operation of shops was subject to only a few rules. The Clayton Act of 1914 and the Pactman Act of 1936 forbade price discrimination and restrictive agreements, vertical concentration and other action-limiting competition. The Federal Trade Commission Act of 1914 set rules of sales practice, and established an agency for checking the content of advertisements (Dupuis and de Maricourt, 1989).

The location of stores was restricted by local 'zoning laws', which classified areas with different uses, and often limited floor size and advertisement signs. The application of these laws has been very flexible as illustrated by the rapid development of shopping centres (Betancourt, 1993).

Until 1960 opening hours were restricted by 'blue laws', which affected most grocery stores. By the end of the 1980s 98 per cent of all larger supermarkets and hypermarkets opened on Sundays and 45 per cent remained open 24 hours (Dupuis and de Maricourt, 1989). The 1984 Merger Guidelines relaxed restrictions on vertical concentration and integration, as it became clear that they raise transaction costs and do not necessarily improve competition. This legal change stimulated manufacturers to internalise the distribution of their products, especially in automobiles, beer, clothing, electric appliances, footwear, hobby goods and supplies. Vertical integration meant that retail chains often gained control of manufacturing. Horizontal integration also increased. Chains with ten outlets or more accounted for 40 per cent of all sales, and 62 per cent of grocery sales in 1987 (Betancourt, 1993).

In Brazil opening a store required approximately ten months in the early 1990s (Oliveira and Mouro, 1997). Legal procedures depended on the type of store, and were more complex for wholesalers than for retailers. Each municipality regulated the location of stores within its own territory, as well as the opening hours. The latter type of regulation was the most severe constraint, although hours have been extended over the past two decades. The enormous amount of paperwork and high costs involved in legally opening or closing a store formed an incentive to function on an informal basis, at least until its profitability and viability was evident. The legal operation of a store was also complex and expensive, requiring detailed bookkeeping of sales and inventories, and the registration of employees with the National Institute of Social Security (INSS) and a labour union.

For many decades the government regulated distributive margins by dictating prices for basic goods, such as bread, cigarettes, gasoline, medicines and milk. During various 'stabilisation' episodes, price freezes prevailed for a much wider range of products, often causing negative margins for retailers. Retailers took evasive action by slightly transforming the merchandise, which they could sell at a higher price. This was legal as no price freeze existed for these slightly modified products. Since 1993 the Brazilian government has cancelled most price controls and freezes.

The Mexican government introduced a large number of regulations which raised the cost of distribution from the 1940s to the 1960s. De La Torre (1991) discusses three types of regulation. Firstly, rules were imposed on the operation of stores which required extensive supervision. Secondly, there were laws determining the number and/or characteristics of stores, which limited possibilities of entry to distribution. Thirdly, certain rules reduced competition among retailers and wholesalers, for example price controls or limits on opening hours. In the 1970s and the 1980s the legal framework was reformed, although the bureaucracy increased.[17] De la Torre estimated that opening a store required at least 70 permits, with a minimum delay of ten months in 1988. The complex legal environment, in addition to motives of escaping price controls and tax laws, stimulated many firms to operate informally.

In his book *The Other Path* (1989), Hernando de Soto demonstrated that an inefficient legal system is one of the major causes of informality. Although his study focuses on Lima, it is also representative of Brazilian and Mexican urban areas. In addition to the 'cost of opening a legal business', he focuses on the 'cost of legally operating a business'. This not only concerns taxes and social security payments, but also the administration of personnel, compliance with bureaucratic procedures and the higher rates for public utilities.[18] In addition to savings, informal retailers bear extra costs compared to their legal counterparts, which include action to avoid detection[19] and undercapitalisation due to limited access to credit facilities.

Excessive government inference had a detrimental effect on productivity performance, as formally operated businesses spent a large amount of time on complying with government regulations, and restrictions caused resources to be used inefficiently. Though informals were more flexible, their productivity was often even much lower because they had limited access to credit to finance capital investments and could not benefit from favourable legal instruments. Moreover, the size of informal establishments was limited, which prevented them from realising economies of scale and scope. The lower productivity performance of informal distributors is confirmed by the results of this study.[20] Other consequences of the large informal economy include reduced rates of investment and technological progress, and an inefficient tax system – the burden of taxes rested upon a small group still operating formally. Moreover, rates for public utilities were often very high due to the large illicit consumption.

Another important aspect of the legal environment is the regulation of foreign direct investment in distributive services. In Brazil and Mexico this was very restricted from the 1930s to the 1970s, a policy that was part of the overall import substitution policy (ISI). The change to export promotion in the course of the 1970s led to an opening-up of the sector for foreign distributors, who became major competitors of domestic firms.

(vi) Technological Progress

The organisation of distributive services has changed enormously with the introduction of computer and information technology in the 1970s (Betancourt, 1993). In the USA, electronic cash registers replaced most of the mechanical registers in the 1970s. The introduction of the Universal Product Code and scanning technology in food retailing raised the productivity of cashiers in the 1980s. Scanning also improved knowledge of customers, which, in addition to closer links between manufacturers, wholesalers and retailers, reduced the size of inventories.

In Brazil and Mexico it was mostly larger firms that invested in new technologies. For small shops and informal traders these investments were often too expensive. Foreign direct investment played an important role in the diffusion of new technologies. In 1994 the largest wholesale and retail firms were foreign-owned. Foreign firms also introduced new management techniques. Rapid technological developments have accentuated the dual structure of the distribution system.

(vii) Scale and Scope

In nineteenth-century USA there was first a rise but later a decline of the wholesaler. This process was driven by changing economies of scale and scope. Economies of scale refer to the larger volume of goods and lower costs per unit in the marketing and distribution of a single line of goods. Economies of scope refers to the handling of a number of product lines and other sale activities through a single set of facilities (Chandler, 1990). As most domestic production and consumption were localised, few intermediaries were needed between producers and retailers. From Independence in 1776 until the Civil War (1861–65) wholesaling grew more rapidly than production and retail trade. In the beginning of this period most wholesalers were importers operating on the east coast. They worked on a commission basis for manufacturers when transmitting their goods to retailers. Producers incurred high risks and inventory costs caused by slow and uncertain communication and transport (Barger, 1955).

The rapid spread of railways and the telegraph from the 1850s to the 1880s reduced risks, transport and inventory costs, and as such increased the volume of distributed goods. Manufacturers grew larger, and the task of selling to an increasing number of retailers at larger distances became heavier. This augmented the need for wholesalers. Distributors, who originally combined the wholesale and the retail functions, now specialised in one of the two. They no longer worked on commission, but bought the goods, and earned their income from mark-up. They were able to distribute goods at a lower cost than a single manufacturer could as they transmitted similar goods of several manufacturers at the same time (economies of scale). Moreover, cost savings were achieved by handling related product groups by one set of facilities (economies of scope). Most wholesalers had central headquarters with large storage space, and many sales people who contacted specialised and general retail stores (Chandler, 1990).

The period after the Civil War marked the decline of wholesalers. Their role was increasingly taken over by mass retailers who wanted to increase their bargaining power *vis-à-vis* manufacturers in order to obtain goods which met specific demands and delivery deadlines. Three types of mass retailers emerged. Firstly, department stores were set up in east coast cities. In the beginning they sold only apparel and textiles, but later also household goods. In the 1880s they also settled in urban centres in the rest of the country. They achieved larger economies of scope than wholesalers as they carried more product lines. Secondly, mail-order houses were established selling mainly to rural families. They became the largest retailers thanks to the large volume of goods sold and many product lines and in consequence they achieved greater economies of scale and scope than department stores. Montgomery Ward and Sears, Roebuck became the two largest in the USA. A high degree of automatisation and advanced scheduling of delivery permitted Sears, Roebuck to handle 100,000 orders a day within a single plant by 1906 (Chandler, 1990). Department stores also engaged in mail orders, of which R.H. Macy and Company of New York was one of the earliest in 1874.[21] Thirdly, chain stores were founded, which achieved scale economies by selling through many outlets.

Wholesalers also disappeared because their functions were increasingly internalised by manufacturers, as an increasing share of their products required special skills for marketing, storage and transportation. These skills were often related to one specific product group. Reduced economies of scope discouraged wholesalers to make the necessary investment to market a product line. At the same time it encouraged manufacturers to incur this cost. Competition on national and international markets created another incentive for producers to invest in marketing. Thanks to new production and transport technologies – railways and steamboats – only a few large factories were enough to meet demand. Manufacturers invested in advertising, delivery, installation, service and repair of their products.

In the early twentieth century markets for perishables (bakery, beer, dairy and meat products) became dominated by a few large companies. They succeeded by investing more in distribution networks than in production, and as such achieved economies of scale. The meat-packing industry was dominated by the company of Gustave F. Swift, who invented the refrigerated railway car. Two other companies dominated the beer market as they invested heavily in temperature-regulated railway cars. For a long time high distribution costs created an entry barrier to these markets. The rapid spread of trucks in the 1920s substantially reduced costs and, as a result, many smaller regional companies emerged who delivered directly to retailers (Chandler, 1990).

In Brazil and Mexico economies of scale in distributive services were realised at least 50 years later than the USA, when a large railway network was established. Since the 1940s the improvements in roads and the large increase in the number of trucks meant further reductions in transport costs and increased economies of scale. Vertical integration on a significant scale did not occur until the 1950s and 1960s, when the first department stores and retail chains were founded. For purchases of goods from manufacturers, these chains and stores increasingly bypassed wholesalers.

Since 1950 further economies of scope or diversification were realised in the USA, while they became important only in this era in Brazil and Mexico. Constraints on the expansion of a firm's major activity, the possibilities of cost-sharing between stores in different product markets and risk reduction fuelled the need for diversification. Retailers grew bigger, especially food stores, and were selling a larger range of (non-food) items. Retailers increased their efforts to identify and exploit opportunities for diversification in four areas. Firstly, they integrated backwards into branding, design and even production of goods. Secondly, retailers provided complementary services to the goods sold, such as financial services. Thirdly, retailers operate different store types within a similar market to attract customers with different profiles. Fourthly, retailers moved into new product segments (for example food retailers opened DIY or consumer electronics stores). The impact of diversification is illustrated by the rise in the number of shopping centres (OECD, 1992a).

(viii) Advertising, Branding, and Packaging

Manufacturers increasingly branded and packaged their goods in the USA in the late nineteenth century, so these could be put directly on the shelves of retailers. Packaging became a standard final phase in the production process (this was aided by the revolution in glass, metal and paper). Only a few companies continued to sell their products in bulk. Branded goods came to play a key role in advertising. This was especially the case in consumer foods, consumer 'chemicals' (drugs, paint, soap and related products) and tobacco: the advertising cost in these categories represented 5 to 14 per cent of sales compared to less than 2 per cent for other products (Chandler, 1990).

In the 1870s advertising agencies emerged, who provided specialised services such as illustrations, layouts and text. They purchased space in newspapers and other periodicals, which was subsequently resold to their clients. In the beginning these were mainly department stores, but soon mass producers became their main clients. Some large firms set up in-house advertising departments, but the majority of the large firms continued to rely on specialised agencies. Since 1950 advertising and brand names have become more popular in Brazilian and Mexican retailing, as radios and televisions have spread rapidly and the population has became more educated.

From the 1950s to the 1990s the share of marketing and distribution expenses grew from 25 to 40 per cent of the final consumer price (Davies, 1995). Advertising and marketing have become much more important. Nowadays manufacturers are much more concerned with the needs and the wants of different groups of consumers than the organisation of production. This transition was accelerated by the increased speed of data transmission, for example information on sales in a shop is transferred instantaneously to the distribution depot, manufacturer and marketing department.

The demand for a wider choice by customers led to an increased number of retail brands. Traditionally these were used for low-priced, and often low-quality, products in food retailing. However, since the 1960s there has been a tendency to provide better quality and higher-priced products supported by large-scale advertising campaigns. Retail brands offer retailers higher margins than manufactured brands. Moreover, customers expect to get good value for the price they pay. Retail brands have become especially popular in beauty and health items and apparel.

(ix) Inflation

In Brazil, and to some extent in Mexico, high inflation had a major impact on the structure of retailing. Between the early 1980s and 1994 Brazil suffered from inflation rates exceeding 100 per cent annually which were comparable to Mexican rates in the late 1980s.[22] Soaring prices reduced real incomes, and as a result, spending on durables fell and were concentrated increasingly on food. This favoured the development of supermarkets and hypermarkets, as there consumers spent their income immediately after having received their monthly salary. In addition to bulk sales, retailers earned high margins as they raised prices faster than the rate of inflation.[23] As the incomes of the poor were not protected against inflation, they suffered most from inflation. In Brazil overall consumer spending fell 23 per cent between 1988 and 1992 (Euromonitor, 1995).

From 1986 to 1992 the Brazilian government launched several stabilisation plans, which tempered inflation for only a few months. Immediately after the price freezes the demand for non-durables surged, while purchases of durables fell as bank deposits were frozen and credits limited. The *Plano Real*, introduced in July 1994, successfully combated inflation. In retailing it led to smaller margins and more competition. Sales were boosted thanks to the increased purchasing power of consumers.[24]

(x) Conclusions

In the USA the distributive sector has enjoyed economies of scale and scope since the transport and communications revolution during the middle of the nineteenth century. With rising incomes consumers spent relatively less on food and more on other items. Wholesalers and retailers handled an increasing volume of goods (economies of scale), and a larger variety by a single set of facilities (economies of scope). Manufacturers contributed to the sophistication of distributive services by investing in packaging and facilities required for the distribution of specific types of goods.

In Brazil and Mexico delayed improvements in the transport and communication network and stagnating per capita income retarded the transformation of the distribution system. Since 1930 rapid income growth, improved transport conditions and urbanisation have accelerated changes in distributive services. From the mid-1970s foreign direct investment in both countries accelerated the modernisation process. High-income inequality combined with complex and costly laws explain the persistence of a massive number of small, underdeveloped and mostly informal retailers.

MEASUREMENT OF OUTPUT AND PRODUCTIVITY IN DISTRIBUTIVE SERVICES[25]

Wholesalers transmit goods from manufacturers to retailers and subsequently retailers sell to consumers. Distributors not only sell goods, but also provide a large range of services such as credit, shopping convenience in terms of location, opening hours, product information and so on. An ideal measure would take account of the goods sold as well as the characteristics and additional services delivered by stores. No such measure exists, although the US Bureau of Labor Statistics is currently constructing a proxy.[26]

In the absence of physical measures output is estimated by monetary aggregates. According to SNA 1993 output should be measured by the total value of the trade margins realised on the goods distributors purchase for resale. This and other studies on productivity, such as Smith and Hitchens (1985), adopt the same measure. Another frequently used output measure is sales (US Department of Labor, Bureau of Labor Statistics, 1999; Hall *et al.*, 1961; Jefferys and Knee, 1962).

Sales data are more readily available at the detailed level than gross margins for many countries. Sales would be valid proxy of output if gross margins are a constant share of sales for all goods and distributors. However, this is not the case in reality.[27] Increasing evidence suggests that even gross margins are not representative for store characteristics as they are biased by consumption patterns, market power, regulation, economies of scale and measurement problems (see Pilat, 1997 for a survey of studies on margins).

Barger (1955) found that gross margins in US retailing rose between 1870 and 1950.[28] He and Schwartzman (1971) found, however, no clear link between the size of margins and the quality of service. While store facilities, physical surroundings and the ease at which merchandise can be returned after purchase improved over time, the service at the point of sale diminished with the increase of self-service. The use of gross margins in international comparisons may be even more problematic, as consumption patterns, market power, regulation and economies of scale are probably more different between countries than between two years within a single country.

In intertemporal comparisons an appropriate price index is needed to deflate sales or gross margins. For this purpose most national accounts use the producer or wholesale price index (PPI) for wholesale trade and the consumer price index (CPI) for retail trade (OECD, 1996). Several authors criticised the use of the CPI, as it often fails to take account of changes in the volume of retail services. Nakamura (1999) illustrated that the real gross margin for US food retailers, when using the CPI to deflate sales and the PPI to deflate purchased goods destined for resale, fell by almost 8 per cent per year between 1977 and 1992. This unrealistic result contrasts with other evidence showing that the volume of their services increased in terms of the amount of personnel per transaction, opening hours, product variety and sales floor area. In contrast Oi (1992, 1998) argued that other types of retail services fell over time, in particular the proximity to the consumer and the mass introduction of self-service retailing. On the whole, however, positive quality changes probably outweigh the negative ones confirming Nakamura's suggested measurement bias.

The recent rise of e-commerce further complicates the measurement of the volume of retail services (Triplett and Bosworth, 2000). The purchase of a book in a conventional store requires a consumer to incur travel costs which are not included in the price of the book. A book bought over the internet, however, incurs handling and shipping costs that are included in the purchase price. Moreover, the internet does not offer the same service as bookstores such as the possibility of browsing through books; the former thus provides less service than the latter. The simple comparison of the book prices in the two settings will omit the value of the retail services (which are not separately priced) to the buyer, and miscount costs to the buyer which are non-market in one case (travel costs to the store) but explicit and charged in the other (shipping and handling for e-commerce sales).

This study relied on census information, that is Brazilian, Mexican and US wholesale and retail trades were matched at a detailed, four-digit, level of the US standard industrial classification (SIC). In the detailed calculations 28 product groups were distinguished, which were subsequently consolidated into durables and non-durables, with food products as a subcategory of non-durables. From these sources we derived comparable estimates of the value of sales and gross value added, as well as employment (which had to be adjusted in the case of the USA to include family workers and working proprietors). In order to get the same coverage for the three countries a number of items had to be excluded from the US censuses of wholesale and retail trade, as they could not be matched with items in the Brazilian or Mexican censuses of distribution. The excluded US trades were 4 per cent of those in our sample, produced 9.5 per cent of value added and accounted for 18.1 per cent of persons engaged in 1977. For Brazil and Mexico a number of trades also had to be excluded which could not be matched with US statistics. Sales of excluded Brazilian trades made up 1.4 per cent of our sample, 1.9 per cent of value added and 1.8 per cent of persons engaged. Sales of excluded Mexican trades were 5.4 per cent of our sample, 6.7 per cent of value added and 3.9 per cent of persons engaged (see Mulder and Maddison, 1993; Mulder, 1994a, 1994b for a list of excluded trades).

The censuses of wholesale and retail trade contained most of the required statistics, but did not provide information on the quantities of goods distributed; only money values of total sales. The US census does not give detailed information on inventory changes and input costs, but the relevant information can be derived from other sources[29] on a somewhat more aggregate level than appears in the census. Information on input costs is only available for merchant wholesalers in wholesale trade. In wholesale trade they accounted for 54 per cent of sales and 80 of establishments in 1977. Non-merchant wholesalers are essentially branches of manufacturing firms who sell goods directly to consumers or to retailers. Ratios of input costs to sales of merchant wholesalers were assumed to be representative for other types of wholesale trade. Our census data for sales in the USA are for 1977 in 1977 prices. In order to compare these with Brazil and Mexico in 1975, US sales data were adjusted to a 1975 basis.[30] Subsequently, ratios of purchased goods were applied, and other inputs to sales derived from the Department of Commerce, Bureau of the Census (1981a, 1981b) to estimate gross margins and value added for individual trades (three or four digits). Value added data in the censuses were adjusted so they correspond with the national accounts concept in use at present by the statistical offices.[31]

Table 5.2 shows the number of establishment per 100,000 inhabitants in 1975/77. Brazil and Mexico had fewer establishments per head of population than the USA, especially in wholesale trade. Brazil had more wholesalers, but fewer retailers per head of population than Mexico. The US figures exclude wholesale establishments without a payroll which are mainly agents and brokers. When these are included the number of wholesalers per 100,000 would almost double.

The average size of establishment is measured by the number of persons employed. Mexican wholesalers and retailers employed more people on average than their Brazilian counterparts in 1975. US wholesalers were about the same size as those in Mexico, though retailers were larger than those in the other two countries.

The lowest margins were found in Brazil, the highest in Mexico with the USA occupying an intermediate position. The lowest margins prevailed in the trade of food products in all countries. High margins were observed in durable goods trade. The censuses also reveal that Brazil had the lowest ratio of intermediate inputs (such as electricity, stationery and so on) to sales (see Table 5.3).

The gross margin as a share of sales is often used as an indicator of efficiency. However, higher margins may have other causes than inefficiency, such as a higher levels of distributive services. Other causes include differences in consumption expenditure patterns, market power, measurement problems, regulation and economies of scale. The higher margins ir the USA relative to Brazil are probably related to the higher service levels in the former country. The high Mexican margins may be explained by the inefficiency expressed in terms of lower labour productivity

Table 5.2 *Number of Establishments in Wholesale and Retail Trade per Capita and Average Size, Brazil, Mexico, and the USA, 1975/77*

	Number of Establishment per 100,000 Population			Average Size (Persons per Establishment)		
	Brazil 1975	Mexico 1975	USA 1977	Brazil 1975	Mexico 1975	USA 1977
Wholesale trade						
Durables	13	5	94	9.6	15.1	12.1
Non-durables	34	13	66	7.0	10.2	13.0
Food	13	7	16	7.2	7.0	17.2
Total (all branches)	47	18	160	7.7	11.6	12.5
Retail trade						
Durables	83	77	209	6.0	5.3	10.5
Non-durables	516	660	335	2.6	1.8	6.4
Food	382	494	101	2.1	1.6	9.2
Total (all branches)	599	737	544	3.1	2.1	8.0
Distribution	646	755	704	3.4	2.4	9.0

Sources: Number of establishments, and employment from distribution censuses as described in Appendix D.

Table 5.3 *Ratios of Purchased Goods to Sales, Other Inputs to Sales and Value Added to Sales in Brazilian, Mexican, and US Distribution, 1975/77*

	Ratio of Gross Margin to Sales			Ration of Other Inputs to Sales		
	Brazil 1975	Mexico 1975	USA 1977	Brazil 1975	Mexico 1975	USA 1977
Wholesale trade						
Durables	22.1	35.5	25.4	3.5	7.6	4.1
Non-durables	17.9	26.9	16.8	2.5	6.8	3.4
Food	13.8	23.9	16.4	3.1	4.5	3.2
Total (all branches)	19.1	29.7	20.5	2.8	7.1	3.7
Retail trade						
Durables	26.1	37.6	28.0	4.7	7.9	4.7
Non-durables	19.2	29.3	26.9	3.8	6.6	5.2
Food	17.9	28.1	23.2	3.3	4.7	4.8
Total (all branches)	22.2	33.2	27.5	4.2	7.2	4.9
Distribution	20.5	32.2	22.9	3.5	7.2	4.1

Source: See Appendix D.

compared to Brazil, as indicated by our double deflation approach (see below). Moreover, Mexican retailers offered more services than their Brazilian counterparts in terms of accessibility (see Table 5.2).

VALUE ADDED AND EMPLOYMENT IN 1975/77

Table 5.4 shows value added and employment in distributive services. The contribution of a sector to overall GDP is best measured by value added.[32] To utilise the advantage of census information over national accounts, which uses a single source rather than multiple sources, this study focuses on census data where possible. Although the coverage of economic activity of the national accounts is superior, census data are often more reliable in countries like Brazil and Mexico. Census data comprise the basic source for wholesale and retail trade.

Wholesale trade accounted for a larger share of value added and a lower share of employment than retail trade in all countries, except for Mexico where it represented only 24 per cent of total value added in distributive services. Therefore, productivity was much higher in wholesale trade than retail trade. The share of non-durables in wholesale trade seemed negatively correlated with income levels, as Brazilian and Mexican shares were higher than those for the USA. No such relationship was found for the share of non-durables in retail trade.

Three types of employment exist: paid full-time and part-time employees, proprietors and unpaid family workers. The Brazilian and Mexican censuses contain data on the number of paid employees, family workers and proprietors combined for each product group. In Brazil family workers and proprietors comprised 48.6 per cent of persons engaged while in Mexico they accounted for 51.9 per cent of persons engaged in wholesale and retail trade in 1975. The US wholesale and retail censuses do not contain information on proprietors and family workers, though there were a substantial number in this category. The proxy measure[33] puts the number of proprietors at 1,240 thousand and family workers at 184,000 in 1977. US proprietors and family workers added 11.4 per cent to paid employees – a much lower proportion than in Brazil and Mexico.

Employment in wholesale trade accounted for 16 per cent of total wholesale and retail employment in Brazil, 12 per cent in Mexico and for 31 per cent in the USA. In Brazil and Mexico trade in food products accounted for more than 40 per cent of the total. Trade in consumer durables provided more than half of distributive employment in the USA. Wholesale and retail trade employment, as recorded in the censuses, accounted for 6.2 per cent, 6.7 per cent of total Brazilian and Mexican employment, respectively. The augmented estimate of US distributive employment (excluding family workers) represented 14.1 per cent of total US employment in 1977.

Table 5.4 *Value Added and Employment in Wholesale and Retail Trade, Brazil, Mexico and the USA, 1975–77*

	Value Added (million 1975 US$)[a]			Persons Engaged (000s)[b]		
	Brazil 1975	Mexico 1975	USA 1977	Brazil 1975	Mexico 1975	USA 1977
Wholesale trade						
Durables	3,309	616	99,693	127	47	2,458
Non-durables	6,780	895	79,373	248	80	1,817
Food	1,439	302	23,630	102	29	613
Total (all branches)	10,089	1,511	179,065	375	127	4,276
Retail trade						
Durables	4,949	2,517	66,991	521	246	4,815
Non-durables	4,537	2,212	58,556	1,425	696	4,652
Food	2,200	1,221	26,265	852	475	2,042
Total (all branches)	9,487	4,728	125,547	1,946	942	9,467
Distribution	19,576	6,239	304,612	2,321	1,069	13,743

Notes:
[a] Converted to US$ by the 1975 prevailing exchange rates.
[b] Distributive censuses in the USA did not include family workers and proprietors, whereas censuses in Brazil and Mexico did. The US number of family workers and proprietors was estimated as described in the text.

Sources: Brazil: IBGE (1981a); Mexico: SPP (1981a); USA: employment from Department of Commerce, Bureau of the Census (1981a, 1981c). Neither census contains data on purchases of goods by distributors and value added. Two other publications of the Department of Commerce, Bureau of the Census (1981b, 1981d) were used to estimate value added as a percentage of sales for different kinds of trade. 1977 US value added was adjusted to a 1975 basis by price indexes derived from Department of Labor, Bureau of Labor Statistics (1978a) (applied to wholesale trade) and Department of Labor (1978b) (applied to retail trade).

COMPARATIVE OUTPUT AND PRODUCTIVITY LEVELS

I. Single Deflation

Comparisons in space require deflators to convert sales, margins and value added to a common set of prices. Various conversion factors can be used for this purpose. Exchange rates are the most simple but little representative for distributive services. Another is final expenditure PPPs. Some studies use a single PPP for total expenditure to convert gross margins of all types of retailing (McKinsey, 1992, 1997). Hall *et al.* (1961), Pilat (1994) and Smith and Hitchens (1985) used detailed expenditure PPPs corresponding to the types of goods sold by wholesalers and retailers to convert sales, gross margins and value added. This single deflation procedure was also adopted at first in this study. Two sets of weights can be used: Brazilian (Mexican) expenditure weights (that is derivation of a Paasche PPP):

$$PPP^{xu(x)}_{SingDef} = \frac{ValueAdded^{x(x)}}{\sum_{i=1}^{T}\left[ValueAdded_i^{x(x)} / PPP_i^{xu}\right]} \tag{5.1}$$

with i=1,..., T types of wholesale and retail trade. US expenditure weights (derivation of a Laspeyres PPP) can also be used:

$$PPP^{xu(u)}_{SingDef} = \frac{\sum_{i=1}^{T}\left[ValueAdded_i^{u(u)} * PPP_i^{xu}\right]}{ValueAdded^{u(u)}} \tag{5.2}$$

The geometric average of the Paasche and Laspeyres estimates represents the Fisher PPP.

Table 5.5 shows the ICP reweighted Paasche and Laspeyres PPPs which we used to convert value added into the other currency. The Fisher PPP of the Brazil/USA comparison was above the prevailing exchange rate. Wholesale price ratios were above the retail price ratios in all comparisons. PPPs of durables were higher than those of non-durables, which, in turn, surpassed those for groceries. The same patterns were found in the implicit PPPs of value added derived by double deflation.

Expenditure PPPs are supposed to reflect not only the price levels of goods sold but also those of retail services. However, retail prices are often not collected in comparable store formats, partly because comparable formats do not always exist. McKinsey (1997) argued that in countries with relatively high wages such as the Netherlands and Sweden, expenditure PPPs overstate retail output and productivity, because they poorly reflect the relative volume of retail services. High wages induce retailers to cut many low-productivity jobs, such as grocery-bagging, which reduces the level of services. PPPs are not adjusted for this.

McKinsey (1997), when comparing Dutch and US retailers, tried to overcome this problem by using the PPP only for the ‘same format’ of stores, that is out-of-town specialised stores. These are the same in terms of retail concept, service and efficiency levels. Their absolute productivity levels were combined with productivities (in terms of value added per hour worked) in other stores in each country to calculate absolute format productivities. Total retail trade productivity was subsequently estimated by weighting the individual format productivities by their respective shares in employment. Retail output was obtained by multiplying labour productivity by the number of hours worked. This approach assumes that when a European and a US store sell the same quantity of goods but the US store has more working hours, then the US store provides more retail services. This is often the case, as US stores have longer opening hours and shorter lines at the check-out counter. This approach showed higher US relative productivity than the PPP comparison.[34]

Table 5.5 *ICP Reweighted Fisher PPPs for Gross Value Added, Distribution, Mexico (1975)/USA (1977) and Brazil (1975)/USA (1977), 1975 prices*

	Brazil, 1975/ USA, 1977 (Cruzeiros per US$)	Mexico, 1975/ USA, 1977 (Pesos per US$)
Wholesale trade		
Durables	9.42	12.08
Non-durables	8.68	11.08
Food	5.56	8.59
Total (all branches)	9.11	11.80
Retail trade		
Durables	9.25	11.70
Non-durables	7.79	9.91
Food	5.44	8.31
Total (all branches)	8.45	10.68
Distribution	8.78	11.36
Exchange rate	8.13	12.50

Notes: The PPPs of this table deviate from those for sales in Table 5.6, because value added was used as weights instead of sales.

Source: See Appendix D.

Mulder and Maddison (1993) and this study also argue that expenditure PPPs are unsuitable converters for the gross margin and value added, mostly because they apply only to sales that equal consumer expenditure. ICP PPPs do not represent relative prices of goods purchased by distributors for resale, nor do they represent relative prices of other inputs like communication costs, fuels and office supplies. In addition to single deflation this study also followed a double deflation procedure for both wholesale and retail trade, in which two sets of converters are used, that is one that applies to sales and another for purchases of goods for resale and other inputs.

II. Double Deflation

(i) PPPs for Sales

The first step was the detailed conversion of Brazilian, Mexican and US sales of 56 types of wholesale and 50 types of retail trade by ICP Paasche and Laspeyres PPPs. Table 5.6 lists the PPPs for broad product categories (derived by weighting the detailed PPPs by the sales of the corresponding wholesale and retail categories).

Table 5.6 *ICP Fisher PPPs for Sales, ICOP Fisher UVRs for Purchases and Other Inputs and Implicit Fisher UVRs for Value Added, Distribution, Brazil (1975)/USA (1977) and Mexico (1975)/USA (1977), 1975 prices*

	Brazil (1975)/USA (1977) Fisher Results (Cruzeiros per US$)				Mexico (1975)/USA (1977) Fisher Results (Pesos per US$)			
	ICP PPP for Sales	ICOP UVR for Purchases	ICOP UVR for Other Inputs	Implicit UVR for Value Added	ICP PPP for Sales	ICOP UVR for Purchases	ICOP UVR for Other Inputs	Implicit UVR for Value Added
Wholesale trade								
Durables	9.4	6.1	6.1	*	11.8	14.0	13.7	9.7
Non-durables	8.4	9.0	6.4	5.5	11.3	13.0	14.0	7.2
Food	5.6	6.6	6.5	4.8	8.7	11.5	14.3	*
Total	8.7	7.9	6.3	14.2	11.6	13.3	13.9	8.7
Retail trade								
Durables	8.9	6.9	6.4	16.3	11.9	15.1	13.1	6.9
Non-durables	7.7	7.8	6.6	7.6	10.0	11.1	14.1	5.5
Food	5.4	5.7	6.7	4.6	8.3	10.0	14.9	*
Total	8.2	7.5	6.5	10.0	10.8	12.5	13.6	6.4
Distribution	8.5	7.7	6.4	11.9	11.4	12.7	13.7	8.3
Exchange rate	8.1	8.1	8.1	8.1	12.5	12.5	12.5	12.5

Note: * Fisher UVR could not be calculated because either the Paasche or Laspeyres UVRs were negative.

Source: See Appendix D.

(ii) UVRs for Goods Purchased

Paasche and Laspeyres UVRs were derived from the Groningen ICOP studies for purchases of goods by distributors from other sectors of the economy for resale. The main difference between the ICP and ICOP approach is that the ICP (or expenditure) approach estimates PPPs by comparing final expenditures (that is private consumer expenditure, investment and government) between countries, whereas the ICOP (or industry-of-origin) estimates are based on ex-factory prices of goods from the commodity-producing sectors. The ICOP UVRs are therefore more suitable to convert purchases than ICP PPPs. This provided the second step in the process of double deflation. Table 5.6 shows the ICOP binary UVRs for broad categories. Subtracting the cost of goods purchased by distributive establishments (that is value of inventories at the beginning of the year, plus purchases of goods during the year less the value of inventories at the end of the year) from sales furnishes a first approximation to gross value added (that is the gross margin). In national accounts terminology the gross margin corresponds to the gross value of output of wholesale and retail trade.

(iii) UVRs for Other Inputs

Next, the 'other inputs' were deducted. The ICOP UVRs for communications, electricity and transport are taken from Mulder (1991, 1994b, 1995). Similar data for fuels and packaging materials are from van Ark and Maddison (1994). The Brazilian, Mexican and US censuses give cost data for these inputs.[35] The inputs included in the double deflation exercise represented 1.4 per cent of total inputs (including purchases of goods for resale), 1.5 per cent in Mexico and 1.7 per cent in the USA. No ICOP UVRs were available to convert the remaining input costs listed in the Brazilian, Mexican and US sources, such as advertising, technical services, rental costs and so on. These conversion-resistant inputs represented 2.8 per cent of total inputs (including purchases of goods for resale) in Brazil, 6.0 per cent in Mexico and 3.4 per cent in the USA. We used a weighted average of the ICOP Paasche UVRs for electricity, packaging materials and transport costs to convert the residual input costs in cruzeiros (pesos) to US$ in the Brazilian (Mexican) case, and a weighted average of the Laspeyres UVRs in the US case to convert its residual from US$ into cruzeiros (pesos).

(iv) Implicit UVRs for Value Added

The implicit Laspeyres UVRs for value added are found by dividing the double deflated US value added estimate in cruzeiros (pesos) by US value added in US$:

$$UVR^{xu(u)}_{DoubDef} = \frac{\sum_{i=1}^{T}\left(\left[Sales^{u(u)}_{ij} * PPP^{xu}_{i}\right] - \left[Purchases^{u(u)}_{ij} * UVRs^{xu}_{i}\right]\right)}{ValueAdded^{U(U)}} \tag{5.3}$$

For Brazil (Mexico), the implicit Paasche UVR is obtained by dividing the value added in cruzeiros (pesos) by double deflated value added in US$:

$$UVR^{xu(x)}_{DoubDef} = \frac{ValueAdded^{x(x)}}{\sum_{i=1}^{T}\left(\left[Sales^{x(x)}_{i} / PPP^{xu}_{i}\right] - \left[Purchases^{x(x)}_{i} / UVR^{xu}_{i}\right]\right)} \tag{5.4}$$

where PPP^{xu} refers to expenditure purchasing power parities for good, and UVR^{xu} to industry-of-origin UVRs for good *i*. Purchases refers to goods for resale and other inputs. Table 5.6 shows the implicit Fisher UVRs.

Van Ark *et al.* (1999) applied the same method for retail trade, but not for wholesale trade. They argued correctly that expenditure PPPs are suitable converters only for retail but not for wholesale sales. They used the ICOP UVRs for the sales and purchases of wholesale trade.

Van Ark and Monnikhof (2000), who compared relative output and productivity levels between 19 countries in the 1990s, further refined this methodology. They argued that not two but three different conversion factors are needed: one for the purchases of the wholesale sector; one for the sales of wholesalers, which equal that for the purchases of retailers, and one for the sales of retailers. For the first ICOP UVRs can be used, and for the third final expenditure PPPs. The second conversion factor is between the UVR and PPP, and can be estimated from either the wholesale or the retail side. Following the first option the UVR is corrected for the relative margin between sales and purchases of the wholesale sector. Let IMP^{xu}_{W} represent the relative intermediate price level between country *x* and the US approximated from the UVR side, then:

$$IMP^{xu}_{w} = UVR^{xu}\frac{1+M^{x}_{w}}{1+M^{u}_{w}} \tag{5.5}$$

with M^{x}_{W} the wholesale margin in country *x* and M^{u}_{W} the wholesale margin in country *u*. The intermediate price level can also be obtained the other way around, that is starting from the retail PPP which is adjusted for the retail margin:

$$IMP_r^{xu} = PPP^{xu} / \frac{1 + M_r^x}{1 + M_r^u} \tag{5.6}$$

with M_r^x the retail margin in country x and M_r^u the retail margin in country u. This procedure assumes that the gross margins of wholesalers and retailers cover the total mark-up from producer to consumer prices. The intermediate price level is now approximated by an average of IMP_{wr}^{xu} and IMP_r^{xu}. The difference between the two results is distributed and the relative intermediate price is estimated as follows:

$$IMP^{xu} = IMP_w^{xu} * \sqrt{IMP_r^{xu} / IMP_w^{xu}} \tag{5.7}$$

The empirical implementation of this procedure turned out to be complicated, as the industry breakdown in the wholesale and retail trade censuses and surveys differs strongly between countries. Moreover, the detail at which UVRs are available also differs strongly from one bilateral comparison to another. To obtain relative prices for particular industries, UVRs were combined using value added weights and PPPs using expenditure weights. The relative prices were calculated using both the gross margin weights of country x, yielding a Paasche index, or those of the USA, yielding a Laspeyres PPP. The geometric of the two, the Fisher, was used for the productivity calculations.

III. Comparing Single and Double Deflation

A comparison of Tables 5.5 and 5.6 indicates the erratic results of the double deflation technique: the ratio of the highest to the lowest Fisher UVR for the Brazil/USA comparison was 3.6 for the double deflation and 1.7 for the single deflation. The Mexico/USA ratios are 1.8 for double and 1.4 for single deflation. Many types of error could arise in the execution of the double deflation procedure: ICP and ICOP UVRs had often limited availability without specific commodity types, and often did not exactly match the type of wholesale or retail trade. Because value added accounts for a small share of sales, a small measurement error in the ICP PPPs or ICOP UVRs is magnified in the implicitly derived value added UVRs. In the case of single deflation, the results are more plausible by branch because there are no negative readings. For this reason the single deflation results are preferred. Nevertheless, it is thought that the double deflation exercise was useful, and cannot be dismissed on the aggregate level as errors may be compensating, that is for wholesale and retail trade as a whole. It should be noted that the erratic character of the double deflation results in this study is not unusual. Szirmai and Pilat (1990) had the same experience in their experiments with double deflation for manufacturing comparisons of Japan and the USA.

Reconciliation of Census and National Accounts Data

To assess whether all economic activity in the wholesale and retail sector was covered by the census, they were reconciled with the national accounts which use other sources in addition to the production censuses (see Table 5.7). It seems that the Brazilian census covered all production and employment. The Mexican census apparently covered only one-third of production and almost two-thirds of employment in wholesale and retail trade. The US census underaccounted employment in distributive services as it excluded proprietors.

Table 5.7 Reconciliation of Census and National Accounts Data, Brazil (1975), Mexico (1975) and the USA (1977)

	Value Added (Million National Currency Units)			Employment (000s)		
	Census	National Accounts	(1)/(2)	Census	National Accounts	(4)/(5)
	(1)	(2)	(3)	(4)	(5)	(6)
Brazil	162,109	148,855	1.09	2,361	2,764	0.85
Mexico	85,448	236,407	0.36	1,118	1,886	0.59
USA	453,049[a]	506,900[a]	0.89	19,206[b]	20,761	0.93

Notes:
[a] Refers to the gross margin.
[b] Excluding self-employed.

Sources: Census estimates of GDP and employment as described in Table 5.8. National accounts: see Appendix E.

The calculations of value added[36] of unregistered activity in distributive services (see Appendix E) shows that the Brazilian national accounts probably modestly overestimated value added. Mexican national accounts seem to have largely overestimated value added. This is confirmed by the suggested larger labour productivity of distributors operating outside formal outlets, that is mostly street vendors, by the national accounts,[37] which is very unlikely.

Labour Productivity Levels in 1975

Labour productivity, measured by value added per worker, can be converted to a common currency using traditional single deflation with expenditure PPPs, or double deflation, which also uses industry-of-origin PPPs for inputs purchased by distributors. Using the double deflation approach, 1975 labour productivity (value added per person engaged) was 26 per cent of the US level in Brazil and 40 per cent in Mexico (see Panel A of Table 5.8). Using the traditional single deflation technique, labour productivity was substantially different: 35 per cent of the US level for Brazil and 29 per cent of the US level for Mexico. When double inflation is used the disaggregated results for different parts of distributive services show an erratic pattern. However, at the aggregate level this procedure has greater validity as the errors are probably compensating. One may conclude that Brazilian and Mexican productivity levels of 1975 lay in a range between 26–35 per cent of the US level for Brazil and between 29–40 per cent for Mexico, but the single deflation results probably deserve greater credence. The wide range between the results yielded by the alternative techniques is caused by the large proportion of purchased goods and inputs in sales, which magnifies differences between expenditure and industry-of-origin PPPs.[38]

The results of Panel A are based on censuses which include only establishments listed in business registers, and which omit all activity outside formal establishments. The labour productivity of informal establishments and street vendors is below that of the formal sector, as the relative productivity performance of the whole sector in Brazil and Mexico diminishes after they have been included (see Panel B).

Long-run Productivity Trends

In the USA labour productivity increased between 1950 and 1996. In Brazil and Mexico shops serving middle- and high-income groups – underwent a rapid process of modernisation, whereas those serving the poor stagnated. Overall there was an increase in productivity up to the 1980s, and then a collapse from 1982 (see Figure 5.2).

Table 5.8 *Labour Productivity in Distribution, Double and Single Deflation Fisher Results, Brazil (1975) and Mexico (1975) as a Per centage of the USA (1977)*

	Brazil (1975)/ USA (1977)		Mexico (1975)/ USA (1977)	
	Single Deflation	Double Deflation	Single Deflation	Double Deflation
Panel A: Results Based on Censuses only[c]				
Wholesale trade[b]				
Durables	55.3	[a]	33.6	42.0
Non-durables	58.8	93.4	28.8	44.5
Food	53.7	61.9	39.5	[a]
Total (all branches)	57.3	36.9	30.1	40.6
Retail trade				
Durables	59.9	34.0	78.7	132.7
Non-durables	26.4	27.0	31.8	57.5
Food	30.0	35.7	30.0	[a]
Total (all branches)	35.4	29.7	44.3	74.5
Distribution	35.2	26.0	29.0	39.5
Panel B: Results Based on Censuses & Activity Omitted in Censuses				
Distribution	33.0	24.4	21.6	29.5

Notes:

[a] A Fisher result could not be derived as the Paasche and/or the Laspeyres PPPs are negative.

[b] The US results cover only merchant wholesaler.

[c] For the Brazil/USA comparison the Paasche single deflated productivity ratio is 42 per cent and the Laspeyres 30 per cent. The Paasche double deflated ratio is 36 per cent and the Laspeyres 19 per cent. For the Mexico/USA comparison the Paasche single deflated productivity ratio is 36 per cent and the Laspeyres 23 per cent. The Paasche double deflated ratio is 57 and the Laspeyres 27 per cent.

Sources: Panel A: value added and employment: Brazil: IBGE (1981a); Mexico: SPP (1981a); USA: employment from Department of Commerce, Bureau of the Census (1981a, 1981c). Value added at national currencies was converted to US$ using expenditure PPPs from Kravis *et al.* (1982). For double deflation, industry-of-origin PPPs from Houben (1990), van Ark and Maddison (1994) and Maddison and van Ooststroom (1993) were used. Panel B: value added and employment from Appendix E.

Figure 5.2 Labour Productivity in Distributive Services: Brazil and Mexico as Per Cent of the USA, 1950–96 (USA=100)

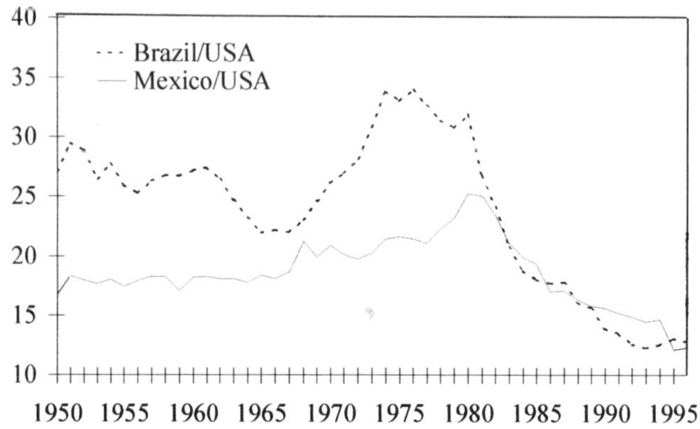

Sources: 1975 benchmark results from Table 5.8, time series of GDP at constant prices from Appendix B and employment from Appendix A.

NOTES

1. The Mexican shares are somewhat overstated as they include hotels and restaurants. These account for about 20 to 30 per cent of employment in distribution. Excluding restaurants and hotels would probably yield shares which are similar to those in Brazil.
2. This was the first year for which information was available for all three countries.
3. These figures should be interpreted with care, as the underreporting of retail outlets decreased over time. Growth rates of outlets may therefore be overestimated.
4. In 1975 they represented about 65 per cent of all stores in Brazil and Mexico (see Table 5.2). Their share fell to 52 per cent in Brazil and to 35 per cent in Mexico in 1993 (Euromonitor, 1995). The Brazilian share remained much higher due to hyperinflation in the 1980s and early 1990s. As a result consumers spent relatively more on food as real income fell. Moreover, food prices rose faster than the average inflation rate (see below).
5. A shopping centre is a cluster of outlets on one site which is easily accessible. It houses a complementary set of shops and offers comfort and security. Consumers benefit from the variety of stores and product ranges, levels of service and ambience, which they get with 'one-stop shopping'. Shop owners benefit from limited competition, and the customer-attracting effect of other shops. Moreover,

cost savings are realised through the sharing of expenses for maintenance, public utilities and security (OECD, 1992a).

6. The much higher share of supermarkets and hypermarkets in total sales in Brazil compared to Mexico is partly explained by the high inflation rates in the former country during recent years (see below).
7. Statistical agencies estimated that sales of informal retailers represented between 30 and 60 per cent of total retail sales in Brazil and approximately 20 per cent of sales in Mexico in the early 1990s (Euromonitor, 1995). In Mexico food sales of informals may have equalled those of formal stores in the same period (Gras and Fraschetto, 1993).
8. Informal retailers are those who operate outside the laws of the state and formal business practices, but whose activities are not clearly illegal in themselves. The goods sold are legal, but the retailers either lack business permits, obstruct zoning codes, fail to pay taxes or do not comply with labour regulations (Cross, 1998).
9. In 1995 Sears distributed a 36-page catalogue jointly with VISA; JC Penney's catalogue was distributed jointly with MasterCard, presenting 30,000 products on 1,360 pages. Mappin Stores was one of the largest mail-order houses, distributing 300,000 copies of a 64-page catalogue covering 500 products (Barbosa *et al.*, 1995).
10. In 1970 the share of people under 15 in the total population was 42, 46 and 28 per cent for Brazil, Mexico and the USA, respectively. In 1995 the share had fallen to 32, 36 and 22 per cent (World Bank, 1997).
11. The share of people of 60 years and older in total population increased from 10 per cent in 1950 to 17 in 1990 in the USA from 4 to 8 per cent in Brazil, and remained stable at 4 per cent in Mexico (see Table 7.6).
12. It increased from 34 per cent in 1950 to 58 per cent in 1990 (Department of Commerce, *Statistical Abstract of the United States,* 1975 and 1995).
13. In 1975 US food retailers employed 20 per cent of the labour force in distribution compared to 40 per cent in Brazil and Mexico (see Table 5.4). US per capita income was about four times that of Brazil and Mexico.
14. In Mexico, for example, the richest 10 per cent of the population only spend 16 per cent on food, whereas the poorest 10 per cent spend almost half of their income on food in the early 1990s (Euromonitor, 1995).
15. In Brazil it is defined as the level of family income necessary to provide a basic level of food and shelter. It was estimated that about 40 per cent of the population lived under this level in the early 1990s (Euromonitor, 1995). In the USA, the percentage of the population living below the poverty line – the cost of a minimum adequate diet multiplied by three to allow for other expenses – decreased from 22 in the late 1950s to 15 per cent in 1994 (Department of Commerce, *Statistical Abstract of the United States*, various issues).
16. Another indicator of urbanisation is the share of the population living in cities surpassing one million inhabitants. In 1980 the share was 27 per cent for Brazil

and Mexico and 36 per cent for the USA. By 1995 the shares increased to 33 per cent for Brazil, 28 for Mexico and 39 for the USA (World Bank, 1997).

17. More than 300 laws were changed. The number of state departments regulating the distribution sector increased from 14 to 15.
18. De Soto (1989, p. 148) found that 21.7 per cent of the costs of 'remaining formal' for an industrial firm in Lima were related to taxes, whereas 72.7 per cent were non-tax related and 5.6 per cent were payments for public utilities in the mid-1980s.
19. The major strategies to avoid detection are the operation of small units instead of larger ones, not advertising goods or services, and bribing of authorities. The risk of detection was the major concern of informal businesses. Bribes represented 10–15 per cent of operating income (de Soto, 1989).
20. Relative productivity of Brazilian wholesale and retail trade decreased from 35 to 33 per cent of the US level in 1975, and that of Mexico from 29 to 22 per cent after accounting for informal activity (see Table 5.8).
21. Macy focused on an urban public with a more refined taste and more insistent on quality than the rural population. Although mail orders helped Macy to spread its name, it was never a very profitable activity. The volume of its products sold grew, but the expenses even faster. Macy stopped its mail-order activities in 1911 (Emmet and Jeuck, 1950).
22. See Chapter 6 and Appendix C for detailed accounts, inflation rates.
23. Two examples are that President Sarney (1985–90) put on trial the supermarket chain *Pão de Açúcar* for price increases above the inflation rate. In December 1993 the government of Itamar Franco protested against a 90 per cent increase in food prices, while inflation and interest rates had remained comparatively stable (Euromonitor, 1995).
24. In 1994 retail sales increased 17 per cent (BNDES, 1996a).
25. This text draws significantly on Mulder and Maddison (1993).
26. It asks individual retailers for their sale prices as well as the replacement costs of goods. Simultaneously, retailers are asked to communicate the characteristics of their stores, such as surface, store area, and type of store (discount, combination outlet, speciality store or warehouse). Using a hedonic function, the variations in margins are explained by the store characteristics.
27. For example, a mass retailer has sales of 1000 US$ with a 10 per cent margin while a mom and pop store has sales of 500 US$ with a margin of 20 per cent. According to the sales measure, the output of the mass retailer was twice that of the small store, whereas in terms of gross margins output was the same.
28. Barger measured the growth of "net output" by retail sales of finished goods adjusted to a constant price basis, and weighted by gross margins in 1869 and 1929. His final index was the mean of the 1869 and 1929 measures. He made no quality adjustment. Prior to 1929, he estimated retail sales by a mark-up on commodity output, i.e. he added transport costs, wholesale and retail trade mark-

ups to the value of commodity production. For the years after 1929, he derived sales directly from the censuses of distribution for 1929, 1939 and 1948. Margins were estimated using census material, and unpublished records of individual enterprises.

29. Department of Commerce, Bureau of the Census, (1981a, 1981b) These sources show sales, purchases of goods, inventory changes and other input costs on a two-digit level for wholesaling and retailing.
30. This was done using consumer price indices in the case of retailing, and wholesale (producer) price indices in the case of wholesaling. Price indexes were taken from two publications of the Department of Labor, Bureau of Labor Statistics (1978a, 1978b). Price indexes are given for individual products at a very detailed level. Annual averages were used to calculate price changes.
31. From the Mexican *valor agregado censal bruto* the following items were deducted: *gastos por uso de patentas y marcas, asistencia tecnica y otros pagos por tecnologia* (cost of patents, licences, technical assistance and technology); and *gastos por rentas y alquileres* (cost of renting). From the US census value added the following items were deducted: lease and rental payments, purchased advertising services, purchased communications services and purchased repair services.
32. The gross value of output as 'contribution measure' means the double counting of production of other industries because of the inclusion of inputs.
33. See Mulder and Maddison (1993).
34. McKinsey admits that the one-to-one relationship between extra employment and extra service may be an exaggeration, but it provides some idea of the quantitative impact of differences in service levels across countries.
35. ICOP Paasche UVRs were available for the following inputs listed in the Brazilian census: communication, electricity, fuels and lubricants, and freight and carriage (that is transport). The Mexican census gives data on electricity and packaging materials. The input output table (SPP, 1981c) is another source from which information can be obtained on input costs: it appears that transport costs were a significant input (that is 10.5 per cent of total 'other' input costs). We applied this percentage to each trade. Neither of the US censuses contained data from which we could derive input costs. Two other sources were used instead (Department of Commerce, Bureau of the Census, 1981b, 1981d). The following inputs were included in the double deflation exercise: communications and electricity, fuels, office supplies and packing and wrapping materials.
36. Value added in the unregistered sector was imputed by multiplying unregistered employment by the labour productivity in establishments with less than five employees as taken from the census. Employment in the unregistered sector, estimated by the difference between the census and national accounts, is shown in column 3. The sum of census value added and imputed value added of the unregistered sector yields the revised estimate of GDP (see column 7). The

employment figures for Mexico are different from those listed in Table 5.4, as the former correspond to the number of persons engaged and the latter to the number of jobs (*puestos renumerados*).

37. As the national accounts made a larger imputation for value added than employment, it is suggested that labour productivity of non-registered workers exceeds that of formal employees.
38. Purchases of goods for resale and inputs accounted for 76 per cent of sales in Brazil, 61 per cent in Mexico in 1975 and 63 per cent in the USA in 1977.

6. Financial Services

LONG-TERM DEVELOPMENT

The Period 1800–1950

In Brazil the development of the financial sector accelerated around the second half of the nineteenth century. In 1850 there were only three commercial banks with deposits accounting for only 5 per cent of GDP, and a minor stock exchange in Rio de Janeiro. There were also several quasi-banks, for example commodity traders and merchant houses who extended credit and accepted deposits. Four decades later, at the end of the Empire (1889), the quasi-banks had disappeared, and new banks and insurance companies had been created. By that time most metallic money was replaced by notes issued by the Treasury and commercial banks. Despite this the financial sector remained small, with a ratio of bank deposits to GDP of only 25 per cent. Banks rarely served as a source of finance for industrial companies.[1] Half the deposits were concentrated in a few banks in Rio de Janeiro, of which *Banco do Brasil* was the largest. Although it was a private bank, it retained close relations with the Imperial government. In 1864 and 1875 major financial crises occurred, caused by failures of quasi-banks which lost large sums in Argentina and Paraguay. Between 1850 and 1890 about a third of the total government debt was financed by foreigners and two-thirds by domestic sources (Goldsmith, 1986).

In the early years of the Republic (1889–91) an almost complete liberalisation of the financial sector, called the *Encilhamento*, induced a rapid increase in the number of banks and a fivefold increase of their assets. An expansionary monetary policy – M2 grew 94 and 43 per cent in 1890 and 1891, respectively – combined with an increase in credit caused high inflation until 1894. The Rio exchange boomed and in the first year of the liberalisation more securities were traded than in the previous 60 years. Many banks were in trouble when the speculative bubble burst in 1894. Moreover, banks suffered big losses on their loans and investments due to high inflation. The government helped cushion these losses, but a new crisis occurred at the turn of the century. From 1889 to 1900 inflation totalled

265 per cent; the exchange rate depreciated by the same amount, that is from 1.87 to 5.19 milréis per US$. In 1906 only ten banks were left of the 68 which had existed in 1891, with only one ninth of the initial capital (Haber, 1991). The share of deposits to GDP fell from 25 to 11 per cent in the same period. From 1906 to 1945 the Brazilian banking system showed steady growth without major disturbances: the number of banks increased to more than 500 in 1945. The ratio of bank deposits to GDP increased to 30 per cent in this period.

From 1890 to 1913 the share of external debt in total government debt grew from one-third to two-thirds. Frequently the government had difficulty in financing its debt and interest payments. In 1898 it arranged a moratorium on interest payments for three years and debt repayments for ten years. From 1913 to 1945 the size of the debt fluctuated, partly because of the exchange rate movements, from 35 per cent of GDP in 1913, to 60 per cent in 1931 and 10 per cent in 1945 (Goldsmith, 1986).

The development of the financial sector in Mexico in the nineteenth century resembled that of Brazil. Most transactions were handled by merchant houses, which also provided short-term loans to well-connected firms at credit rates varying between 12 and 40 per cent. They also financed government debt, at interest rates often exceeding 100 per cent a year. The first commercial bank, *Banco de Avio*, was established in 1830, but failed 12 years later. The second bank, the British-owned *Banco de Londres y México*, was established during the 1860s, and the third, the French owned *Banco Nacional de México*, was founded in 1884.

A major difference between Brazil and Mexico was the role of silver in the money supply. In Brazil copper, gold, and silver coins accounted for one-fourth to one-third of the money supply in the 1850s. However, as the milréis was quoted 10 to 40 per cent below its gold parity during the 1860s, all coins disappeared from circulation and were exported. In Mexico silver coins remained an important part of the money supply (Goldsmith, 1986).

The Mexican system experienced relatively rapid growth during the last decade of the Porfiriato, when assets grew 13 per cent per year. In 1909 assets held by 47 banks amounted to 700 million pesos or 25 per cent of GDP. These banks issued money, facilitated international trade and offered commercial credit. The banking sector was highly concentrated. In 1910 the two largest banks accounted for 75 per cent of the deposits in Mexico's nine largest banks, and issued half of the notes in circulation. The small and concentrated financial sector made it difficult for manufacturers to obtain bank credit.[2] Mortgage banks were the only other financial institutions of any importance, representing 13 per cent of all bank assets in 1909. There were no savings banks, insurance companies or government financial institutions. During the Porfiriato capital imports grew rapidly, though they were not channelled through the financial system as they consisted mostly of direct investments and government bonds sold to foreign investors (Goldsmith, 1966; Haber, 1991, 1997).

The Porfirian government mainly relied on foreign funds to cover government credit needs. In 1885, when government finances were in bad shape, Mexico faced a financial crisis. The government suspended payments on all short-term debts. Successful negotiations with foreign bondholders resulted in a conversion of debts and a large sum of unpaid interest obligations accumulated over the previous decades. The process of debt conversion was completed in 1888, with a £10 million loan, which also signified the re-entry of Mexican bonds on European capital markets. New bond issues were placed on the Berlin and London exchange in 1889, 1890 and 1893 (Marichal, 1997).

The financial sector suffered greatly from the Revolution (1910–17), as many banks defaulted. The peso depreciated 60 per cent in 1914, 340 per cent in 1915 and 213 per cent in 1916. In the decades following the Revolution, growth slowed down and the system did not regain its pre-Revolution level of assets to GDP ratio until 1940. Commercial banks remained the main component of the financial sector. From 1920 to 1940 their number increased from 30 to 60, though assets grew only 2 per cent per year. The Central Bank and other major financial government institutions were founded during this period (see below).

In the USA the development of the banking system accelerated in the early nineteenth century and was concentrated in the north-east of the country. The number of banks in New England increased from 17 in 1800 to 84 in 1819, to 172 in 1830 and to 505 in 1860. Their capital increased from US$5.5 million in 1800 to US$123.6 million in 1860. Banks gradually broadened their portfolios to include loans to industrial firms, applied more flexible lending requirements and increased the duration of loans to a maximum of ten years.

The National Banking Act of 1863 accelerated the development of the banking system, as it unified the regionally based capital markets into one national market. The Act created a national network of chartered banks, and organised the widespread sale of government bonds to the public (Haber, 1991). Panics plagued the financial system in 1873, 1884, 1890, 1893 and 1907, years in which a large number of banks failed and the public withdrew cash fearing a complete failure of the system. The small size of banks contributed to the substantial risk of bank failure.

The Period 1950–96

From 1950 to 1996 the relative importance of financial services in total GDP grew in all the three countries. Figure 6.1 shows that in 1950 banking and insurance were relatively more important in Brazil than in Mexico and the USA. In Brazil the share increased rapidly during periods of hyperinflation, and fell during the stabilisation plans of 1986, 1990 and 1994. Several months after the 1986 and 1990 plans inflation accelerated again, and banking activity and its share in GDP exploded. By 1993 the financial services share reached 12 per cent of GDP. The successful price stabilisation in 1994 reduced inflation and the financial services share to 6 per cent in 1996.

Figure 6.1 Share of Financial Services in GDP at Current Prices, Brazil, Mexico and the USA, 1950–96

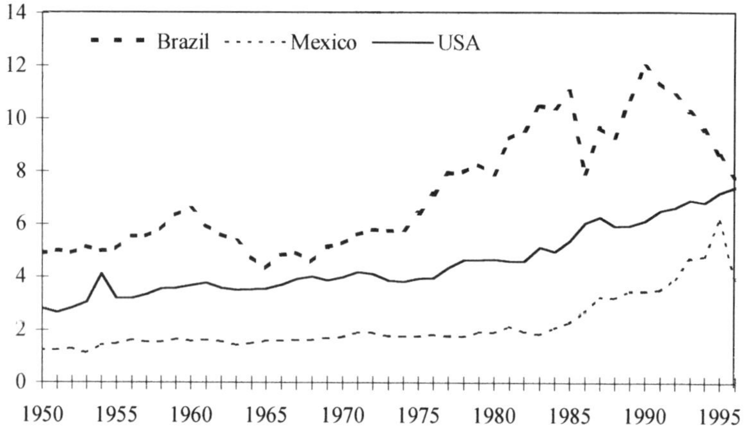

Sources: GDP at constant prices from Appendix B, converted to current prices with GDP deflators of Appendix C.

In Mexico the financial services share remained relatively stable until the 1980s, after which it rose steadily until 1994. The US financial services share showed constant growth throughout the whole period. The importance of banks and credit institutions grew in the course of time at the expense of insurance companies and other financial intermediaries in the USA, whereas the opposite occurred in Mexico. For Brazil no breakdown is available for banks and other credit institutions on the one hand, and insurers and other financial intermediaries on the other.

The share of financial services in employment was proportionally much lower than that in GDP (see Figure 6.2). In 1950 the US share was higher than Brazil's and Mexico's share. Afterwards employment grew most rapidly in Brazil, where the financial services share in total employment tripled. Nevertheless, in 1996, the US share remained four times that of Mexico and three times that of Brazil. The US breakdown of employment within financial services shows that the share of banks and other credit institutions increased from less than half of all employees in 1950 to 58 per cent of the total in 1996.

Figure 6.2 Employment in Financial Services as Percentage of the Total, Brazil, Mexico and the USA, 1950–96

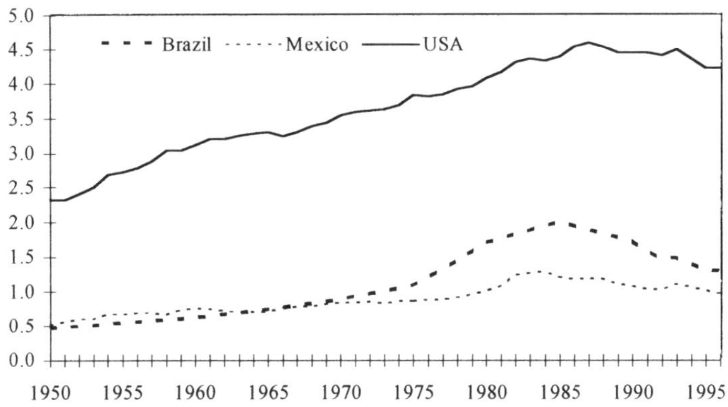

Source: Appendix A.

The number of banking establishments per 100,000 inhabitants can be used as a proxy indicator of access to financial services (Berg *et al.*, 1993; see Table 6.1). A banking establishment refers to an office (a physical location) providing financial services. In 1950 the three countries had approximately the same number of bank branches per capita. The picture changed drastically in the course of time: in 1992 the USA had almost four times as many establishments per capita as Brazil and seven times as many as Mexico. The banking density indicator as a proxy for service levels has to be interpreted with care, as larger banks tend to offer a larger variety of services than smaller ones. In the USA, banks were not allowed to set up branches in other states until the mid-1990s. Due to this legal restriction banks remained relatively small, and provided few types of services, that is mostly deposit and loan activities. In Brazil and Mexico, no restrictions on interstate banking existed.

Table 6.1 *Banking Establishments in Brazil, Mexico and the USA, 1950–92*

	Brazil		Mexico		USA	
	Number	Per 100,000 Persons	Number	Per 100,000 Persons	Number	Per 100,000 Persons
1950	1,897	3.7	846	3.1	4,934	3.2
1975	12,592	12.0	2,373	3.9	46,931	21.3
1992	17,000	10.9	4,400	4.9	92,000	36.0

Sources: Brazil: 1955 establishments from Goldsmith (1986, p. 266); 1975 and 1992 from IBGE, *Anuario Estatístico do Brasil* (various issues). Mexico: 1950 from Goldsmith (1966, p. 92), 1975 figure refers to private credit institutions (*instituciones privadas de credito*) from INEGI, *Anuario Estadístico de los Estados Unidos Mexicanos* (various issues). USA: 1950 from Department of Commerce, Bureau of the Census (1975, p. 1037); 1975 from Department of Commerce, *Statistical Abstract of the United States 1977*. Data for 1992 from McKinsey (1994, p. 1-b). Population from Maddison (1995b).

DETERMINANTS OF LONG-TERM DEVELOPMENT

i) The Economic Context

The development of the financial sector depends on the macroeconomic context. Economic growth (stagnation) increases (reduces) the demand for financial intermediaries. In the nineteenth century low per capita income and unequal income distribution in Brazil and Mexico slowed their financial development in comparison to the USA. From 1950 to 1980 the financial sector in Brazil and Mexico benefited from high GDP growth of more than 6 per cent per year on average from 1950 to 1980. Manufacturing was among the fastest growing sectors in this period. High growth created a high demand for loans to finance investment. The high demand for funds also stimulated the growth of the stock markets in Brazil and Mexico.

Crises in the real economy had a negative impact on the financial sectors in both countries. The Mexican Revolution and its aftermath halted the development of the financial sector for about 20 years. In Brazil and Mexico many banks ended up in trouble during the debt crisis of 1982, because loan and interest repayments by the government stopped. Moreover, as the economies plunged into a depression, many individuals and firms were also unable to repay loans. In the USA the crisis in real estate and falling oil prices in the 1980s – in combination with moral hazard behaviour of fund managers – caused the default of many banks and saving and loan associations.

The causality also runs the other way: a well (poor)-functioning financial sector fosters (inhibits) economic growth. The retarded development of the banking system and equity markets in Brazil and Mexico in comparison to the USA slowed economic growth and industrialisation in the Latin American countries. Limited access to equity markets and bank loans restrained the founding or the enlargement of industrial firms, as Haber (1991) illustrated for the textile industry in the three countries. In Brazil the number of textile companies listed on the Rio stock exchange increased rapidly after the liberalisation of financial markets, from 18 in 1894 to 54 in 1914, representing 28 per cent of all textile companies. In Mexico only 3 per cent of all textile companies were listed on the Mexico City stock exchange in 1910.

ii) Government Intervention

In the nineteenth century the financial systems in Brazil and Mexico were highly regulated, in contrast to the system of the USA. In Brazil the government restricted entry to the banking sector. Strong regulation at that time may have two reasons. Firstly, the governments were more preoccupied with creating a secure, stable source of funds for themselves, than with the establishment of a large number of institutions to channel credit to the private sector. Moreover, the owners of the existing banks had close ties to the governments and used these to obtain special rights and limited market entry. Another factor retarding growth of the financial sector in the Latin American countries was the absence, until the 1880s, of laws governing commercial banks and corporations. This made it difficult to enforce loan contracts (Haber, 1991).

In Mexico the government granted many privileges to the *Banco de México*.[3] Moreover, entry to banking was limited by high minimum capital requirements for new banks, the obligation to hold two-thirds of the deposits in reserves and the prohibition to open banks without prior approval of the secretary of the treasury and the congress.

The fragmented banking system of the USA in the nineteenth century resulted from privileges retained by the states, under the federal system of government (Bordo *et al.*, 1993, p. 4). Prior to the Civil War individual states controlled the banks. Except for some southern states, state governments allowed banks to operate only one or a few establishments, and did not permit banks to open branches in other states. Nevertheless, few restrictions existed to establish new banks. During the Civil War in 1863 the US government proclaimed the National Banking Act. A new institution, the Comptroller of Currency – part of the Department of the Treasury – administered the new regulations.

The financial system in each country was directly controlled by the government until the founding of the central banks in 1964 in Brazil (*Banco Central do Brasil*), in 1925 in Mexico (*Banco de Mexico*) and in 1913 in the USA (Federal Reserve System). In Brazil and the USA, this occurred after a major crisis,[4] whereas in Mexico it was part of a longer period of institution building. In Brazil the *Banco do Brasil* gradually obtained more supervisory powers over the financial system in the early twentieth century. It became the sole issuer of money and regulated the entire financial sector. The *Superintendencia de Moeda e Credito* (SUMOC) took over the supervisory functions of the *Banco do Brasil* in 1945. Finally, the Central Bank of Brazil (*Banco Central do Brasil*) was founded in 1964, after a period of recession and rapid inflation in 1961–64.

The *Banco de Mexico* performed more functions than its counterparts in Brazil and the USA. It accepted deposits (until 1925) and lent money to private and public firms. The Brazilian and Mexican central banks were never fully independent as the government often intervened in the formulation of monetary policy and regulation, in contrast to the USA. In the USA the Federal Reserve System (FED) was founded in 1913. The functions attributed to the FED was to act as a lender of last resort, and to regulate its member banks. Membership was obligatory for national banks and optional for state banks.

In Brazil and Mexico governments set up development banks in the 1930s to the 1950s, intended to provide cheap credit to firms in manufacturing and other sectors which were considered of key importance in the economic development process. The most important were the *Banco Nacional de Desenvolvimento Economico* (BNDE)[5] founded in 1951 in Brazil, and *Nacional Financiera* established in 1933 in Mexico. The US government never owned or operated commercial banks in the twentieth century.

The laws defining the regulatory environment of the financial sector in the second half of the twentieth century in Brazil originated in the early 1930s and mid-1960s. Its Mexican counterpart was the General Law of Credit Institutions and Auxiliary Organisations of 1941, and in the USA such laws were enacted in the late 1920s and early 1930s. The main regulations included interest rate ceilings, intended to control the cost of credit, and reserve requirements. The *Banco do Brasil* introduced the Usury Law in 1933, which prohibited nominal interest rates above 12 per cent. In Mexico the introduction of interest rate ceilings was part of the 1941 law. In the USA the FED introduced Regulation Q in 1933, which restricted interest on time deposits and prohibited interest on demand deposits. In all three countries the banking systems suffered from these restrictions in the 1970s and 1980s (see below).

The second major rule forced banks to hold fixed reserves. These provided a guarantee for deposit-holders and a tool for monetary policy. In Brazil and Mexico they also provided a source of government finance in the 1970s and 1980s. In 1962 three types of compulsory reserve requirements were introduced in Brazil. The first, which applied to demand deposits, varied between 40 and 50 per cent depending on the region where the bank was located. Banks were forced to transmit an additional 25 per cent of the demand deposit holdings as loans to the rural sector and a similar share to the manufacturing sector. These sectors paid preferential interest rates which were identical to those on the market. The second type, applied to saving deposits, varied between 10 and 15 per cent; and the third type was used for interest earning assets. Of the total deposits received by banks only 16 to 23 per cent could be allocated freely (Karoly Kaznar, 1994). In Mexico the reserve requirements formulated in the 1941 law depended on the geographic location of the bank, whether deposits were denominated in national or foreign currency, and the type of deposit. Two elements were added to this law in 1949: banks were required to deposit at the central bank part of the increase in deposits, and the central bank acquired the power to set reserve requirements to allocate credit (Gil, 1992).

In the USA reserve requirements were fixed by law between 15 and 25 per cent in 1863. The Federal Reserve Act of 1913 centralised the reserves of banks which were member of the Federal Reserve System in the 12 Federal Reserve Banks around the country. The required reserves depended on the type of deposit – demand or time – and the location of the bank – rural and urban. The law was changed in the course of time: since 1972 the distinction between rural and urban banks has been dropped, and since 1980 non-FED members have been subject to the same rules as the FED members. The reserve requirements were an important tool for monetary policy, especially between 1936 and 1965, when the ratio was changed more than 50 times (Durand, 1986).

In all three countries the sphere of operations of each type of institution in financial services was clearly limited by law. In Brazil and Mexico governments believed that segmentation would benefit specialisation, lower transaction costs and, therefore, would encourage capital formation. In Brazil the regulation introduced in 1964–66 divided the financial system into commercial banks, investment banks, credit and finance companies and the housing finance system. These new rules reduced the number of banks from 350 in 1964 to 120 in 1973. In Mexico the 1941 law defined the different financial institutions and their sphere of operations: deposit banks, savings banks,[6] financial societies, mortgage credit banks, capitalisation banks and trust funds. Clearing houses, the stock market, and credit unions were labelled auxiliary organisations. In the USA laws from the first third of this century separated commercial and investment banks. Both were not allowed to engage in insurance activities. The savings and loans institutions and credit unions, also referred to as thrift institutions, were subject to yet another set of regulations.

In Brazil and Mexico the policy of financial specialisation was partly successful as capital formation increased during the 1960s and 1970s. However, the policy came at a high price. The measures induced the concentration of banks, created inefficiency and a wide spread between lending and deposit rates. Moreover, the allocation of credit was far from optimal, as funds were channelled to individuals and firms which had access to information and privileges and not to those investors whose investments seemed most promising (Contador, 1992).

In addition to the standard types of regulation, each country had specific rules which had a major impact on the development of the financial sector, in particular the indexation mechanism in Brazil, and limits on opening branches in other states and deposit insurance in the USA. In Brazil the indexation of assets was introduced in 1964–66 after several years of negative real interest rates resulting from fixed nominal rates (as dictated by the Usury Law) and high inflation. Indexation of financial assets aimed to substitute the costly informal indexation, intended to stimulate voluntary savings and long-term contracts, and reduce the redistributive and allocative effects of inflation. At first indexation applied to fiscal debts only, but later the *Banco Central* extended it to other financial instruments such as time and saving deposits. Banks earned high profits, as demand deposits remained exempted from indexation, in contrast to loans and other financial instruments. Indexation was ex-ante for some instruments and ex-post for others. The former type of indexation meant that the asset value was corrected at the beginning of a period on the basis of the predicted rate of inflation, while in the latter case the value of an asset was adjusted at the end of a period on the basis of the actual inflation. The correction for inflation became progressively less complete over time, causing negative real interest rates.

In the USA the present fragmented structure of the banking system stems from a historical process of more than two centuries. The McFadden Act of 1927 delegated the regulation of bank branches to state governments, which resulted in a dual banking system. Restrictive states, such as Illinois, allowed banks to have only one branch, whereas liberal states, such as California, permitted multiple branches. Until the end of the 1980s this law produced a system with thousands of small banks, each operating one or a few branches.

A second distortion unique to the USA is the Federal Deposit Insurance Corporation (FDIC). This was created in 1934 as a response to the 1933 panic. Insolvent banks were not allowed to go bankrupt; instead they were put under new management or merged with a financially healthy bank. Depositors knew that their money was safe and would not 'run' if the bank was endangered. The new law resulted in a 97 per cent insurance rate of all commercial banks (Friedman and Schwartz, 1963, p. 434). The system reduced bank failures to almost zero until the late 1970s.

From the 1950s to the 1970s, when GDP grew at a high rate in all three countries, the banking sector also grew steadily. From the late 1970s onwards, when the economic growth slowed down and inflation accelerated, more and more banks ended up in trouble, due to the strict limitations on the sphere of operations and interest rate ceilings. In Mexico the authorities changed laws and allowed banks to form financial conglomerates or multiple banks,[7] and lifted restrictions on the portfolio of banks. As a result the number of banks decreased from 497 in 1975 to 50 in 1982. In Brazil multiple banks were not allowed until 1988.

In reaction to the 1982 debt crisis the Mexican government took far-reaching measures, including the nationalisation of all banks and the imposition of exchange rate controls. The 1982–88 policy restructured the financial sector by consolidating bank institutions, resulting in a further decrease in the number of banks to 8 in 1988. Bank size increased substantially as a result of this process. Non-banking institutions grew rapidly in the 1980s because they were subject to less regulation. Their freedom to set their own interest rates proved profitable.

Reforms announced at the end of 1989 led to the privatisation of banks. From 1991 onwards foreigners were allowed to own shares in Mexican banks, the autonomy of banks was increased and a market-oriented approach was encouraged. The strict reserve requirements were replaced by a more flexible arrangement, where they became dependent on the composition of the bank's loan portfolio. The free trade zone created in 1994 between Mexico, Canada and the USA (NAFTA) envisaged the gradual opening of the Mexican financial sector letting Canadian and US banks and other financial institutions perform the same tasks as domestic financial institutions. Other countries also gained better access to the financial market.

In the USA bank failures increased in number during the late 1970s. Part of the failures resulted from the rapid growth of mutual funds in the late 1970s, which sucked deposits away from banks as they were allowed, in contrast to banks, to pay interest on demand deposits. The government tried to overcome this by passing the Depository Institutions Deregulation and Monetary Control Act in 1980, which, among other things, allowed retail banks to create deposit accounts on which banks could pay interest. The

1980s brought a further relaxation of Regulation Q. The division between commercial and investment banking remained. Parties involved lobbied for the abolition of this law, only with partial success.[8]

Commercial banks and savings and loans institutions faced major problems in the 1980s. This was, among other things, a result of eased restrictions on bank activity in real estate lending and the Deposit Insurance Act introduced in the 1930s. This act guaranteed that in case of a bank's insolvency, depositors would be bailed out by the Federal Deposit Insurance Cooperation. This insurance induced bankers to undertake risky investments (White, 1992, p. 11). In the second half of the 1980s many banks ended up in trouble by poor or negative returns on investments. With the help of the FDIC healthy banks absorbed those who failed.[9] Insolvency risk stimulated healthy banks to merge.[10] The 1991 Federal Deposit Insurance Corporation Improvement Act improved accounting methods in order to signal earlier insolvency, and introduced risk-based deposit insurance premiums.

The FED recognised that the fragmented structure contributed to the bank failures of the 1980s. Barriers to competition with foreign banks also contributed to their troubled situation. After the second half of the 1980s the FED relaxed restrictions on opening branches in other states.[11] However, the US banking system remains fragmented compared to the Brazilian and Mexico situation.

The post-war period saw a spectacular expansion of Savings and Loan Associations (S&Ls, also referred to as thrift institutions). They doubled their assets every five years and reached half the size of assets of commercial banks by 1980 (White, 1991, p. 59). The stable gap between lending and deposit rates from 1950 to 1980 and regulation that prevented competition among S&Ls explains this expansion. S&Ls were a safe haven for demand and saving deposits as they were insured by the government through the Federal Savings and Loan Insurance Corporation (FSLIC). S&Ls borrowed short, demand and savings deposits, and lent long, mostly 20–30 year mortgage loans at fixed interest rates. Therefore, they could not afford to pay higher rates on their deposits than they would receive for their loans over extended time periods. Such a shortfall could occur in periods of rising interest rates, as happened in the late 1960s – early 1970s, and a decade later. During the first period Regulation Q, which imposed a ceiling on deposit rates, prevented the jeopardy of the S&Ls.

However, in the late 1970s, Money Market Mutual Funds (MMMFs), which were not subject to Regulation Q, rapidly sucked deposits out of S&Ls. Regulation Q was loosened to some extent, but this could not prevent increasing losses of the S&Ls in 1980–82. The government further deregulated the S&Ls. It allowed newly issued mortgages to be adjustable to market interest rates and thrifts to diversify loans and investments. The control on S&Ls was also loosened (White, 1991, p. 6). In this new institutional setting S&Ls grew rapidly by increasing their federally insured deposit base. In the second half of the 1980s many of the new loans and investments decreased in value due to the recession, which brought hundreds of thrifts into trouble. The FSLIS had to cover the shortfall to the depositors. The federal government did not act until 1989, when it accelerated the process of liquidating insolvent thrifts by supplying extra funds, abolished the FSLIC and introduced new institutions and regulations to prevent similar disasters from happening again in the future. The thrift crisis cost the US taxpayer approximately US$ 180 billion (Bartholomew, 1993).[12]

The main causes of the thrift crisis, according to Barth (1991), Bartholomew (1993) and White (1991), are: (1) high and volatile interest rates in the late 1970s and early 1980s (see below); (2) moral hazard induced by the deposit insurance system;[13] (3) great losses due to the deterioration of credit quality;[14] (4) fraud and mismanagement of thrift institutions; and (5) the late recognition of the severity of the crisis by Congress and thereby the retarded clean-up.

iii) Inflation and Interest Rates

Table 6.2 and Figure 6.3 compare inflation rates in Brazil, Mexico and the USA from 1880 to 1996. Brazil had already experienced high inflation in the 1890s. Though the annual rate was only 11 per cent, it was high in the context of that period. Brazilian prices fell in 1900–1909. Mexican inflation increased during the Revolution of 1910–17. During the 1920s and the Great Depression both countries had low inflation. In the 1950s and 1960s price levels remained fairly stable in Mexico, while in Brazil inflation rates reached 100 per cent in the mid-1960s. From the 1970s onwards inflation accelerated in both countries. The trend got steeper every five years in Brazil reaching annual rates of more than 1,400 per cent in the 1990–94 period, despite efforts to stop inflation like the Cruzado Plan, and the Collor I and II Plans. In July 1994 the Real Plan was introduced and turned out to be successful: inflation was brought down to less than 17 per cent in 1996. The Mexican government managed to bring inflation down to 16 per cent annually in 1990–94. In 1995 this country faced an economic and financial crisis, which increased inflation to 38 per cent. The USA experienced deflation from 1880 to 1900, during the 1920s and the Great Depression of the 1930s. Inflation accelerated during World War II and the oil crises in the 1970s, but never reached levels above 7 per cent annually.

In addition to the rate of inflation, the variation is also important as it expresses the variability of price increases. This is shown in the right-hand panel of Table 6.2. In Mexico the average inflation rate was very low in the

1890s, but the variation was high as it experienced years of inflation as well as deflation. The same phenomenon was observed in all three countries in the 1920s and 1930s. In the 1980s and 1990s an increase in the rate of inflation was accompanied by an increase in the standard deviation in Brazil and Mexico.

Table 6.2 Average Annual Growth of Prices (Per Cent), Brazil, Mexico and the USA, 1880–1996

	Annual Growth Rate			Standard Deviation		
	Brazil	Mexico	USA	Brazil	Mexico	USA
1880–89	0.2	1.7	–0.8	5.3	9.7	1.5
1890–99	11.8	0.9	–0.8	15.3	11.0	1.5
1900–09	–3.3	5.6	0.8	10.8	8.0	2.3
1910–19	11.4	5.3	6.7	15.4	11.5	6.6
1920–29	4.6	–2.3	–0.1	14.2	6.7	6.5
1930–39	0.1	2.1	–2.1	10.7	7.8	4.6
1940–49	12.1	10.3	5.6	5.0	8.4	4.5
1950–59	18.0	8.3	2.0	7.9	5.7	2.2
1960–64	54.9	2.7	1.0	22.9	1.9	0.3
1965–69	33.1	1.6	2.6	13.2	1.3	1.1
1970–74	20.1	11.1	5.2	4.7	9.6	2.1
1975–79	40.6	18.4	7.1	8.3	8.8	1.1
1980–84	131.9	53.7	6.4	47.1	27.8	2.6
1985–89	386.6	77.3	4.0	442.1	39.9	0.6
1990–94	1,440.9	16.1	3.9	871.3	7.5	0.9
1995–96	44.3	34.7	2.3	30.1	3.5	0.4

Notes: No data were available for Mexico for the 1878–85, and 1913–17 period. These years were estimated using annual average compound growth rates for the 1877–86 and 1912–18 period.

Sources: Brazil: 1850–89 from Goldsmith (1986, pp. 30–31), linked to new series for 1889–1944 from Villela and Suzigan (1977); linked to 1944–88 series from IBGE (1990, p. 226–37); series were updated to 1996 using GPD deflator from national accounts as from IMF (various issues). Mexico: 1877, and 1886–1980 from INEGI (1994b) (refers to wholesale prices in Mexico City); linked to 1980–94 series of INEGI, *Anuario Estadístico de los Estados Unidos Mexicanos* (various issues) (national consumer prices). USA: 1880–1960 from Department of Commerce, Bureau of the Census (1975, pp. 210–11); 1960–96 from IMF (various issues).

Figure 6.3 shows the price stability during the final years of the second Brazilian monarchy (1880–89) and the Mexican Porfiriato (1876–1910), the 1920s, and the 1930s. It also shows the acceleration of inflation in the 1970–92 period in Brazil and Mexico, with a much steeper trend in Brazil.

Table 6.3 shows the prevailing nominal and real interest rates from 1950 to 1996. Nominal rates in Brazil rose rapidly after 1978, corresponding to the acceleration of inflation. Real rates were negative during the early 1960s and late 1970s. In Mexico real rates were negative during the late 1970s and 1980s. US real interest rates were mostly above those of Brazil and Mexico. The governments of the latter two countries kept real interest rates low to favour investment, but also to borrow money from the financial sector at favourable terms.

Figure 6.3 *Trends in Price Level, Brazil and Mexico, 1880–1996 (1880 = 100), (Semi-logarithmic Scale)*

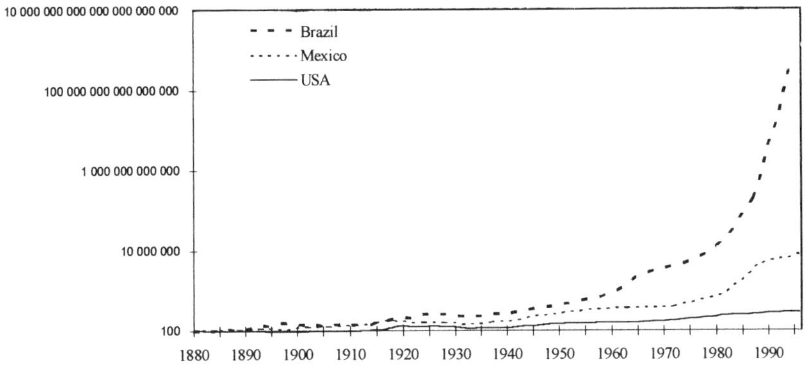

Source: See Table 6.2.

Inflation stimulated the growth of the Brazilian banking system through various mechanisms. Firstly, it made the intermediation services more complex. Banks developed, with help from the government, a variety of monetary and non-monetary assets to protect depositors and the banks against inflation. Secondly, banking became an increasingly profitable activity because of the large spread between the real debit and credit interest rates, that is interest rates paid to depositors were below the rate of inflation, while the rates charged to borrowers increased by using market devices (such as illegal side payments) that circumvented the 1933 Usury Law. To attract depositors banks expanded at a high rate in terms of branches, employees and modern facilities offered. Thirdly, as money lost its value rapidly, banks invested heavily in computers and personnel to ensure that transactions were carried out rapidly.

Inflation had significant effects on the financial structure, that is a rise of the ratio of non-monetary assets, real estate bills and government bonds, to monetary assets (currency and demand deposits), and a large decline in the value of non-indexed assets. The share of time deposits in total assets drop-

Table 6.3 *Nominal and Real Interest Rates, Brazil, Mexico and the USA, 1950–96*

	Brazil Discount Rate	Mexico Saving Deposits	USA Discount Rate		Brazil Discount Rate	Mexico Time Deposits	USA Discount Rate
			Nominal Rates				
1950	6.0	4.5	1.8	1978	33.0	15.1	9.5
1955	6.0	4.5	2.5	1979	35.0	16.4	12.0
1960	8.0	4.5	3.0	1980	93.4	20.7	13.0
1961	8.0	4.5	3.0	1981	121.0	28.6	12.0
1962	8.0	4.5	3.0	1982	173.9	40.4	8.5
1963	8.0	4.5	3.5	1983	194.2	56.7	8.5
1964	8.0	4.5	4.0	1984	272.0	51.1	8.0
1965	10.0	4.5	4.5	1985	379.8	56.1	7.5
1966	12.0	4.5	4.5	1986	89.5	80.9	5.5
1967	17.0	4.5	4.5	1987	401.4	94.6	6.0
1968	22.0	4.5	5.5	1988	2,282.0	67.6	6.5
1969	21.0	4.5	6.0	1989	38,341.0	44.6	7.0
1970	20.0	4.5	5.5	1990	1,082.8	37.1	6.5
1971	20.0	4.5	4.5	1991	2,494.3	22.6	3.5
1972	20.0	4.5	4.5	1992	1,489.0	18.8	3.0
1973	18.0	4.5	7.5	1993	5,756.8	18.6	3.0
1974	18.0	4.5	7.8	1994	56.4	15.5	4.8
1975	18.0	11.9	6.0	1995	39.0	45.1	5.3
1976	28.0	11.8	5.3	1996	23.9	30.7	5.0
1977	30.0	12.9	6.0				
			Real Rates				
1950	–5.5	–6.5	1.3	1978	–5.7	4.8	2.4
1955	–10.3	–12.7	2.9	1979	–19.0	–2.0	3.6
1960	–21.1	–1.7	1.4	1980	–6.8	–5.5	2.7
1961	–29.2	3.7	2.0	1981	11.1	0.6	3.3
1962	–43.9	3.0	2.4	1982	78.4	–18.5	3.1
1963	–65.7	3.0	2.5	1983	39.7	n.a.	4.3
1964	–82.7	1.1	3.1	1984	51.4	–14.4	4.3
1965	–47.1	0.5	3.6	1985	154.3	–1.7	3.7
1966	–26.5	3.5	2.6	1986	–52.8	–5.4	2.5
1967	–11.6	4.5	1.8	1987	176.6	–37.2	1.9
1968	–2.2	2.8	1.6	1988	1,633.4	–46.5	2.2
1969	0.9	3.1	2.3	1989	37,018.3	24.6	2.0
1970	0.5	0.2	1.1	1990	–1,502.0	10.4	1.3
1971	–0.3	1.6	0.3	1991	2,096.1	–0.1	–1.1
1972	2.7	0.2	1.2	1992	456.3	3.3	–0.7
1973	3.1	–15.7	2.8	1993	3,708.8	8.8	0.0
1974	–10.7	–21.2	–1.6	1994	–2,512.6	8.5	1.9
1975	–9.9	–1.9	–2.1	1995	–38.6	6.9	2.6
1976	–13.2	–3.7	–0.3	1996	6.6	–0.6	3.1
1977	–12.7	–22.7	–0.4				

Source: IMF, *International Financial Statistics* (various issues).

ped, while the demand for real assets and durable goods rose. Savings banks, *Caixas Economicas*, suffered most from inflation, because of the Usury Law which prohibited the incorporation of inflation in the nominal interest rates, causing a loss of deposits.

In contrast to Brazil inflation had a negative impact on the growth of the banking system in Mexico and the USA. In the 1970s a combination of interest rate ceilings and inflation caused real rates to be negative. In Mexico this caused a drop in the volume of deposit and savings account, and an increase in the money held abroad. Even though restrictive laws on interest rates were abolished in the late 1970s, real rates of interest remained negative in the 1980s, increasing the capital flight. In the USA people transferred their assets from banks to mutual funds, because the latter were not subject to interest rate ceilings (Regulation Q).

iv) Financing Budget Deficits

In the 1970s and 1980s the Brazilian and Mexican governments increased their borrowing from the financial sector. Brazil suffered greatly from the oil crises, as it was dependent on imports which became much more expensive. The government absorbed an increasing share of bank loans and lent money abroad to maintain the domestic oil supply, while at the same time it introduced an expensive programme to substitute imported oil by domestically produced fuel alcohol. Mexico benefited from the oil crisis, as oil was one of its major export products. Anticipating substantial revenues in the future, the Echeverria and Lopez Portillo administrations embarked on expansionist policies, financed by bank reserves and increased foreign borrowing. The default of the Mexican government on interest and loan repayments in 1982 caused great problems for many banks.

In Brazil and Mexico an important instrument for government borrowing from the banking system was the reserve requirement. In Brazil the Central Bank increased the requirement from 4 per cent in 1964 to 69 per cent in 1974, decreased this requirement gradually to 8 per cent in 1983 and then increased it again to 45 per cent in 1984 (Welch, 1992). In Mexico the reserve requirement averaged 43.6 per cent in the 1960s. From 1972 to 1976 the average reserve requirement rose to 64 per cent and the marginal rate to 100 per cent. All the increases in reserves were used to finance the growing fiscal deficit (Gil, 1992).

In Brazil the inflation tax or seignorage was another important means of financing the government deficit, especially in the 1970s and 1980s. Seignorage may be defined as the percentage loss in the real value of government bonds due to inflation. Although, since 1964, government bonds have been indexed the inflation tax remained positive. This was because the actual rate of inflation was above the rate used for indexation. The latter was based on the expected rate of inflation for a fixed period of time. The inflation tax increased in the course of time, and reached a maximum rate of 3.9 per cent of GDP or 40 per cent of the federal government debt in 1979–80. As such, seignorage was an important additional source of inflation (Contador, 1992; Welch, 1992).

v) Technological Developments

The financial sector has invested heavily in information technology and automation, though this happened at a faster pace in the USA compared to Brazil and Mexico. The use of computers and on-line terminals reduces administrative costs at centralised locations as all information is collected and processed at its entry point. Moreover, computers facilitate the deposit and credit functions, improving labour productivity by as much as 60 per cent. In 1992 the number of terminals per 100 employees was 27 in Brazil, 34 in Mexico and 74 in the USA. In 1992 the USA had 87,300 automated teller machines (ATMs) compared to 2,200 in Brazil and 3,300 in Mexico. ATMs substantially improved the service quality in terms of 24-hour banking and shorter waiting times (McKinsey, 1994).

In Brazil the banking industry became a major purchaser of data-processing equipment, installing its first mainframes in the 1960s. From 1980 to 1987 the financial sector accounted for one-quarter of total Brazilian demand for data-processing equipment. This high demand for computer equipment originated from the high rates of inflation from the 1970s onwards, requiring an increased velocity of transactions. Banks earned high profits by absorbing interest-free resources from the public and the government, which were subsequently reinvested in a real interest earning government paper. To attract clients, banks opened new branches, broadened the scope of their product line and increased the speed at which transactions were carried out.[15] There were two additional sources of demand for fast transactions services: (i) commercial banks substituted special government outlets for the payments to and transactions within the government; and (ii) commercial banks increasingly served to receive payments to utility companies (Frischtak, 1992).

In the USA the gross capital stock per employee in financial services and insurance rose 380 per cent compared to only 20 per cent on average in the total non-farm economy from 1958 to 1987 (Baily and Gordon, 1988). The introduction of information technology increased labour productivity in cheque processing by 8 per cent per year between 1971 and 1986, yet the productivity performance of the whole industry rose very little. Three possible explanations may be given for this paradox (Baily and Gordon,

1988; Firschtak, 1992). Firstly, these new technologies required organisational changes, and therefore there may be a time lag between the innovation and observed productivity increase. The fragmented structure of the US financial system, that is many banks each serving a small local market, complicated these changes. Each bank used its own procedure, which made the introduction of standardised software very difficult. New software often also created problems and therefore many banks continued to use paper-based procedures. Secondly, the measurement of value added may be subject to errors, as it may fail to account for changes in the quality of output. Thirdly, gains in productivity may have been offset by the opening of too many branches leading to diseconomies of scale. According to Baily and Gordon (1988), small banks perform worse than large ones not because of diseconomies of scale, but because of their organisational and technological backwardness compared to larger banks. The latter have easier access to modern technology. In Brazil this problem does not seem to have occurred in this period, as labour productivity in banking increased 8 per cent per year.

vi) Conclusion

In Brazil and Mexico banking experienced rapid growth in terms of offices, GDP and employment from 1950 to 1996. In relative terms, the size of the financial sector in Brazil and Mexico converged to that of the USA. Brazil even surpassed the USA in terms of the share of the financial sector in total GDP. The output growth of the financial sector was above that of the total economy in all three countries. Above all the rapid growth of the financial sector in Brazil is explained by the way it has profited from the high inflation in the 1970s and 1980s.

In the nineteenth century the US financial sector developed more rapidly than the financial sectors in Brazil and Mexico. The different developments may be explained by the stronger regulation, lower per capita income and a slower pace of industrialisation in the Latin American countries in comparison to the USA. The Mexican Revolution delayed the financial development by at least 20 years.

Since the 1940s the financial sector has played a key role in the development policy of Brazil and Mexico. For this purpose the government owned and operated part of the banking system and introduced strong regulations including the allocation of credit, high reserve requirements, interest rate ceilings and measures favouring the segmentation of the financial sector. Moreover, governments absorbed a large share of credit to finance their spending. In Brazil indexation was introduced in 1964 to mitigate the effects of high inflation. One may conclude that the government intervention has been partly successful in Brazil and Mexico, as the financial sector contributed to mobilise more savings, which were translated into higher investment rates in the 1960s and 1970s (see Figure 6.4). This has greatly contributed to the rapid industrialisation in this period. However, this conclusion should be interpreted with care, as it is unknown how the financial sector would have developed with less intervention. Government intervention also had a high cost, that is inefficient government-owned banks were a major part of the system, there was little competition, high concentration rates, a large spread between deposit and lending rates, overemployment, strict regulation and limited investment in new technologies. Since the late 1980s the government of Mexico, and to a lesser extent that of Brazil, started to deregulate the financial sector.

Figure 6.4 *Investment as Percentage of GDP in Current Prices, Brazil, Mexico and the USA, 1950–94*

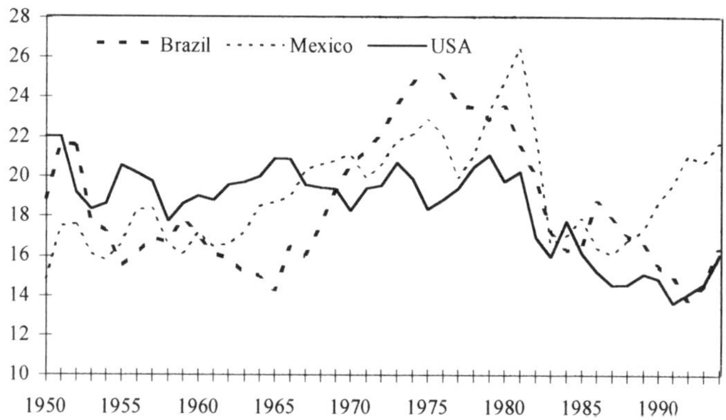

Source: Hofman (1998).

The US banking system has suffered from tight supervision. Restrictions on opening branches in other states, interest rates and the type of services offered resulted in a highly fragmented system of thousands of small banks. Deposit insurance contributed to the Savings and Loan crisis in the late 1980s. Restrictions on interest rates were gradually abolished in the 1970s and 1980s, and limits on interstate banking were eased in the early 1990s. The banking system has recently undergone a process of takeovers and mergers, which has reduced the number of banks from 14,000 in 1980 to 9,000 in 1996.

Investment rates are one way to judge the success of financial intermediation (see Figure 6.4). In Brazil the rate rose from 15 per cent in 1955–64 to 30 per cent in 1975–76. In addition to the introduction of indexation, other factors contributed to this increase. These include the foundation of institutional investors, laws imposing the allocation of resources of insurance companies and pension funds, and incentives to private firms to issue bonds. The investment rate dropped with the acceleration of inflation after 1975. The Mexican saving rate increased steadily from 1960 until the 1982 debt crisis, whereas the US rate remained relatively stable until 1980.

There are several other ways to judge the success of the development of the financial sector, such as operating margins, the spread between the deposit and loan rate, the M2 to value added ratio, total credit to value added ratio and operating cost to assets ratio (Welch, 1992, pp. 171–72). In this study labour productivity has been used, that is value added per employee, to measure the success of financial development. To express value added in a common currency, unit values and PPPs have been estimated. These are derived using (i) the gross value of output, and (ii) the physical output produced by banks or insurance companies. The former was estimated by operating revenues of financial institutions. The measurement of the latter will be discussed in the next section.

OUTPUT AND PRODUCTIVITY LEVELS

Banking

Banks provide services to borrowers in terms of loans, to savers in terms of checking and saving accounts and the facilitation of payments, and a range of other services such as advice on investment and taxation, currency exchange, equity and bond management, insurance services and so on. The measurement of the output is complicated by the fact that many of these banking services are not explicitly priced. Instead banks charge clients for these services in an indirect way, by retaining some of the payable interest to depositors or by charging a higher interest rate to lenders relative to a reference rate of interest. The latter rate excludes intermediation costs and the risk premium; for example the inter-bank or central bank lending rates.

According to SNA 1993 the output of banks equals gross revenues from services for which clients are explicitly charged plus the value of the financial services indirectly measured (FISIM) for the services for which banks do not charge explicitly. The FISIM approach is also referred to as the interest margin or user cost approach (Berger and Humphrey, 1992; de Boer, 1999; Fixler, 1993; Fixler and Zieschang, 1999). In the FISIM approach revenues are generated in an indirect way by paying lower interest rates than would otherwise be the case to those who lend money and by charging higher rates to those who borrow funds. The resulting interest receipts represent the output for this service. The interest margins are estimated by the difference between the deposit and lending rates on the one hand and a 'reference' rate of interest on the other.

SNA 1993 does not prescribe a price index for banking services. In practice most OECD countries using input indices as a proxy of output, using either the number of workers or working hours, or labour compensation deflated by the CPI. Others simply deflate banking revenue by a consumer or producer price index from another sector (OECD, 1996).

The Eurostat Task Force on Financial Intermediation (2000) proposes a weighted volume index that cover all loan and deposit activities that generate FISIM, using the share of each activity in profits as weights. Output indicators should take account of differences between the consumer and business markets. Moreover, they should be adjusted for quality changes, such as the use of the internet, extended opening hours of banks and so on.

The Dutch national accounts (de Boer, 1999) developed such an index, although no adjustment was made for quality changes. The composite volume index is obtained by weighting detailed volume indices by their cost components. Banking is split into almost 20 activities. For each activity, a separate volume index was constructed. Output indicators represented both 'administrative' activities such as the number of savings accounts as well as 'movements' like acquisitions of new credit and money transfers.

For the Eustostat Task Force a second-best index would be based on the application of base period interest margins on loans and deposits to the stocks of loans and deposits revalued at base year prices. Another possibility is to adjust deposit, lending and reference rates to the general rate of inflation. The resulting interest rate differentials are referred to as the price or the user cost of financial services. The changes in the user cost from one year to another yield the price index for FISIM.

Fixler (1993) proposed a price index that is superlative and of the Törnqvist type. For n types of financial services for which clients are not explicitly charged, the price index is a weighted average of the annual changes in the user costs of all financial services, using the share of each service in total profits as weights:

$$I(p) = \prod_{i=1}^{n} \left| \frac{p_i^1}{p_i^0} \right|^{(\omega_i^0 + \omega_i^1)/2} \tag{6.1}$$

where $p_i = |u_i| =$ user costs and ω_i is the share of service i in profits. The superscripts refer to two consecutive years. As the user costs are implicitly calculated and ω_i based on accounting data, the index is slightly modified to convert the implicit in 'accounting' user costs.

Fixler and Zieschang (1999) measure the price deflator indirectly by the ratio of FISIM to an output quantity index. The latter is estimated by an output distance function first used by Malmquist (1953), further developed in the literature on technical efficiency (see Berger and Humphrey, 1992) and multifactor productivity (Caves *et al.*, 1982). The output index is a kind of weighted average of the growth rates of the real volume of assets and liabilities, each weighted by their user costs.

In addition to FISIM, other yardsticks proposed in the literature include:

i) *The M2 to GDP ratio* (Goldsmith, 1983; Pilat, 1994) represents the ratio of cash currency, demand deposits and time and savings deposits (for example M2) to total wealth (using GDP as a proxy). A higher M2/GDP ratio indicates a relatively larger financial sector or more services provided. The M2/GDP ratio is available for a large number of countries and long periods of time, and is comparable among countries. However, this measure has three major disadvantages: it includes cash which is not part of banking output; it leaves out other parts of banking output which are included for example in M3, M4 or M5,[16] and it focuses on the liability side of the bank's balance sheet and excludes assets from banking output.

ii) *The Asset approach* (Berger and Humphrey, 1992; Peñazola Webb, 1985; Welch, 1992) views banks as intermediaries between liability holders and those who receive bank funds. Therefore, only items on the asset side of a bank's balance sheet (mainly loans) are considered as output. Objections to using the value of loans (or other assets) as a proxy for bank output include that loan values cannot be added,[17] the use of balance sheet measures (for example loans), which represent a stock at a particular time, whereas output is a flow measure, and the exclusion of the liability side of the bank's balance sheet.

iii) *The Liquidity approach* (Gorman, 1969) states that banks produce money to hold in order to fulfil the liquidity preferences of depositors. Output equals the value of deposits times average bank earnings per deposit. This approach neglects the asset side of the bank's balance sheet.

iv) *The Transactions approach* (Dean and Kunze, 1991; Frischtak, 1992; Gorman, 1969; Mark, 1982; McKinsey, 1992, 1994, 1998; Speagle and Kohn, 1958) estimates production by the volume of services performed by each banking function. Some studies only use one output indicator, such as the number of cheques cashed (Frischtak, 1992), while others (Dean and Kunze, 1991; McKinsey, 1992, 1994, 1998) use a variety of output indicators for different banking functions, like credit services, deposit and saving accounts services and transaction services. McKinsey weighted the detailed output indices by employment in each activity to derive a total output index.

Except for the M2/GDP ratio and transactions approach, all other approaches have been applied exclusively to intertemporal comparisons. The SNA recommended the FISIM approach and its deflators have not yet been applied in international comparisons. This can be explained by the difficulty of obtaining detailed internationally comparable information on the asset and liability activities in terms of volume measures. These are required, in combination with user costs, to estimate the unit values of banking services for which clients are charged implicitly.

The approaches (i) to (iii) are also difficult to implement as they measure output in terms of values which are expressed in different currencies across countries. Instead McKinsey used the transactions approach to compare banking output and productivity across countries. After dividing by some measure of input, the output measured in values assesses financial efficiency, while output measured by transactions addresses technical organisational efficiency. Each group of methods therefore tells only part of the story (see Bruggink, 1989, 129–34).

In this study the transactions and value approaches are combined. A quantity relative is derived using McKinsey's approach. It distinguished activities on the liability side of the bank's balance sheet (handling of transactions and facilitating demand and time deposits), and the asset side (issuing of loans). Output of these services is measured, respectively, by the number of demand deposits in the Mexico/USA comparison and the number of cheques cashed in the Brazil/USA comparison (*C*), the number of time deposits (*D*), and the number of loans issued (*K*) (see Table 6.4). The quantity relative is obtained as follows:

$$\frac{Q^x}{Q^u} = \left[\frac{L_C{}^u}{L_T{}^u} \frac{C^x}{C^u} + \frac{L_D{}^u}{L_T{}^u} \frac{D^x}{D^u} + \frac{L_K{}^u}{L_T{}^u} \frac{K^x}{K^u} \right] \qquad (6.2)$$

with L_C, L_D, L_K and L_T indicating the US employment in the handling of demand deposits and cheques, time deposits, loan activities and the sum of the three, respectively. The employment breakdown was available only for the USA and was assumed to be representative also for the other two countries.[18] Subsequently, the quantity relatives were combined with the gross revenues to derive UVRs as shown in equations (4.10) and (4.11).

Financial services were excluded from the economic censuses in Brazil, Mexico and the USA and therefore alternative sources were used: (i) data on revenues and physical output were taken from central bank publications, statistical yearbooks and information from branch organisations of banks (see Table 6.4 and Appendix D);[19] and (ii) value added and employment were derived from the national accounts (see sources of Figures 6.1 and 6.2).

Table 6.4 *Output in Banking and Insurance, Brazil, Mexico and the USA, 1975*

	USA (Million)	Brazil (Million)	Mexico (Million)	Persons Engaged in each Function in the USA (000s)
Banking output				
Cheques cashed	6,275	619	n.a.	419 }
Demand deposits	308	n.a.	1	
Time deposits	129	5	16	89
Commercial loans	8	5	n.a.	99
Insurance output				
Life insurance policies	380	10	2	
Health insurance policies	718	1	1	

Notes: In the Brazil/USA comparison total relative output (US output as a percentage of Brazilian output) was estimated by the weighted sum of the relative outputs in cheque cashing, time deposit keeping and commercial loan activities, weighted by the US employment in each function. In the Mexico/USA comparison, total relative output equals the weighted sum of relative outputs in demand deposit keeping and time deposit keeping, using US employment in each function as weights.

Sources: Brazil: cheques cashed and number of time deposits from worksheets of the *Banco Central do Brasil*; Number of commercial bank loans and insurance output from IBGE (1976), *Anuario Estatístico do Brasil*. Mexico: data refer to private banks and other credit institutions (*instituciones privadas de credito*), as from INEGI (1977), *Anuario Estadístico de los Estados Unidos Mexicanos*. USA: banking output and number of persons engaged in each function from Federal Reserve Bank (1977); insurance output from Department of Commerce, *Statistical Abstract of the United States 1977*.

Insurance

According to SNA and ESA nominal output of insurance equals total premiums earned minus total claims due plus income from investments into actuarial reserves. This output concept is derived from the *risk-pooling* model, according to which the insurance company facilitates and administrates a large pool created by policyholders for sharing risk. Holders pay a fee to cover administrative costs.

Although widely used this concept has been criticised (see Sherwood, 1999; Triplett and Bosworth, 2000), as in practice clients contract insurance companies for covering a certain amount of risk and not for performing administrative tasks. Households and firms protect themselves from risk by transferring it to an insurance company in exchange for a premium. Under this *risk-assumption* model output equals the amount of premiums paid for risk protection. The premium reflects not only the efficiency of administrating premiums and claims, but also the efficiency of administrating risks. The second concept yields a much larger gross output than the first. For the US casualty insurance the former equals between only one-fifth to one-third of the latter (Sherwood, 1999).

Even though both models include earnings from invested reserves in nominal output, they omit this financial activity. These reserves arise because insurance companies collect premiums before claims liabilities. Owing to competitive pressures insurance companies transfer these earnings to their policy-holders in the form of reduced premiums. Most insurance companies do not cover the total cost of their claims from the premium earnings.

The SNA and ESA manuals provide no guidelines on real output measurement, as 'the breakdown into price and volume components can usually only be made on arbitrary grounds and would have to be based on conventions' (ESA 95, paragraph 10.40). In contrast the Eurostat Task Force (2000) proposes several real output measures. The preferred method would estimate output as the real value of assets and services available to settle claims or to assume risk (see also Sherwood, 1999); that is, the deflated value of provisions or funds available – premiums plus investment income less administrative costs – to cover risk. The deflator equals a weighted price index for replacement cars, buildings, repair and medical services and the maintenance of purchasing power (all items of the CPI). The weights are determined by the number of settlements of each policy type. The Eurostat Task force (2000) pointed to some weaknesses of this method, such as the impact of institutions, for example new social security legislation, on the funds available and the fact that funds will be little representative in the case of unexpected excessive claims.

A second-best method, the direct services method, uses indicators that describe the acquisition of policies and administration of claims. Real output equals the number of contracts of different types weighted by base year premiums. This approach assumes that risks are constant over time and excludes the investment activity. All methods should incorporate changes in the quality of service, such as the possibility of purchasing policies through the internet.

In the OECD countries real output measures are mostly based on the number of policies, the number of persons covered weighted by base year premiums (in health insurance), premiums paid deflated by the consumer price index for insurance or input indicators (OECD, 1996). No international comparisons of insurance output and productivity are available.

This study measures real output by the number of life and health insurance policies. These were used to derive a quantity relative, which in combination with gross revenues yielded the UVRs.

Table 6.5 shows the resulting UVRs for financial services. The UVRs for total banking and insurance were derived by weighting the specific UVRs by the gross value of output (GVO) of each branch. Two sets of weights can be used: Brazilian or Mexican GVO weights yield a Paasche UVR, while US weights generate a Laspeyres UVR. A Fisher UVR represents the geometric average of the Paasche and Laspeyres UVRs. The Table also shows the 1975 prevailing exchange rates. Both binary comparisons revealed a higher UVR for banking than for insurance.[20] The UVR for total financial services was 11.0 cruzeiros per US dollar in the Brazil/USA comparison and 14.8 pesos per US dollar in the Mexico/USA comparison (Fisher results). Both values were above the exchange rate in both countries, indicating that financial services were more expensive in Brazil and Mexico in comparison to the USA.

Table 6.5 Unit Value Ratios for Banking and Insurance, Brazil/USA and Mexico/USA, 1975

	At Brazilian or Mexican Quantity Weights (Paasche)	At US Quantity Weights (Laspeyres)	Geometric Average (Fisher)	Laspeyres/ Paasche Spread
	Brazil/USA (Cruzeiros per US$)			
Banks and credit institutions	14.4	14.4	14.4	1.0
Insurance and other financial intermediaries	2.7	9.4	5.1	3.5
Total	11.3	10.8	11.0	1.0
Exchange rate	8.1	8.1	8.1	
	Mexico/USA (Pesos per US$)			
Banks and credit institutions	15.8	15.8	15.8	1.0
Insurance and other financial intermediaries	14.6	12.0	13.2	0.8
Total	15.5	14.1	14.8	0.9
Exchange rate	12.5	12.5	12.5	

Source: See Appendix D.

Gross value added was converted to a common currency by the UVRs of Table 6.5. Labour productivity was subsequently calculated by dividing value added by the number of persons engaged in financial services. Table 6.6 shows that the relative performance of Brazil and Mexico was about the same, that is 56.6 and 56.4 per cent of the US performance in 1975, respectively.

Table 6.6 Labour Productivity in Financial Services, Brazil and Mexico as a Percentage of the USA, 1975

	At Brazilian or Mexican Quantity Weights (Paasche)	At US Quantity Weights (Laspeyres)	Geometric Average (Fisher)	Laspeyres/ Paasche
		Brazil/USA		
Financial services	55.5	57.8	56.6	1.0
		Mexico/USA		
Financial services	53.9	59.1	56.4	1.1

Sources: 1975 GDP of Figure 6.1 was converted by PPPs of Table 6.5, and divided by the number of employees from Appendix A.

The 1975 benchmark results of labour productivity were extrapolated to cover the 1950–96 period using time series of GDP at constant prices (see Appendix B) and labour inputs (see Appendix A). Figure 6.5 presents Brazilian and Mexican productivity as a percentage of the US level in 1950–96. McKinsey (1994, 1998) also estimated productivity in financial services in Brazil and Mexico, comparing these with the USA. The McKinsey study and this study yielded very different results due to major differences in coverage and methodology.[21] This study's extrapolated 1992 productivity levels of Brazil and Mexico were 78 and 77 per cent of the US level, respectively (see Figure 6.5). The McKinsey (1994) results were much lower at 31 and 28 per cent, respectively. Their 1996 update showed an improvement of the Brazilian performance to 40 per cent of the US level, which was again much lower than my estimate of 72 per cent for the same year.

Brazilian relative productivity showed wide fluctuations in the post-war period: it grew in the 1950s, but fell when inflation accelerated in 1959–66. At that time banks were not protected against inflation, and suffered from negative interest rates. In 1964–66 several profitable schemes were introduced which protected banks and clients against inflation. The opposite impact of inflation on output, profits and productivity growth is observed in the period 1966–81. The economic slowdown in 1981–84 reduced finance's relative performance. From the introduction of the Cruzado plan in 1986 until 1990, the relative performance improved. The various attempts to stabilise inflation between 1986 and 1990 were successful for few months only. Banks benefited from the following accelerating inflation inducing high output growth in banking. The relative productivity performance declined after 1990 due to smaller earnings out of inflation and the successful stabilisation of prices in 1994 which meant an even further reduction of bank earnings.

Figure 6.5 *Labour Productivity in Banking and Insurance: Brazil and Mexico as a Percentage of the USA, 1950–96*

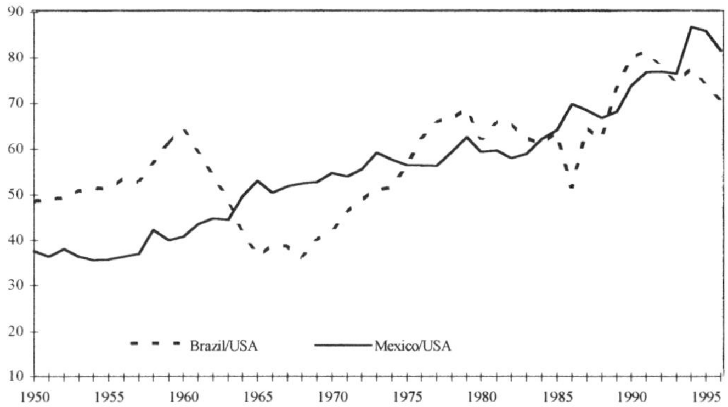

Sources: 1975 benchmark results from Table 6.6, and time series for GDP from Appendix B and employment series from Appendix A.

In 1950 Mexican performance was lower than Brazil. The lesser performance is also indicated by the smaller number of bank establishments per head and the lower proportion of bank loans to the private sector in Mexico relative to Brazil in the same year. From 1950 to 1996 Mexico's labour productivity showed a catch-up process with US productivity levels. Productivity growth was highest in 1955–70 and 1987–94. The rapid growth in the second period corresponds to an improvement of the M2/GDP ratio, an increase in the ratio of commercial bank to total bank assets, a rise in the share of loans to the private sector and a fall in the share of loans to the government. Moreover, since 1989 the financial sector has been gradually liberalised and banks were reprivatised in 1991. Banks suffered from major economic downturns and, in contrast to Brazil, the acceleration of inflation in 1980–83, 1986–87 and 1995–96.

The crisis at the end of 1994 reversed the positive trend, as it had a large impact on the banking system. Due to the sudden rise in interest rates in December 1994, combined with high inflation and a recession, many individuals and firms could no longer repay loans and interest. Several banks ended up in trouble. To prevent their collapse the government set up a scheme FOBAPROA, which lent emergency cash to some banks, helped others to restructure their loans and assisted large debtors to make repayments. It also bought overdue loans with 'zero-coupon' bonds that repaid the loans and interest after ten years. FOBAPROA bought all bad loans of the weakest banks. The total cost of this scheme reached 65 billion dollars in 1998, equal to 15 per cent of GDP. A large part of the past-due loans were already accumulated before the 1994 crisis, and resulted from three years of a huge careless expansion of credit. Loans were often made against fictitious or overvalued assets. Supervision during these years was weak (*The Economist*, 25 July 1998).

NOTES

1. From 1850 to 1885 only one manufacturing company was listed on the stock exchange. Its shares were traded during only 3 of those 36 years. Banks were small in number and size and did, therefore, rarely serve as a source of finance (Haber, 1991).
2. From 1895 to 1910 bank credit did not exceed 3 per cent of the capital of manufacturers. In 1915 manufacturers in Brazil financed an average of 47 per cent of their capital with bonds and loans (Haber, 1991).
3. It was subject to only half of the reserve requirement of other banks, it was the only intermediator for government transactions, the payment of all taxes and fees paid to the government passed through the *Banco de México* and it was exempted from taxes (Haber, 1991).
4. A bank panic occurred in 1907, the fifth in a period of 30 years.
5. The aim of this bank was to provide medium- and long-term loans to private firms engaged in activities of national importance (such as power, steel and transport), and to a limited extent to the government. The BNDE and other state development banks grew rapidly. During the first decade of its existence more than half of its resources were invested in transport and energy.
6. Deposits at deposit and savings banks were limited to checking accounts and time deposits. Credit operations were limited to the period of the outstanding loan (maximum of 180 days) and volume (no more than 20 per cent of the total of deposits and reserves (Gil, 1992).
7. Integration of the services of traditional banks, savings and loans institutions, mortgage banks, brokers and other financial intermediaries in one institution. The main advantages of multiple banks are spreading of risk and economies of scale.
8. In the 1980s banks were allowed to engage in more types of operations.
9. The 'bailing-out' of insolvent banks decreased FDICs' resources by US$ 40 billion to a deficit of US$ 7 billion by 1991.

10. Seventy-five per cent of the 4,103 banks absorbed in the 1985–91 period were healthy banks (White, 1992, p. 12).
11. The new rules allow banks to buy insolvent banks in other states, and to open up more branches. Some states set up reciprocal arrangements allowing state banks to set up branches in other states.
12. The first savings and loan institution was set up in 1831. The number of S&L institutions grew steadily in the subsequent 120 years. Some state and federal supervision developed in the course of time. Failures occurred in the 1890s, and during the 1930s. During the Great Depression savings were withdrawn and assets fell in value because of real estate delinquencies and failures. In 1932 the federal government introduced the Federal Home Loan Bank Act which created 12 regional banks that were to supply a source of funds to which members would have access in turbulent times. The act also introduced heavier regulations on its members (Barth, 1991, p. 15).
13. When deposits were not government-insured, a smaller number of depositors would have invested in undercapitalised funds, and many funds would have been forced to raise additional funds or cease operations. Deposit insurance made investors careless of the health of the thrift institution they managed.
14. Since the early 1980s thrifts were allowed to diversify their portfolios. They made consumer and commercial loans, took equity positions and bought purchased residential and commercial properties. Owing to the economic recession, which caused property values to drop, and falling energy prices, many investments turned out to be very poor. Many of the failing thrifts were located in the south-west and suffered from the latter cause.
15. The transfer of funds via cheques took less than a day in Brazil in 1992, compared to two to three days in Mexico. In the USA, the transfer of cheques took more than a week (McKinsey, 1994).
16. However, the use of M3, M4 and so on as output measures for cross-country comparisons is limited because the definitions of these aggregates vary between countries. Moreover, for most countries, including Brazil and Mexico, no long-run series are available of these measures.
17. For example a consumer loan requires more banking services (that is bookkeeping, credit analysis, information gathering and riskbearing) per dollar of loan than a loan to a corporate customer. Adding dollar amounts of loans provides therefore a poor indication of the total volume of loan services.
18. In the Mexico/USA comparison the liability side functions only were considered because no volume indicators were available on the loan activity of Mexican banks.
19. Claudio Frischtak kindly provided unpublished worksheets of the *Banco Central do Brasil* on the volume of services produced by banks.

20. The Brazilian and Mexican national accounts list 'insurance companies' and 'other financial intermediaries' as one group. It was therefore assumed that the insurance PPP was valid also for the category 'other financial intermediaries'.
21. Firstly, the discrepancy results from differences in coverage: McKinsey included private retail banking only, whereas this study covered the whole financial sector, including wholesale banking and other credit institutions, insurance and other financial intermediaries. The higher results may result from superior relative productivity levels in other parts of finance. Secondly, McKinsey's labour productivity concept was different because it measured physical output per employee instead of value added per employee. McKinsey estimated physical output along the same lines as this study, but neglected the price at which this output was produced. Their productivity yardstick measures technical-organisational efficiency only, but not the financial efficiency. In contrast, this study also captured financial efficiency by looking at the relative price at which the services were produced. Thirdly, it was assumed that the 1992 and 1998 price structure for banking was the same as the one prevailing in 1975. Brazilian and Mexican banks went through a process of mergers after the mid-1970s which increased the capital intensity by incorporating high-tech machinery. This may have changed the price structure in each country.

7. Health Care

INTRODUCTION

Health care[1] is a major social service in Brazil, Mexico and the USA, representing 3 per cent of employment in the former two countries, and 7 per cent in the USA in 1996. The growth of the health care sector has been largely financed by public funds. From 1955 to 1990 public expenditure on health care as a share of GDP has grown sevenfold in Brazil, tenfold in Mexico and fivefold in the USA.[2] Together with improved nutrition, water supply, sewerage and other socio-economic conditions, better health care has contributed greatly to the improvement of health conditions in the three countries in 1950–96 (see Table 7.1). The mortality rate of children under five years old has declined in all three countries, although the decline in Brazil and Mexico was much steeper than in the USA. Life expectancy at birth was higher in the USA than in Brazil and Mexico, but the gaps have narrowed in the course of time. The percentage of Mexican babies with a low birth weight was more than twice the Brazilian and the US percentages in 1990. The incidence of tuberculosis (TB) increased in Mexico. The USA initially experienced a decline in the incidence of TB, after the initiation of anti-TB measures in 1953. However, TB rates began to climb in the late 1980s and have reached epidemic proportions in some populations. Public health officials link this alarming increase to AIDS and poverty. The prevalence of tuberculosis in Brazil was half the Mexican rate in 1990.

All countries experienced a sharp decline in the mortality rates due to infectious diseases (see the bottom panel of Table 7.1). The treatment of non-infectious diseases requires more health care resources than infectious diseases, because these diseases tend to require chronic, rather than acute, care (see Bobadilla *et al.*, 1993, p. 59). Infectious diseases remained relatively more common in Brazil and Mexico relative to the USA, probably reflecting inadequate immunisation and sanitation in certain parts of the Latin American countries. In the USA the number of deaths due to both groups of diseases declined in the course of time.

Table 7.1 Health Outcomes, Brazil, Mexico and the USA, 1960 and 1990

	Brazil		Mexico		USA	
	1960	1990	1960	1990	1960	1990
Under 5 year mortality (death per 1,000 children)	159	83	148	38	31	11
Life expectancy at birth (years)	52	66	56	70	70	76
Babies with low birth weight (per cent)	n.a.	8	n.a.	15	n.a.	7
Incidence of tuberculosis (deaths per 100,000)	82	56	80	110	31	10
Mortality by cause (deaths per 100,000 population)						
Infectious diseases & maternal/perinatal causes	*331*	*12.9%*	*376*	*156*	*94*	*54*
Non-infectious diseases and injuries	*683*	*87.1%*	*183*	*543*	*906*	*505*

Source: 1960 Brazil from United Nations (1965, pp. 762–67), data refer to the state of Guanabara only. Mexico and USA from World Bank (1993); Brazil: mortality by broad cause from Pan American Health Organisation (1994), data refer to 1989. Mexico: 1960 from INEGI (1994b); mortality by broad cause from Bobadilla *et al.* (1993); USA data for 1990 from OECD (1993).

A final indicator, not shown in Table 7.1, is the global burden of disease measured by disability-adjusted life years (DALYs). The number of DALYs is calculated by taking the present value of the future years of disability-free life that is lost as a result of premature death or disability occurring in a particular year (see World Bank, 1993, Appendix B). The burden of countries in Latin America – no results were available for Brazil and Mexico in particular – was almost twice that of the USA in 1990: 232 DALYs compared to 117 DALYs per 1,000 population.

Despite these improvements, health standards – such as infant mortality, life expectancy and the share of the population with access to care – are below what would be expected, when compared to those of countries with similar per capita income levels in other parts of the world (Inter-American Development Bank, 1996). The larger income inequality and share of the population living in poverty in Brazil and Mexico, compared to (especially) Asian countries with similar per capita income levels, contribute to these poorer outcomes. Moreover, the inadequate organisation of health care in Brazil and Mexico may also play a role, as it concentrates on curative care for the middle- and high-income groups rather than preventive care for the poor. Other deficiencies include the poor quality of public care and the exploding costs. The disappointing health outcomes in Mexico do show up also in the comparatively low levels of labour productivity of care providers: the Mexican performance was only 46 per cent of the US performance in 1987/88 (see Table 7.1). The relatively superior performance in Brazil, that is labour productivity was 65 per cent of the US level in 1980, did not produce better health outcomes than in Mexico, partly because the poor had limited access to good quality care.

LONG-TERM DEVELOPMENT

Developments before 1950

The colonisation of the Americas involved the transfer of infectious diseases formerly unknown, such as measles and smallpox. As the indigenous Indian populations had no immunities to these infections, some have suggested that more than 90 per cent died from new diseases in the first century of European settlement.[3] The Spanish were much more active than the British and Portuguese in providing care in their colonies. In Mexico the Spanish built 125 hospitals in the first one hundred years of occupation, of which many provided care to the Indians. Medical care was regulated from 1525 onwards and lasted the entire colonial period. Formal medical education started in 1579, while in 1570 the first major medical publication, *Opera Medicinales* by Francisco Bravo, was issued in Mexico City (Cassedy, 1991).

In contrast to the Spaniards, the Portuguese showed little interest in providing care in Brazil. Some care was provided by religious brotherhoods from Portugal, of which the *Irmandades de Misericórdia* were the most important. The first *Casa de Misericórdia* was opened in Santos in 1543. Others followed in Rio de Janeiro, Salvador, Santos and São Paulo. Some only admitted the poor, while others accepted only patients who could pay a fee. Until today these remain important health care providers in urban areas. The first medical schools were founded in Rio and Salvador shortly after the capital of the Portuguese empire was moved to Rio de Janeiro in 1808, more than 200 years later than in Mexico (Ludwig, 1985; van Stralen, 1996).

The British also paid little attention to medical care in their US colonies, which was partly due to the small size and limited resources of British colonial towns in the early colonial period. In the seventeenth century only few physicians were willing to exchange their comfortable situation at home for colonies that were unappealing. In England the Church, the private sector and the government also failed to improve medical care in the colonies. This attitude reflected the common opinion people held in the seventeenth century that physicians could do little about diseases.

In all three countries many patients did not rely on doctors but relied on folk healers, herb doctors, midwives, nurses and surgeons without academic credentials. Often these alternative care providers also came from Europe.

Many had to supplement their medical income by other occupations such as farming. Religion played a key role in caring for the sick (Cassedy, 1991).

In colonial North America the number of qualified physicians slowly increased after 1700, stimulated by a growing population, urbanisation and the rise of an upper class demanding the best care available. Trained doctors started to teach medical courses in the 1730s, but it was not until 1765 that a formal medical school was founded in Philadelphia. Physicians started to organise themselves in small societies, of which the first was founded in Boston in 1736. Physicians visited patients at their homes, where they performed difficult surgical procedures. Victims of accidents were also taken to their homes for care. Some surgeons and physicians provided free care for the poor who could not afford the medical fees.

Though hospitals for special groups[4] were founded much earlier in the USA, the first general hospital was not established until 1752. During the eighteenth and nineteenth century, hospitals provided care for the poor, mostly immigrants with chronic illnesses. Their care was paid for by charities. Hospitals were unknown to most US-born citizens, who relied on self-medication and on other home remedies in case of illness.

In Brazil and Mexico the development of the health care sector stagnated during most of the nineteenth century. In Brazil this was partly due to the lack of interest in health issues of the imperial governments. In Mexico political turbulence and public disinterest were the main causes. In Brazil several private initiatives were undertaken, which, however, provided care for only a small number of people. Following the European example, several mutual-aid societies were founded. Some targeted people of one nationality, such as the *Sociedade Portuguesa de Beneficiência* (1840), covering 20,000 Portuguese. Other societies were for skilled workers who paid lump sums in the case of illness or invalidity. One of the largest mutual-aid societies was founded by a railway company in 1884 and had 5,000 members in 1914. At the end of the nineteenth century other railway companies and large firms set up company funds, which covered medical expenses among other social benefits.

The Eloy Chaves Law of 1923 represented the first step towards the establishment of the Brazilian social security system. It provided *for Caixas de Apesentadoria e Pensões* (Retirement and Pension Funds, CAPs). The CAPs provided health care, job security and pensions. At first members were only entitled to outpatient care and cheap medicines, but a 1926 law added hospital care. Funding came from contributions of the employers, employees and the state. The impact of the Eloy Chaves Law was small, as it covered only a fraction of the labour-force. Several attempts in the 1920s to include more categories of workers failed. Therefore most urban workers remained exempted from medical care, while the rural population was completely deprived of any type of medical care.

The government undertook various actions to combat infectious diseases and improve hygiene. For this purpose several health services were merged to form the first General Department of Public Health (*Diretoria Geral de Saúde Publica*) in 1897. It was the predecessor of the Ministry of Health that was founded in 1953. Most of the public responsibility remained with the states, as dictated by the 1891 constitution. Some, like the state of São Paulo,[5] were very active, whereas others, especially in the north-east, undertook few initiatives. Compulsory vaccination was introduced in 1904. A campaign against yellow fever in Rio de Janeiro, led by Oswaldo Cruz, led to the virtual elimination of the disease a few years later. He was appointed as director to a research institute for infectious diseases along the lines of the Parisian Pasteur Institute. The institute engaged in research, trained health professionals and advised on public health policy. Research in bacteriology made clear that instead of a dirty environment, specific germs were responsible for the spread of diseases. The spread of this knowledge had a large impact on the organisation of care. Many laboratories were set up, and tests were developed to detect infectious diseases. In the 1920s the Cruz institute worked closely with the US Rockefeller Foundation.

In the 1910s several reports demonstrated the disastrous medical situation in rural areas, and the large differences in care offered across states. The government took various measures to improve the medical situation of the most poorly served regions, such as the introduction of centres (*postos rurais*) for maternal care and immunisation in 1923. Another new development was the introduction of health centres in urban areas, directed at the provision of maternal and other first-line care. These clinics were set up in collaboration with Johns Hopkins University. The federal government broadened the scope of public health care, that is it took measures in the areas of food inspection, control of hygiene in commercial establishments and housing, and the provision of child care, hospitals and vaccination. Moreover, it sharply reduced the autonomy of states. Despite its efforts in rural areas, most federal efforts were limited to large cities.

The Vargas administration (1930–45) increased the commitment to health care at the federal, state and municipal levels. Vargas extended the retirement and other social security benefits to civil servants in 1930 and to miners in 1932. The CAPs were reformed, as many encountered financial difficulties. Another problem of the CAP arrangements was that they were too expensive for small firms. In 1933 social security coverage was increased by the foundation of another institution: the *Instituto de Aposentodoria e Pensões* (IAPs). They differed from the CAPs, as they were organised by occupational category rather than by company. Funding remained tripartite, but the contribution of the government was larger. Several IAPs were established, covering employees in banking, distribution, manufacturing and the public sector. The health benefits offered differed strongly between the IAPs. The number of employees covered by the CAPs and IAPs increased from 142,000 in the early 1930s to two million at the end of the decade. Some IAPs operated their own facilities, while others contracted hospitals. Despite the growth of social security its coverage remained tiny. Most of the population continued to be dependent on public care (van Stralen, 1996).

In 1934 Vargas reactivated health campaigns in rural areas, fighting diseases such as malaria and yellow fever. In 1937 he centralised decision making in the reorganised Ministry of Education and Health. From 1940 onwards the budget allocated to health increased, partly to finance the construction of new centres for health care and hygiene. In 1942 the Brazilian and US governments agreed to improve care in regions of strategic importance to the Americans (the Amazon for the extraction of rubber and the Rio Doce valley for magnesia). This programme was funded by the Rockefeller Foundation, and realised an important transmission of knowledge.

In the 1930s and 1940s some states and municipalities also undertook initiatives, of which São Paulo and Rio were the most active. Following the first hospital census in 1944 new hospitals were planned in regions not yet served by a hospital. Despite the major efforts of Vargas, the supply of care remained very unevenly spread across regions and income groups.

In Mexico a national health system was not created until the 1930s. The many different governments during most of the nineteenth century and the Porfiriato (1877–1910) showed little interest in providing health care, except sanitary measures in urban areas and the fight against infectious diseases in economically important areas of the country. The Revolution and its aftermath of political instability also retarded the development of a national policy. Until the 1920s most private health care was provided by charities and religious organisations. Moreover, labour unions provided health services for its members. In the early 1920s the state created the Salubrity Department to increase the volume of public services and to coordinate the private provision of health care. However, the difficult economic situation in the 1920s and 1930s prevented major improvements in the provision of public care.

In 1937 a second Ministry was created (*Secretaria de Asistencia Publica*), which started special medical programmes for children, civil servants and the military. It also constructed health centres in some urban and rural areas. The execution of the health care programmes was delegated to the state governments. In the 1940s the health care system was consolidated with a range of institutions serving different groups based on their occupational status. In 1943 the two Ministries were consolidated into the Ministry of Health (*Secretaria de Salubridad y Asistencia*). Its responsibilities were the care for the poor and the public health policy. In the same year the social security schemes of the many labour unions were put together under the Social Security Institute (*Instituto Mexicano del Seguro Social*, IMSS). Several social security funds for the military, those working in the oil industry and civil servants, remained independent from IMSS (OECD, 1997).

In the USA the government became involved in health care much earlier than the authorities in Brazil and Mexico. At the federal level a central medical staff was formed for the permanent armed forces in 1818, and for the Navy in 1848. From 1798 onwards the government provided care for seamen through hospitals in sea ports and along the Mississippi and Great Lakes. The Civil War also permanently enlarged the medical functions of the government: the US Soldiers' Home was created to provide care for veterans, the Freedmen's Bureau for blacks and the Bureau of Indian Affairs for Indians. The federal government also stimulated the founding of state universities, medical schools and science departments. The involvement of state governments in medical care grew very slowly. At first they delegated matters such as the supplying of medical licences to state and local medical societies. In the course of the nineteenth century they set up asylums and hospitals for the blind, deaf, and mentally ill, and employed physicians to inspect the health of new immigrants and prisoners. Some states also improved the registration of births and deaths, although few functioned well before the next century.

Municipalities also delegated most responsibilities to medical committees or individual physicians. In the middle of the nineteenth century city councils became more committed to sanitation and health care, as medical problems worsened due to the overpopulation of cities. Municipalities invested heavily in the provision of drinking water, garbage disposal and sewerage systems. Medical conditions also improved by free vaccination, the inspection of sanitary conditions of schools and other buildings, food inspections in markets and other measures associated with health and disease. By the end of the nineteenth century discoveries in bacteriology changed the health activities of city councils. They opened public health laboratories, initially for testing the purity of water but later to make routine diagnostic tests to check the presence of infectious diseases. Health education programmes were set up to improve the conditions of new immigrants, pregnant women and school-children. Some cities opened special hospitals for patients with infectious diseases.

Between the 1870s and 1900 the states formed boards and health departments, which later played a key role in organising services related to hygiene and medical care of the counties, towns and communities. At first, the states mostly gave advice, and did some research. Later, they also performed numerous other functions such as the inspection of food, milk and water, providing licences for health professionals, planning of sewerage and water systems and extensive research. Within states the provision of public health services in poor and rural areas progressed only little by little. The development of health agencies varied widely between states, depending on their level of industrialisation, population density, urbanisation and wealth.

From the 1880s onwards the federal government also became more involved in health care. Efforts to create a federal department of health failed, and different programmes remained located in various government departments. Military medical services were extended to fight infectious diseases, research and training – with the formation of the Army Medical School in 1893 –. The Marine Hospital Service expanded its work to combat (infectious) diseases in rural areas; it was renamed the Public Health Service in 1912. The Animal Industry Bureau and Chemistry Bureau of the Department of Agriculture fought animal diseases and inspected meat. At the turn of the century the Children's Bureau was created to combat infant mortality. With help of the Sheppard-Towner Act, which granted financial assistance for this purpose to states, some 3,000 centres for prenatal and child care were created by 1929.

Several private initiatives helped to create health agencies at all levels of government. Voluntary health organisations, composed of academics, civil servants, health workers and philanthropists, undertook many initiatives to conduct surveys, provide health education, raise money and stimulate research. An association for tuberculosis was founded in 1904, followed by one devoted to child health (1909), mental diseases (1909), public nursing (1912) and cancer control (1913). Large life insurance companies stimulated improvements in sanitation and vitality statistics, offered free examinations, supported health organisations and local health departments, and stimulated research. Philanthropic foundations, of which Rockefeller was the largest, was a third major private group which supported medical research and training, and provided medical services.

In the 1920s the federal government withdrew much of its support for medical care. The access to medical care for blacks, farmers, recent immigrants and infants remained minimal. The middle and upper classes, on the other hand, commanded increasingly high levels of care. The Great Depression of the 1930s represented a major change. The New Deal put health care at the centre of economic relief. For this purpose it provided funds for hospitals, rural health programmes, sanitation, and in 1937 the restoration of the child and maternity programmes.

The two World Wars, with the major participation of the US military, further increased the commitment to health care of the government. It constructed and equipped hospitals and other care facilities at home and abroad for the military. The treatment of the wounded had improved thanks to rapid evacuation, and availability of new types of surgery and medicines such as penicillin and quinine. After the war the government continued to provide free care for the veterans. The federal administration also increased its commitment to care for the non-military, as expressed by the Hill-Burton Act of 1946. This law envisaged the construction of hospitals in smaller towns and rural areas, and the renovation and extension of existing hospitals (Cassedy, 1991).

In the nineteenth century several large companies formed associations with physicians, clinics and hospitals to provide care for its members. Formal health insurance did not exist, as insurance companies considered health care an uninsurable risk. In the 1920s several prepayment plans were introduced, which offered employee groups a fixed number of days per year of care, in exchange for a monthly fee. In 1933 four prepayment plans started, which were not attached to enterprises or a profession but to an entire community. These four plans meant the start of the Blue Cross, which grew rapidly to 56 plans covering more than six million people in 1940. Their rapid growth was favoured by new legislation, which exempted the non-profit Blue Cross plans from reserve requirements imposed on insurance companies, as well as from taxes on earned revenues. Blue Cross insured hospital expenses only. Another organisation, Blue Shield, started in 1946, and covered expenses on physicians. Following the success of the Blue Cross commercial insurance companies also started to sell health insurance in the 1930s. By 1940 they included 3.5 million people. In the 1940s and 1950s the population covered by Blue Cross/Shield and commercial insurers increased to 50 million and 30 million, respectively (Drake, 1994).

Only few international comparable statistics are available to evaluate the impact of the improvements in care and sanitation on the health status before 1950. One measure presented here is infant mortality, as shown in Table 7.2. A quarter of all new-borns in Mexico did not reach the age of five in 1903, compared to 16 per cent in the USA. Infant mortality decreased in the course of time, most rapidly in the USA. In 1950 infant mortality in Brazil and Mexico was still three times the US rate.

Developments after 1950

Table 7.3 presents trends on expenditure on health care. Brazilian public expenditure rose from 0.4 per cent in 1955 to 2.7 per cent in 1994. Mexican public expenditure care rose from 0.3 to 4.4 per cent of GDP in 1950–75, and then dropped to 2.8 per cent in 1994. US expenditure started at a much higher level and rose almost sixfold over the period as a whole. Private expenditure was 4.7 per cent of GDP in Brazil and 2.6 per cent in Mexico in 1994 (World Bank, *World Development Indicators, 1998*). US private care expenses rose from 3.4 per cent to 7.8 per cent of GDP from 1950 to 1994.[6]

Table 7.2 *Infant Mortality and Inputs, Brazil, Mexico and the USA, 1903–50*

	Infant Mortality (Deaths per 1,000)			Employment in Health Care (000s)*	
	Brazil	Mexico	USA	Brazil	USA
1903		255	158		
1922	210	223	85	37	
1930		216	75		749
1940	202	132	58	33	841
1950	136	96	34	64	1 239

Notes: * No employment data were available for Mexico.

Source: Brazil: 1922 from Ludwig (1985, p. 84); 1940 and 1950 from Singer *et al.* (1978, p. 122). Mexico: INEGI (1994b). USA: Department of Commerce (1975, p. 60).

Table 7.3 *Public Expenditure on Health Care as a Percentage of GDP, Brazil, Mexico and the USA, 1955–94*

	Brazil	Mexico	USA
1955	0.4	0.3	1.1
1975	2.2	4.4	3.5
1994	2.7	2.8	6.3

Notes: Expenditure on health includes items which are excluded from health care value added.

Source: Brazil: 1975 from ECLAC (1993, p. 3); Mexico: 1955 and 1975 from INEGI (1994b); US 1955 and 1975 health expenditure from Department of Commerce, *Statistical Abstract of the United States 1977*, p. 94; 1994 from World Bank (1997).

Kravis *et al.* (1982) also compared expenditure levels countries in 1975, accounting for differences in relative prices across countries: Brazilian medical consumption per capita was 13.5 per cent of the US level, and Mexico 18.9 per cent. No breakdown was shown in private and public expenditure. Unfortunately no more recent estimates are available.

Trends in expenditure on medical care are not fully representative for the development of health care providers, as it includes items which are not part of the output of the health care sector, such as drugs and medical equipment, health insurance and medical research. Expenditure on health care providers also only overstates the size of the sector, as it includes intermediate inputs which are not produced by the sector itself. In the USA, for example, inputs accounted for 35 per cent of expenditure on health care in 1987 (Department of Commerce, *Bureau of Economic Analysis Survey of Current Business*, April 1994). To study the long-term development of the health care sector, we therefore focus on value added, which equals total expenditure minus intermediate inputs. From 1950 to 1990 the share of the health care sector in total GDP more than doubled in the USA, whereas in Mexico it increased no more than 50 per cent. From the 1970s to 1990s the Brazilian share was about 2 per cent (see Table 7.4).

Table 7.4 *Value Added and Employment as a Percentage of Total GDP and Employment, Health Care, Brazil, Mexico and the USA, 1950–96*

	Value Added as a % of GDP			Employment as a % of the Total		
	1950	1975	1996	1950	1975	1996
Brazil	n.a.	2.0	2.2	0.8	1.1	2.5
Mexico	2.0	2.6	3.0	0.6	1.8	2.9
USA	2.2	3.7	5.8	1.9	4.6	7.3

Source: National accounts, see Appendices A and B.

Employment in health care is another indicator illustrating its long-term development. The number of employees increased fifteen old in Brazil (from 117,000 to 1,713,000), twelve old in Mexico (from 50,000 to 633,000) and sevenfold in the USA (from 1,244,000 to 8,467,000). These trends resulted in a growing share in total employment from less than 1 per cent in 1950 to 3 per cent in 1996 in Brazil and Mexico; and from almost 2 per cent to over 7 per cent in the USA.

Table 7.5 shows the growth of health care inputs. In the course of time the number of physicians per capita increased in all three countries. The number of beds per capita, on the contrary, decreased in Brazil and the USA, while this was not the case in Mexico. The US population was much better served overall than the Brazilians and Mexicans in terms of the number of per capita medical staff and beds. Mexico's input growth in the 1950–92 period was, however, much higher than that of the USA, though it started from much lower levels. In Brazil the number of nurses and beds per 1,000 inhabitants decreased from 1975 to 1990.

Table 7.5 Inputs in Health Care, Brazil, Mexico and the USA, 1965–92

	Brazil			Mexico[b]			USA		
	1965	1975	1990	1965	1975	1992	1965	1975	1992
Doctors per 1,000 population	0.3	0.7	1.5	0.3	0.6	1.7	1.6	1.8	2.4
Nurses per 1,000 population	0.5	0.4	0.4[a]	0.3	1.1	0.9	3.2	4.4	8.7
Nurse to doctor ratio	2.1	0.7	0.3	0.9	1.6	0.5	2.0	2.5	3.6
Hospital beds per 1,000 persons	2.8	3.9	3.5	0.5	0.7	1.0	8.8	6.8	5.2

Notes:
[a] Refers to 1992.
[b] Public health services only.

Sources: Brazil: 1965 from IBGE, *Anuario Estatístico do Brasil*, various issues; 1975 from ECLAC (1993); 1990 from World Bank (1997). Number of nurses in 1992 from Dal Poz and Varella. Mexico 1965 and 1975 from INEGI (1994b). USA: 1965 and 1975 from OECD (1993, pp. 170–78). 1992 Mexico and USA from Pan-American Health Organisation (1995).

The rising number of physicians per capita indicates that the access to health care improved in the course of time in all countries. The falling number of nurses and hospital beds per capita did not restrict the access to hospitals, as the average length of stay has sharply decreased in the course of time, requiring less input per patient.

DETERMINANTS OF LONG-TERM DEVELOPMENT

Important differences exist between the Brazilian, Mexican and US systems: (i) in Mexico most health care facilities are provided directly by the IMSS and ISSSTE, whereas in Brazil the INPS, and in the USA Medicare and Medicaid, reimburse health care suppliers for providing services; (ii) in Mexico health care is mainly financed by centralised public funds, whereas Brazil and the USA are characterised by a mixture of public and private, centralised and decentralised funds; (iii) the private sector plays a minor role in Mexico, in contrast to Brazil and the USA; (iv) Brazilian and Mexican patients have little effective power to complain about the quality of care, in contrast to the situation in the USA (Academia Nacional de Medicina, 1992, pp. 9–12).

Health Care Demand

Important socio-economic changes took place, which affected the demand for health services, as Table 7.6 illustrates. The Brazilian and Mexican population grew faster than that of the USA.[7] This reflects higher fertility in Brazil and Mexico. Although fertility dropped by 30 per cent in Brazil and by half in Mexico between 1975 and 1990, it remained at almost twice the US level. As a result the share of obstetric care in overall hospital services was relatively higher in Brazil and Mexico.

The per capita income gap between Brazil and the USA slightly narrowed (US GDP per capita was 5.7 times that of Brazil in 1950 and 4.7 in 1990), while the Mexico–USA gap remained stable (Mexican per capita income grew 2.4 times and the US 2.3 times). The Brazilian and US population aged significantly: in Brazil and the USA the share of the population aged 60 and above grew from 4 and 10 per cent in 1950 to 8 and 17 per cent, respectively, in 1990, whereas in Mexico it remained stable. The elderly group consumes more health care services than younger generations, which explains an important part of the increase in health care demand in the USA. Americans smoked almost three times as much as Mexicans in 1975; tobacco use had decreased by 30 per cent by 1990 in both countries. Brazilians smoked more than Mexicans, although consumption decreased in the 1975–90 period.

The post-war era saw significant improvements in socio-economic conditions in Brazil and Mexico (see bottom panel of Table 7.6). Similar changes took place in an earlier period in the USA. The share of the population living in rural areas was much higher in Brazil than in Mexico and the USA in 1990. In general people living in urban zones have better access to health care than those in rural areas. Suicides occur far more frequently in the USA than in Brazil and Mexico. By contrast Brazil and Mexico experienced more violent crime than the USA.

Scientific Improvements

The demand for health care depends heavily on the possible impact of medicine on the course of diseases. Until the late eighteenth century physicians were able to pull diseased teeth, set fractures and relieve some of the symptoms of several ailments. They could do little about other medical problems, such as child diseases, epidemics and internal disorders. In the early nineteenth century this situation changed slightly when vaccination against smallpox was introduced in the USA. Careful examination of the body, food and water improved with the spread of microscopes in the 1840s

Table 7.6 *Population Characteristics and Socio-economic Development, Brazil, Mexico and the USA, 1950–1990*

	Brazil			Mexico			USA		
	1950	1975	1990	1950	1975	1990	1950	1975	1990
Population (000s)	51 941	104 851	150 368	27 376	60 153	86 154	152 271	215 973	249 924
Per capita income (1990 Geary Khamis dollars)	1 673	4 230	4 812	2 085	4 408	4 997	9 573	16 060	21 866
Population of 14 years and below (percentage)	42	40	34	43	46	38	31	25	22
Population of 60 years and over (percentage)	4	6	8	4	3	4	10	11	17
Fertility (births per woman):	6.2	4.7	3.3	6.7	6.5	3.3	2.7	2.2	1.9
Tobacco consumption per year (kg per capita)	n.a	2.1	1.8	n.a	1.4	1.0	n.a	3.8	2.6
Socio-economic developments									
Adult literacy rate (%)	49.3	70.4	81.1	55.9	78.4	87.6	96.8	99.0	99.0
Population in villages < 2.500 inhabitants	63.9	43.9	24.8	56.7	37.1	28.7	36.0	26.5	24.8
Houses with running water (%)	15.6	43.9	82.6	17.0	65.8	79.4	n.a.	94.0	97.9
Houses with sewerage (%)	13.1	34.9	52.8	20.3	46.1	63.6	92.2	94.0	99.4
Suicide rate (death/100,000 people)	5.0	3.2	3.1	0.9	2.1	2.2	11.4	12.5	12.1
Crime rate (death/100,000 people)	10.8	n.a.	24.8	43.6	22.1	20.3	5.3	9.1	10.2

Source: Population and GDP per capita from Maddison (1995b); Brazilian population structure 1950 and 1975 from IBGE (1990, p. 35); 1990 from IBGE, *Anuario Estatístico do Brasil 1992*, p. 209; Mexico population structure and characteristics from Bobadilla *et al.* (ed.) (1993, p. 56). 1950 and 1975 Brazilian suicide rate from Ludwig (1985, pp. 87–88). Brazilian and Mexican suicide and crime rates from UN, *Demographic Yearbook*, various issues. 1950 US population structure and 1950 suicide and crime rates from Dept. of Commerce (1975, pp. 10, 414); 1975 structure from Department of Commerce, *Statistical Abstract 1977*, p. 27. Brazilian and Mexican fertility rates in 1950 from Wilkie (1992, p. 144). Brazilian fertility rate in 1975 and 1990 and percentage of houses with sewerage from ECLAC (1993, pp. 16, 66). US social-economic conditions from Dept. of Commerce, *Statistical Abstract of the United States* (various issues). Urban population from World Bank (1993b), *World Tables*. Tobacco use and fertility rate from World Bank (1993a, pp. 204–05). Deaths caused by suicides, homicides and other violence from WHO (1979, 1992).

and 1850s, although its use for diagnostic purposes remained unknown for several decades. Many US physicians went to Britain, France and Germany to carry out research, and subsequently duplicated it at home. In the USA the number of research laboratories grew very rapidly after the Civil War. By 1920 every sizeable health department, hospital, medical school and pharmaceutical company had a research laboratory where analytical and diagnostic services, medicines and new therapeutic techniques were developed, and new physicians and scientists were trained. The number of libraries and museums also expanded (Cassedy, 1991).

In the last quarter of the nineteenth century, the role of hospitals changed drastically. Looser family ties and higher life expectancy increased the dependence on hospitals. Moreover, discoveries in germ theory and advances in surgery rendered treatment at home impossible. Hospitals attracted more people from the middle and upper classes thanks to improvements in diagnostic and therapeutic equipment, such as X-rays. These contributed to a fall in the death rate as a result of surgery from 40 per cent in the 1880s to 5 per cent in 1900. Medical advances caused a rapid rise in costs, making hospitals more dependent on patient fees. In the USA the number of hospitals increased from one hundred in 1870 to 6,000 in 1930. Until the 1950s governments contributed little to medical care (Vogel, 1979). In Brazil and Mexico the large expansion in the number of hospitals occurred several decades later. Hospitals became the major institution for the provision of care in all three countries.

During and after World War II enormous improvements were made in medical technology in various domains, including (a) laboratory techniques for diagnostic and therapeutic purposes, (b) pharmacotherapy for cardiovescular disease, infections, psychiatric illness and various types of cancer, (c) surgical techniques including cardiovascular and transplantation, (d) radiological and nuclear medicine techniques for diagnosis and treatment and (e) preventive medicine techniques such as diagnostic tools for determining genetic diseases. These new technologies account for a large proportion of the increased demand for health care and the rise of health care costs since the 1950s. Application of these technologies has led to an ongoing ethical and political debate in all three countries, since choices have to be made as to which patients benefit.

Social Security Schemes

In Brazil and Mexico social security funds play a central role in the provision of health care for civil servants and formal workers in the private sector. Operated by the public sector, they are financed by premiums of employees and employers, and direct government subsidies. In Brazil health services of the social security system are largely provided by contracted private hospitals and clinics, whereas in Mexico the social security institutes operate their own care infrastructure.

In Brazil the percentage population of working age (15 to 65 years) covered by the social security institutes (IAPs) grew from 13 to 23 per cent between 1940 and 1960. This resulted from increased membership of the IAPs founded in the 1930s, as well as the foundation of a new IAP for civil servants in 1954. Each IAP delivered health care to its members, but in practice the types of care offered strongly differed between IAPs. This practice ended in 1960 when the health care benefits of all IAPs became standardised. In 1967 the IAPs were absorbed by the newly created Institute of Social Security (INPS). The tripartite funding remained intact, but the control over funds was transferred from sector-specific institutes to the state.

The INPS provided outpatient care through its own facilities, but most of the inpatient care continued to be provided by private hospitals under contract. It had little choice, as the facilities inherited by the former IAPs were largely insufficient to meet demand. From 1964 to 1985 the number of private hospitals beds grew from 144,000 to 395,000, whereas the number of public hospital beds only increased from 84,000 to 138,000. Until 1982 hospitals were paid on a fee-for-service basis, which created an incentive to bill for non-existing patients, non-performed procedures and an excessive use of high-technology equipment and medicines. Low daily payments for patients to hospitals also stimulated the abuse of billing. This practice, in combination with overcrowding, and poor managements led to a deterioration of the quality of care during the Military Regime (1964–85).

In 1982 the fee-for-service reimbursement system was replaced by the Diagnosis Related Groups system under the CONASP plan. This system was also used in the USA to reimburse hospitals for treating Medicare or Medicaid patients. CONASP's objective was to reduce hospital expenditures. However, hospitals rapidly discovered ways to maintain their income, for example they selected patients whose treatment would be most profitable or they treated 'phantom' patients. The CONASP plan also improved outpatient services, where waiting times were very long, by increasing the number of physicians.

In 1987 the introduction of the Decentralised Unified Care System (SUDS) ended the provision of care by the INPS. The state secretariats of health gradually absorbed the functions of the INPS, that is the budgeting and planning of social security funds, the control on expenditure and the provision of care. The states were expected to transfer the management of local health facilities to the municipalities. In practice only some states did so, while many others remained centralised. The SUDS resulted in an increase of public hospitals and out patient facilities, and caused a fall in the provision of private facilities. Nevertheless, the private sector continued to dominate hospital care and specialised outpatient services, whereas the public sector provided most ambulatory services (van Stralen, 1996).

Mexico's health care system is divided into two vertically integrated segments that cover a different population group. Each segment runs its own network of physicians, hospitals and other care institutions. Formal employees are covered by the Institute of Social Security (IMSS) and the Institute of Social Security and Services for State Employees (ISSSTE). These were founded in 1943 and 1959, respectively, and also supply many other social needs (kindergarten, occupational risk coverage, pensions and so on. The former covers employees and self-employed of the formal private economy, and the latter cares for civil servants. The share of the population covered by these institutions increased from 20 per cent in 1965 to more than 50 per cent in 1990. Financial support comes from employees' and employers' contributions, transfers from the federal government and returns on investment of the two agencies. Health services accounted for 60 per cent of total expenditure by ISSSTE and 40 per cent of IMSS expenditure in 1990. A large share was spent on expensive equipment which was often under utilised. Workers in the informal economy can enrol in the IMSS, but in practice few do. In addition various state enterprises, for example PEMEX (the state oil company) and the railways, and the military operate their own health care facilities for employees.

Public Schemes for the Old and the Poor

In Brazil the Ministry of Health historically provided care to rural workers and the urban poor. In the largest cities the urban poor were served by a network of public (poor-quality and overcrowded) hospitals. In other cities facilities for the poor were virtually absent, except for some first-aid health posts (*prontos soccorros*). The government subsidised private charity hospitals, of which the *Santas Casas de Misericórdia*, in rural areas. The Ministry also ran special programmes to fight infectious diseases in rural areas. In 1970 the military government implemented a special social security programme for rural areas, FUNRURAL. Its funding came from compulsory contributions of urban workers. FUNRURAL did not provide services directly, but contracted charity hospitals, or labour unions which delivered care. In 1975 the programme was extended to fishermen. The provided care was rudimentary compared to the urban social security due to a lack of resources. In 1977 FUNRURAL was abolished and the provision of health care to the rural poor was transferred to the INAMPS. In the late 1980s the care for the poor was shifted to the municipalities and states.

In 1974 a programme was introduced (*Amporo Previdencial*) which provided a small pension allowance to those of 70+ years old, and some basic health care. The benefits remained small from the outset (van Stralen, 1996).

In Mexico the Department of Health (*Secretaría de Salud*), IMSS-Solidaridad (public assistance managed by the IMSS), and the Department of the Federal District (DDF) in Mexico City provide care to the population not covered by other schemes. This group includes most people from rural areas and poor urban zones. In 1996 some 34 million people used these services (Maddison, 1992; OECD, 1997).[8]

In the USA, the government introduced two public health programmes, Medicare and Medicaid, in the 1960s. Medicare covers people 65+ years old and the disabled of any age. In 1990 they covered 13 per cent of the population. Together, payroll taxes, federal revenues and premiums finance Medicare, representing an intergenerational transfer from working people to the elderly.

Medicare offers two types of coverage. Beneficiaries are entitled to free inpatient hospital care, certain home nursing services and other home services to those who paid payroll taxes during their working years. Other beneficiaries are not entitled to these free services, but receive free services once their eligibility for Medicare has been established. The latter coverage focuses on acute needs and excludes long-term nursing home care and outpatient prescription drugs. Less than half of the health care expenses of the aged are covered by Medicare. Almost 70 per cent of the elderly have supplementary private co-insurance to pay for uncovered benefits.

Medicaid covers poor people who are old, blind, disabled, pregnant or parent of a dependent child. In 1990 it provided preventive, acute and long-term care services for 10 per cent of the population. The Federal government and the governments of the states finance Medicaid and the states implement it. The federal contribution varies from 50 to 83 per cent of total expenses, depending on the per capita income level of the state involved. More than half of the people living below the federal poverty line (US$ 13,359 for a four-person family in 1990; see Department of Commerce, *Statistical Abstract of the United States 1994*) are excluded from Medicaid benefits because they do not meet these criteria. Mothers and their children consumed almost 70 per cent of the Medicaid services in 1990, the elderly 13 per cent and the blind and disabled 15 per cent. Medicaid covers long-term nursing home care. As a result many of the middle-class elderly have deliberately transferred income and wealth to their children in order to become eligible for Medicaid. In 1990 more than 40 per cent of the programme's expenses provided nursing home and care facilities other than hospitals (OECD, 1994, pp. 319–20). There is also a scheme for ex-military personnel (veterans). The coverage provided by these schemes increased from 25 to 44 per cent of the population from 1965 to 1990 (OECD, 1994, p. 266). In the 1990s the exploding costs of Medicare and Medicaid made their coverage, funding and organisation a major political issue.

Private Care

In Brazil and the USA most care is provided by privately owned clinics and hospitals, while in Mexico the public sector is the main supplier. In Brazil most private care is paid for by public social security funds. In the USA insurance companies pay most of the care. In Brazil and Mexico out-of-pocket payments are also a major source of growth of private practice. These payments are made by the poor without any coverage, or by the middle and upper classes, who are dissatisfied with social security care.

In Brazil the private health care sector matured well before World War II. Social security funds and the state governments subsidised private hospitals, as their own facilities were insufficient to provide all kinds of care. Throughout the post-war period subsidies from the public sector remained a major source for the expansion of the private sector. Private hospitals accounted for 53 per cent of all beds in 1950, 72 per cent in 1975 and 74 per cent in 1985 (van Stralen, 1996).

Since the 1960s the share of health care funded by the private sector steadily increased. The social security institutes increasingly delegated the arrangement of health care to private companies in exchange for a reduction of social security contributions. In turn these enterprises signed contracts with medical group companies. Similar to the US Health Maintenance Organisations (HMOs) medical group companies provide health insurance and manage care facilities. Subscribers pay a fixed fee for which they receive a predefined set of services in turn. Some medical group companies operate their own facilities, while other contract physicians, clinics and hospitals. The first was established in 1954 in São Paulo. Often workers also insure themselves directly with insurance companies.

From 1968 onwards physicians formed medical cooperatives. They differed from medical group companies, as they were managed by doctors themselves. They were better able to operate in rural areas as the cooperatives consisted of numerous private practices at different locations and not at one clinic or hospital. In 1989 21 per cent of the population was covered by private health insurance. Half of them had a contract with a medical group company, one quarter with medical cooperatives and the rest with company-managed plans (van Stralen, 1996).

Compared to Brazil and the USA, the private care sector in Mexico is small. It includes many types of care for people of all income categories. Private clinics for high income groups, which predominate private care, are often funded with private insurance plans. Although expanding, the coverage of these plans remained small, that is 3.6 million people or 5 per cent of the population in 1993. In the same year half of the privately insured were also covered by IMSS. Private insurance is either complementary to IMSS insurance, or in some cases (such as the banking sector) replaces the IMSS scheme. The low- and middle-income groups also take private care, which they have to pay themselves. The volume of care consumed by these groups is difficult to measure, but it may represent 40 per cent of all their medical consultations (OECD, 1997).

In the USA private health insurance covered three-quarters of the population, public programmes included one quarter and *ad hoc* arrangements covered one-seventh of the population in 1990.[9] Approximately 80 per cent of those with private insurance are enrolled in an employer-based group insurance plan, while the other 20 per cent are covered by an individual insurance policy. Most employers have purchased a group policy from a large private insurance company. To contain costs some employers have cancelled their contracts and pay medical costs when they arise. Many small firms do not insure their employees at all.

Since the early 1970s many private insurance companies have started to contract or operate care health care facilities themselves in order to control costs. Subscribers to these Health Maintenance Organisations (HMOs) receive care from the providers contracted, that is the choice of providers is constrained. Administrators of HMOs review the medical practice and utilisation in order to save costs by abolishing unnecessary procedures (OECD, 1992b).

Problems of the Care Systems

Despite the growing coverage of health care since 1950, about 30 per cent of the population still had no access to care in Brazil and Mexico (Inter-American Development Bank, 1996) compared to 14 per cent in the USA (OECD, 1992b) in 1990. Moreover, spending is concentrated on those covered by social security in Brazil and Mexico, or by insurance plans in the USA. Thus, the allocation of health care resources depends more on socio-economic status than health needs.

In Brazil the SUDS and the SUS should guarantee universal access to health care. However, in practice, the publicly funded care is concentrated in urban areas in the central and southern parts of Brazil. Most of the poor living elsewhere are practically excluded from care. In Mexico the social security sector spends twice as much per capita for its members than the government does for the uninsured population. The uncovered population is concentrated in certain states, especially in the south. This results from the link between public health spending per capita and per capita tax revenues. States that generate little tax income, often those that have most needs, are endowed with minimal resources (OECD, 1997).

In Brazil and Mexico a second major obstacle is the allocation of resources in the care for the poor. The share devoted to preventive care is much lower when compared to other countries at similar per capita income levels. Moreover, the share spent on expensive technologies which is used for only a few cases/patients, hospital care and non-priority health problems is high. Money is also wasted on corruption. Moreover, the quality of public care is often poor. Health professionals are often underpaid and have to work under difficult conditions. Waiting times for patients are long and often no medication is prescribed. In Brazil and Mexico difficulties also stem from conflicting interests within the Ministries of Health, as they provide and regulate care at the same time. In Brazil another obstacle is that most services for the poor are delivered by so-called for-profit hospitals. As the reimbursements by the state for these services are very low, these hospitals admit only poor patients when they have additional insurance or are able to pay extra money (OECD, 1997; van Stralen, 1996).

A third major problem in all countries is the exploding costs of health care. As care is free for (insured) patients, demand has risen fast. Moreover, the continuous invention and improvement of sophisticated and costly diagnostic and treatment options has also contributed to the increase in costs. The open-end character of reimbursement on a fee-for-service basis formed an incentive for physicians to prescribe costly and profitable treatments (OECD, 1992b).

Reforms in the early 1990s

In Brazil and Mexico the governments have recently implemented or planned reforms to solve the problems of cost, coverage and quality. In Brazil the *Sistema Unico de Saúde*, implemented in 1990, aimed to provide equal access to care for the whole population. In practice this meant a reallocation of resources according to the demographic and epidemiological profile of an area. This reorganisation was extremely difficult to achieve in a country with a consolidated system of private care provision and a limited budget for care for the poor. Up to 1995 few guidelines have been implemented due to the resistance to redistribute resources from the rich to the poor and from hospital to primary care. In particular the unequal regional distribution constrained improvements in the access to care. The improvement of preventive and primary care has been small so far, as hospital care continues to dominate the system. The decentralisation of care to municipalities has somewhat improved the access to basic facilities in many places. However, this was not the case in most small municipalities, which have increased in number over the last couple of years (van Stralen, 1996).

In Mexico *the Programa de Reforma del Sector Salud*, 1995–2000 replaces the vertically segmented system by a horizontal structure, under which the SSA keeps only its regulatory functions. Insurance contributions, taxes and user fees finance the new system. Public and private providers are supposed to compete for delivering services. The care for the poor is supposed to be fully delegated to the states. Changes in social security is another part of the overall reforms. Cost containment and regulatory changes should decrease the contributions to favour affiliation to the IMSS. Decentralisation and competition from the private sector are also expected to increase the efficiency and quality of IMSS. The reforms implemented until mid-1997 all occurred within the fragmented framework. There are great doubts on how the major reforms should be implemented (OECD, 1997).

Conclusion

In Brazil health care is provided by private and public bodies. Most hospital care is privately paid for on a fee-for-procedure basis, supplied by a mixture of private and public insurance. Most primary care is public. In the USA most care is purchased by private insurance companies, although the government is also a major supplier of funds through the Medicare and Medicaid programmes. Mexico has a segmented system with social security covering formal workers, the public sector covering the remaining part of the population and a private sector for those who pay directly or have private insurance. Brazil resembles the USA as in both countries private providers predominate and similar organisations are found, such as health management organisations. In Mexico the majority of care is provided by the public sector. Recently Brazil and Mexico have implemented major reforms, but so far these seem to have had a limited impact.

OUTPUT AND PRODUCTIVITY LEVELS

The past four decades have shown a rapid increase in health care resources in Brazil, Mexico and the USA. Was this growth of resources accompanied by an increase of the efficiency at which these resources were deployed? Labour represents the most important production factor in health care, and labour productivity serves therefore as a reliable proxy of overall efficiency.

Data availability dictated the use of the year 1980 for the Brazil/USA comparison, and 1987 and 1988 for Mexico/USA.[10] Table 7.7 shows value added and employment as being derived from the census and national accounts. Private services accounted for 65 and 41 per cent of total health care value added in Brazil (1980) and Mexico (1988), respectively. US national accounts give no breakdown between private and public services. Private institutions were the main employers in Brazil and the USA but not in Mexico.

Table 7.7 *Value Added and Employment in Health Care, Brazil/USA, 1980 and Mexico/USA, 1987/88*

	Value Added (Million National Currency)		Employment (000s)	
	Brazil (Cruzeiros) or Mexico (Pesos)	USA (US$)	Brazil or Mexico	USA
	Brazil/USA, 1980			
Health Care	246 492	108 834	941	5 770
	Mexico/USA, 1987/88 (1988 prices)[b]			
Census and other sources				
Private health care				
Hospital services	163 518[a]	139 911	28	4 331
Physicians and dentists	494 696[a]	105 084	67	1 933
Laboratories	117 212[a]	5 436	12	132
Other services	5 590[a]	31 161	1	1 845
Total	781 016[a]	281 592	109	8 241
Public health care	4 108 404[a]	n.a.	331	n.a.
Total health care	4 889 419	281 592	440	8 241
National accounts				
Total health care	10 542 427	247 536	591	7 388

Notes:
[a] Refers to census value added.
[b] The private-public split was available only for Mexico. Census data in Mexico refer to private services only, while in the USA they cover both private and public. Value added in Mexican public care was estimated by multiplying the value added share in gross output, as taken from the national accounts, by health care expenditure from Salinas de Gortari (1993).

Source: Brazil: IBGE (1989b). Mexico: census data from INEGI (1993); national accounts data from INEGI (1994a). USA: census data from Department of Commerce, Bureau of the Census (1991); national accounts data from Department of Commerce, Bureau of Economic Analysis (January 1992; May 1993), *Survey of Current Business*; and 1980 from Department of Commerce, Bureau of Economic Analysis (1986).

Unfortunately, neither price nor cost data on medical services are available for the three countries. Therefore, these unit costs have been estimated implicitly by dividing total costs by the quantity of services produced. The validity of the UVRs depends on finding appropriate volume indicators to represent health care production.

Measurement of Health Care Output

Most OECD countries measure real output using input or throughput indicators. Some follow the price approach, deflating expenditure on inputs, or the indicator approach which extrapolates inputs in a base year using quantitative information. The Dutch national accounts use throughput indicators such as the number of treatments broken down by diagnosis related groups.

Weisbrod (1992, pp. S131–37) and others argue that output should be measured using health (outcome) measures instead of the input or 'throughput' measures suggested by SNA 1993 and ESA 1995. Outcome measures include the incidence of infant mortality, life expectancy, quality-adjusted life years (QUALYs) and satisfaction with care. Only few micro studies have been done using these measures, as it is difficult to separate the contribution of health care from other factors affecting health outcomes.

Cutler *et al.* (1999) constructed two price indices for the treatment of cardiovascular disease in the USA. The first was based on the cost of treatment of elderly heart attack victims in a large teaching hospital. Using claims records, they found that most of the price increase between 1984 and 1991 resulted from more intensive treatment of heart attacks. This differed only slightly from a conventional index based on input costs which was about 3 percentage points above the CPI in 1984–91. When they also took account of the spectacular increase in the treatment efficacy, measured by the drop in mortality rates in and outside the hospital,[11] the price index fell by 4 percentage points per year to 1 percentage point below the CPI.

Similar results were found by Frank *et al.* (1999) for the price index of the treatment of acute depression. On the basis of treatments tested in the clinical trial literature, they identified nine different bundles of psychotherapy, antidepressant drugs and medical management necessary to arrive at similar outcomes of different forms of depression. Price indexes were constructed for each bundle for the period 1991–95 and aggregated using Törnqvist index formulae. Their index declined 30 per cent over the period, which is very different from the conventional price index based on inputs which increased 25 per cent over the same interval.

A third example incorporating improvements in treatment efficacy and side-effects relates to cataract surgery in Sweden (Roos, 1997) and the USA (Shapiro and Wilcox, 1996). In the 1950s this surgery involved a ten-day hospitalisation in intensive care whereas today it is an outpatient procedure.

These studies not only adjusted their price index for the decline in discutility of treatment, but they also accounted for improvements in visual activity such as reading newspapers and text on television.

The only international comparison of health care output and productivity incorporating outcomes of treatment is McKinsey (1996). They compared the productivity of the treatments of diabetes, gallstones, breast and lung cancer between Germany, the UK and the USA in 1990. Outcomes of the treatments of the former two diseases were measured by improvements in QUALYs, and those of the latter by additional years of life expectancy.

Instead of outcome measures the first and second rounds of the international comparison project (ICP I and II) used inputs per capita, such as the number of physicians, dentists and nurses, and bed-days or beds. ICP III (Kravis *et al.*, 1982, pp. 140–54)[12] also relied on inputs, although they made an adjustment for the differences in the capital intensity of medical care[13] and productivity.[14]

In this study real output is measured by throughput measures as recommended by the Eurostat Task Force: inpatient days for hospital services and patient visits for services of dentists and physicians. Brazilian and US statistics cover private and public services, while Mexican health statistics exclude private care providers (see Appendix D).

Throughput data do not reflect differences in 'case-mix' and quality of service, for which separate adjustments were made. The case-mix refers to the different compositions of patient groups in terms of types and severity of illness between countries as well as changes over time within a country. Each case-mix requires different amounts of health care inputs. Suppose an inpatient day in surgery requires twice as many services as one in internal medicine. Output measured by inpatient days would underestimate the volume of health services for countries with a relatively high share of treatments in surgery and overestimate services in countries with a concentration in internal medicine.

The case-mix effect was estimated using detailed data on hospital discharges, broken down by almost five hundred diagnoses-related groups (DRGs). For each discharge the hospital statistics show average costs and number of inpatient days. The average cost represents a proxy of the resource requirement of each discharge. The Brazilian and Mexican DRG classifications were matched with that of the USA. Subsequently, the case-mix effect is estimated by the ratio of the weighted to the unweighted quantity relative using either US cost weights:

$$CME^{xu(u)} = \left[\frac{\sum_{i=1}^{T} \left(Q_i^x * C_i^u\right) / \left(Q_i^u * C_i^u\right)}{Q_T^x / Q_T^u} \right] \tag{7.1}$$

with Q the number of discharges per DRG, C the average cost per discharge, and i=1,...,T the DRGs. The discharges in the nominator are also weighted by cost weights of country x:

$$CME^{xu(x)} = \left[\frac{\sum_{i=1}^{T} \left(Q_i^x * C_i^x\right) / \left(Q_i^u * C_i^x\right)}{Q_T^x / Q_T^u} \right] \tag{7.2}$$

The final case mix effect is the geometric average of the USA and country x weighted CMEs. The CME adjustment showed that compared to Mexico the USA had a much higher concentration of resource intensive diagnoses and treatments in 1993, as the weighted quantity relative was 50 higher than the unweighted one. In contrast the DRG composition of treatments in Brazilian hospitals was very similar to that of US hospitals. This surprising result mainly stems from the for-profit character of most Brazilian hospitals, which favour profitable resource-intensive treatments.

The quality of health service can be assessed by evaluating the structure, processes and outcomes of health services (see Boerkamp, 1995; Loegering *et. al.*, 1994 for a discussion of quality measurement in health care). Structure refers to health care inputs, processes to the way procedures are carried out and outcomes to the results of care. Access to care, measured by the number of doctors per 100,000 population, in the USA was more than twice that of Mexico and 1.7 times that of Brazil in 1990. Other indicators show that Brazilian doctors had 87 per cent and Mexican doctors 77 per cent of the volume of capital equipment available compared to that of their US colleagues in 1975 (Kravis *et al.*, 1982). Brazilian and Mexican physicians scored much lower than US ones on common exams (a 29 and 34 per cent pass rate compared to a 92 per cent pass rate) in the same year (Kravis *et al.*, 1982). In 1990 73 per cent of all births were attended by health staff in Brazil, compared to 79 per cent in Mexico, and almost all births in the USA.

No information was available on the quality of the process of care. Quality of outcome indicators show that US health care scored much higher in terms of patient satisfaction (85 per cent compared to 60 per cent in Mexico)[15] and maternal[16] and child mortality, both at much lower rates than Brazil and Mexico (see Table 7.8). Mexican throughput was adjusted by

0.60/0.85 = 0.7, the ratio of Mexican to US patient satisfaction, to account for the lower quality of Mexican care. This ratio approximates the ratios of capital input and birth attendance. Patient satisfaction was preferred to other outcome indicators, because its level is mainly determined by the health care institutions. In contrast other factors influence the other indicators, such as socio-economic conditions. As no data were available on patient satisfaction of Brazilian health care, Brazilian output was decreased by 0.62, the average of the four ratios of Brazilian to US health indicators, excluding health insurance coverage.

Table 7.8 Quality of Health Care, Brazil, Mexico and the USA

	Unit	Brazil	Mexico	USA
Structure				
Health insurance coverage, 1990	Share of population	21*	52	83
Doctors per 100,000 population, 1990	Number	146	104	240
Capital input per doctor, 1975	USA = 100	87	77	100
Test scores of doctors, 1975	Percentage passed	34	29	92
Births attended by health staff, 1990	Percentage	73	79	100
Outcomes				
Patient satisfaction	Percentage	n.a.	60	85
Maternal mortality, 1990	Death per 1,000 births	35	68	10
Child specific mortality rate, 1990	Death per 1,000 births	69	30	11

Notes: * Private insurance only as from Medici (1991), p. 49.

Source: Doctors per 100,000 population from Table 8.5; capital input per doctor and doctors' test scores from Kravis *et al.* (1982); percentage of births attended by physicians from Pan-American Health Organisation (1994); patients and doctors' satisfaction: see text; maternal and child specific mortality rates from Table 7.1.

Unit Value Ratios and Labour Productivity, 1950–96

UVRs were derived using the throughput data, adjusted for differences between countries in case-mix and quality of care, in combination with the gross value of output (see Table 7.9). UVRs based on crude throughput data show that the price of Brazilian health care services was one-fourth of the US level in 1980, and that of Mexico one-seventh of the US level. Case-mix adjustment increases the Fisher UVR only 3 per cent in the Brazil/USA case, compared to 50 per cent in the Mexico/USA case. The quality adjustment has the largest impact on the relative price levels, that is it increases the Brazil/US UVR by more than half, and the Mexico/US UVR by 40 per cent.

Table 7.9 Unit Value Ratios for Health Care, Brazil/USA, 1980 and Mexico/USA, 1987/88

	Brazil/USA, 1980			Mexico/USA, 1987/88 (1988 prices):		
	Paasche UVRs	Las-peyres UVRs	Geometric Average	Paasche UVRs	Las-peyres UVRs	Geometric Average
			A. Unadjusted			
Hospital services				188.3	188.3	188.3
Physicians & dentists				482.1	482.1	482.1
Total (all branches)	12.86	12.86	12.86	324.9	345.7	335.1
			B. Adjusted for case-mix			
Hospital services				283.4	283.4	283.4
Physicians & dentists				725.7	725.7	725.7
Total (all branches)	13.25	13.25	13.25	489.1	520.4	504.5
			C. Adjusted for case-mix and quality			
Hospital services				404.9	404.9	404.9
Physicians & dentists				1 036.7	1 036.7	1 036.7
Total (all branches)	21.36	21.36	21.36	743.4	698.7	720.7
Exchange rate	52.71	52.71	52.71	2 273.1	2 273.1	2 273.1

Source: See Appendix D.

Labour productivity was derived by dividing value added (converted to a common currency by use of the UVRs in Table 7.9) by employment from Table 7.7. Relative labour productivity levels are shown in Table 7.10. The productivity results in the first and the fourth columns are based on crude measures of output, that is numbers of patient days and doctors' visits. Output was adjusted for differences in the types of diseases treated (case-mix) between countries (columns 2 and 5), and quality differences (columns 3 and 6).

The Brazilian relative health care performance was 65 per cent of the US level in 1980. The Mexico/USA comparison based on census information shows a very low relative performance of Mexican clinics and offices of health practitioners, and a somewhat smaller gap between Mexican and US hospitals. This had been expected because new techniques and types of care are probably adopted sooner by hospitals than by clinics and offices. Overall Mexican productivity in private care equalled 29 per cent of the US level. The relative performance of public services equalled 60 per cent of the US level, producing an overall result of 45 per cent. The relative productivity result based on the national accounts was 74 per cent, which seems to be rather high, especially compared to the result of the private part of Mexican health care. As Mexican national accounts tend to overestimate economic activity (GDP), the results based on census information are preferred.

Table 7.10 Labour Productivity in Health Care, Brazil/USA, 1980 and Mexico/USA, 1987/88

	Brazil/USA, 1980 (Fisher results)			Mexico/USA, 1987/88 (Fisher results)		
	Un-adjusted	Adjusted for Case-mix	Adjusted for Case-mix and Quality	Un-adjusted	Adjusted for Case-mix	Adjusted for Case-mix and Quality
	Census and other Sources					
Private health care						
Hospital services				94.4	62.7	43.9
Physicians & dentists				28.0	18.6	13.0
Laboratories*				71.8	47.7	33.4
Other medical services*				88.3	58.6	41.0
Total				63.5	42.2	29.5
Public health care (a)				113.0	75.0	51.1
Total health care				100.7	66.9	45.8
	National Accounts					
Total health care	108.0	104.8	65.0	238.1	158.2	110.7

Notes: * Value added converted by using UVR for total health care.

Source: Value added from Table 7.7 converted by UVRs in Table 7.9, and subsequently divided by employment from Table 7.7.

The benchmark results were extrapolated to cover the period 1950–96 on the basis of series of GDP and employment (see Appendices A and B) as shown in Figure 7.1. Time series for Brazil were available only from 1971 only. The performance of Brazil *vis-à-vis* the USA worsened steadily in the 1970s until 1987, and was caused by growing inefficiency, exploding costs and other problems mentioned above. The 1987 and 1990 reforms (SUDS and SUS) have been successful as they reversed this negative trend. Brazilian productivity caught up with US levels from 1987 to 1996. Mexican relative performance in health care was 39 per cent of that of the USA in 1950, and fell until 1965; from 1965 to 1985 its relative performance improved to 50 per cent of the US level in 1985. Its relative performance stagnated during the rest of the period. The reforms introduced in the early 1990s were not improved labour productivity until 1996.

Figure 7.1 Labour Productivity in Health Care: Brazil and Mexico as a Per Cent of the USA (USA = 100), 1950–96

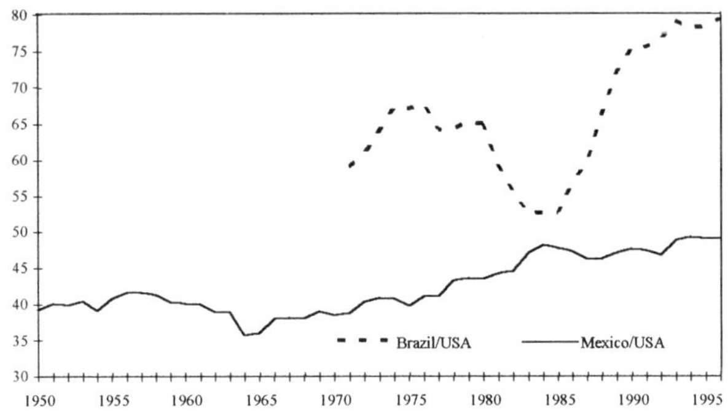

Source: Benchmark results from Table 7.10 extrapolated with time series of GDP (see Appendix B) and employment (see Appendix A).

The higher relative productivity of Brazil when compared to Mexico only partly confirms the better outcomes of health care observed in the first part of this chapter. Brazil had a better score in terms of the incidence of tuberculosis and the percentage of babies with an acceptable birth weight in 1990. However, Brazil scored lower than Mexico on life expectancy and infant mortality rates in the early 1990s. The relatively higher productivity in Brazil when compared to Mexico probably stems from the predominance of private care providers in the former country. Many private hospitals are profit-oriented and have an incentive to maximise the efficiency of the resources used. In Mexico most hospitals are public and lack incentives to increase productivity. As labour productivity is a measure of economic efficiency and not of allocative efficiency, it is possible that Brazil had poorer health outcomes than Mexico, despite its higher productivity levels.

NOTES

1. Health care is defined, according to the standard industrial classifications of Mexico and the USAZ, by the services provided by general, psychiatric and speciality hospitals; offices and clinics of doctors, dentists and other health practitioners; medical and dental laboratories and miscellaneous health services.

2. Oxley and MacFarlan (1995) found a significant relationship between health care spending and life expectancy at age 60 for OECD countries excluding Mexico.
3. See Maddison (1995a, p. 310) for a detailed account of estimates of the population during the colonial period in Mexico.
4. A hospital for new settlers was founded along the James River in 1612; isolation hospitals emerged in the early seventeenth century, and a hospital for the mentally ill was erected in Williamsburg in 1773 (Cassedy, 1991).
5. Several institutes were founded in São Paulo which included the Pharmaceutical Institute, the Laboratory of Chemical Analysis and a Vaccination Institute in the 1890s. The state was divided into several sanitary districts with one inspector for each district (van Stralen, 1996).
6. These trends confirm the weak correlation between the expenditure share of health in GDP and per capita income across countries, as found by the 1993 issue of the World Development Report, *Investing in Health* (World Bank, 1993).
7. The Brazilian and Mexican population tripled in the 1950–90 period, whereas in the USA it rose by 64 per cent.
8. This figure also includes those who used the services of the National Institute for Indigenous People (INI) and the Integrated Family Programme (DIF). The number of potential users would be much higher (OECD, 1997).
9. As some people are covered by more than one scheme, the total surpasses one.
10. In Brazil the censuses of 1975, 1980 and 1985 excluded health care; detailed national accounts estimates for this sector were available only for 1980. In Mexico and the USA, revenue and cost data of care were available every five years as part of the *Censos de Servicios* (INEGI) and *Census of Service Industries* (Department of Commerce), respectively. The Mexican census covers private health care only, while US census information included public and private services.
11. The age-adjusted population death rate from heart attacks fell almost 60 per cent between 1975 and 1995. Of those people hospitalised, adjusted for age and sex, the 30 day hospitality rate fell by40 per cent over the same period. Cutler *et al.* (1999) valued the additional years of life expectancy of the heart attack victims by an estimate of the value of an additional life year (US$ 25,000) computed in other research.
12. They distinguished seven categories of health expenditures: drugs and medical preparations, medical supplies, therapeutic equipment and four types of medical services (dentists, nurses, hospitals and physicians,). The first three types of expenditure, not part of the health care industry, were dealt with by direct price comparisons.
13. ICP III estimated the capital stock in health care for eight countries within the low-, middle- and high-income range, assuming equal capital productivity across countries. Relative output of country x compared to the USA (u) was calculated firstly by labour alone, that is $Q^x/Q^u = L^x/L^u$, and subsequently by combining

labour and capital inputs (that is $Q^x/Q^u = 0.85 * L^x/L^u + 0.15 * K^x/K^u$). Relative output was reduced in countries with lower *K/L* ratios than the USA. On the basis of the eight country sample, quantity ratios for each professional category were divided by 1.30 for low-income countries and 1.15 for middle income countries.

14. GDP per capita was used as a proxy for lower productivity of health services in lower income countries, including Brazil and Mexico. The Brazil/US quantity ratio was divided by 1.54, and the Mexico/US ratio by 1.24 (Kravis *et al.*, 1982, p. 153).
15. For a discussion of patient dissatisfaction and other aspects of the poor quality of Mexican health services, see Fundación Mexicana para la Salud (1994a, 1994b). US patient satisfaction was derived from Blendon (1989, p. 7). No data on this were available for Brazil.
16. Number of perinatal death per 1,000 births, late fetal deaths occurring at 28 weeks of gestation or thereafter, and early neonatal death occurring within the first seven days of life.

8. Education

INTRODUCTION

Education is the largest non-market service sector in Brazil, Mexico and the USA. The important role of education stems from its fulfilment of at least five societal goals (Maddison, 1995a). Firstly, the accumulation of knowledge yields satisfaction throughout life and as such education is a means of personal development. Secondly, education is considered important to promote social continuity and cohesion. In the USA, and to a lesser extent in Brazil and Mexico, education has been used to build a homogeneous society from an immigrant population. However, after the education system has reached a certain level of development, education is no longer a source of cohesion, but a force producing unpredictable social change. Thirdly, free access to all levels of education promotes social mobility. Fourthly, education produces a greater equality of earnings, as the share of educated people increases and that of the less-educated decreases. This decreases the relative wages of the well-educated and increases the wages of the uneducated. Finally, education raises worker productivity and earnings.[1] Empirical research has confirmed the positive contribution of education to economic growth in Brazil, Mexico and the USA.[2] Investment in human capital occurs largely through the educational system, although other forms of learning also exist, such as training on the job. This chapter focuses on the educational system.

In Mexico and the USA education is compulsory from the age of 6 and from 7 in Brazil. School attendance is obligatory until the age of 14 in Brazil and Mexico and 16 in the USA. Except for the secondary level, the three educational systems have significant similarities.[3] In Brazil and Mexico enormous efforts have been made to achieve universal and free schooling. From 1950 to 1990 its relative importance strongly increased in Brazil and Mexico: student enrolment grew twice as fast as the population, and employment in education grew even more. Expenditure on education as a share of GDP increased sevenfold in Brazil and fourfold in Mexico. In the

USA, the spread of mass education had already occurred in the late eighteenth and nineteenth centuries.

Thanks to these massive investments in Brazil and Mexico, the gap in their educational level *vis-à-vis* the USA were narrowed substantially between 1950 and 1990, as illustrated by rapidly falling illiteracy rates in Brazil and Mexico, and the increase in the number of years of schooling of the working population. Nevertheless, educational levels in Brazil and Mexico could be considered as disappointing when they are compared to those of countries with similar per capita income levels in other parts of the world. This gap is mainly due to the large deficiencies of the schooling systems in both countries. The major bottleneck does not seem to be the lack of resources (especially in Mexico) but the low quality of inputs, inequality of access to education, lack of quality control, and political obstacles (Inter-American Development Bank, 1996).

LONG-TERM DEVELOPMENT

Enrolment

The long-term development of education is illustrated by enrolment figures and enrolment ratios[4] at different levels of education (see Table 8.1). In the twentieth century enrolment grew much faster in Brazil and Mexico than in the USA. Starting from much lower enrolment ratios, the more rapid growth in the Latin countries reveals a catch-up phenomenon, *vis-à-vis* the USA. From 1907 to 1950 school enrolment grew fastest in Brazil (from 700,000 to 6.2 million). During this period higher education showed the most rapid growth in Brazil. In Mexico and the USA secondary education was the fastest growing part. From 1950 to 1990 total enrolment grew fourfold in Brazil, sevenfold in Mexico and twofold in the USA. The biggest increase in student numbers took place in higher education: the 1990 enrolment figure was 40 times that of 1950 in Mexico and 9 times in the USA. In Brazil the 1990 figure was 16 times that of 1960. These significant increases can be explained by both demographic movements (see Table 2.4), and a rise in enrolment ratios (see Table 8.1).

In Brazil and Mexico primary school ratios exceeded 100 because a large number of children repeated the first grade (see Schiefelbein and Wolff, 1993). In Brazil relative enrolment grew in primary schools, decreased in secondary schools and doubled in higher education in the 1970–90 period. Mexican enrolment ratios grew more than 18 times in secondary schools and

Table 8.1 *Number of Students by Level of Education, Percentage of the Age group and Number of Pupils per Teacher, Brazil, Mexico and the USA, 1900–90*

	Brazil				Mexico				USA			
	Pre & Primary	Secondary	Higher	Total	Pre & Primary	Secondary	Higher	Total	Pre & Primary	Secondary	Higher	Total
Panel A: Number of Students (000s)												
1900					696	7	10	713	16,131	630	258	17,019
1907	638	56	6	700	667	6	10	682	16,140	751	315	17,206
1930	2,085	73	127	2,285	1,300	17	24	1,341	23,534	4,740	1,101	29,375
1940	3,303	170	260	3,733	1,950				20,928	7,059	1,494	29,481
1950	5,240	407	571	6,218	3,112	70	67	3,249	25,342	6,397	2,281	34,020
1960	7,477	1,177	96	8,750	2,997	107	30	3,134	20,466	7,130	1,494	29,090
1970	17,066	4,086	430	21,582	9,248	1,584	248	11,080	28,410	22,847	8,581	59,838
1990	28,944	3,499	1,540	33,983	14,402	6,704	1,311	22,417	26,784	19,344	13,820	59,948
Panel B: As a Percentage of Total Persons in Age Group												
1960	100.0	11.0	1.6		71.6	3.1	1.3		139.8	86.5	13.0	
1970	82.0	43.0	5.1		105.5	22.8	5.8		100.0	94.0	51.8	
1990	108.0	39.0	11.6		112.7	56.0	13.6		106.0	96.0	72.2	
Panel C: Number of Pupils per Teacher												
1960	33	13			45	8			33	18		
1970	22	15			45	17			22	19		
1990	23	15			30	16			18	15		

Notes: The figures in Panel B are calculated by the ratio of total enrolment of all ages in the school level to the population of the specific age group, which corresponds to the school level. Ratios can exceed 100 because of participation of students outside the normal age group.

Sources: Brazilian data, 1950 US enrolment and 1970 and 1990 figures from Department of Education (1993, pp. 410–11), based on UNESCO data. Brazil: student numbers 1890–1950 from Ludwig (1985); number of students per teacher from ECLAC (1993, pp. 58–59). Mexico: total enrolment and population by age group in 1950 from INEGI (1994b). 1950 US population by age group from US Department of Commerce, Bureau of the Census (1975, p. 15).

almost 10 times in higher education from 1950 to 1990. In the USA most of the 6–11 and 12–17 age group were already enrolled in 1950. In the USA only higher education enrolment ratios increased substantially in the 1950–90 period. The primary school ratio dropped from 140 per cent to 106 per cent, indicating a drop in the proportion of people outside the 6–11 age year group who were enrolled (that is fewer repeaters).

Quality of Education

The outcome of education depends not only on enrolment ratios, but also on the quality of schooling. A frequently used quality indicator in primary and secondary education is the student/teacher ratio. In Brazil these remained constant in the 1970–90 period (see the bottom panel of Table 8.1). In Mexico the number of students per teacher decreased in primary education and increased in secondary education in the 1950–90 period. Both ratios declined in the USA. In contrast to Brazil the difference between the primary and secondary education ratios narrowed over time in Mexico and the USA. By 1991 the student/teacher ratio in secondary education was half of that in primary schools in Mexico, whereas in the USA classes became almost equal in size.

The relationship between class size and educational outcomes is, however, not robust (see Harbison and Hanushek, 1992, p. 24). Other quality indicators for the benchmark years are shown in Table 8.2. Dropout rates refer to the percentage of first-year students who fail to finish an educational cycle. In primary and secondary education dropout rates were much higher in Brazil and Mexico[5] than in the USA. In primary education the Brazilian dropout rate surpassed that of Mexico, whereas in secondary schooling the rate was similar in both countries.

A second quality indicator is the share of first-grade students in primary school repeating the first year. In Brazil they represented 62 per cent of the first-grade classes in 1980 compared to 33 per cent in Mexico in 1988. No data are available for the USA. The bottom panel of Table 8.2 shows the most commonly used indicator to measure the quality of education, that is achievement levels. In 1994 Mexico has been included for the first time in cross-country tests of pupils.[6] However, the Mexican government refused to release its results. Brazil was included in several international comparisons of achievements in mathematics and science. The 1991 comparison was coordinated by the Educational Testing Service and published in *Learning Mathematics* and *Learning Science.* The results show that Brazilian students scored 20 points lower on average than their US counterparts (scale 1 to 100).

Table 8.2 *Indicators of the Quality of Education, Brazil/USA, 1980 and Mexico/USA, 1987/88*

	Unit	Brazil/USA, 1980		Mexico/USA	
		Brazil	USA	Mexico 1988	USA 1987
Dropout rates					
• Primary school	Ratio of dropouts	68.3[a]	n.a.	43.7	n.a.
• Secondary school	to 1st year enrolment	56.2[a]	12.7	54.5	12.7
First grade repetition level in primary	Share of repeaters in first grade	61.9	n.a.	32.8	n.a.
Educational testing, 1991					
• Mathematics test scores	Average % correct	34.7[b]	55.3	n.a.	55.3
• Science test scores	Average % correct	49.6[b]	67.0	n.a.	67.0

Notes:
[a] Estimated by the ratio of number of students in the fifth grade of elementary school in 1980 to first grade enrolment five years previously (that is 1975) (primary school dropout rate) or enrolment in the third grade of secondary school by number of students in the fifth grade of primary school six years ago (that is 1974) (secondary school dropout rate).
[b] Figure refers to 13-year-old students from Brazil.

Sources: Brazil dropout rate from IBGE, *Anuário Estatístico do Brasil 1982*; Mexico dropout rate from Secretaría de Educación Publica (1990); US dropout rate from Department of Education (1993); first grade repetition from Schiefelbein and Wolff (1993, p. 85). Test results from Educational Testing Service (1992a, 1992b).

Outcomes

Outcomes of education are illustrated by illiteracy rates and average years of schooling of the working population. In 1890 the share of the Brazilian and Mexican population able to read and write was about the same as the share of illiterates in the US population (see Table 8.3). From 1890 to 1950 the share of literate people doubled in Mexico, whereas in Brazil illiteracy decreased less. In 1950 only 3 per cent of Americans were illiterate. From 1950 to 1990 the share of illiterates decreased to 18 per cent in Brazil and 11 per cent in Mexico.

Another outcome indicator is the average number of years of schooling of population of working age, that is 15–65 years old (see Table 8.4). From 1970 to 1990 the share of workers lacking any education decreased from 42 per cent to 18 per cent in Brazil and from 24 to 11 per cent in Mexico. In Brazil the share of those who had not completed primary school increased from 27 per cent to 40 per cent, while in Mexico it dropped from 44 to 22 per cent. In 1990, a higher share of people of working age had (partly) completed secondary and higher education in Brazil and Mexico. In the USA the share of people with a primary education degree only decreased substantially and the share of people with a higher education degree increased correspondingly.

Table 8.3 Share of Illiterates in Total Population (Per Cent), Brazil, Mexico and the USA, 1890–1950

	Brazil	Mexico	USA
1890	85.2	82.1	13.3
1900	74.4	77.7	10.7
1910	n.a.	72.3	7.7
1921	75.5	66.1	6.0
1930	n.a.	61.5	4.3
1940	61.2	64.0	2.9
1950	57.2	44.2	3.2
1970	42.3	23.6	0.0
1990	18.1	10.6	0.0

Sources: Brazil: Ludwig (1985) and IBGE, *Anuário Estatístico do Brasil 1992*; Mexico: INEGI (1994b); USA: Department of Commerce, Bureau of the Census (1975, p. 382). 1970 and 1990 from Table 8.4.

DETERMINANTS OF LONG-TERM DEVELOPMENT

Expenditure, Value Added and Employment

The impact of education on the schooling of the population largely depends on the size of the educational system, for example the number of schools and teachers. These, in turn, depend on private and public expenditure. Table 8.5 shows that in 1955 public expenditure as a share of GDP in the USA was eight times that of Brazil, and five times that of Mexico. In Mexico and the USA relative expenditure increased rapidly from 1955 to 1975, while in Brazil expenditure only rose after 1975. In 1990 the relative expenditure gap between the three countries had narrowed, although the Americans still spent 50 per cent more in relative terms. In each country the expenditure per student in higher education was much higher than that in primary and secondary education.[7]

Table 8.4 Educational Attainment of Working Population, Brazil, Mexico and the USA, 1970–90 (Percentage Distribution)

	Brazil		Mexico		USA	
	1970	1990	1970	1990	1970	1990
Zero	42.3	18.1	23.6	10.6	0.0	0.0
Primary						
• not completed	26.7	40.3	43.5	21.5	12.3	2.1
• completed	19.4	8.1	17.0	20.3	23.3	7.8
Secondary						
• not completed	5.9	15.3	6.3	19.1	10.1	18.8
• completed	3.7	12.4	5.5	15.6	35.1	35.8
Higher	2.0	5.7	4.1	10.8	19.2	35.6
Non-specified				2.1		
Total	100.0	100.0	100.0	100.0	100.0	100.0
Average years of schooling	2.8	4.8	4.2	6.7	10.6	12.6

Sources: Brazil: 1970 from Wilkie (1980, p. 126); 1990 from IBGE, *Anuário Estatístico do Brasil 1992*. Mexican and US data from Latapi (1994); estimates were compiled from population censuses of Mexico and the USA.

Table 8.5 Public Expenditure on Education as a Percentage of Total GDP, Brazil, Mexico and the USA, 1950–90

	1955	1975	1990
Brazil	0.5	0.6	3.7
Mexico	0.8	2.8	3.5
USA	3.9	6.6	5.5

Sources: Brazil: 1955 and 1975 from IBGE (1990), Mexico: 1955 and 1975 from INEGI (1994b), 1990 from INEGI (1998). USA: 1955 and 1975 from Department of Education (1993), 1990 from OECD (1993, p. 66).

Table 8.6 illustrates the size and growth of the education sector, including private education. The Mexican education sector was relatively larger in terms of its share in value added than that of the USA in 1950. This seems an unlikely result. An overestimation of the Mexican national accounts of value added, which was also found for other sectors (see Appendix E), may explain this result. From 1950 to 1990 the US share increased 2.5 times.

The Brazilian share doubled from 1975 to 1996. In Brazil and Mexico the share of education in total employment grew four times from 1950 to 1996, while in the USA it almost tripled. The share of education in employment in Mexico in 1990 was surprisingly high compared to Brazil and the USA.

Table 8.6 *Value Added and Employment as a Percentage of Total GDP and Employment, Education, Brazil, Mexico and the USA, 1950–96*

	Value Added as a % of GDP			Employment as a % of the Total		
	1950	1975	1996	1950	1975	1996
Brazil	n.a.	1.7	3.3	1.2	3.1	4.1
Mexico	3.6	3.6	5.2	2.1	5.3	10.0
USA	1.9	4.5	4.6	3.3	7.1	8.5

Sources: National accounts (see Appendices A and B).

Public and Private Initiatives: A Long-run View

Brazil

The colonial government of Brazil showed little interest and almost all education was provided by the Jesuits. They introduced dualism in the education system, with secondary schools for sons of landowners, who could study to be lawyers or priests, and separate primary schools for the poor, who were taught some bible knowledge, reading and writing. In 1759 the Jesuits were expelled and replaced by new teachers. Scientific and technical subjects were added to the curriculum. The Portuguese also established advanced schools for military officers and public administrators. Unlike the Spanish colonies, no universities were created in the colonial period.

During the Empire (1821–1889) basic education was almost entirely neglected, despite the establishment of the universal right to free primary education in the Constitution of 1824. In 1834 the provision of primary education was delegated to provincial and municipal governments which lacked resources to fund schools. Some technical and scientific-orientated schools were established, as well as institutions focusing on arts, humanities and law. By 1889 259,000 children were enrolled in schools, representing 14 per cent of those in the 7–11 year age group.

In the new Republican Constitution of 1891 states became entirely responsible for primary and vocational education, while they shared authority with the federal government for secondary and higher education. In wealthy states, such as São Paulo, enrolment in primary schools increased, while in others this stagnated.

In the 1920s educational reformers (*escolanovistas),* influenced by Europe and the USA, organised themselves in the Brazilian Education Association (ABE). In 1932 they proposed compulsory, free and secular education. The ABE proposals were adopted in the Constitution of 1934. The foundation of the Ministry of Education and Health in 1930 signified a more active role of the federal government. A period of political turmoil led to the withdrawal of the ABE propositions in the Constitution adopted in 1937, and their re-establishment in the Constitution adopted after World War II and the 1961 Basic Education Law.

The military government (1964–85) focused on the expansion of higher and vocational secondary education. In 1971 a reform extended compulsory primary schooling from four to eight years. The reform was intended to reduce the dualism in education. However, the opposite occurred, as the budget for public education was reduced and the gap between public and private schools widened. The 1971 reform transferred the responsibility for education to municipalities and states without providing the necessary resources. After 1971 enrolment ratios in primary education declined, but those in higher education increased.

Primary education was given a much larger role in the new constitution of 1988. The federal, state and municipal administrations were mandated to spend at least 50 per cent of their resources for education on primary schooling. This policy should achieve universal primary schooling and reduce illiteracy. Up to 1996 public action to achieve this goal had been limited and only few states and municipalities had changed their spending patterns (Ludwig, 1985; Plank, 1996).

Mexico

Centuries before the Spanish conquest the indigenous peoples of Meso-america had already established an advanced system of public schooling. The Aztecs' system was the best known; their educational system was much more advanced than that of the Indians living in present-day Brazil and the USA. Education was provided only to the elite group of the hierarchic Aztec society, called the *calpulli.* The system stressed arts, astronomical calculation, calendar reading, dance, defence, religion and self-sacrifice. The education of Aztecs depended on the position of their fathers. For example the sons of nobility attended the seminary-like *calmeac* where they were taught to be military leaders, priests or public officials (Osborn, 1976).

The Spanish destroyed all forms of indigenous education. Under the new system education became the responsibility of clerical orders and aimed at the conversion to Catholicism. Its educational benefits were negligible, as shown by the 99.5 per cent share of illiterates in the indigenous population in 1821. In 1523 the first school was founded in Texcoco by the Franciscan Pedro de Gante, who became responsible for the development of education in colonial Mexico. In 1536 the first institute for higher learning in the Americas, the Santa Cruz de Tlatelolco Academy, was established by the Jesuits. In the late sixteenth century the Academy was closed, as the colonisers disliked its move towards emancipation of the Indians. The oldest, still existing institution for higher education, is the Colegio de San Nicolás Obispo de Pátzcuaro founded in 1540. The first university of the Americas, the Royal and Pontificia University of Mexico, was created in 1551. Before the opening of Harvard College in 1636, the first US university, more than 8,000 students had already graduated in Mexico.

The most active order offering education was the Jesuits. They introduced liberal education, including Greek and Latin, as well as history, mathematics and physics. The Augustians, the Dominicans and the Franciscans established 300 convents during the first century of occupation, of which 145 remained by the end of the colonial period. Non-formal education on *haciendas* was much more important than formal education. Agricultural techniques and farming skills were instructed a mixture of apprenticeship and force.

In the seventeenth and eighteenth centuries education advanced little, due to a shortage of priests and a refusal to secularise education. In 1767 many schools were closed following a decision to expel the Jesuits (Osborn, 1976).

During the first decades after Independence only a few schools were founded. By 1850 Mexico had about 350 schools, of which only 30 per cent were public. In the same period 26 secondary and higher educational institutions were added to the 12 existing ones. As such education remained a privilege of the upper class. The new constitution adopted by Juarez in 1857 was an important step towards democratisation: it provided compulsory secular education free of charge. Although the number of schools increased to 8,000 by 1874, providing tuition for 350,000 students, enrolment remained low, as there were two million children of school-age. This disappointing outcome was mostly due to the lack of finance to pay for extra schools and teachers. Porfirio Diaz provided some further funding. By 1910 there were 12,000 schools for one million children, a fifth of the school-age population. Most schools were located in urban areas, especially in Mexico City. In the same year only one university, the National University of Mexico, was functioning.

The new Constitution adopted after the Mexican Revolution not only provided for compulsory and free schooling between the age of 6–14, but also provided finance in the form of special taxes and obligatory financial contributions of large companies to the education of their workers' children.

In 1921 the Ministry of Education, *Secretaria de Educación Publica* (SEP), was founded, which was to play a key role in the popularisation of schooling. By 1926 2,600 new primary schools and four universities were founded in rural areas. From 1930 to 1950 the government promoted technical-vocational education, establishing several national and regional polytechnic institutes and providing scholarships (Osborn, 1976).

From the 1950s onwards increased public expenditure contributed to the spread of primary and secondary schools, universities and vocational institutions. The expansion was almost entirely directed by the SEP. This centralised policy provoked many problems (see below) which contributed to the disappointing results of the system. Special policies to promote education in rural areas had limited success, due to a shortage of funds and lack of qualified teachers.

From 1982 to 1987 public spending decreased by 7 per cent annually, while enrolment increased. The real income of teachers fell sharply. In 1992 the government decentralised the system, transferring operational and technical responsibility to the states. SEP expected states to participate in financing, depending on their ability to pay and with a federal government equalisation policy between states. The decentralisation turned out to be very limited, as the federal government maintained complete control over technical education, part of the teachers at all levels, a 50 per cent control of the total budget for education and the monopoly in the evaluation of the quality of the system (Maddison, 1992).

USA[8]

During the colonial period education was fully controlled by the colonial powers. The French and Spanish copied their home institutions, that is they installed convents and monasteries, where Indians and whites were taught bible knowledge, reading and writing. The British and the Dutch, on the contrary, incorporated new features in the educational system they put into place in New England. As in their home countries religion played a key role in learning. However, in the colonies there was much more emphasis on the development of skills. These were taught at academies, of which the first was established in 1751. The subjects taught included bookkeeping, geography and shipping.

In 1647 Massachusetts passed a law which required towns to establish and maintain schools. A special tax was introduced for this purpose. Other parts of New England soon followed this practice. Children entered school at age six or seven and remained there three or four years on average. Social background remained the main determinant of the length of stay in schools. The children of the early poor settlers received little education. The first higher education institution, Harvard College, was founded in 1636. At the time of the Revolution there were nine colleges with 750 students.

The new federal government of the independent Union of States did not establish a national policy on education, but stimulated education indirectly by granting federal land to states to establish colleges and schools. In the late 1700s seven states explicitly mentioned education in their constitution. However, only three of them required each county to establish a school with support from the state. Massachusetts was the first state to adopt the new district system in 1789, that is freedom of each local community to regulate its schools, and to accept girls. The first national educational institution, the military academy for engineers, was established in West Point in 1802. In the absence of public schools in many places private initiatives promoted schooling for the poor. From 1806 to 1830 monitorial schools providing inexpensive education to masses spread rapidly. Teachers selected students as monitors who, in turn, instructed small groups of children. Around 1800 religious groups started Sunday schools. The education for the poor was coordinated by school societies, which were established first in Connecticut and New York.

At the elementary level kindergartens were founded in 1848, well after the introduction of infant schools in 1818. Kindergartens stimulated learning through play, songs and stories. Their numbers remained small until the 1960s when they spread rapidly due to private donations. By the 1980s more than 90 per cent of all five-year-olds attended kindergartens.

At the secondary level the number of academies grew rapidly from Independence until the Civil War. In addition to private donations, many were supported by local governments. Each academy had a different curriculum, often including classical subjects as well as botany, chemistry, modern languages and music. Many offered preparatory courses for college, while others prepared for professions such as teachers. Special academies for girls were also founded. Some efforts were made to educate minority groups such as the slaves. At the beginning of the Civil War there were 6,000 academies, of which most were located in the eastern states.

In 1824 a new form of secondary education was established in Boston, that is the high school. In the beginning this school form was intended for middle- and upper-class boys not going to college. Later on high schools also accepted girls, as well as children from lower-income groups. By 1900, half of the students were female. Pupils could choose among a classical, commercial or English curriculum. The number of high schools grew slowly until the Civil War, as they competed with the well-established academies. Moreover, many towns were reluctant to introduce taxes for secondary education. This changed when in 1872 the Supreme Court of Michigan acknowledged the link high schools formed between elementary school and university, and thus justified the levying of taxes. With the use of public funds, high schools expanded rapidly,[9] causing a rapid decline of the popularity of the academies. The high school overtook the function of the academy to prepare for college. Enrolment levels increased rapidly in the twentieth century. From 1930 onwards more and more states divided the high school into a junior and senior branch of three years each.[10]

As for higher education, many colleges and universities were founded in areas lacking institutions of higher learning from 1800 onwards. The number of private colleges increased from 30 in 1810, to 50 in 1830 and to 182 at the beginning of the Civil War. Many state universities emerged in new settlement areas in the West. Three universities opened departments for scientific and technical education around 1850. The extension of the university curriculum to agriculture and mechanics was favoured by the two Morrill Acts. The first, adopted in 1862, donated public lands to states which created colleges teaching these subjects. The second, adopted in 1890, granted federal funds for the same purpose. These laws were successful as 65 new colleges and universities were created by 1900.

In 1876 the Johns Hopkins University opened in Baltimore. It was the first to concentrate itself on scientific research and teaching. The unique graduate programme stressed more research than the transmission of knowledge. Its practice of faculty members involved in research was also new. Johns Hopkins founded the first medical college with full-time professors. Soon other universities adopted the Johns Hopkins model. By 1900 more than 530 professional schools were operating around the country, which increasingly replaced the practice of apprentice offices and self-education.

After 1910 the number of junior colleges has increased rapidly. These offered two-year courses, and often provided the start of standard college education. Public colleges spread more rapidly than private ones. Tuition at the former was free or inexpensive.

After the 1920s the involvement of the federal government in education grew rapidly. A separate Office of Education was created in 1930, which became part of the Department of Health, Education and Welfare in 1953. During the Great Depression vocational training was stimulated, as well as adult education. Moreover, the government provided loans to construct libraries and schools. During the two World Wars large numbers of people were trained as physicians or technicians. In the late 1950s and 1960s several Acts were passed to promote education at all levels.[11] At the elementary and secondary levels funds were made available for text books and other instructional materials, to ensure adequate teaching for poor children, and for research in education. At the higher education level the acquisition of books for libraries, teacher training and financial assistance to poor students was promoted. In the 1970s little federal legislation was introduced, resulting from an oversupply of teachers, and a fear of overregulation (Pulliam, 1982).

Teaching Quality and Adequacy of Facilities

In Brazil and Mexico the low quality of schooling results partly from the low quality of input. Teachers in public schools are often poorly trained[12] and underpaid. In many parts of Brazil teachers' salaries were below US$ 20 dollars per month in the early 1990s. In Mexico teachers' salaries decreased 56 per cent in real terms between 1982 and 1987. In private schools teachers are often better educated and trained, and they receive higher salaries than their colleagues in public schools. In public schools long strikes are common.[13]

In Brazil and Mexico public educational buildings are often in a poor condition. In Brazil a 1985 survey showed that only one quarter of all buildings was in good condition, and that half of the school buildings in the north-east needed repair. Almost 30 per cent of all schools had too few seats for the number of enrolled students, and many lacked books and other educational materials. In Mexico maintenance of buildings and equipment has been very poor since the debt crisis of 1982 (Guevara Niebla, 1995; Harbison and Hanushek, 1992; Plank, 1996).

Inequality in Education

In Brazil and Mexico the quality of schools strongly varies between regions. In Brazil those in the south and south-east are systematically better off than those in the north and north-east.[14] In Mexico central and northern states are better equipped than southern ones. The disparity in the quality of schooling has, in addition to large socio-economic discrepancies, led to wide differences in the outcomes of schooling. To reduce inequality in schooling the government and international organisations allocated special funds for the poorly served regions with little success. In Brazil a disproportionate share, compared to the southern regions, has been used for administrative purposes and the finance of local electoral campaigns instead of improvements in the classrooms. In Mexico, a special programme for rural education was abandoned in 1992.

Urban schools are generally better off than rural ones, in terms of expenditure per student, the quality and salary of teachers, buildings and equipment. In Brazil the urban rural disparity is worsened by the separate provision of schooling by the state and municipalities. In the north-east state schools, providing better quality teaching, are concentrated in towns, while most municipal schools are located in rural areas. Most private schools, subsidised by the government, are also located in urban areas.

Within the educational systems of Brazil and Mexico, the free provision of higher education is another major source of inequality. Defenders of free higher education argue that charging fees would exclude the poor. However, most students in universities come from private secondary schools and middle- and upper-class households (Guevara Niebla, 1995; Plank, 1996).

Lack of Quality Control

Until recently the governments in Brazil and Mexico measured the efficiency of the schooling system by the amounts of physical inputs, such as the numbers of schools, teachers and students, enrolment ratios, dropout and repetition rates. The lack of knowledge of educational performance served the interests of many incompetent administrators and teachers, as their quality could not be judged from these figures. Recently both countries have started to use standardised examinations to measure the learning of students.[15] The use of these examinations for policy purposes has remained limited. Other problems in Brazil and Mexico include the inadequate supervision of teachers, a missing incentive structure for teachers in Brazil and a lack of participation of local administrations in education in Mexico (Inter-American Development Bank, 1996). For many years achievement tests have been used in USA even though their outcomes are frequently not translated into policy measures, as learning performance depends on many other factors than schooling.[16]

Political Obstacles

In Brazil one of the major causes of the low quality of schooling, according to Plank (1996, p. 45), is *clientelismo*, that is 'a style of politics in which political support is acquired and maintained by using public resources to benefit supporters and clients'. As public sector jobs are the most important resource, the influence and power of politicians largely depends on the number of jobs under their control. Jobs are exchanged for political support and votes, a practice referred to as *empreguismo*. As the education sector is often a main public employer, that is in many states it accounts for over 70 per cent of all public sector jobs, it is subject to this practice at all levels.[17] *Empreguismo* leads to a lack of continuity and to the appointment of people on the basis of political affiliation instead of competence. Another consequence of *empreguismo* is that many employees hold jobs outside the educational system or are not even working at all.

Federal funding and scholarships were also manipulated for political purposes. The home state of the President and his allies received a disproportionate share of all scholarships. Moreover, as part of the allocation of scholarships was delegated to members of Congress, they are often traded for cash or support. Many states – especially the poor ones – remained dependent on federal funding in order to keep their educational systems running, despite the transfer of taxing authority from the federal government to the states and municipalities in 1988. Only a fraction of the federal funds are redistributed on the basis of objective criteria such as the size of the population and local tax revenues. The largest share flowed into special projects to promote education in poor rural and urban areas, of which the distribution largely depends on the political ties of mayors (Plank, 1996).

In Mexico the financing of education was highly centralised until 1993. This is in contrast to the Brazilian situation, where the states provide most of the funding (around 65 per cent in 1995), The centralised bureaucracy was highly politicised, illustrated by the allocation of key jobs in the Ministry of Public Education to political allies, who may not be the most competent employees. Like Brazil high officials often used resources in education for personal gains. Centralisation led to a multiplication of management levels, as many as 17, between the federal government and the teachers. Central planning ignored the differences in educational needs between the different regions. The Reform of 1993, which formally transferred the responsibility for education from the federal to the state governments, had little effect on the improvement of the functioning of the system. This is mainly because the federal government retained control over most of the system (Guevara Niebla, 1995; Ornelas, 1995).

Conclusion

The economic laggard position of Brazil and Mexico relative to the USA is partly explained by the historical development of their respective educational systems. The determinants discussed here are not exhaustive, as the more rapid development of education in the USA may also be explained by the more rapid urbanisation and quicker improvements in transport and communication networks (see Chapter 4). The spread of education in all countries has been favoured by international developments, such as the advancement of educational science, and the promotion of education by international organisations such as the Inter-American Development Bank, UNESCO and the World Bank. The racial mix has also affected the development of the educational system in all three countries. For example, in southern US states with substantial non-white populations, the expansion of education was much slower than in the predominantly white states of the north. The racial mix in poor states in Brazil and Mexico also slowed down the development of education. Independence has accelerated the spread of education in the USA, this in contrast to Brazil and Mexico (Meyer *et al.*, 1977; Meyer *et al.*, 1992).

OUTPUT AND PRODUCTIVITY LEVELS

In Brazil and Mexico the rapid growth of employment in education has improved educational standards, although the quality of education remains generally low. This assessment is verified here by comparing labour productivity levels with the USA using the industry-of-origin approach. The benchmark years for the comparisons are 1980 for Brazil/USA and 1987/88 for Mexico/USA. The benchmark year used for the other sectors, 1975, could not be used here due to data limitations.

Table 8.7 shows value added and employment in education for the benchmark years. In Brazil and Mexico private education accounted for a larger share of value added relative to the USA. In terms of employment the private sector represented a much smaller share in Mexico and the USA when compared to Brazil.

Measurement of Output

Output of education can be defined by its contribution to human capital formation. The SNA 1993 views educational services as teaching provided by producers of education services – schools, colleges, universities – to pupils and students who consume such services. Nominal output is commonly measured by total revenues in market-oriented institutions and total costs in public outfits. Real output measures are constructed using quantity relatives of each service weighted by their share in costs or revenues. The SNA stresses the importance of distinguishing as many kinds of education services as possible, as their relative costs and qualities may vary substantially. Quality depends on the number of pupils per teacher or the amount of capital equipment in the form of laboratories, libraries, computers and so on.

Nominal output can be deflated using volume measures based on outcome indicators, 'throughput' measures and inputs. SNA 1993 and ESA 1995 recommend the use of 'throughput' indicators, such as the number of students. This is also the practice in most OECD countries, in addition to the use of input indicators such as the number of teachers or teachers' salaries deflated by the CPI (OECD, 1996).

Table 8.7 *Value Added and Employment in Education, Brazil/USA, 1980 and Mexico/USA, 1987/88*

	Value Added in Million National Currency Units		Employment (000s)	
	Brazil (Cruzeiros) or Mexico (Pesos)	USA	Brazil or Mexico	USA
	Brazil/USA, 1980			
Private education	106,879	16,428	409	1,376
Public education	236,690	104,372*	1,334	7,330
Total	343,569	120,800	1,743	8,706
	Mexico/USA, 1987/88 (1988 prices)			
Census:				
Private Education	1,048,778	4,256	162	153
National accounts:				
Private education	2,828,472	31,892	231	1,713
Public education	10,666,430	182,248*	1,876	7,949
Total	13,494,902	214,139	2,107	9,662

Notes: * Value added is estimated by the total compensation of employees, see Department of Commerce, Bureau of Economic Analysis (May 1993), *Survey of Current Business*, p. 43.

Sources: Brazil: IBGE (1989b). Mexico: census from INEGI (1993); national accounts data from INEGI (1994a). USA: Census from Department of Commerce, Bureau of the Census (1991); national accounts from Department of Commerce, Bureau of Economic Analysis (January 1992 and May 1993), *Survey of Current Business*; 1980 from Department of Commerce, Bureau of Economic Analysis (1986).

Few studies used outcome indicators. Jorgenson and Fraumeni (1992, 2000) consider education as an investment good whose value equals its effect on the lifetime income of an individual. The value is measured by the impact of one year of additional schooling on the income of a person over his or her lifetime. This income is estimated by comparing two individuals of the same sex and age and an identical number of years of education. However, one is enrolled in school but not the other. The output of schooling of the latter person is determined by the expected additional income he or she will earn over his or her lifetime compared to the individual not enrolled in school. It is supposed that all income differences are due to differences in schooling and do not result from ability, training on the job or work experience.

The approach of Jorgenson and Fraumeni was used in other intertemporal comparisons, for example by Ahlroth (1997) in Sweden, but has not been tested in international comparisons. This is probably because of the difficulty in finding international comparable data on labour income and its characteristics in terms of sex, age and schooling.

Other authors also viewed education as an investment in human capital (see Blaug, 1976; Maddison, 1974). They defined output as the '*opportunity costs*' of remaining in school instead of working, which equals the increase the average wage a person will earn over his or her working life thanks to the additional education.

A more frequently used output indicator are test scores. Tests are not only carried out in individual countries, but also between countries (see Department of Education, Educational Testing Service, 1992a, 1992b). This indicator is a valid proxy of output as long as the contents of the curriculum and exams remain stable, as well as the learning environment (family and neighbourhood conditions and so on). Rivkin (2000) controlled for these variables at the micro-level. However, this seems impossible at the level of total education or between countries.

International comparisons used mostly input indicators such as the number of teachers or a combination of input and 'throughput' measures. The UN international comparisons project (ICP) measured output in their first and second rounds by the number of teachers, adjusted for their level of education. In ICP III Kravis *et al.* (1982) took a geometric average of the quantity indices of teacher numbers and student numbers. They refer to this measure as a teacher-based quantity index, adjusted for productivity differentials. For primary and secondary education an adjustment was made for quality differences, using per capita income as a proxy. Pilat (1994) used student numbers as output measure to compare productivity between Japan, Korea and the USA.

In this study the quantity of educational services is measured by the number of students enrolled in education, adjusted for the desire of education and the quality of education. These crude enrolment figures do not however reflect: (i) the desire for education by people remaining in school after statutory age (see Blaug, 1976; Maddison, 1974); and (ii) quality differences among Brazilian, Mexican and US education systems.

The quantity figures were adjusted to account for this in the following way:

(i) '*Opportunity costs of education* are measured by the additional income a person is likely to earn over his or her working live thanks to completing the secondary or tertiary educational cycle. For this purpose Brazilian and US data on the median annual incomes of full-time workers of 25 years old and over, by years of schooling completed, have been used (Ramos, 1991, Department of Education, 1993).

In the 1980s income differences by level of education were much larger in Brazil when compared to the USA: an employee with a higher education degree earned 4.6 times as much as one with elementary school only in Brazil, whereas the USA showed an income differential of 2.5 to one. The number of secondary school students were multiplied by the ratio of the median annual income of workers with a high school degree to the income of employees with elementary school only in 1980. The number of students in higher education was multiplied by the ratio of the median income of workers with a four-year college degree to the income of employees with elementary school only. This procedure increased the 'weight' of secondary and higher education students in the total (Blaug, 1976):

$$\frac{Q^x}{Q^u}=\left[\frac{B_p{}^x}{B_p{}^u}+\frac{\left(W_s{}^x/W_p{}^x\right)B_s{}^x}{\left(W_s{}^u/W_p{}^u\right)B_s{}^u}+\frac{\left(W_t{}^x/W_p{}^x\right)B_t{}^x}{\left(W_t{}^u/W_p{}^u\right)B_t{}^u}\right] \tag{8.1}$$

with B indicating the number of students, W the wage level, and the underscores p, s and t refer to primary, secondary and tertiary education, respectively. Owing to the lack of information on Mexican income differences per level of education, the Brazilian income differences as a proxy were used.

(ii) *Quality of Education*: several studies (Blaug, 1976; OECD, 1990; Pilat, 1994) adjust output to account for quality differences between countries or over time. A double adjustment was made to account for quality differences. Firstly, the enrolment data were adjusted by the dropout ratio, that is the share of the pupils not completing an educational cycle. Secondly, test scores were used to adjust for the lower quality of Brazilian and Mexican education. As Mexico has not published any scores on international standardised tests, the Brazilian ones were used as a proxy. As dropout rates and test scores for higher education were lacking, those of secondary education were used as a proxy.

Unit Value Ratios and Labour Productivity

The UVRs from the comparisons are shown in Table 8.8. The UVRs obtained with student numbers as quantity relatives are extremely low: the Brazil/USA UVR was one-fifth of the exchange rate in 1980, and the Mexico/USA UVR was one-tenth of the exchange rate in 1988. Surprisingly, the relative price of Brazilian private education was below that of public education in 1980, while the opposite was found in Mexico. The adjustment for opportunity costs of attending secondary and higher education yielded somewhat lower UVRs, as these costs in Brazil and Mexico were higher relative to the USA. The double quality adjustment triples the Brazil/USA UVRs, and doubles the Mexico/USA UVRs.

Table 8.8 *Unit Value Ratios for Education, Brazil/USA, 1980 and Mexico/USA, 1987/88*

	Brazil/USA, 1980			Mexico/USA, 1987/88 (1988 prices)		
	Paasche UVRs	Laspeyres UVRs	Geometric Average	Paasche UVRs	Laspeyres UVRs	Geometric Average
			A. Unadjusted			
Private education	6.10	6.18	6.18	313.1	313.1	313.1
Public education	6.95	22.85	12.60	144.9	258.3	193.5
Total	6.69	20.59	11.73	163.3	266.5	208.6
			B. Adjusted for Opportunity Cost			
Private education	5.44	5.44	5.44	285.4	285.4	285.4
Public education	6.64	13.98	9.64	129.9	172.8	149.8
Total	6.22	12.82	8.93	146.6	189.6	166.7
			C. Adjusted for Opportunity Cost and Quality			
Private education	19.10	19.10	19.10	1,027.1	1,027.1	1,027.1
Public education	27.58	46.55	35.83	380.2	770.2	541.2
Total	24.23	42.82	32.21	438.1	808.4	595.1
Exchange rate	52.71	52.71	52.71	2,273.1	2,273.1	2,273.1

Sources: See Appendix D.

The comparative levels of labour productivity are presented in Table 8.9. These results were obtained after output (in terms of student enrolment) was adjusted for the opportunity costs of education (panel B), and quality differences (panel C). In both countries the relative performance of private education, which represents only a small share of the total system, surpassed that of public education. The results without the quality adjustment are highly implausible, as Brazilian and Mexican productivity would be 60 per cent in 1980 and 73 per cent in 1987/88 above the US level, respectively. After the quality adjustment Brazilian and Mexican productivity equalled 44 and 49 per cent of the US level, respectively.

Table 8.9 Labour Productivity in Education Brazil/USA , 1980 and Mexico/USA, 1987/88

	Brazil/USA, 1980			Mexico/USA, 1987/88		
	At Brazilian Prices	At US Prices	Geometric Average	At Mexican Prices	At US Prices	Geometric Average
			A. Unadjusted			
Private education	354.0	354.0	354.0	210.5	210.5	210.5
Public education	179.3	54.5	98.9	171.1	96.0	128.2
Total	212.3	69.0	121.0	177.0	108.4	138.5
			B. Adjusted for Opportunity Cost			
Private education	402.2	402.2	402.2	231.0	231.0	231.0
Public education	187.5	89.1	129.3	190.9	143.5	165.5
Total	228.5	110.8	159.1	197.1	152.4	173.3
			C. Adjusted for Opportunity Cost and Quality			
Private education	114.5	114.5	114.5	64.2	64.2	64.2
Public education	45.2	26.8	34.8	65.2	32.2	45.8
Total	58.6	33.2	44.1	66.0	35.7	48.6

Sources: Value added of Table 8.7 was converted with UVRs from Table 8.8, and subsequently divided by employment of Table 8.7.

The benchmark productivity results were extrapolated to the period 1950–96 using time series of GDP and employment (see Figure 8.1). Brazilian productivity decreased in the early 1980s. The Mexican performance largely improved in the 1960s, when student numbers rose rapidly. The US level performance showed a moderate negative trend over the whole period.

Relative to the USA the Brazilian performance improved during the 1970s, while that of Mexico increased in the previous decade. For both countries the 1980s was a period in which productivity stagnated, even though in Mexico the downward trend had already started in the 1970s. The inferior relative performance of Brazil relative to Mexico confirms the lower outcomes of the educational system, in terms of dropout levels, illiteracy rates and repetition levels in the former country.

Figure 8.1 *Labour Productivity in Education, Brazil and Mexico as a Per Cent of the USA (USA = 100), 1950–96*

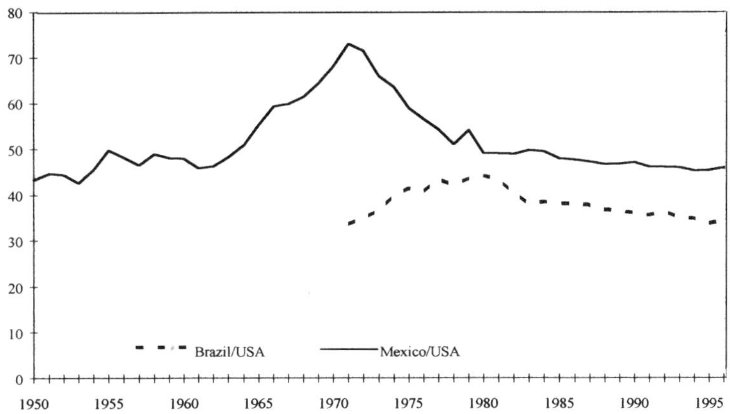

Sources: Benchmark results from Table 8.9 and time series (see Appendices A and B).

NOTES

1. A large corpus of literature exists on the relationship between human capital and economic growth (see Abramovitz, 1989; Romer, 1990; Schultz, 1961).
2. For the contribution of human capital to economic growth in Brazil and Mexico, see Hofman (1998), Lau *et al.* (1993), and in the USA, see Denison (1967), Jorgenson and Fraumeni (1992) and Kendrick (1961).
3. In Brazil secondary schooling (*segunda grau*), from the age of 15 onwards, is voluntary and consists of three- to four-year courses. There is no formal entry examination from the first level (*primeira grau*) (see Cowen and McLean, 1985, pp. 611–13). In Mexico secondary schooling consists of the obligatory *secundaria* of three years (basic secondary, age 12–14), after which different types of 'higher secondary' schools can be followed (optional): preparatory (for university), professional and technical. Completing successfully higher secondary education results in a professional certificate or *bachillerato* (see Cowen and McLean, 1985, pp. 732–33). US secondary education consists of obligatory (junior and senior) high schools (see OECD, 1990, p. 144).

4. Measured by the number of students in an educational cycle to the population in the corresponding age group. Enrolment ratios may exceed 100, indicating the presence of students older than the normal age group.
5. The number of dropouts in elementary education was calculated by the ratio of the number of students in grade six to the enrolment figure in the first grade six years earlier. Dropout ratios in secondary education are calculated in the same way. The secondary school dropout ratio was the weighted average of three types of schools: 0.5 * obligatory secondary school dropout rate plus 0.5 * (professional medio plus bachillerato)/2). The first type corresponds to the Phase I secondary education (12–14 years) and the latter two types are part of Phase II (14–18 years). This method somewhat overestimates the dropout ratio, as pupils repeating a grade were excluded.
6. Mexico was, among more than 40 countries, included in the 1994–95 round of the *Achievements in Mathematics* and *Achievements in Science* of the Boston-based International Association for the Evaluation of Educational Achievement. It tested the performances of nine and thirteen year olds in biology, chemistry, mathematics and physics.
7. In Brazil the expenditure per student was US$ 526 in primary, 621 in secondary and 5,258 in higher education in 1990 (Inter-American Development Bank, 1996).
8. This overview draws on Pulliam (1982).
9. The number of students increased from 25,000 in 1875, to 200,000 by 1890 and to 500,000 in 1900. The number of schools grew from 300 in 1862 to 6,000 in 1900.
10. Several motivations led to the establishment of a separate junior high school, including its special curriculum with a limited number of introductory courses, and the separation of young adolescents from older pupils.
11. The most important are the National Education Defence Act of 1958, the Elementary and Secondary Education Act of 1965 and the Higher Education Act of 1965.
12. In Brazil rural areas teachers often have not completed primary schooling. On standardised tests the scores of many teachers were only slightly better than their students (Plank, 1996).
13. In Brazil the distribution of students in primary education was 58 per cent in state schools, 30 per cent in municipal schools and 12 per cent in private schools in 1991. In secondary education the distribution was: 74 per cent in state schools, 1 per cent in municipal schools, 21 per cent in private schools and 5 per cent in federal schools (Plank, 1996).
14. Per child expenditure in the south-east was six times that in the north-east in 1987. In the north-east 26 per cent of all teachers, and 60 per cent in rural regions had not finished primary schooling in the same year (Plank, 1996).

15. In Brazil the evaluation of primary and secondary schooling started in 1990, using an annual sample of pupils from four different grades. In Mexico testing started in 1993 (Inter-American Development Bank, 1996).
16. The learning performance of pupils depends on many factors, as shown in Harbison and Hanushek (1992, pp. 18–26), who reviewed 152 studies for industrialised countries and 30 studies for developing countries. Most showed no significant relationship between class size and learning performance; the few that did showed either a positive or a negative one. Other factors affecting student performance include the education, experience and salary of teachers; and the expenditure on pupils, administration and facilities. The outcomes of these studies vary a lot between 'rich' and 'poor' countries. No systematic relationship was found between the various components and learning outcomes in the industrialised countries, except for the teacher performance on verbal ability tests (an indicator of skills). In developing countries it seems that education and experience of teachers matter, as do school inputs (textbooks and so on). However, there are many problems involved in conducting and interpreting these studies, not only because of poor data quality or incorrect measurement of 'administration and facilities' characteristics, but also because family background seems to matter more than the factors mentioned above.
17. At the federal level, members of the highest authority – the Federal Education Council – are appointed by the President. At the state level governors appoint their own Ministers of Education who, in turn employ many others. Nearly 20 per cent of all state jobs in education are occupied by political appointees. At the municipal level new mayors appoint administrators and teachers (Plank, 1996).

9. Commodity-producing Sectors

AGRICULTURE

Since the start of the ICOP programme in 1983 agriculture was the first sector for which international comparisons were carried out. This was because of the similarity of products, and the availability of standardised information on output, inputs, farm prices and farm accounts from the Food and Agriculture Organisation (FAO). Moreover, problems of quality, product differentiation, coverage and the application of double deflation are smaller for agriculture than for other sectors. Production statistics on agriculture distinguish only about 200 products compared to more than 15,000 for manufacturing.

Brazil, Mexico and the USA were included in a 14-country comparison for 1975 by Maddison and van Ooststroom (1984, revised in 1993). The main results are summarised in Table 9.1. On the basis of the FAO data 76 products were matched in Brazil/USA comparison, and 83 in the Mexico/USA comparison. The produced quantities of each country were valued at US producer prices, as price information of other countries was much weaker. In Maddison and Rao (1996) the analysis was extended by calculating Paasche, Laspeyres and Geary-Khamis measures of agricultural output net of feed and seed. In order to fill the gaps in the data they used the CPD (country product dummy) method which is also adopted by the International Comparisons Programme (ICP), instead of shadow prices. In combination with employment statistics labour productivity of Brazil was estimated at 10 per cent of the US level and that of Mexico at 7 per cent.

Maddison and van Ooststroom (1993) questioned the reliability of the FAO data for Brazil, as they differed strongly from the data of the Brazilian census of agriculture for various products.[1] The Mexican data also seemed questionable, as the national accounts value of output estimate for meat and vegetables production was twice that of the FAO.

Table 9.1 *Gross Value of Output, Inputs, Value Added, Employment and Labour Productivity in Agriculture: Brazil, Mexico and the USA, 1975*

	Brazil	Mexico	USA
Gross value at country's own prices (million national currency units)	173,311	121,712	92,863
Gross value at US prices (million US$)	23,600	9,042	92,863
Paasche PPPs	7	13	1
Feed and seed inputs at US prices (million US$, converted by output PPPs)	2,999	1,176	16,966
Fertilisers, pesticides and energy (million US$, valued at US unit values)	1,149	979	12,297
Other non-agricultural inputs (million US$)	1,149	863	16,619
Value added (million US$)	18,303	6,024	46,981
Paasche PPPs for value added	7.47	13.52	1.00
Employment (000s)	12,468	6,134	3,208
Labour productivity (US = 100)	10.0	6.7	100.0

Source: Maddison and van Ooststroom (1993, pp. 1–13).

MINING

Brazil, Mexico and the USA were also included in the first ICOP study on mining by Wieringa and Maddison (1985, revised), which covered the same countries and used the same benchmark year as Maddison and van Ooststroom (1993). Produced quantities of 45 types of minerals were valued at US prices. A more detailed comparison for the three countries only was made by Houben (1990, see also Table 9.2), who used the mining censuses as the basic source. He calculated Paasche, Laspeyres and Fisher PPPs based on 17 product matches for Brazil/USA, and 27 matches for the Mexico/USA comparison. In Mexico mining is dominated by oil extraction, while in Brazil and the USA a much wider range of minerals is extracted. According to Houben labour productivity equalled 55 per cent of the US level in Brazil and only 32 per cent in Mexico. Wieringa and Maddison's estimates were substantially lower, mostly because of the large differences in the employment estimates.

Table 9.2 *1975 Benchmark Results for Mining: Wieringa and Maddison (1985) and Houben (1990)*

	Gross Value Added (Paasche PPPs, US = 100)		Employment (000s persons)		Labour Productivity (Paasche) US = 100.	
	Wieringa and Maddison	Houben*	Wieringa and Maddison	Houben	Wieringa and Maddison	Houben
Brazil	2.75	6.12	93	61	22.2	55.4
Mexico	5.21	5.61	241	96	16.2	32.4
USA	100.00	100.00	752	554	100.0	100.0

Notes: * Refers to US census concept of value added which includes non-industrial services.

Sources: Wieringa and Maddison (1985, revised) and Houben (1990).

MANUFACTURING

Brazil, Mexico and the USA were the countries selected for the first pilot study on international comparisons in manufacturing by Maddison and van Ark (1988).[2] They used one single source for gross output, produced quantities, inputs, value added and employment: the census of manufactures for 1975 for Brazil and Mexico and for 1977 for the USA. This was a pioneering study in developing general guidelines for manufacturing comparisons in the framework of the ICOP project.

This study set the stage for more than 30 bilateral comparisons, including OECD countries and countries in Asia and Latin America. Their performances are compared with that of Germany or the USA for one, two or three benchmark years (most often 1975, 1987 and 1996). The Brazil/USA and Mexico/USA comparisons were updated by Mulder *et al.* (2002) for 1985 and 1988, respectively, using a refined methodology. Currently updates of both comparisons are under way for the late 1990s.

The manufacturing sectors in Brazil and Mexico underwent large changes in the past two decades. Until the late 1970s they were still highly protected against foreign competition, received large subsidies and part of manufacturing was state-owned. The debt crisis of the 1980s meant the bankruptcy of these import substitution policies and marked the beginning of more outward-oriented policies. In the late 1980s and 1990s the institutional environment completely changed as state enterprises were privatised, subsidies cut and competition reinforced through deregulation. Moreover, foreign trade was liberalised by reducing tariffs and eliminating quotas and licences. Both countries reinforced their multilateral and in particular regional trade relations through free trade agreements, of which the most important are their entrance in the regional trade agreements Mercosur and NAFTA. The increased exposure to foreign competition on the home market and abroad provided an important stimulus for firms to improve their productivity and cost performances. This process was reinforced by a large influx of foreign direct investment.

The main trends in output, employment and productivity growth in manufacturing in the 1970s to 1990s are shown in Figure 9.1. Brazil and Mexico show very different trends compared to the USA, in particular in terms of employment growth. Whereas employment grew in the Latin countries, in the USA it remained almost constant throughout the period in almost all branches, except for textiles and clothing which experienced a substantial decline.

During the entire 1970–99 period the USA experienced positive output and labour productivity growth, even though these rates were relatively low in the 1970s. Productivity growth accelerated in the second half of the 1990s and mostly in machinery. The spectacular productivity growth of this branch originates almost exclusively from the computer industry, where the volume of production increased very rapidly due to rapid price declines.

Brazil and Mexico lived periods of upturns and downturns in employment and output growth. Value added grew at relatively high rates in the 1970s and the 1990s. In the second half of the 1990s Mexico benefited from an increased demand from the USA which boosted its output growth. The most important downturns in output growth were during the debt crisis of the 1980s, in particular in Brazil. Both countries show very different trends in employment growth. In Brazil employment grew in the 1970s and between 1983 and 1989 and fell around 1980 and in the 1990s. In Mexico employment growth was relatively constant over time, with a deceleration in the first half of the 1980s and acceleration in the second half of the 1990s.

Figure 9.1 shows that labour productivity growth was slightly higher in Mexican manufacturing compared to Brazilian manufacturing, except for food and transport equipment where Brazil outperformed Mexico. Both Latin American countries showed significantly lower productivity growth than the USA. In addition to growth rates productivity *levels* should also be taken into account. Some countries may register high growth rates because they have low *levels* of productivity which allow them to benefit from the large catch-up potential or productivity gap. This study aims to check whether a link exists between the growth rates and levels of productivity.

Figure 9.1 Indices of Value Added, Employment and Labour Productivity (1970 = 100): Brazil

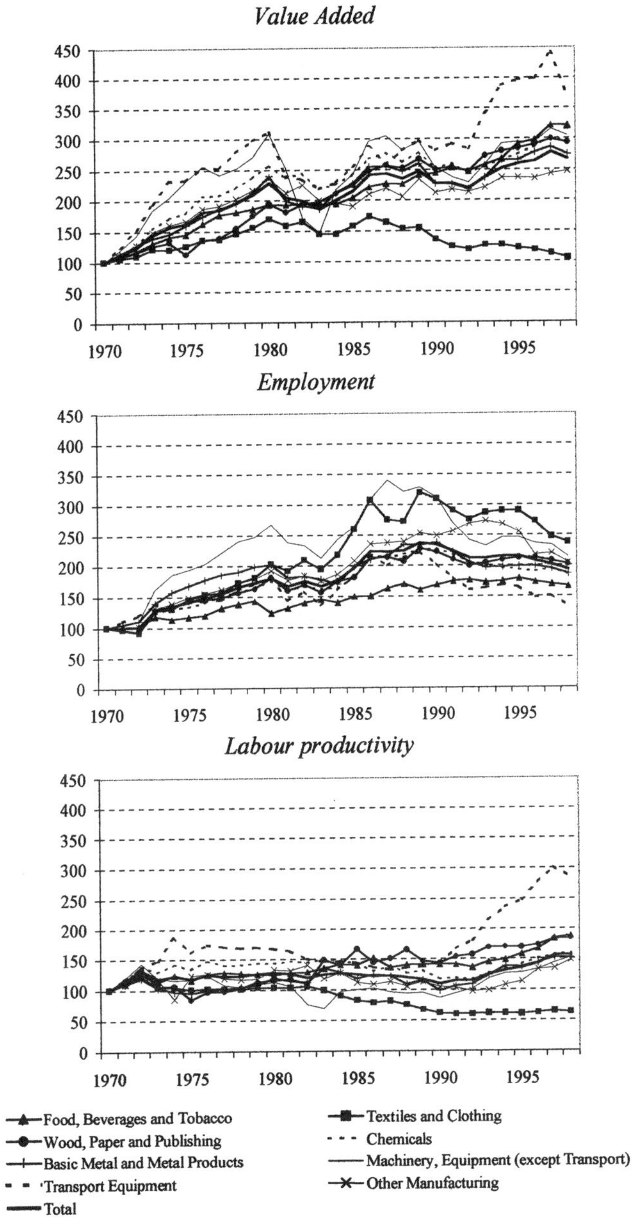

Figure 9.1 (cont.): Mexico

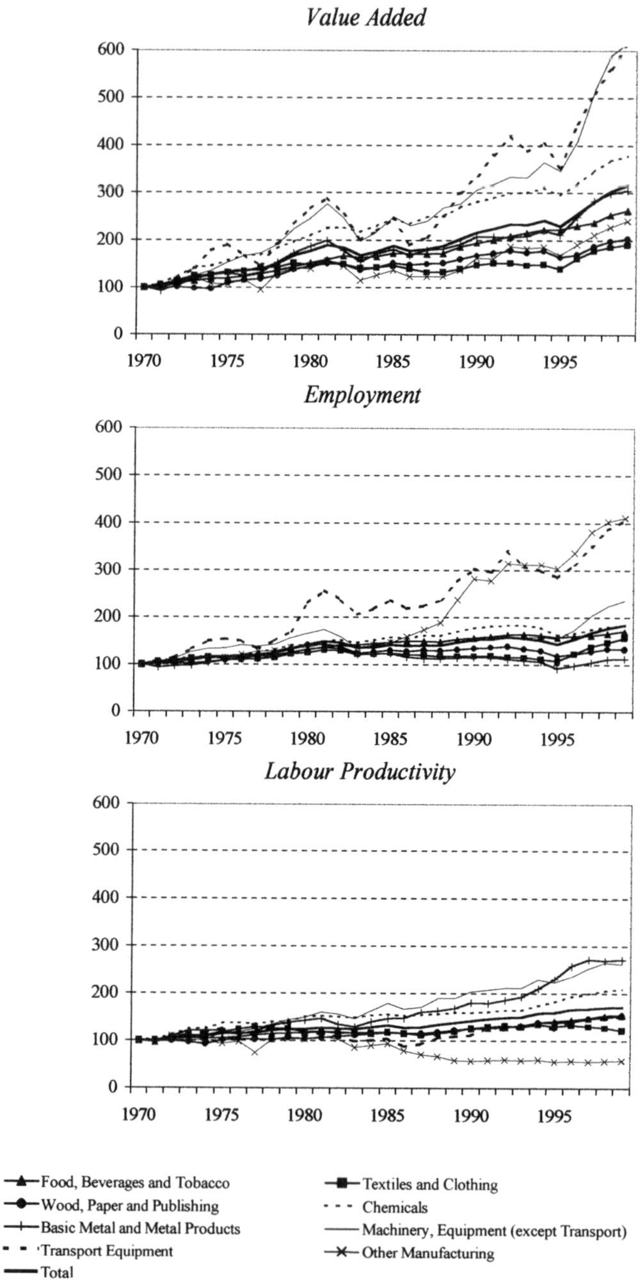

Figure 9.1 (cont.): USA

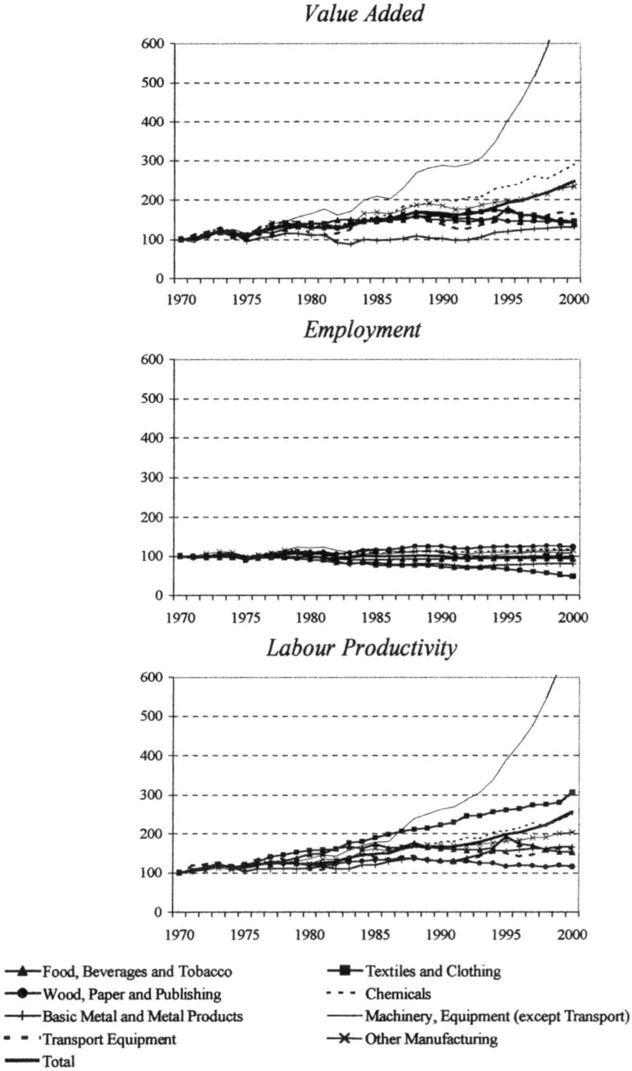

Sources: Brazil: 1970–85 from IBGE (1990), *Estatísticas Históricas do Brasil*; 1985–99 from IBGE, *Contas Nacionais* (various editions). Mexico: INEGI, *Sistema de cuentas nacionales* (various editions). USA: Department of Commerce, Bureau of Economic Analysis, *National Income and Product Accounts* (various editions). Value added series for 1947–87 are at fixed 1982 prices but reweighted at current dollar value added every five years (1947, 1952, 1957 and so on). The series from 1987–99 are chain weighted series at 1992 dollars. Employment refers to full-time and part-time employees plus self-employed.

Methodology for International Comparisons: 1975 and 1985/88

The data used for the bilateral comparisons are drawn from the censuses of production: for Brazil the *Censo industrial 1975* and *Censo industrial 1985* from IBGE, for Mexico the *X Censo industrial–1976* and *XIII Censo industrial–1989* from SPP and INEGI, respectively, and for the USA the *1977 Census of Manufactures* and *1987 Census of Manufactures* from the Bureau of the Census.

Mexico and Brazil are compared via the USA; as a comparison with this international productivity leader provides an indication of the productivity gap and the potential for catch-up for the Latin American countries. Moreover, as the US census has much more product data than the Brazilian and Mexican censuses, a link through the USA allows us to take account of more information than a direct comparison between Brazil and Mexico.

For the 1975 comparisons 14 common branches were defined in each bilateral comparison. Within these branches 27 sample industries were selected for which 129 products were matched in the Brazil/USA comparison and 130 in the Mexico/USA comparison (see Table 9.3). Most matches were made in food, beverages and tobacco and chemicals. The derivation of unit values of products, the ratio of unit values between two countries and the aggregation of UVRs is the same as for services; see equations (4.1) to (4.6). In contrast to services the UVRs often do not cover total output of an industry, as information in quantity is often missing or comparable products cannot be found in the two countries. The matched products can be considered as a sampled subset of products within an industry where relative price, under certain conditions, may be judged representative for the non-matched part.

The UVRs of the sample of matched products were considered reliable for an entire industry if they covered, on average, at least 25 per cent of its output in the two countries. Sample industries were selected on the basis of the possibility of matching a significant part of output between two countries; as such the product matches covered between 28 and 96 per cent of industry output. However, the matches covered much lower shares of branch output (see Table 9.3), that is between 11 and 44 per cent of output. The highest coverage ratios were in food, beverages and tobacco and in chemicals.

The branch UVRs were obtained by weighting the UVRs of the representative industries with value added according to equations (4.15) and (4.16). In the final stage branch UVRs are weighted at branch value added to obtain a UVR for total manufacturing. No products were matched in 'other manufacturing', and instead total manufacturing UVRs were assumed representative. The international price level of a country is defined as the ratio of the UVR to the exchange rate: a ratio above 1 indicates that producer prices in Brazil or Mexico are above those in the USA. In 1975 Brazilian prices were on average slightly below those in the USA, whereas Mexican prices were 9 per cent above the US level. In both Latin American countries the lowest prices were in food, beverages and tobacco. The highest were in chemicals in Brazil and wood, paper and publishing in Mexico.

Table 9.3 *Number of Product Matches, Unit Value Ratios and Percentage of Matched Sales, Brazil/USA and Mexico/USA, 1975*

	Number of	Unit Value Ratios (National currency/US$)			Price Level	Matched as % of Total Output	
	Product Matches	At Other Country Weights	At US Weights	Geo-metric Average	(US = 100)	Brazil	USA
		Brazil/USA					
Food, beverages, tobacco	31	4.59	6.49	5.46	67.1	39.6	25.5
Textiles and clothing	12	7.18	9.56	8.28	101.9	38.1	24.7
Wood, paper and publishing	10	9.78	11.35	10.54	129.6	23.1	14.7
Chemicals	41	10.26	12.05	11.12	136.8	29.2	30.5
Basic metals, metal products	12	6.20	8.07	7.07	87.0	30.7	15.9
Machinery and equipment	23	7.14	7.50	7.32	90.0	18.0	22.3
Other manufacturing	0	6.91	8.77	7.79	95.8	0.0	0.0
Total	129	6.91	8.77	7.79	95.8	27.9	22.9
		Mexico/USA					
Food, beverages, tobacco	31	8.07	12.59	10.08	80.7	29.8	25.3
Textiles and clothing	8	15.46	18.41	16.87	135.0	20.9	24.4
Wood, paper and publishing	15	18.38	22.69	20.42	163.3	27.7	16.4
Chemicals	43	11.82	13.09	12.44	99.5	43.8	30.5
Basic metals, metal products	13	11.50	12.35	11.92	95.4	33.6	14.7
Machinery and equipment	20	15.17	15.43	15.30	122.4	24.0	10.8
Other manufacturing	0	11.99	15.62	13.68	109.5	0.0	0.0
Total	130	11.97	15.62	13.67	109.4	31.8	22.8

Notes: The percentages of matched output were available only at a more detailed level. It was assumed that within branches value added is a constant share of output, which allowed us to aggregate coverage ratios using value added weights.

Sources: van Ark (1993) and van Ark and Maddison (1994).

In the 1985/88 comparisons carried out in 2001 the procedures were refined incorporating the experiences of almost two decades of international comparisons in manufacturing (see Timmer, 2000, Timmer *et al.*, 2001). Instead of the more or less arbitrary selection of 27 broadly defined 'sample' industries in the 1975 comparisons, an industry is defined in the new comparisons as the most detailed common entity between two countries for which data are available for output, inputs and employment. As such 229 detailed common industries were identified in the Brazil/USA comparison and 223 industries in the Mexico/USA comparison covering total production. The advantage of this procedure is that matches will represent a larger variety of industries. Moreover, the more detailed the industries, the more realistic the assumption of the representativity of matched output for the non-matched part of an industry.

In the new comparisons the representativity of the UVRs of the matches does not only depend on their coverage of industry output, but also their variance. Given the homogeneous character of the products belonging to an industry, it is expected that product UVRs in an industry do not differ much. Hence, if the variation of the product UVRs is high, this is deemed an indication of unreliability. As reliability increases with the percentage of industry output covered by matched products, the coverage ratio is also taken into account. This is done by using the so-called finite population correction in calculating the variance. The variance of the industry UVRs is given by the mean of the weighted deviations of the product UVRs around the industry UVR (see Selvanathan, 1991):

$$Var\left[UVR_J\right] = (1 - f_{j)})\frac{1}{I_j - 1}\sum_{i=1}^{I_j} w_{ij}\left(UVR_{ij} - UVR_j\right)^2 \qquad (9.1)$$

with I_j the number of products matched in industry i and f_j the share of industry output covered by the matches. $(1 - f_j)$ is the 'finite population correction', and ensures that an increase in sample coverage reduces its variance. This equation can be applied to either the Laspeyres or Paasche UVRs using output value weights of the base country for the Laspeyres variance, and quantity weights of the other country valued at US prices for the Paasche variance. To determine the reliability of a sample the (geometric) average is taken of the Paasche and Laspeyres variances.

The coefficient of variation of industry j (cv_j) is measured as follows:

$$cv\left[UVR_j\right] = \frac{\sqrt{var[UVR_j]}}{UVR_j} \qquad (9.2)$$

The following decision rule is used: when the coefficient of variation is less than 0.1 the industry is assigned to $J_k(a)$, other wise to $J_k(b)$:

$$\begin{array}{llll} \text{if} & cv\lfloor UVR_j \rfloor < 0.1 & \text{then} & j \in J_k(a) \\ \text{otherwise} & & & j \in J_k(b) \end{array} \tag{9.3}$$

The aggregation to branch UVRs is done by weighting the industry UVRs by either US quantities:

$$UVR_k^{xu(u)} = \sum_{j=1}^{J_k} \left(UVR_{jk}^{xu(u)} \times w_{jk}^{u(u)} \right) \tag{9.4a}$$

The aggregation to branch UVRs is done by weighting the industry UVRs by either US quantities:

$$UVR_k^{xu(u)} = \sum_{j=1}^{J_k} \left(UVR_{jk}^{xu(u)} \times w_{jk}^{u(u)} \right) \tag{9.4b}$$

with j = 1,..., J_k the number of industries in branch k for which at least one UVR has been calculated; w_{jk} the output share of the jth industry in branch k. The industries for which the UVRs are reliable ($J_k(a)$) are weighted with the total industry output at own prices: $o_{jk}^{T\,u(u)}$. The UVRs from the other industries (belonging to $J_k(b)$) are weighted only by the output value of the matched products in the industry: $o_{jk}^{M\,u(u)} = \sum_{i=1}^{I_j} uv_{ij}^{u} q_{ij}^{u}$. Hence the weights are given by:

$$\begin{array}{ll} w_{jk}^{u(u)} = o_{jk}^{T\,u(u)} / o_k^{M\,u(u)} & \forall j \in J_k(a) \\ w_{jk}^{u(u)} = o_{jk}^{M\,u(u)} / o_k^{M\,u(u)} = \sum_{i=1}^{I_j} uv_{ij}^{u} q_{ij}^{u} / o_k^{M\,u(u)} & \forall j \in J_k(b) \end{array} \tag{9.5}$$

with $$o_k^{M\,u(u)} = \sum_{J_k(a)} o_{jk}^{T\,u(u)} + \sum_{J_k(b)} o_{jk}^{M\,u(u)}$$

To arrive at the Paasche index the US weights are replaced by the Brazilian or Mexican output valued at US prices:

$$UVR_k^{xu(x)} = \sum_{j=1}^{J_k} \left(UVR_{jk}^{xu(x)} \times w_{jk}^{u(x)} \right) \tag{9.6}$$

with

$$\begin{aligned} w_{jk}^{u(x)} &= o_{jk}^{T\,u(x)} / o_k^{M\,u(x)} & \forall j \in J_k(a) \\ w_{jk}^{u(x)} &= o_{jk}^{M\,u(x)} / o_k^{M\,u(x)} = \sum_{i=1}^{I_j} uv_{ij}^{u} q_{ij}^{x} / o_k^{M\,u(x)} & \forall j \in J_k(b) \end{aligned} \tag{9.7}$$

with

$$o_k^{M\,u(x)} = \sum_{J_k(a)} o_{jk}^{T\,u(x)} + \sum_{J_k(a)} o_{jk}^{M\,u(x)}$$

The aggregation of branch to total manufacturing UVRs is done in the same way as that from the industry to the branch UVRs. US country output weights are used to arrive at the Laspeyres index, and the 'other' country quantities valued at US prices are used to arrive at the Paasche index. The Laspeyres and Paasche indices are combined into a Fisher index when a single currency conversion factor is required.

There is one important difference between aggregation steps two and three, that is the output weights of the branch do not depend on the reliability of their UVRs. The branch UVRs always enter the weighting system with their total production, as they are considered the most 'characteristic' for the branch even when their variance is high and/or their representativeness low. Nevertheless, it should be stressed that the UVRs for branches with a coefficient of variation above 0.1 should be interpreted with care.

Branch variance is calculated, as indicated by the stratified sampling theory, by the quadratic output weighted average of the corresponding industry UVRs:

$$Var\left[UVR_k\right] = \left(1 - f_k\right) \sum_{j=1}^{J_j} w_{jk}^2 var\left[UVR_{jk}\right] \tag{9.8}$$

with f_k the share of branch output covered by matched products. Two variances are estimated: one using US and one using 'other' country weights, of which a geometric average is taken.

Finally, the sample variance of the UVR for total manufacturing is given by the quadratic output weighted average of the corresponding branch UVR variances:

$$Var[UVR] = \sum_{k=1}^{K} w_k^2 var[UVR_k] \qquad (9.9)$$

In the new 1985 Brazil/USA comparison 213 matches were made compared to 129 in 1975. In the 1988 Mexico/USA comparison 435 matches were made compared to 130 in 1975 (see Table 9.4). The larger number of product matches covered a substantially higher share of output: 39 instead of 28 per cent of output in 1985 compared to 1975 in Brazil, and 46 compared to 32 per cent in Mexico. The share of US output covered was also higher in the Mexico/US comparison (33 versus 23 per cent), but lower in the Brazil/USA comparison (19 versus 23 per cent). In both bilateral comparisons most matches were made in food, beverages and tobacco and machinery and other equipment. Other branches with many matchings in the Brazil/USA comparison were wood, paper and publishing, and in the Mexico/USA comparison chemicals. In contrast to van Ark and Maddison matches were also made in other manufacturing, even though they represented only a small share of output.[3]

Industry, branch and total manufacturing UVRs were calculated using the old (van Ark and Maddison) and new methodologies. The main differences between the two are that the latter uses the coefficient of variation instead of the 25 per cent rule to determine representativity. Moreover, the latter aggregates UVRs using gross output instead of value added. Although the two methods yield almost the same result for total manufacturing, they produce outcomes which differ up to 15 per cent of the branch level (see columns 2 and 3).[4]

The aggregate UVRs obtained with the new method were divided by the exchange rate to derive the average price level. On average Brazilian manufacturing products were less expensive than those of Mexico (66 and 77 per cent of the US price level) in 1985 and 1988, respectively. Brazil and Mexico each had price advantages and disadvantages in different branches. In Brazil the lowest price levels were in transport equipment, and food, beverages and tobacco and the highest in chemicals. In Mexico the lowest relative prices were in food, beverages and tobacco and other manufacturing, and the highest in machinery and other equipment, and basic metals and metal products.

The UVRs for total manufacturing of both Brazil/USA and Mexico/USA comparisons turn out to be very reliable, as the coefficients of variations are well below 0.1 (see columns 5 and 6). The variation coefficients of the Brazil/USA comparison are twice as high as those of the Mexico/USA comparison indicating that the latter are even more consistent. With regard to individual branches, the coefficient of variation for machinery and other equipment in the Brazil/USA comparison and the one for other manufacturing in the Mexico/USA comparison are relatively high.

Table 9.4 Number of Product Matches, Unit Value Ratios, Coefficients of Variation and Percentage of Matched Sales, Brazil/USA, 1985 and Mexico/USA, 1988

	Number of Product Matches	UVRs, Fisher (Curr. per US$) New Method	UVRs, Fisher (Curr. per US$) Old Method	Price Level (USA = 100)	Coefficient of Variation Other Country Weights	Coefficient of Variation US Weights	Matched as % of Total Output Other Country	Matched as % of Total Output USA
		Brazil/USA, 1985						
Food, beverages, tobacco	50	3,068	3,006	49	0.038	0.083	63.9	39.2
Textiles and clothing	17	4,081	4,280	66	0.142	0.024	24.1	8.6
Wood, paper and publishing	41	3,343	3,935	54	0.016	0.051	50.2	23.5
Chemicals	31	6,667	5,940	107	0.049	0.073	33.0	9.0
Basic metals, metal products	20	4,319	4,147	70	0.038	0.056	27.6	17.5
Machinery/other equipment	45	4,035	3,950	65	0.105	0.077	27.3	11.3
Transport equipment	7	2,899	3,228	47	0.010	0.008	56.3	25.4
Other manufacturing	2	4,613	6,102	74	n.a.	n.a.	8.1	5.6
Total	213	4,095	4,118	66	0.029	0.029	39.1	19.4
Exchange rate		6,202	6,202					
		Mexico/USA, 1988						
Food, beverages, tobacco	75	1,457	1,461	64	0.030	0.033	62.3	67.4
Textiles and clothing	72	1,552	1,533	68	0.018	0.038	54.1	62.0
Wood, paper and publishing	44	1,968	1,816	86	0.020	0.020	51.2	31.3
Chemicals	75	1,826	1,914	80	0.028	0.040	31.8	19.4
Basic metals, metal products	54	2,064	1,980	90	0.027	0.026	45.8	35.0
Machinery/other equipment	83	2,179	2,134	95	0.030	0.041	28.4	13.4
Transport equipment	21	1,961	1,690	86	0.029	0.050	49.8	34.6
Other manufacturing	11	1,603	1,593	70	0.210	0.101	16.4	8.5
Total	435	1,758	1,779	77	0.012	0.015	46.1	33.3
Exchange rate		2,290	2,290					

Source: Mulder *et al.* (2002).

Reconciliation of Industrial Census Data with the National Accounts

Before calculating relative productivity levels, it is important to assess the consistency of the information in the censuses with estimates of output and employment in the national accounts (see Table 9.5). A major difficulty in reconciling census information with the national accounts is that the value added concepts in the censuses differ strongly from those in the national accounts.[5] Using detailed definitions and data from the production censuses, van Ark and Maddison (1994) and Mulder *et al.* (2002) harmonised the value added data between the censuses and the national accounts for Brazil and Mexico. US census value added could not be harmonised with national accounts value added, as the census lacks information on non-industrial service inputs.

Table 9.5 Comparison of Census and National Accounts Estimates of Value Added and Employment, Brazil, Mexico and the USA, 1975/80/85/87/88

	Value Added (Million national Currency)			Employment (000s)		
	Census (Present NA Concept)	National Accounts	Ratio	Census	National Accounts	Ratio
Brazil, 1975	263,269	268,927	0.98	n.a.	n.a.	
Brazil, 1980				4,839	6,939	0.70
Brazil, 1985[a]	375,182	419,960	0.89	5,231	8,063	0.65
Mexico, 1975	168,100	232,077	0.72	1,674	2,003[b]	0.84
Mexico, 1988[a]	59,450	88,215	0.67	2,576	2,981[b]	0.86
USA, 1977	442,485[c]	341,123	1.30	18,302	18,685	0.98
USA, 1987	1,138,204[c]	866,541	1.31	18,751	19,318	0.97

Notes:
[a] Value added expressed in billion national currency.
[b] Employees only.
[c] Not directly comparable with national accounts value added, as census value added could not be adjusted to the national accounts concept.

Sources: 1975 and 1980 from van Ark and Maddison (1994) and 1985/87/88 from Mulder *et al.* (2002).

In Brazil, non-industrial services[6] were deducted from census value added (*valor de transformação industrial*) to compare it with national accounts value added. In 1975 adjusted census value added was only 2 per cent smaller than national accounts value added. National accounts understated industrial output by relying almost exclusively on activity registered in the census. The national accounts made almost no imputation for activity of the industrial workers outside the census (referred to as *autonomos* or non-census establishments). This result was confirmed by other authors cited in van Ark and Maddison (1994), and the employment gap of 30 per cent between the census and national accounts in 1980. In 1985 national accounts value added seems more realistic as it is 10 per cent higher than census value added, while the employment gap even slightly increased between the census and the national accounts.

In Mexico the value added definitions of the census and national accounts are similar, except for the inclusion of the costs of patents, licences, technical assistance and technology transfers, and rental costs of machinery, equipment and other goods in the former. Census value added was adjusted correspondingly.[7] Mexican census value added also include indirect taxes. The most important cases for which a correction was made are alcoholic beverages and tobacco and tobacco products.

The Mexican national accounts make substantial adjustments for activity excluded from the census, as the value added estimates are 38 and 48 per cent higher than those of the census in 1975 and 1988, respectively. The census seems to exclude more than just the small establishments of the informal sector, as value added per person is lower in the census than in the national accounts figures. This paradoxical result may be due to the fact that the national accounts only include paid employees, whereas in the informal sector there is a high proportion of low and unpaid family employees. Nevertheless, the Mexican national accounts are likely to make too big imputations for informal activity outside the census.

For the USA census and national accounts value added cannot be compared as the census provides no detailed information on inputs of non-industrial services. Census value added was 31 per cent higher than national accounts value added, reflecting mostly the inclusion of the non-industrial services. The employment estimates of the two sources are almost the same, despite the fact that the census excludes firms without employees. However, they account for only a small share of manufacturing output, for example 0.5 per cent in 1975 (van Ark and Maddison, 1994).

In principle national accounts are preferred to censuses in order to assess the performance of the entire manufacturing sector, census establishments and informal production. However, with the likely underestimation and overestimation of value added in the Brazilian and Mexican national accounts, respectively, these sources would produce odd results. It was decided to stick to the census for Brazil and Mexico, and the national accounts for the USA; for the latter census value added could not be adjusted.

Labour Productivity Levels, 1975 and 1985/88

Brazilian and Mexican labour productivity in 1975 were 48 and 37 per cent, respectively, of the US level in 1975 (see Table 9.6). The most productive branches in Brazil were chemicals and food, beverage and tobacco, and in Mexico basic metals and metal products, and chemicals. From 1975 to 1985/88 Brazilian and Mexican relative levels each fell by 6 percentage points. In Brazil productivity fell most in chemicals, followed by food, beverages and tobacco, and clothing. Despite the overall drop in relative performance, productivity in basic metals and metal products grew 10 percentage points. In Mexico no branch succeeded in increasing its relative performance and only wood, paper and publishing and machinery and equipment maintained their relative levels. Productivity in all other branches fell, most of which was in basic metals and metal products.

Table 9.6 *Relative Levels of Labour Productivity, Value Added, Employment and Prices, Brazil/USA and Mexico/USA, 1975, 1985 and 1988 (USA = 100)*

	Relative Labour Productivity	Relative Value Added	Relative Employment	Relative Price Level	Relative Labour Productivity	Relative Value Added	Relative Employment	Relative Price Level
	Brazil/USA, 1975				*Brazil/USA, 1985*			
Food, beverages, tobacco	57	21	36	67	45	23	49	49
Textiles and clothing	52	14	26	102	52	12	50	66
Wood, paper, publishing	29	6	20	130	28	24	19	54
Chemicals	67	11	16	137	33	17	36	107
Basic metals & products	42	10	24	87	53	10	25	70
Machinery, equipment	52	8	15	90	56	24	16	65
Transport equipment					52	8	15	47
Other manufacturing	39	6	16	96	34	1	29	74
Total	48	10	20	96	42	12	27	66
	Mexico/USA, 1975				*Mexico/USA, 1988*			
Food, beverages, tobacco	36	9	24	81	25	8	32	64
Textiles and clothing	38	4	12	135	33	7	21	68
Wood, paper, publishing	22	1	6	163	22	2	8	86
Chemicals	39	6	16	99	31	5	17	80
Basic metals & products	43	4	10	95	29	3	12	90
Machinery, equipment	31	2	6	122	17	1	9	95
Transport equipment					51	4	8	86
Other manufacturing	29	1	4	109	19	2	10	70
Total	37	3	9	109	27	4	13	77

Sources: 1975 from van Ark and Maddison (1994) and 1985/88 from Mulder *et al.* (2002).

The fall in productivity levels from the mid-1970s to the mid-1980s in Brazil and Mexico originated from the more rapid growth in employment than output in the Latin American countries relative to the USA. There seems to be no inverse relationship between productivity and price levels, as both productivity and price levels fell from the mid-1970s to the mid-1980s. The 1975 and 1985/88 comparisons showed that in Brazil chemicals were the most expensive and food products and transport equipment the cheapest. In Mexico the most expensive products in 1985/88 include wood, paper and publishing and machinery and other equipment.

Relative Prices and Productivity, 1970–99

The 1985 and 1988 price levels were extrapolated with trends in manufacturing prices and exchange rates (see Figure 9.2). Brazilian and Mexican relative price levels were similar between 1970 and 1990. The trends reflect major changes in exchange rate regimes. In the 1970s Brazil and Mexico maintained a fixed peg, even though Brazil depreciated its currency a little every year. As inflation was higher in the Latin American countries than in the USA, these countries' relative prices strongly increased. Only when Mexico dropped its fixed exchange rate in 1976 and when Brazil depreciated its currency by 30 per cent in 1979 the two countries became more price competitive. The 1982 debt crises led to a massive depreciation of the Brazilian and Mexican currencies lowering their price levels.

From 1985 onwards the Brazilian government strongly controlled the nominal exchange rate while inflation accelerated, causing a steep rise in the price level. This policy changed in 1989 with a range of stop-and-go policies, fixing the exchange rate for some months and introducing subsequently major devaluations. This led to a sharp drop in the price level between 1989 and 1991. In the subsequent years the exchange rate was stabilised using massive market interventions, until the introduction of the real in July 1994.

The Mexican monetary policy also constrained devaluations from 1986 to 1994, which in combination with higher inflation compared to the USA led to an overvaluation of its currency. The peso crisis at the end of 1994 caused a major devaluation and large drop in the price level, followed by several years of relative price increases.

Figure 9.2 also shows the price levels of the total economy, estimated by the ratio of the PPP for total final expenditure to the exchange rate. In Mexico the overall price level was below that of manufacturing during the entire period, as expected by the Balassa hypothesis. The trends for manufacturing and the total economy were almost the same. The few years for which PPPs are available for Brazil show the contrary. This is explained by the introduction of the real in 1993–94, which led to a strong increase in the relative price level. Sectors exposed to international competition, such as manufacturing, limited much more than the non-tradable sector the price increases to limit the loss of market shares on their home and foreign markets.

Figure 9.2 *Trends in Brazilian and Mexican Relative Price Levels in Manufacturing (ratio of UVR to exchange rate) and the Total Economy (ratio of PPP to exchange rate), USA = 1*

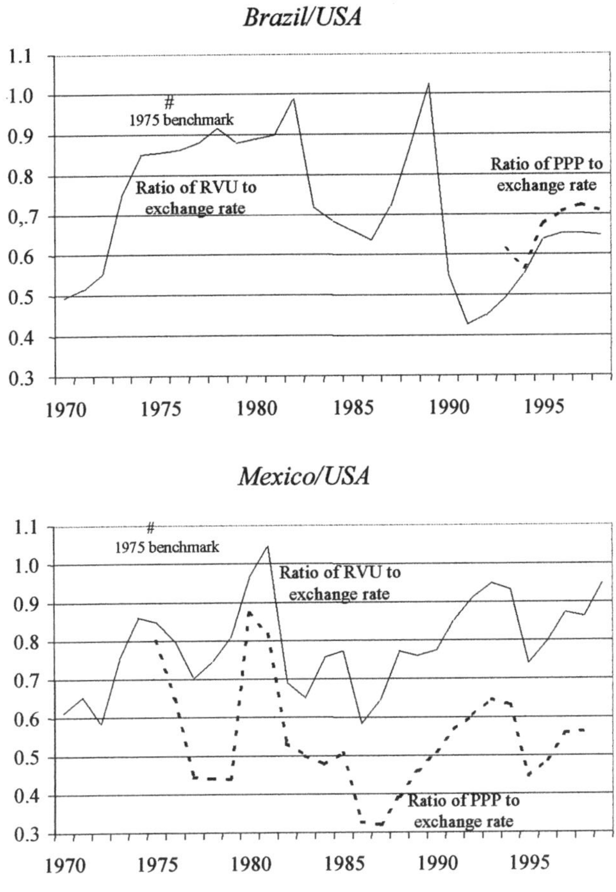

Sources: Benchmark UVRs from Table 9.4, extrapolated with time series of manufacturing deflators, derived by dividing current value added by constant value added from the national accounts as described in Figure 9.1. PPPs are from World Bank (2001), *World Development Indicators*. Price levels of the total economy are measured by the ratio of the PPP to exchange rate; and those of manufacturing by the ratio of the UVR to exchange rate. Series of nominal exchange rates from CEPII, the CHELEM database.

The productivity estimates for 1985 and 1988 are extrapolated with time series for value added at constant prices and employment for the 1970–99 period (see Figure 9.3). As productivity growth was faster in the USA than in Brazil and Mexico (see Figure 9.1), the productivity gaps widened over time. The largest drop occurred during the 'lost decade' of the 1980s. In the 1990s Brazil managed to stabilise the productivity gap, whereas Mexico's position further eroded after the peso crisis at the end of 1994. As productivity growth in the USA accelerated in the 1990s, the performance of Mexico until 1995 and that of Brazil throughout the decade are rather remarkable.

Figure 9.3 Labour Productivity Levels in Manufacturing, Brazil and Mexico as Per Cent of the USA, 1970–98 (USA = 100)

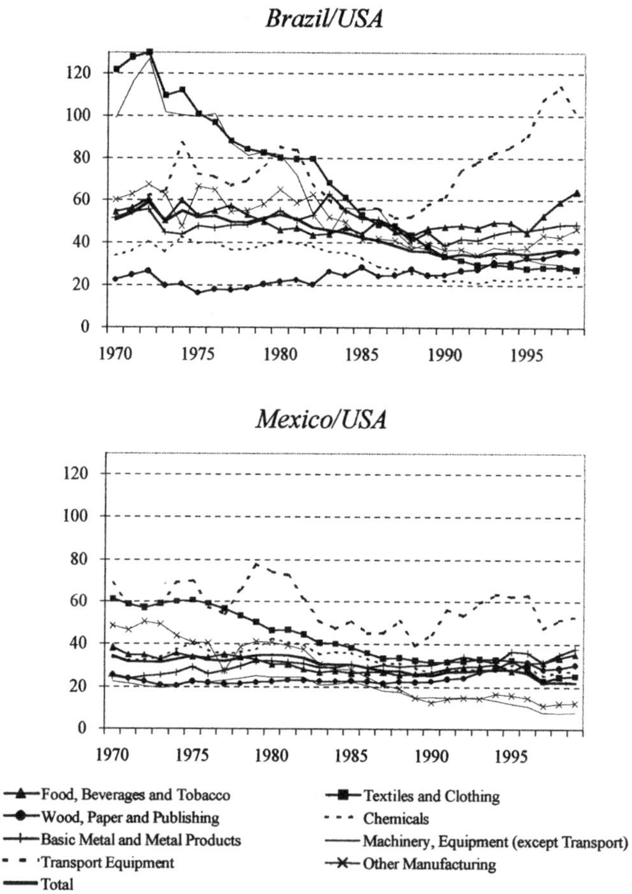

Sources: Benchmark productivity levels from Table 9.6, extrapolated with time series of value added and employment, as described in Figure 9.1.

In Brazil most industries lost ground *vis-à-vis* the USA, except for transport equipment, wood and paper and to a lesser extent food, beverages and tobacco. For Brazil consistent series of value added and employment only exist for the 1990s. These had to be combined with two other series for the 1980s and the 1970s. In particular for textiles and clothing, machinery and equipment, and transport equipment, the final series produce odd results in terms of trends in relative productivity levels.[8]

In Mexico the only branches that did *not* lose ground relative to their counterparts in the USA are basic metals and metal products and wood and wood products. As in Brazil the largest relative productivity decline was observed in textiles and clothing. The Mexican time series produce more plausible results than those of Mexico, partly because of the availability of long-run time series of the national accounts for value added and employment.

An important question is whether the differences in growth rates between Brazil and the USA in textiles and clothing, machinery and transport equipment are real or due to inconsistencies in the time series. For this purpose the plausibility of the time series is checked by using them to backdate our 1985 benchmark estimates to 1975.[9] The retropolated productivity result from 1985 to 1975 was 56 per cent of the US level, which was 7.5 percentage points higher than the result of Maddison and van Ark (see Table 9.7). Although the results for food products and basic metals and metal products were close, those for the other branches show major discrepancies. This seriously questions the Brazilian time series.

The same exercise was carried out for the Mexico/USA comparison. In contrast to the Brazil/USA comparison, the extrapolated results for Mexico from 1988 to 1975 are very close to those of van Ark and Maddison. This finding holds for total manufacturing, as well as most branches except textiles and clothing and other manufacturing.

Unit Labour Costs

Relative productivity levels are an important determinant of international competitiveness. However, some countries may not be handicapped by low productivity if at the same time labour compensation is also low. The net result of relative productivity and relative remuneration is expressed by the concept of unit labour costs. It divides labour compensation in country x relative to that in the USA by the labour productivity in x relative to that in the USA:

$$ULC^{xu} = \frac{\left(\frac{(W/N)^x}{ER^{xu}}\right)}{\frac{(W/N)^u}{RLP^{xu}}} \quad (9.10)$$

where ULC are unit labour costs, *W/N* compensation per employee, *ER* exchange rate and *RLP* relative level of labour productivity. Labour costs of country *x* are expressed in US$ using the exchange rate, as this is the rate at which international investors compare labour costs between countries. Labour productivity of country x, however, is converted into US$ by the UVR as this is the rate that should be applied to compare real output per person between countries.In Brazil and Mexico the relatively low productivity levels were largely compensated by even lower levels of labour compensation: in Brazil unit labour costs were only 23 per cent of the US level in 1985 and in Mexico only 37 per cent of the US level in 1988 (see Table 9.8). The lowest unit labour costs in Brazil were in food products and textiles and clothing, and in Mexico in chemicals and transport equipment.

Conclusion

Two benchmark comparisons of manufacturing performance are presented here: those of van Ark and Maddison (1994) for 1975, and an update for 1985/88. In 1975 Brazilian and Mexican productivities were 48 and 37 per cent of the US level, respectively. In 1985 and 1988 Brazilian and Mexican relative levels fell by 6 percentage points. Relative productivity levels strongly vary across branches.

The reliability tests of the UVRs in the 1985/88 comparisons indicate that in some branches our measures need to be improved. However, the most problematic issue, which falls outside the immediate scope of the ICOP methodology, concerns the Brazilian time series of value added and employment. In particular the time series for textiles and clothing, and machinery and transport equipment seem very implausible. An alternative and probably more reliable method to derive relative productivity estimates is to redo a full benchmark comparison each decade.[10] To obtain more reliable results for the 1990s, the way forward therefore seems to be to carry out new bilateral comparisons instead of relying on the extrapolated results from 1985 and 1988.

Table 9.7 *Extrapolation of Relative Productivity Levels from 1985/88 to 1975 and Comparison with Results of van Ark and Maddison (USA = 100)*

	Brazil			Mexico		
	1985	1975		1988	1975	
		Retro-polated	van Ark and Maddison		Retro-polated	van Ark and Maddison
Food, beverages and tobacco	43.9	52.5	56.6	25.5	33.9	36.1
Textiles and clothing	52.7	100.6	52.5	33.4	60.5	38.2
Wood, paper and publishing	28.3	16.2	28.6	22.3	22.5	22.3
Chemicals	32.6	39.2	66.6	31.0	40.0	39.3
Basic and metal products	50.8	47.5	42.4	29.4	35.4	42.8
Machinery, other equipment	55.3	99.8	51.6 }	17.5	22.8	31.3 }
Transport equipment	55.9	72.2		50.8	69.8	
Other manufacturing	41.3	80.8	39.0	18.9	42.6	29.2
Total	42.5	56.0	48.5	27.4	37.6	37.1

Sources: Benchmark results from Table 9.6, extrapolations based on time series, as described in Figure 9.1.

Table 9.8 *Relative Levels of Unit Labour Costs, Brazil/USA, 1985 and Mexico/USA, 1988 (USA = 100)*

	Brazil/USA, 1985			Mexico/USA, 1988		
	Unit Labour Costs	Compen-sation per Employee	Labour Produc-tivity	Unit Labour Costs	Compen-sation per Employee	Labour Produc-tivity
Food, beverages and tobacco	17.4	7.9	45.1	36.4	9.3	25.5
Textiles and clothing	19.8	10.2	51.6	33.8	11.3	33.4
Wood, paper and publishing	31.0	8.7	28.2	39.5	8.8	22.3
Chemicals	30.7	10.0	32.5	32.3	10.0	31.0
Basic metal and metal products	21.0	11.2	53.2	35.5	10.4	29.4
Machinery and other equipment	23.0	12.9	56.2	54.0	9.3	17.3
Transport equipment	21.2	11.0	51.8	32.5	16.5	50.8
Other manufacturing	30.3	10.4	34.2	36.1	6.8	18.9
Total	22.7	9.6	42.5	36.8	10.1	27.3

Sources: Relative productivity levels from Table 9.6, labour compensation from censuses of manufacturing, as described in text.

Another area which requires further investigation is the comparability of Brazilian and Mexican national accounts methods to estimate value added in informal activity. In Mexico the census estimate of value added is augmented by 30 per cent, whereas the imputation in Brazil is much smaller, in spite of evidence from employment statistics that informal activity is proportionally comparable between the two countries. Van Ark and Maddison (1994) already observed this for 1975. It would be interesting to check this with new evidence for the 1990s.

CONSTRUCTION

To compare the Brazilian and US performances, censuses of construction for 1975 (Brazil) and 1977 (USA) were used as the basic source.[11] These show revenues, input costs, employment and the value of completed construction (building and non-building) on a detailed level by branch of the construction.[12] In Mexico construction was excluded from the production censuses until 1988. Instead information from a survey was used,[13] which showed no breakdown by branch.

These sources list values of the completed structures, but lack physical output measures (such as surface of buildings, length of roads constructed); therefore, no PPPs could be derived. Instead ICP expenditure PPPs[14] were used as a proxy for the relative price of construction output. Conceptually output PPPs of the construction sector and expenditure PPPs on construction are similar, because there are no trade and transport margins involved and most construction is non-traded. Even so construction output is all part of final demand, as there is no intermediate component. The major drawbacks of using expenditure PPPs as a proxy for output do therefore not apply to construction. Only taxes and subsidies may distort the ICP PPPs (see Pilat, 1994). Labour productivity is about the same in Brazil and Mexico, that is 45 per cent of the US level.

Output by type of construction[15] was converted to a common currency by the ICP PPPs. For Brazil the cruzeiro value of construction was divided by the dollar value to derive a reweighted Paasche ICP PPP. For the USA the cruzeiro value was divided, obtained by multiplying the dollar values by the corresponding Laspeyres PPPs, by the US value to derive a reweighted Laspeyres PPP. Note that this procedure does not derive a new set of PPPs, but that it uses different weights to aggregate the PPPs of the basic headings. The same procedure was followed in the Mexico/US comparison (see Table 9.9). Brazilian and Mexican labour productivity were about the same level, that is 45 per cent of that of the USA. The breakdown for Brazil shows that highway and street construction was the least, and special trade contractors the most productive branches in construction.

Table 9.9 *Value Added, PPPs, Employment, and Comparative Productivity Levels by Major Branch of Construction, Brazil/USA, 1975 and Mexico/USA, 1975/77 (1975 prices)*

	Value Added (million 1975 US$)[a, b]	Fisher Purchasing Power Parities (National Currency per US$)	Persons Engaged (000s)	Value Added per Person Engaged (US = 100)
	Brazil, 1975			
Building construction	1,574,	5.06	343	41
Highway and street construction	911,	5.25	144	37
Heavy constr., except highway	800,	4.57	147	39
Special trade contractors	928,	4.70	154	57
Total	4,212,	4.89	788	45
	Mexico, 1977			
Construction	5,258	6.48	1 163	44
	USA, 1977			
Building construction	21,165	1.00	1,181	100
Highway and street construction	7,197,	1.00	268,	100
Heavy constr., except highway	16,231,	1.00	649,	100
Special trade contractors	39,868,	1.00	2,175,	100
Total	84,461,	1.00	4,273,	100

Notes:
[a] The Brazilian concept of value added could not be adjusted to the national accounts concept. Therefore, the census value added concept was used for both Brazil and the USA (including rental payments for machinery, equipment and structures, and purchased services).
[b] PPPs for total construction in the Brazil/US comparison were derived by weighting the PPPs of the branches by their value added.
Brazilian and Mexican data were converted to US$ using the exchange rate. Mexican and US figures were adjusted to 1975 prices by the GDP deflator for construction.

Source: Brazil: IBGE (1982); Mexico: INEGI (1994a); USA: US Department of Commerce, Bureau of the Census (1981e). Detailed Paasche and Laspeyres expenditure PPPs derived from Kravis *et al.* (1982), which were subsequently aggregated using construction output as weights. Fisher equals geometric average of Paasche and Laspeyres PPPs.

NOTES

1. For example, the price listed in the census for coffee was one-fifth of that of the FAO, and the production volume was twice as high (Maddison and van Ooststroom, 1993, p. 20).

2. A slightly revised version of this study was published in van Ark and Maddison (1994), whose results are shown here.
3. In the Brazil/USA comparison, in 122 common industries it was impossible to match any products, in 56 industries it was possible to match one product, in 27 industries two products, in 10 industries three products, in 10 industries four products and in 4 industries five or more products. In the Mexico/USA comparison, in 61 common industries it was impossible to match any products, in 40 industries it was possible to match one product, in 42 industries two products, in 41 industries three products, in 19 industries four products and in 20 industries five or more products.
4. An outlier is other manufacturing in the Brazil/USA comparison, with a difference of 30 per cent between the new and old methods. This results from the large differences between the two UVRs and the large differences in the shares of value added in output in the two countries.
5. In general the former only deduct intermediate goods and industrial services from gross output, while the latter also exclude non-industrial services. Moreover, although the concept of value added in national accounts is similar in the three countries due to the international guidelines of UN/IMF/OECD/Eurostat, each census adopted a different value added concept.
6. Rents (*alugueis condominios e arrendamentos de imoveis*), other rents and leasing (*alugueis e 'leasing' de maquinas e equipamentos e veiculos*), freight and carriage (*fretes e carretos*), excise duties and other indirect taxes (*impostos e taxas*), insurance premiums (*premios de seguro*), repair and maintenance (*serviços de reparação e manutenção da maquinas*), and other costs (*outros despesas e costos*).
7. In 1975 the necessary adjustments could be made using detailed census data. However, the 1988 census did not provide data for these input categories. Instead the subsequent census for 1993 had information on rental costs (*pagos por alquileres*). The 1993 ratios of rental costs to census value added were applied in order to adjust 1988 census value added to the national accounts concept.
8. For textiles the Brazilian series show a fall in absolute productivity levels between 1970s and the 1990s, whereas according to the US series, important productivity gains were achieved in this sector. The two trends combined yield relative productive levels above 100 per cent in the early 1970s. Another explanation for the high relative level of Brazil in textiles in the early 1970s is that the 1985 relative productivity level is probably overestimated due to the exclusion of non-census establishments, which had much lower productivity. For transport equipment the Brazilian series show a substantial cut in employment with continuous positive output growth resulting in a very high rate of productivity growth in the 1990s. Combined with a moderate rate of productivity growth in the USA, the relative productivity level of Brazil exceeded 100 per cent after 1995.
9. It should be stressed that even with exactly the same sources, extrapolated estimates will never exactly compare with benchmark results for the corresponding year, because of inconsistencies in index numbers.

10. As such the ICOP estimates of comparative labour productivity in textiles and clothing, wood, paper and publishing, machinery and transport equipment and other manufacturing between the 1975 and the 1985 benchmark estimates seem much more plausible than the huge relative productivity changes suggested by the backward extrapolation procedure.

11 For Brazil, see IBGE (1982) and for the USA, see Department of Commerce, Bureau of the Census (1981e).

12. Four branches were matched within the construction industry: building construction, highway and street construction, heavy construction other than highways,and special trade contractors: plumbers, electrical work, masonry, plastering, tile setting, carpentering and flooring, and miscellaneous trade contractors (see also Office of Management and the Budget, 1972, pp. 15–17).

13. SPP and Cámara Nacional de la Industria de la Construcción (1980). This source does not distinguish branches, but specifies commodity output according to private and public purchasers. The following types of public demand were distinguished: the federal government, states and municipalities, decentralised government bodies and other public institutions. The US census does not provide such a breakdown. Public demand accounted for 81 per cent of total output in 1977·

14. ICP III (Kravis *et al.*, 1982) distinguished two types of residential buildings (one and two dwelling buildings, and multi-dwellings), eight types of non-residential buildings (hotels, industrial buildings, commercial buildings, office buildings, educational buildings, hospital buildings, agricultural buildings and other buildings), and only four types of other construction (roads, transport and utility lines, other construction and land improvement).

15. The Brazilian census shows completed construction of seven types of buildings (residential and non-residential), and 45 types of non-building construction. The US census is less detailed than the Brazilian, that is it shows for each branch the value of completed construction disaggregated into 12 types of building construction and 22 types of non-building construction.

10. Comparative Performances of the Service and Commodity Sectors

INTRODUCTION

From 1950 to 1982 Brazil and Mexico achieved faster labour productivity growth than the USA. Since 1982 their growth has lagged behind that of the USA, which caused a widening of the gap between the three countries. An inverse relationship between productivity growth and levels may be observed. Countries with low productivity levels have a 'catch-up' potential that is not available to those with higher productivity levels such as the USA. This is because such countries operate much closer to the frontiers of technological progress.

In our benchmark year, 1975, the overall labour productivity level in Brazil was 21 per cent of the US level, while in Mexico it was 27 per cent (see Figure 10.1). However, in Brazil there was a large variation between the different sectors: productivity in the primary sector was only 3 per cent of the US level, in the secondary sector 45 per cent and in services 37 per cent. In Mexico the intersector variations were somewhat smaller: 10 per cent for the primary sector, 31 per cent for the secondary, and 36 per cent for the tertiary sector.

From 1950 to 1996 the share of primary sector employment fell, while the share of the services, and to a lesser extent industry, increased in Brazil and Mexico. Considering the much higher relative performance of Brazil and Mexico in the secondary and service sector, it is not surprising that movement of labour into those activities accelerated the catch-up process of these countries.

Figure 10.1 *Labour Productivity Levels by Sector, Brazil; Mexico and the USA, 1975 (1975 US$ 1,000, national currency converted by ICOP Fisher UVRs)*

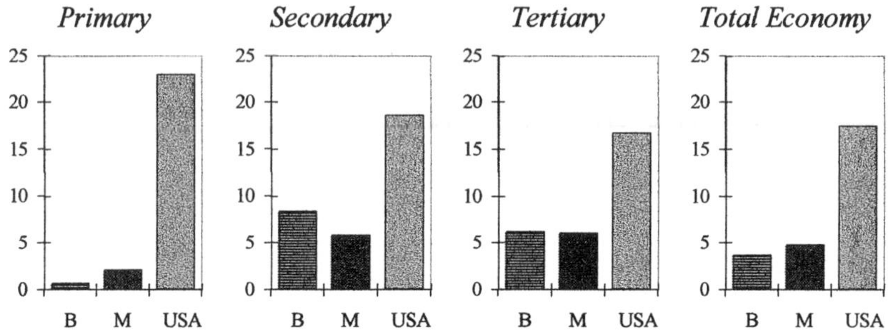

Notes: B = Brazil; M = Mexico and US = USA.

Sources: See Tables 10.3 and 10.4.

THE IMPACT OF SECTORAL CHANGE ON LABOUR PRODUCTIVITY

Sectoral shifts in employment raise the labour productivity performance of the total economy, if there is a net labour transfer from sectors with low levels of productivity to those with high levels. To check whether this was the case in the three countries, productivity levels are analysed in each sector in the long run. These are obtained by dividing for each sector its share in GDP in current prices by its share in employment (see Table 10.1). From 1920 to 1996 labour productivity in the secondary and tertiary sectors in Brazil and Mexico was indeed higher than in the primary sector.

Productivity in services was the highest for all sectors at the beginning of the period in all three countries. This may be attributed to the lower relative output prices and higher educational levels or workers in services when compared to those in the goods sector. In the course of time productivity levels in services and other sectors converged, as productivity growth in the former was below that of the rest of the economy. The shrinking productivity gap between sectors is also observed in the growth process of many other countries (Maddison, 1980; Ohkawa, 1993; Syrquin, 1986).

Table 10.1 Relative Levels of Labour Productivity for each Sector Compared to the Total Economy, Brazil, Mexico and the USA, 1900–96 (Current Prices)

	Brazil			Mexico			USA			
Sector	1920	1950	1996	1929	1950	1996	1900	1929	1950	1996
Primary	65	42	36	42	39	40	48	42	82	104
Secondary	167	143	158	66	163	119	89	109	107	112
Tertiary	392	212	107	411	191	113	154	86	100	97
Total	100	100	100	100	100	100	100	100	100	100

Sources: Appendices A, B and C.

Agriculture had the lowest productivity levels in all three countries in the first half of this century.[1] After the 1960s relative productivity levels remained much below the average performance in Brazil and Mexico, while in the USA the productivity level surpassed the average. The strong productivity improvements in the USA occurred thanks to technological innovations, large capital investments and a massive outflow of labour to other sectors.

In Brazil the secondary sector showed the highest growth of labour productivity of all sectors from 1950 to 1973. In Mexico the secondary sector growth was slightly less than that of the primary sector. Since 1973 the secondary sectors have performed worse than the rest of the economy and have converged to the average level of the economy in Brazil and Mexico.[2]

From Table 10.1 it can be concluded that the shift of labour from agriculture to manufacturing and services raised the overall performance of the economy. The contribution of employment shifts from low to high productivity sectors in overall productivity growth is measured as follows (van Ark, 1995; Nordhaus, 1972; Timmer and Szirmai, 1997).[3] Productivity of the economy as a whole is the sum of the productivity *levels* by sector multiplied their employment shares (10.1):

$$P_m = \frac{Y_m}{L_m} = \sum_{k=1}^{n} \left(\frac{Y_k}{L_k}\right)\left(\frac{L_k}{L_m}\right) = \sum_{k=1}^{n} (P_k S_k) \qquad (10.1)$$

with Y and L representing output and employment by sector ($k = 1...n$) and the total economy (m), P representing productivity (Y/L), and S representing the sectoral employment share (L_k/L_m).

Including a time perspective this expression can be rewritten as (10.2):

$$\Delta P_m = \sum_{k=1}^{n} (\Delta P_k * S_k) + \sum_{k=1}^{n} (P_k * \Delta S_k) \tag{10.2}$$

In a discrete form the latter can be rewritten into three components (10.3):

$$\frac{P_m^t - P_m^0}{P_m^0} = \frac{\sum_{k=1}^{n} (P_k^t - P_k^0) * S_k^0}{\sum_{k=1}^{n} P_k^0} + \frac{\sum_{k=1}^{n} P_k^0 * (S_k^t - S_k^0)}{\sum_{k=1}^{n} P_k^0} + \frac{\sum_{k=1}^{n} (P_k^t - P_k^0) * (S_k^t - S_k^0)}{\sum_{k=1}^{n} P_k^0} \tag{10.3}$$

for the current year (t) and a base year (0).

The first term on the right-hand side of the equation (10.3) represents the intrasectoral productivity growth, and corresponds to that part of the productivity change which is caused by productivity growth *within* the sectors. The second term is referred to as the static shift effect, and represents the effect of the change in sectoral employment shares on overall growth. This effect is positive when labour moves to branches with relatively high productivity levels in the beginning of the period. The third effect measures the dynamic shift effect, and is positive when labour shifts to sectors which improve their productivity performance. The sum of the second and third terms is referred to as the total structural change effect.

Each term of equation (10.3) is divided by the total productivity growth to estimate its contribution (see Table 10.2). In Brazil and Mexico productivity growth is mainly explained by productivity growth *within* sectors; structural change accounted for a quarter of total growth in the 1950–96 period. In Brazil the contribution of structural shifts increased after 1973. In contrast, in Mexico its magnitude fell. In the USA, structural change affected productivity negatively throughout the whole period, indicating a shift of labour to sectors with low or stagnating labour productivity, for example education, health care and other services.

Table 10.3 shows a sectoral breakdown of the intrasectoral productivity growth and the total shift effect for 1950–96. Productivity growth *within* sectors accounted for most of productivity growth, for example 68 per cent in Brazil, 57 in Mexico, and more than 100 per cent in the USA. Columns (1), (3) and (6) show that the primary sectors contributed most to the labour productivity growth *within* sectors in Brazil and Mexico, when compared to the secondary sector in the USA. The second largest contributors were the secondary sectors in Brazil and Mexico and the primary sector in the USA.

Table 10.2 Decomposition of Labour Productivity Growth: Intrasectoral Effect, Static and Dynamic Shift Effects, Brazil, Mexico and the USA, 1950–96

	Brazil			Mexico			USA		
	1950 –73	1973 –96	1950 –96	1950 –73	1973 –96	1950 –96	1950 –73	1973 –96	1950 –96
Labour productivity growth rate per year	4.0	1.5	2.7	3.1	0.6	1.9	1.9	0.9	1.4
Decomposition in %:									
Intrasectoral growth	81	53	74	64	87	79	109	149	140
Structural change, of which:	19	47	26	36	13	21	–9	–49	–40
static effect	14	98	27	24	80	31	7	–12	6
dynamic effect	5	–51	–2	12	–67	–10	–16	–37	–46
Total	100	100	100	100	100	100	100	100	100

Sources: Value added at constant prices from Appendix B and employment from Appendix A.

Table 10.3 Sectoral Contributions to Labour Productivity Growth, Brazil, Mexico and the USA, 1950–96 (Average Percentage Annual Compound Growth Rates)

	Brazil			Mexico			USA		
Sectors	Weighted Productivity Growth	Total Shift Effect	Total Sectoral Effect	Weighted Productivity Growth	Total Shift Effect	Total Sectoral Effect	Weighted Productivity Growth	Total Shift Effect	Total Sectoral Effect
Primary	0.7	–0.6	0.2	0.9	–0.8	0.1	0.4	–0.4	0.0
Secondary	0.6	0.2	0.8	0.3	0.3	0.6	0.9	–0.6	0.3
Tertiary	0.7	1.1	1.8	0.3	0.9	1.2	0.7	0.4	1.1
Total	2.0	0.7	2.7	1.5	0.4	1.9	2.0	–0.6	1.4

Sources: Appendices A and B.

Columns (2), (4) and (6) show the sum of the static and the dynamic shift effects. In Brazil and Mexico the largest negative shifts were in agriculture, accounting for about 60 per cent of employment in 1950. Its share dropped to about 24 per cent in 1996. The shift effect was positive in the secondary sector, but above all in the tertiary sectors (mainly distribution, finance and other services). In the USA, the shift effect was not only negative in the primary, but also in the secondary sector and even in some service branches.

When the two effects combined are looked at (column 3, 6 and 9), the large differences between the sectoral contributions to productivity growth become apparent. That of agriculture was small, and even negative in USA. In Brazil and Mexico manufacturing and mining accounted for almost a third. By far the largest contribution came from services, mainly distribution and other services.

The importance of structural change in productivity growth as estimated here may be too low because of the high level of aggregation which hides resource shifts within sectors. Chapters 5 to 9 discuss in detail the structural changes within particular branches of services. These shifts are not accounted for here. The static and partial nature of the studies is another source of underestimation, because it is assumed that sectoral productivity growth is unaffected by structural change. The high rates of productivity growth in agriculture in Brazil and Mexico in 1950–96 would not have been possible if the agricultural sector had continued to employ almost 60 per cent of the labour-force, as it did in 1950 in both countries. To take this criticism into account, the effect of structural change was recalculated following an alternative method (see Broadberry, 1995; Denison, 1967; Kindleberger, 1967)[4] for the 1950–96 period: its contribution increased from 0.7 to 1.2 per cent in Brazil, from 0.4 to 1.3 in Mexico and from –0.6 to 0.2 per cent per year in the USA.

The results presented here may be overestimated due to the assumption of input similarity, that is it is assumed that workers transferred to another sector would have the same productivity as those already existing in that sector. However, in reality, differences in labour productivity between sectors often reflect quality differences. The shift of workers from a low to a high productivity sector involves costly investments in human and physical capital. An economy can only benefit from fast changes in the composition of employment in combination with high levels of growth and investment (Chenery *et al.*, 1986; Maddison, 1995b).[5]

Thus a comparison of the labour productivity growth of the different sectors showed that services in Brazil and Mexico contributed most to overall labour productivity growth in 1950–96. This is largely due to the large expansion in employment that occurred in this sector, and not because of the labour productivity growth, which lay below that of other sectors. The poor growth performance in services may be related to the fact that productivity levels in the service sectors of Brazil and Mexico are already close to the 'world's best standard', and therefore the possibilities for catch-up and rapid growth have been exhausted. The international comparison of productivity levels is the subject of the next chapter.

THE CONTRIBUTION OF LABOUR REALLOCATION TO OVERALL ECONOMIC GROWTH

To analyse the contribution of the reallocation of labour to economic growth, its contribution was compared to that of other sources, as demonstrated in Table 10.4. The estimates are derived from Hofman (1998) for Brazil and Mexico and from Maddison (1995b and unpublished worksheets) for the USA. Using a traditional growth-accounting framework, GDP growth is explained by increases in employment and physical capital weighted by the share of their remuneration in GDP.

Table 10.4 Sources of GDP Growth, Brazil, Mexico and the USA, 1950–94 (Annual Average Compound Growth Rates)

	Brazil		Mexico		USA	
	1950 –73	1973 –94	1950 –73	1973 –94	1950 –73	1973 –94
GDP	6.9	3.6	6.5	3.4	3.9	2.6
Sources of growth						
Employment	1.7	1.7	1.4	1.8	0.9	1.0
Hours per employee	0.1	–0.3	–0.1	0.0	–0.2	–0.2
Education	0.8	1.8	1.0	2.0	0.3	0.7
Machinery and equipment	0.9	0.5	1.5	0.7	0.5	0.5
Non-residential structures	1.1	0.7	0.6	0.5	0.3	0.3
Total factor input	4.6	4.4	4.4	4.8	1.8	2.3
Total factor productivity, of which	2.4	–0.8	2.1	–1.4	2.1	0.3
Labour reallocation	0.8	0.3	0.9	0.4	–0.2	–0.3

Sources: Brazil and Mexico from Hofman (1998, p. 117); USA from Maddison (1995b and unpublished worksheets), except for contribution of labour reallocation which is taken from this study.

From 1950 to 1973 economic growth in Brazil and Mexico is mainly explained by capital accumulation. From 1973 to 1994 the growth of employment and improvements in educational levels overtook capital as the engine of growth due to falling investment rates. The residual shown in the table proxies total factor productivity growth, though it contains items which are normally excluded.[6] The residual explains half of economic growth in the USA, compared to about a third in Brazil and Mexico in 1950–73. The reallocation of labour positively contributed to economic growth in Brazil and Mexico in this period, explaining about 10 per cent of economic growth. Although its contribution remained positive in 1973–94, the overall residual turned negative in the Latin American countries. In the USA the reallocation effect was negative due to the move of labour to lower productivity sectors.

UNIT VALUE RATIOS

Sectoral UVRs are presented in Table 10.5. UVRs within branches were weighted by the value added. The use of Brazilian or Mexican weights yields a Paasche UVR, while US weights give a Laspeyres UVR (see also Chapter 4). The geometric average of the two is the Fisher UVR. To derive UVRs for sectors and the total economy, value added weights were used. The ratio of the UVR to the exchange rate indicates whether the price (or the cost) of an activity in Brazil or Mexico is below its equivalent in the USA (ratio below one), equal or superior (ratio above one). This ratio is referred to as the comparative or relative price.

The results of the Brazil/USA and Mexico/USA comparisons show large variations in UVRs and comparative prices across sectors (see Table 10.5). In Brazil the primary and secondary sectors, as well as some services (education, government, health care, real estate and transport), revealed relatively low UVRs and prices. Brazilian communications, financial services, public utilities and to a lesser extent distribution, on the contrary had relatively high UVRs and prices. The UVRs of total services lay below that of the primary and secondary sector. In Mexico the UVRs of the primary and secondary sector were relatively high and those of services relatively low.

The UVRs for total GDP were slightly below the exchange rate of 1975. The aggregate final expenditure PPPs in ICP III (Kravis *et al.*, 1982) for Brazil/USA and Mexico/USA were about 40 per cent below the results. The largest differences were observed in services where the estimates were more than twice those of ICP. This may be explained partly by the different price concepts used CP uses market prices whereas we use factor costs. In Brazil and Mexico several (public) services were relatively more subsidised than in the USA, which leads to a lower PPP at market prices than at factor cost. The higher UVRs for services stem from the higher price of intermediate services (such as freight transport and distribution) in Brazil and Mexico, which do not figure explicitly in the ICP approach. A third reason is that larger adjustments were made for quality differences, particularly for education and health care.

Table 10.5 Unit Value Ratios by Sector and the Laspeyres Paasche Spread, Brazil/USA and Mexico/USA, 1975

	Brazil/USA			Mexico/USA		
Sector	At Brazilian Quantity Weights	At US Quantity Weights	Laspeyres/ Paasche spread*	At Mexican Quantity Weights	At US Quantity Weights	Laspeyres/ Paasche Spread*
Primary	6.74	7.56	1.12	12.36	13.07	1.06
Secondary	6.06	8.14	1.34	9.94	13.96	1.40
Tertiary	5.22	8.51	1.63	8.79	12.03	1.37
Total	5.68	8.35	1.47	9.63	12.61	1.31
Exchange rate	8.13	8.13		12.50	12.50	

Notes: * The Laspeyres Paasche spread is estimated by the ratio of the Laspeyres to Paasche UVRs.

Sources: Primary sector is a weighted average of agriculture (Maddison and Rao, 1996) and mining (Houben, 1990); secondary sector is a weighted average of manufacturing (van Ark and Maddison, 1994) and construction (Chapter 9); services is a weighted average of UVRs of service activities presented in Chapters 4 to 8, and the ICP PPPs for government from Kravis *et al.* (1982). The UVRs for real estate, health care and education were retropolated to 1975 using GDP deflators.

Kravis *et al.* (1982) demonstrated the degree of similarity of price and the quantity structures of each pair of countries by the Laspeyres Paasche spreads (LPS), see column (3) and (6) of Table 10.5. The ratio of the Laspeyres to the Paasche UVR approaches unity as the structures of two countries become more similar. For Brazil/USA the spread in the commodity sector was smaller than in services. Brazil had relatively higher shares for transport, distribution and finance, and smaller shares for health care and 'other services' than the USA. For Mexico/USA the spread was lowest in the primary sector, followed by services and the secondary sector. The spread for total GDP was somewhat lower than in the Brazil/USA comparison. The spreads found here were similar to those obtained by ICP III, for example 0.63 for Brazil/USA and 0.71 for Mexico/USA (Kravis *et al.*, 1982).

The benchmark UVRs for 1975 were extrapolated to cover the whole period 1950–96, using GDP deflators presented in Appendix C. In Brazil prices rose several million times in the 1980s and early 1990s.[7] The exchange rate followed the acceleration of prices, although not always at the same speed. This caused substantial variations in the comparative price levels, as illustrated by the ratios of UVRs to the exchange rates in

Figure 10.2. In the early 1950s and 1990s Brazil had an overvalued exchange rate, with an aggregate price level more than 50 per cent above that in the USA. From the 1960s to the late 1980s the currency was undervalued and the aggregate price level fell below the US level. Finance, wholesale and retail trade services were exceptions as they surpassed US prices for most of the period. After the stabilisation in 1994 the price of Brazilian financial services dropped sharply to almost half the US level in 1996.

Figure 10.2 Comparative Price Levels, Brazil/USA and Mexico/USA, 1950–96

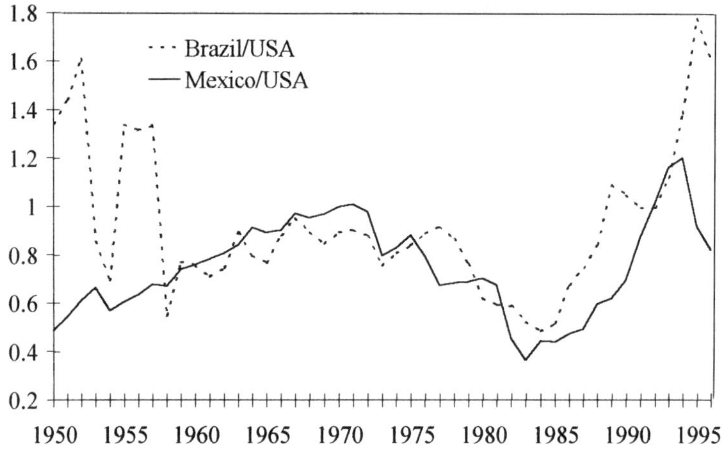

Notes: Comparative price levels are measured by the ratio of unit value ratios to the exchange rates. Ratios equal one indicate that prices in Brazil and Mexico were the same as those in the USA. Ratios above (below) one indicate that the Brazilian or Mexican price level is above (below) that in the USA.

Sources: Table 10.1 and Appendix C.

In 1950 Mexico had a significantly undervalued exchange rate, so its price level was almost half the level in the USA. Between 1955 and 1975, it tied the exchange rate at 12.50 pesos per US$. During this period the UVR converged towards the exchange rate. This was due to the higher rate of inflation in Mexico. The exchange rate was strongly devalued in 1976–77 and in 1980–88; and as such improving Mexico's price competitiveness. From 1988 to 1994 Mexican prices increased faster than those in the USA. This was caused by a higher inflation rate and minor exchange rate devaluations. In 1995 the overvalued Mexican currency, a large current account deficit and speculative attacks against the peso caused a strong devaluation of the peso and a major recession.

Various studies have indicated that due to the 'Balassa-effect' comparative price levels in low and medium-income countries are the lowest in the tertiary sector (Balassa, 1964; Froot and Rogoff, 1996; Kravis and Lipsey, 1983, 1988; Lahrèche-Révil, 1998). Labour productivity differentials between high- and low-income countries are larger in the tradable (commodity) sector, compared to the non-tradable sector (mostly services). However, as wages tend to converge between sectors, services are relatively more expensive in high-income countries. Since services are included in the estimation of UVRs, but have little effect on the exchange rate, the total economy UVR of a poor country in comparison with a rich country will lie below the exchange rate.

LABOUR PRODUCTIVITY LEVELS, 1975

Relative productivity levels are summarised in Table 10.6. In Brazil and Mexico labour productivity varied strongly between different service activities. Brazilian communications and public utilities were characterised by very low productivity levels. Telecommunications were of very poor quality, as illustrated by the high share of local calls which could not be completed and the long delays (often for several years) in having a telephone line installed. Inefficiency was also found in state enterprises distributing electricity, gas and drinking water as they often did not charge customers. Mexico showed a somewhat better performance, particularly in telecommunications.

In Brazil and Mexico years of public neglect turned railways and water transport into the poorest productivity performers. Intensive use of bus transport contributed to relatively high productivity levels in road-passenger transport. The predominant position of road-passenger transport in both countries partly compensated the low performance in the other transport branches, resulting in a total performance of a third of the US level in Brazil and 42 per cent of the US performance in Mexico.

Wholesale and retail trade was the predominant branch of the tertiary sector, accounting for about one-third of total employment in all three countries. Food retailing in Brazil and Mexico performed poorly due to the

Table 10.6 UVRs, Productivity Levels and Relative Prices, Brazil/USA and Mexico/USA, 1975

	Brazil/USA			Mexico/USA		
	Unit Value Ratio (Fisher, Cruzeiros/US$)	Value Added per Person Engaged (US = 100)	Relative Price Level (US = 100)	Unit Value Ratio (Fisher, Pesos/ US$)	Value Added per PersonEngaged (US = 100)	Relative Price Level (US = 100)
Agriculture	7.56	5.6	93	14.67	9.7	117
Mining	4.80	45.0	59	9.43	39.1	75
Total primary sector	7.14	4.3	88	12.71	9.5	102
Manufacturing	7.78	46.4	96	13.66	25.2	109
Construction	4.89	53.6	60	6.48	73.1	52
Total secondary sector	7.03	45.4	86	11.78	31.4	94
Public utilities	11.11	14.3	137	12.15	18.3	97
Transport	5.53	35.4	68	9.42	41.5	75
Communications	17.23	12.5	212	16.59	24.5	133
Distribution	8.78	42.8	108	11.36	33.5	91
Financial services	11.05	51.3	136	14.78	58.7	118
Real estate	7.39	33.5	91	13.08	33.4	105
Health care	3.25	52.4	40	14.26	53.7	114
Education	7.15	52.4	88	6.52	73.6	52
Government	3.35	96.4	41	6.31	59.6	50
Other services	6.66	41.8	82	10.29	47.5	82
Total tertiary sector	6.66	47.8	82	10.29	42.9	82
Total (all sectors)	6.89	23.3	85	11.02	29.0	88

Sources: UVRs from Table 10.5; value added and employment from Chapters 4 to 8 and Appendices A, D and E.

predominance of small (informal) retail outlets in the total. The productivity gap between the countries in wholesale trade was smaller. Banking and insurance were among the most productive services in Brazil and Mexico. In Brazil banks developed many profitable instruments to protect clients against high inflation. Moreover, they invested in computer technology to accelerate the processing of transactions.

In Brazil health care was poorly adapted to the needs of the population. Expensive and inefficient hospital care for the rich and middle-income class dominated, and resources to fight maternal, infant and infectious diseases of the poor were relatively scarce. In Mexico inefficient public hospitals mainly catered to the urban and insured people. Free care for the poor was rather scarce. In Brazil and Mexico the quality of the educational system was also poor, as demonstrated by high repetition rates, high dropout rates and low scores on international tests. Surprisingly, the relatively high productivity in 1975 resulted from the very low price of education in both countries, even after adjustments for quality differences.

Productivity performance in Brazilian services was below that of the secondary sector, whereas Mexican services performed somewhat better than the secondary sector. Total economy performance was much lower than that of the secondary and tertiary sector, at 21 per cent of the US level in Brazil and 27 per cent in Mexico. This is mainly due to the large weight agriculture has in Brazil and Mexico.

Brazil showed very low productivity in agriculture, which stems from the dualistic nature of this sector. Most of the land is owned by a small elite and is cultivated with relatively modern machinery. The majority of farmers, however, own only small plots of land and have little or no machinery. As a consequence their productivity is low. The huge expansion of the agricultural area has not improved the distribution of land very much. Although productivity is substantially higher in mining, the overall performance in the primary sector remained very low, as mining accounted for only 0.3 per cent of employment in the primary sector in Brazil, as opposed to 18 per cent in the USA. Mexico performed relatively better than Brazil in agriculture, which may be related to its more equal distribution of land (Maddison and Associates, 1992). In manufacturing and construction the Brazilian performance was about half, and that of Mexico one-quarter of the performance in the USA. Results by branch show that in Brazil food products were the best performing branch, whereas in Mexico basic and fabricated metals was the top performer (see Appendix D). Manufacturing was the key sector of the post-war development policy of import substitution industrialisation (ISI) in these Latin American countries. Its development has been stimulated by cheap credit, state ownership of certain industries (for example the steel industry) and protection from foreign competition (see van Ark and Maddison, 1994, for a more detailed discussion of the results).

COMPARATIVE LABOUR PRODUCTIVITY PERFORMANCE, 1950–96

The labour productivity results for 1975 were extrapolated to 1950–96 (see Figures 10.3 and 10.4). This was done by using time series of real GDP (Appendix B) and employment (Appendix A).[8] The low productivity levels of Brazilian and Mexican services, when compared to the USA in 1950, reflect their slow development in the previous century. The development of transport infrastructure was very retarded in the two Latin American countries when considered in relation to the USA. In 1870 there were already 85,000 km of railways in the USA as opposed to just a few hundred in Brazil and Mexico. The USA built extensive canal and road networks in the nineteenth century, whereas road building on a large scale did not start until the 1930s in Brazil and Mexico. Aviation developed rapidly in Brazil and Mexico. Compared to the USA the Latin American countries showed only a relatively small delay in development, partly on account of the poor situation of other modes of transport. In both Latin American countries the telegraph and telephone were introduced only a decade later than in the USA, but the spread of these mediums was rather slow.

In the USA department stores and supermarkets were introduced at the end of the nineteenth and early twentieth centuries. In Brazil and Mexico, these formats were uncommon until after the 1950s. Heavy regulation in Brazil and political chaos in Mexico in the nineteenth century delayed the development of the financial system at the end of the nineteenth century, whereas the USA already had a banking network in the early nineteenth century. In Mexico the Revolution retarded the development of the financial system by at least 20 years.

Health care and education in Brazil and Mexico also developed at a very slow pace in the nineteenth century. In Brazil this was mainly due to the lack of interest of the imperial government, whereas in Mexico political turmoil was the major cause. At the turn of the century the governments of both countries showed increased activities both in fighting infectious diseases and the improvement of public health. It was not until the 1930s that a public health system was established in the two Latin countries, which had already been developed in the USA in the nineteenth century. The development of education occurred at a very low pace in Brazil and Mexico. By 1890 less than 15 per cent of the Brazilian and Mexican population could write, compared to 85 per cent in the USA. From the 1930s onwards major efforts in both Latin American countries improved schooling levels a little. In 1950 half of the population was still illiterate.

Figure 10.3 Value Added per Person Engaged, Brazil/USA, 1950–96, USA = 100

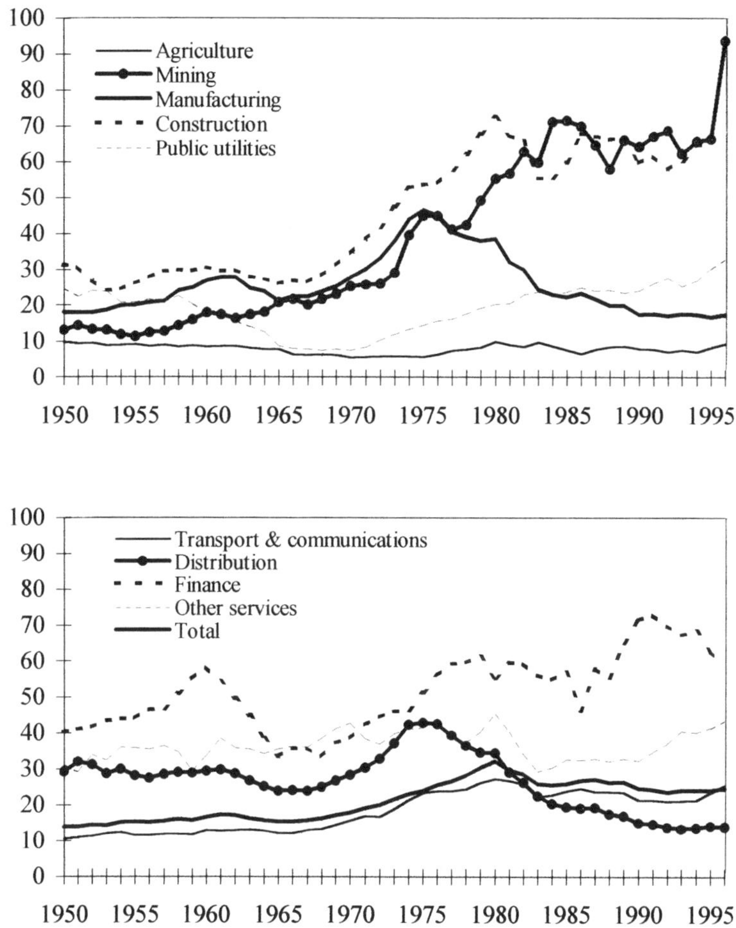

Sources: 1975 benchmark from Table 10.7 extrapolated with time series from Appendices A and B.

Figure 10.4 Value Added per Person Engaged, Mexico/USA, 1950–96, USA = 100

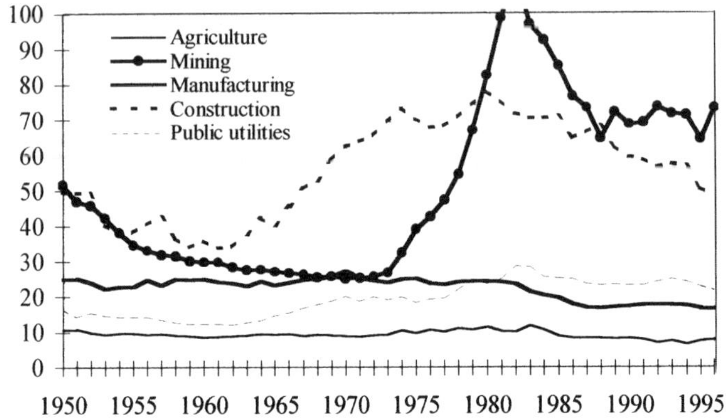

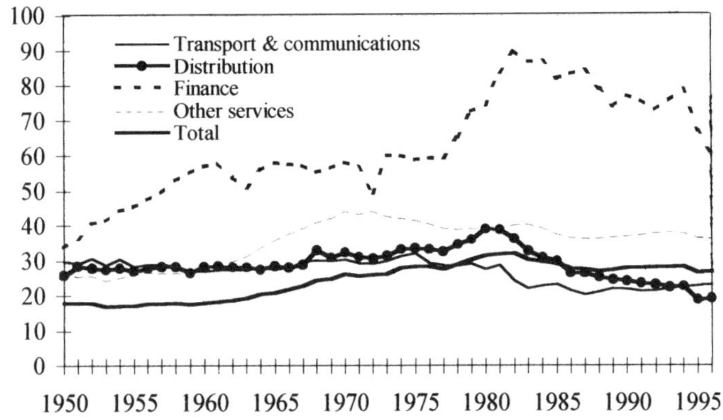

Sources: 1975 benchmark: Table 10.8, extrapolated with time series of Appendices A and B.

The overall performance in Mexican services remained stable when compared with other sectors; this in spite of the productivity increases in several service industries in 1950–82. This paradoxical result stems from the increasing weight of industries in the service sector with relatively low productivity levels and a decrease of the weight of those with high levels. Productivity in transport, communications and distribution somewhat increased until the early 1980s, after which it declined. These sectors were heavily regulated until the late 1980s, as was the case in Brazil. The financial sector improved its relative performance in the 1960s and 1970s, but the trend was reversed after the nationalisation of the banking sector in 1982. The privatisation of banks between 1989 and 1991, the merger process within this sector and the resumption of economic growth did not reverse the negative trend. The financial crisis in 1994–95 had a negative impact on their productivity performance. The productivity of other services increased until the early 1970s. Afterwards it stagnated in comparison with US levels, as a result of the rapid expansion of employment in health care and education in this sector and the slow output growth.

The top panels of the two previous figures show the performance in the commodity sector and public utilities. The performance in Brazilian and Mexican agriculture stagnated during the entire period when considered against the US performance. In Mexico, and to a lesser extent in Brazil, mining showed large productivity gains, which considering a poor US performance resulted in a fast catch-up. These gains seem closely related to the evolution in oil prices. The rise of oil prices following the first oil crisis boosted oil extraction, which required only small increments in employment. In the early 1980s Mexican productivity levels even surpassed those in the USA. In the second half of the 1980s oil prices fell sharply and the productivity trend was reversed.

In Brazil and Mexico the government stimulated the development of the manufacturing sector from the 1930s until the 1980s, which is also referred to as import substitution industrialisation. This was done by offering large subsidies to enterprises in key branches, by state ownership and by protecting firms from foreign competition on the domestic market. In Brazil this policy improved the relative productivity performance in 1950–77 from 18 to over 46 per cent of the US level. Mexico's relative manufacturing performance, on the contrary, did not show any signs of improvement. After 1982 both Brazilian and Mexican manufacturing lost ground to the USA. From the late 1980s onwards the government stopped protecting the manufacturing sector. Subsidies were cut, the borders opened to foreign firms and products and most state enterprises were privatised. This policy change incited firms to increase labour productivity. However, only the negative trend of the 1980s was stopped, but productivity growth did not accelerate until 1996.

The relative productivity of construction in Brazil and Mexico showed a similar pattern: it improved until the late 1970s. In both countries the crisis of the 1980s led to a fall in the performance in this sector. The growth recovery in the early 1990s only had a positive impact on performance in Brazilian construction.

IMPACT OF DIFFERENCES IN PRODUCTION STRUCTURE ON PRODUCTIVITY

The productivity performance of the total economy depends not only on the performance in the individual sectors, but also on differences between countries in the sectoral composition of GDP and employment. In 1950 the relatively low productivity levels of Brazil and Mexico were primarily due to the large share of agriculture in employment in both countries and their poor performance in this sector. In the course of time employment shifted from agriculture to sectors with higher productivity levels. Employment shifts improved the overall productivity performance of Brazil and Mexico *vis-à-vis* the USA. To assess the impact of differences in sectoral structure, the time variables in equation (10.4) were replaced by country variables and the shift effects were summed (as it is not very useful to distinguish a dynamic effect in international comparisons), see equation (10.4).

$$\frac{P_m^x - P_m^u}{P_m^U} = \frac{\sum_{k=1}^{n}(P_k^x - P_k^u) * S_k^u}{\sum_{k=1}^{n} P_k^u} + \frac{\sum_{k=1}^{n} P_k^x * (S_k^x - S_k^u)}{\sum_{k=1}^{n} P_k^u} \qquad (10.4)$$

with Y and L representing output and employment by sector ($k = 1...n$) and the total economy (m), P representing productivity (Y/L), and S representing the sectoral employment share (L_k/L_m); x refers to Brazil or Mexico and u to the USA. Equation (10.4) decomposes the productivity gap between two countries in two parts: the first indicates the part due to labour productivity differences *within* sectors, and the second indicates the part due to differences in structure. The ratio of each part to the total productivity gap indicates how much of the total gap it 'explains'.

Table 10.7 shows that these intrabranch productivity differentials accounted for more than 90 per cent of the total productivity gaps. The part ascribed to structural differences was small, despite the distinct sectoral composition of the Latin American and US economies. The limited role of structural differences mainly resulted from the rather similar relative productivity levels between sectors, especially in the 1950s and after the 1980s. From 1950 to 1975 the size of the catch-up potential for structural change productivity increased a little due to the growing productivity differentials between sectors. Nevertheless, the part ascribed to structural differences always remained below 10 per cent of the total productivity gap between countries. From this the conclusion may be drawn that the elimination of structural differences between the three countries would have only marginally reduced the productivity gap with the USA.

Table 10.7 Decomposition of Labour Productivity Differences: Brazil/USA and Mexico/USA, 1950–96

	Brazil/USA, Contribution of:			Mexico/USA, Contribution of:		
	Intrabranch Productivity Differences	Structural Differences	Total	Intrabranch Productivity Differences	Structural Differences	Total
1950	97.8	2.2	100.0	94.5	5.5	100.0
1975	91.4	8.6	100.0	93.5	6.5	100.0
1982	94.8	5.2	100.0	94.2	5.8	100.0
1989	97.0	3.0	100.0	96.5	3.5	100.0
1996	97.3	2.7	100.0	97.2	2.8	100.0

Sources: 1975 from Tables 10.7 and 10.8, other years obtained by extrapolating the 1975 benchmark with time series of GDP at constant prices and employment.

CONCLUSION

The aim of this chapter was to compare Brazilian and Mexican productivity performance in services with that of other sectors of the economy, as well as to consider it in relation to the USA. In this way we may come to see how far the Latin American countries lagged behind the 'best practice', and assess their potential for catch-up. Until 1982 the two Latin American countries showed a modest catch-up with US productivity levels, but their relative performance worsened later. When compared to the USA performance in services in Brazil and Mexico after 1950 was slightly better than their relative performance in their secondary sectors. In both Latin American countries performance in the tertiary sectors was much better than in the primary sectors. In Brazil productivity levels in the secondary and tertiary sectors rose approximately 10 percentage points from 1950 to 1982, reaching 35 per cent of the US level. In Mexico the comparative performance in both sectors remained stable. From 1982 to 1996 the secondary sectors experienced a larger fall in productivity than services in both countries,[9] despite the faster rate of employment growth in services. Productivity growth was most rapid in agriculture in Brazil and Mexico, but did not advance faster than in the USA.

From 1950 to 1982 the growth of output and labour productivity in services was stimulated by increasing per capita incomes, industrialisation and urbanisation, which raised the demand for final and intermediate services. Governments in both Latin American countries promoted the development of public utilities, transport, communications, finance, education and health care by state ownership and subsidies. Productivity growth in services was somewhat higher in Brazil than Mexico. Brazil started from a lower level in 1950 and was able to achieve higher growth rates. In Brazil inflation was an important stimulus to the expansion of the banking sector. At the same time this lowered demand for other services due to its negative impact on real incomes of the poor.

More research needs to be done to explain the tendency of faster catch-up (and smaller divergence after 1982) of productivity levels in the service sector, relative to the manufacturing sector, in Brazil and Mexico *vis-à-vis* the USA. Some argue that service production is much more homogeneous than goods production. Catch-up in services may be more rapid as similar types of technology are used in different countries and therefore technical diffusion is easier. In manufacturing countries tend to specialise in the production of goods in which they have a comparative advantage. As countries produce a greater variety of goods, there are no a priori reasons why production technologies should be the same or why they should converge in the course of time. Some catch-up does however occur in manufacturing, as there are spillovers across goods (Bernard and Jones, 1996).

For the translation of productivity levels of each country into a common currency, UVRs based on sectoral comparisons have been used, with 1975 as the benchmark year. Prices in services often cannot be determined clearly, on account of intercountry variations in the quality of output, and therefore UVRs have to be derived implicitly. Quantities are relatively easy to measure in services like transport and communications, but measurements are extremely difficult for comparison-resistant services such as education and health care. These difficulties arise from the intangible characteristics of services and the large quality differences between countries. In several Brazilian and Mexican services quality adjustments were made, which increased their relative price and reduced their relative productivity levels.

In Brazil and Mexico relative prices in services were below those of the commodity sector in 1975. In Mexico lower relative prices in services partly resulted from smaller productivity differentials in this sector, when compared to the secondary sector in the USA. In Brazil relative productivity in services was below that of the secondary sector despite the lower relative prices in the service sector. The UVRs for total GDP in both countries were below the exchange rate. Nevertheless, there are large differences in the price and productivity levels between service industries. In Brazil and Mexico communications, financial services and public utilities were relatively expensive, while education and government services were cheap in 1975. In turn, relative labour productivity levels were closely linked to prices, except for financial services which showed quite high productivity in Brazil and Mexico in 1975.

The measurement of output and prices in services still needs to be refined to improve its reliability. Conceptual and measurement problems still contaminate our results. A lack of consensus on how to measure output leads to the use of various proxy indicators which may distort comparisons. Moreover, in Brazil and Mexico, the statistical apparatus for services is often inadequately developed, which limits the range of output indicators available.

NOTES

1. Kuznets (1971) observed the same for a large range of countries at early stages of development in 1958, that is labour productivity in industry and services was about five times as high as the level in agriculture.
2. The patterns observed in Brazil and Mexico are typical of developing countries, as illustrated in Chenery and Syrquin (1975) and Chenery *et al.* (1986). In the early phases of development the productivity performance of manufacturing accelerates in response to domestic demand shifts in a country's comparative advantage and government policies promoting industrialisation. High productivity growth implies that the share of manufacturing in GDP grows faster than in employment. Industry is a leading sector in economic growth, as it improves the performance of the total economy, generates technological innovations and increases exports. As a country has become industrialised, the share of industry products in consumer demand falls, which lowers the share of industry in production. Labour productivity also decreases in relation to the total economy performance as the share of industry in employment falls with a time lag.
3. Similar formulations of the contribution of the reallocation of labour to productivity growth can be found in Chenery *et al.* (1986), Denison (1967), Kuznets (1957), Ohkawa (1993) and Syrquin (1984). The formulation used here is also referred to as the gross allocation effect, that is the observed aggregate labour productivity growth minus the growth that would have occurred if the share of each sector in the labour-force would have remained constant over time. This measure ignores aspects of structural change other than labour shifts, and uses average instead of marginal labour productivities to calculate gains and losses.
4. It is assumed that if labour was shifted back to agriculture, output in that sector would not have increased but would only have lowered the productivity growth rate. This is because all labour that moved out of agriculture is considered

surplus labour. On the other hand, the shift of labour away from manufacturing and services would have reduced output, leaving productivity unchanged. For this purpose, equation (10.2) is divided by P_M, and the first term on the right-hand side is multiplied and divided by P_k. We get (10.4): $\frac{\Delta P_m}{P_m} = \sum_{k=1}^{n} \frac{\Delta P_k}{P_k} * \frac{P_k}{P_m} * S_k + \sum_{k=1}^{n} \frac{P_k}{P_m} * \Delta S_k$. The first term on the right-hand side of equation (10.4) is rewritten as (10.5), $\sum_{k=1}^{n} \alpha_k \frac{P_k}{P_m} S_k$. The counterfactual productivity growth rate of each sector is given by equation $\alpha_k = \frac{\Delta P_k}{P_k} - (\frac{\Delta L_m}{L_m} - \frac{\Delta L_k}{L_k})$ if $\Delta S_k < 0$ or $\alpha_k = \frac{\Delta P_k}{P_k}$ if $\Delta S_k \geq 0$.

5. Some authors took account of this as they dropped the assumption that the marginal labour productivity remains constant after new employees are added to a sector (Syrquin, 1986). This is because the amount of capital per worker and correspondingly labour productivity decline after workers are added. The gross effect minus the expected change in labour productivity equals the 'net reallocation effect'.
6. It includes the accumulation of residential structural, natural resources and capital productivity. However, Maddison (1995b) did not include these items for the USA.
7. Due to high inflation new currencies were introduced in 1986, 1989, 1990 and 1994 (see Appendix C).
8. Labour productivity increases when real value added grows faster than employment. The growth of the Brazil/USA productivity ratio is calculated by dividing the productivity change in Brazil by the productivity change in the USA.
9. From 1982 to 1996 the relative productivity level of services fell 9 points in Brazil compared to 5 points in Mexico. The performance of the secondary sector fell 12 points in Brazil and 9 points in Mexico.

Appendix A: Population and Employment

POPULATION

The population estimates for 1820–1994 are from Maddison (1995b), which are linked to data from the Department of Commerce, Bureau of the Census (1998).

EMPLOYMENT

The analysis of labour productivity trends by sector of the economy requires the construction of employment series. This is a difficult task for Brazil and Mexico, as most information on employment comes from population censuses which are only available on a decade basis. In recent years additional sources have become available such as labour force surveys, which are published more frequently. The statistical basis of these countries is too weak to estimate hours worked on a sectoral basis.

Brazil

For the period prior to 1950 employment information by sector of the economy was only available from the population censuses, which were taken in 1900, 1920, 1940 and 1950. The 1900 census included a large category 'not elsewhere classified', which included persons from, among others, construction, utilities and financial services. The 1940 census also had a large category 'not elsewhere classified'. The census data are listed in Ludwig (1985).

From 1950 to 1970 employment information by sector of the economy was only available from the population censuses taken in 1950, 1960 and 1970. For the post-1970 period two basic sources are available. Firstly, population censuses for 1970, 1980 and 1990 and population surveys for intermediate years (IBGE, *Pesquisa Nacional por Amostra de Domicilios*, PNAD, various issues). Secondly, since 1975 the national accounts published employment figures on a quinquennial basis until 1990, and annually afterwards. Employment levels and trends from the PNAD often differ from those of the national accounts. On the sectoral level the PNAD often shows large breaks in their series. Moreover, the level of sectoral disaggregation varies over time. Important changes have also taken place in the questionnaire, the samples and methods to impute total employment based on the samples. For these reasons the PNAD data are hardly useful to construct trends in employment, and this study therefore relied on the national accounts series from 1975 onwards.

The 1950, 1960, 1970 data were taken from population censuses as presented in IBGE (1990, p. 75); except for agriculture for 1970, which was taken from IBGE, *Censos Economicos*, as its value was much larger than the population census indicated. The years 1975, 1980, 1985 and 1991–96 were taken from IBGE, *Matriz de Insumo-Produto* (various issues). The years between 1950, 1960 and 1970, 1975, 1980, 1985 and 1990 were interpolated using average annual compound growth rates. Census employment in mining in 1975 was similar to that of the national accounts, though only one-third of the level indicated by the 1976 PNAD. As the census systematically (in 1960, 1970 and 1980) underestimates employment by about two-thirds, it was assumed the same underestimation was made for 1975. A breakdown of employment into finance and real estate was available for 1980, 1985, and 1990–96, and shows that the shares remained relatively stable. Therefore, the 1980 breakdown was applied to estimate employment in finance and real estate separately for 1950–80. Health care: 1980 benchmark from Chapter 8; 1978–86 extrapolated with IBGE, *Pesquisa de Assistencia Medico Sanitaria* (various issues). 1990, 1993 and 1995 from IBGE, *Pesquisa Nacional por Amostra de Domicilios* (PNAD). 1970–78, 1987–79, 1991–92 and 1994 were estimated using annual average compound growth rates. Health care employment in 1996 was estimated by the 1995–96 trend for government and private non-market services. Education: 1970 and 1980 levels were interpolated using average annual growth rates. The public education trend for 1980–91 was used to estimate employment in private education. 1993 and 1995 from IBGE, PNAD; 1992 and 1994 were extrapolations based on employment in education as taken from IBGE, *Anuario Estatístico do Brasil* (various issues). Employment in education in 1996 was estimated as for health care.

Mexico

For the period prior to 1950 employment information by sector of the economy was only available from the population censuses held in 1900, 1910, 1921, 1930, 1940 and 1950. The results of the *Censos Generales de Población* are presented in Nacional Financiera (1978).

Employment in 1950, 1960, 1970, 1980 and 1990 were taken from SPP and INEGI, *Censos Generales de Poblacion*, 1950, 1960, 1970, 1980 and 1990. Intermediate years were interpolated with trends on the number of employees, which were taken from the Government of Mexico (1979) for the period 1950–67, and from INEGI (1994b, 1998) for the period 1970–96. 1968 and 1969 were estimated using the annual average compound growth rate of the 1967–70 period. Health care and education: 1970–91 from INEGI (1994a) (series refer to the number of employees), linked to 1950–70 series of the number of teachers in all levels of education from INEGI (1994b). Employment in health care in the 1950–67 period was estimated using Hernandez Laos' (1973) time series of GDP and labour productivity for 'services'. Employment figures for 1968–69 were estimated by using annual average compound growth rates for the 1960–67 period.

The number of employees in services in 1950–67 from Government of Mexico (1979) and 1970–96 from INEGI, *Cuentas Nacionales de México* (various issues). The years 1968 and 1969 were estimated by using the annual average compound growth rate of the 1967–70 period.

USA

Employment in the 1889–1950 period are from Kendrick (1961). Employment in the 1950–88 period are from Department of Commerce, Bureau of Economic Analysis (1992); linked to series of Department of Commerce, Bureau of Economic Analysis, *Survey of Current Business,* January 1992, July 1994 and August 1997.

Appendix B: GDP Indices and Levels of GDP

Output is measured by gross domestic product (GDP), because it gives the best account of the contribution of a sector to the overall income. Moreover, GDP is available for many sectors and countries and it is widely used to assess productivity performance. Major efforts have been made by international organisations (Eurostat, IMF, OECD and United Nations) to harmonise concepts across countries, as part of the System of National Accounts. The latest revision of the *System of National Accounts* (Inter-Secretariat Working Group on National Accounts, 1993) was implemented in Brazil, Mexico and the USA in the mid-1990s.

In Brazil the national accounts were the responsibility of the Fundação Getúlio Vargas until 1986, after which it was transferred to the Fundação Instituto Brasileiro de Geografia e Estatística (IBGE). The GDP levels are based on economic censuses covering most sectors. The estimates for years between censuses are less reliable. The final economic census was taken in 1985. In 1995 the five-year interval census has been replaced by annual surveys. Input output tables[1] served as indicators for ratios of value added to gross output. IBGE made little imputations for economic activity not covered in the census. It does, as such, understate the level of output. In contrast to Brazil, Mexico makes extensive allowances for informality (see also Appendix F and Maddison and Associates, 1992). The level estimates presented here corrected the underestimation of Brazilian GDP and the overestimation of Mexican GDP by using a standardised method to account for unregistered activity in both countries.

In Mexico the national accounts were compiled by the Central Bank until 1978, when the INEGI took over. The first extensive *Sistema de Cuentas Nacionales de México* (SCNM) was produced by a group of experts, funded by the United Nations, in the late 1970s and early 1980s. Several volumes, published in 1981, explained in detail the compilation of GDP in current and constant prices for 1970–78 and the first detailed input output table for 1970. A major revision, updating the base year from 1970 to 1980, was made in the second half of the 1980s. The revision of the SCNM which incorporated the 1993 SNA guidelines was finished in 1997.

The Brazilian national accounts provide a limited sectoral breakdown for services: public utilities, transport, communications, distribution, finance and real estate, government and other services. The Mexican national accounts are more detailed: constant prices' series from 1960 provide a breakdown into 13 branches of services. From 1988 onwards a detailed account of more than 60 service industries has been available. The US national accounts provide a breakdown of about 40 branches of services.

The Brazilian national accounts do not provide long-term series at constant prices, but present annual real growth rates. The Mexican national accounts provide series in 1970 prices for 1970–84, in 1980 prices for 1960–83 and in 1993 prices for 1988–96. The US national accounts provided long-term series in 1982 and 1987 prices, using fixed weights for the whole period since 1947. Recently the US Department of Commerce has replaced the fixed weights by a chain-weighted index, changing weights every five years (see Department of Commerce, *Survey of Current Business*, May and November, 1997). The change from the fixed 1987 to the chain-weighted index increased the growth rate prior to 1987, and decreased it after 1987. The series provided here are based on a single base year weight, 1982, which is in line with the practice adopted by the Mexican national accounts.

SOURCE NOTES

Brazil

The series of real GDP for 1900–50 are estimated from indexes of real GDP at 1939 prices for 1900–47 from Haddad (1978, pp. 7–8, 11 and 161–62); linked to 1947–50 series from Goldsmith (1986, pp. 224–25).

The GDP series at 1975 constant prices was derived as follows. The levels of GDP in 1975 cruzeiros are derived from Appendix Table E.2. The 1975 levels were extrapolated to 1950–80 with indexes of real GDP for all sectors from Gusmão Veloso (1987). The real GDP in finance and real estate from 1980 to 1990 was estimated by deflating current GDP series with the price index for finance and real estate. The 1950–80 series were linked to new series of IBGE (1992, 1995a, 1998). Health care and education GDPs were extrapolated with the trend for 'total services' for the 1971–80 period. For the 1980–90 period the GDP-index of 'other services', derived from IBGE (1995a), has been used. For 1991–96, the real GDP index of government services and private non-market services was used. No proxies of real GDP for health care and education were available before 1970. GDP at constant prices in other services was estimated as a residual, that is deducting from total GDP the sum of all sectors.

Mexico

The 1900–50 real GDP series are from Nacional Financiera (1978, pp. 23–28). The 1900–39 series in constant 1950 prices were linked to a series for 1939–50 in 1960 prices. No data are available for the period of the Mexican Revolution and its aftermath (1910–21).

The 1950–96 series at 1975 prices were derived as follows. The 1975 levels of GDP in 1975 pesos are derived from Appendix Table E.3. The 1975 levels were extrapolated to 1960–93 with indexes of real GDP for all sectors 1960–93 from INEGI (1994a), linked to 1950–60 series in 1960 prices from Nacional Financiera (1978), and 1993–96 series from INEGI (1998).

USA

The 1900–50 real GDP trends are from Kendrick (1961). The 1950–96 series at 1975 US$ were estimated as follows: the 1975 levels of GDP in 1975 US$ are derived from the Department of Commerce, Bureau of Economic Analysis, *Survey of Current Business*, August 1996. The 1975 levels were extrapolated with 1950–77 GDP series from Department of Commerce (1986); linked to 1977–87 series from Department of Commerce, Bureau of Economic Analysis, *Survey of Current Business*, January 1991. 1988–90 from Department of Commerce, Bureau of Economic Analysis, *Survey of Current Business*, May 1993. The years 1990–93 from Department of Commerce, *Survey of Current Business*, October 1994 and April 1995, and 1993–96 from Department of Commerce, *Survey of Current Business*, November 1997.

NOTE

1. Detailed input output tables were produced every five years since 1970. From 1990 onwards, annual (more aggregated) tables are available.

Appendix C: Exchange Rates and Prices

EXCHANGE RATES

Brazil

Exchange rates of 1889, 1900 and 1938–80 from Maddison *et al.* (1992, pp. 215–17). 1913–37 from Goldsmith (1986, p. 180). 1980–91 from Baer (1995, pp. 392–93); 1992–97 from IMF, *International Financial Statistics* (various issues). From 1953 to 1966 Brazil had a system of multiple exchange rates. The 1955–57 rates were an average of the different prevailing rates; the 1953–54 and 1958–66 rates correspond to the free rates (Maddison and Associates, 1992). Brazil has changed its currency various times. On 31 October 1942 the milréis was replaced by the old cruzeiro. In 1967 the new cruzeiros, equal to 1,000 old cruzeiros, were introduced. On 28 February 1986 the cruzado, equal to 1,000 new cruzeiros, was introduced. On 15 January 1989 the new cruzado, equal to 1,000 old cruzados, was introduced. On 16 March 1990 the cruzeiro replaced the new cruzado at a rate of one new cruzado for one cruzeiro. On 1 August 1993, the cruzeiro Real, equal to 1,000 cruzeiros, was introduced. On 1 July 1994 the real replaced the cruzeiro real at a rate of 2,750 cruzeiro reis for one real.

Mexico

The pesos/US$ exchange rate for 1821–1992 from INEGI (1994b); 1992–97 from IMF, *International Financial Statistics* (various issues). On 1 January 1993 the new peso, equal to 1,000 old pesos, was introduced.

PRICE DEFLATORS BY SECTOR OF THE ECONOMY

The evolution of prices by sector of the economy was estimated by GDP deflators obtained by dividing the series of GDP in current prices by the series of GDP in constant prices. Brazil experienced very high rates of inflation in the 1980s and early 1990s, which makes the presentation of a single index difficult. Therefore, three benchmark years were chosen, for example 1980, 1986 and 1990. For reasons of comparability, the same benchmark years were used for Mexico and the USA. The sources for the series of GDP at constant prices are described in Appendix B. The sources of the series of GDP at current prices are as follows.

Brazil

GDP at current prices for 1900–08 from Goldsmith (1986, pp. 82–83); 1908–47 from Haddad (1978); 1947–50 from Goldsmith (1986, p. 224); 1950–85 from Gusmão Veloso (1987); 1985–90 from IBGE (1992); 1990–96 from IBGE (1998).

Mexico

The 1900–70 series from Nacional Financiera (1978); linked to 1970–80, and 1980–88 series from INEGI (1994a); 1988–96 from INEGI (1998).

USA

GDP for 1950–59 from Department of Commerce, Bureau of Economic Analysis (1986); linked to the 1959–94 series from Department of Commerce, Bureau of Economic Analysis, *Survey of Current Business*, August 1996; 1995–96 extrapolated with series from Department of Commerce, Bureau of Economic Analysis, *Survey of Current Business*, November 1997.

Appendix D: The Service Sector

This appendix presents the underlying sources for the bilateral comparisons of output in services. The underlying data are available in Mulder (1999), and upon request from the author.

PUBLIC UTILITIES

Public utilities consist of the production and distribution of gas, electricity and water. Volume data: for Brazil electricity production was derived from IBGE (1990, p. 497); for Mexico from INEGI (1982); and for the USA from Department of Commerce, *Statistical Abstract of the United States 1979.* Volume of water distribution: Brazil was estimated by the – urban and rural – per capita consumption times the size of the urban and rural population. This figure was corrected for the share of houses connected to (piped) water works as taken from ECLAC (1993, pp. 16, 166). Mexico from Cessti (1989) and *Comisión del Plan Hidraulico* (1981); USA: see source electricity distribution. Gas distribution is from Wilkie (1990, p. 511).

Value of output: cost of public utilities was derived from the national accounts of Brazil and the USA (see IBGE, 1987; Department of Commerce, Bureau of Economic Analysis, 1986), and for Mexico from INEGI (1994a). Cost of water distribution was taken from Mulder (1991).

TRANSPORT

Passenger km, passengers, ton km, tons and value of output: Brazil from *Ministerio do Transportes* (1982); IBGE, *Anuario Estatístico do Brasil* (various issues); and IBGE (1990); Mexico from SPP (1979), SPP (1981b), and SPP, *Anuario Estadístico de los Estados Unidos Mexicanos*; and USA: from Department of Transportation, *National Transportation Statistics* (various issues); and Department of Commerce, *Statistical Abstract of the United States* (various issues).

WHOLESALE AND RETAIL TRADE

Sales, inputs and value added: Brazil: IBGE (1981a); Mexico: SPP (1981a, Table 35): '*Ventas netas mas ingresos diversos, insumos totales y valor agregado censal bruto por clase de actividad y estrato de personal ocupado*'. USA: Department of Commerce, Bureau of the Census (1981a, 1981c). Neither census contains data on purchases of goods by distributors and value added. Two other publications of Department of Commerce, Bureau of the Census (1981b, 1981d) were used to estimate purchased goods and value added as a percentage of sales for different kinds of trade. The 1977 US wholesale prices were adjusted to a 1975 basis by wholesale price indexes derived from the Department of Labor, Bureau of Labor Statistics (1978a). The 1977 retail prices were adjusted to a 1975 basis by consumer price indexes derived from the Department of Labor, Bureau of Labor Statistics (1978b).

The ICP augmented binary PPPs for sales are from worksheets of Kravis *et al.* (1982); ICOP binary UVRs for purchases and other inputs from Houben (1990), van Ark and Maddison (1994) and Maddison and van Ooststroom (1993).

FINANCE

Brazilian number of loans granted by *Banco do Brasil*, and operating revenues (*rendas operacionais*), and insurance policies from IBGE (1976), *Anuario Estatístico do Brasil*, Rio de Janeiro. Mexico: demand and time deposits, bank revenues, number of life and health insurance policies, and premium income are from INEGI (1977), *Anuario Estadístico de los Estados Unidos Mexicanos*, Tables 15.24, 15.37 and 15.38; Output of the *Instituciones Privadas de Credito* was taken from INEGI (1994b). USA: Federal Reserve Bank (1977). Number of US life and health insurance policies and premium revenues from US Department of Commerce (1977), *Statistical Abstract of the United States 1977*, Tables 881, 885 and 887.

REAL ESTATE

The major share of real estate output refers to paid rents for residential structures and imputed housing services. The volume of real estate services has been estimated by the utility derived from the housing stock, measured by the physical characteristics of dwellings in terms of number of rooms and the availability of facilities. Data for 1980 were used as no data are available for 1975. Brazilian rural houses had only a few amenities, as only 4 per cent were connected to piped water, more than half lacked sewerage facilities and four-fifths lacked access to electricity.

In contrast to the Brazilian census, the Mexican census shows the size of homes measured by the number of rooms and bedrooms, and the type of material used to build the walls and roof. The latter type of information was lacking in the US survey. The USA had seven times more housing units than Mexico, and Mexico had more than twice the number of occupants per home as the USA. US homes were larger than Mexican ones in terms of the number of rooms. More than a third of Mexican houses lacked access to piped water, half had no sewerage and one quarter had no access to electricity.

The volume of housing services was estimated by the number of housing units, adjusted for the smaller size and the larger share of houses lacking basic facilities in Brazil and Mexico compared to the USA. The number of (bed)rooms per house has been used as an indicator for size, and the connection to public sewerage or a septic tank as a proxy for quality.

Gross output, value added and employment in real estate: Brazil from IBGE (1989b); Mexico from INEGI (1994a); and USA from Department of Commerce (1992). Characteristics of housing stock: Brazil: from IBGE, *Anuario Estatístico do Brasil 1987–88*, pp. 251–52 (data compiled from the population census), Mexico from INEGI (1984, pp. 331–83); and USA from Department of Housing and Urban Development and Department of Commerce, Bureau of the Census (1983).

HEALTH CARE

Brazil: number of admissions, medical and dental consults from IBGE, *Anuario Estatístico do Brasil 1980*; and value of output from IBGE (1989b). In Mexico the following institutions were included: *Secretaria de Salud* (SSA), *Instituto Mexico del Seguro Social* (IMSS) and *IMSS Solidaridad, Instituto de Servicios Sociales y Salud para Trabajadores del Estado* (ISSSTE). Services provided were derived from *Secretaria de Salud* (1994); costs of SSA from *Secretaria de Salud* (1989). Costs of IMSS and ISSSTE from Salinas de Gortari (1993), which were allocated to hospitals, physicians and dentists services by using shares listed in Chaves *et al.* (1988, p. 46). USA: hospital services and total expenses from American Hospital Association (1990). Physicians' and dentists' visits from Department of Commerce, *Statistical Abstract of the United States 1993*, p. 119. Gross value of output was estimated by national expenditure on physician and dentist services from the Department of Commerce, *Statistical Abstract of the United States 1991*, p. 108.

Breakdown of hospital stays by diagnosis related groups (DRGs): for Brazil: *Ministério da Saúde, Fundação Nacional de Saúde, Depto. de Informática do Sistema Único de Saúde, Sistema Síntese*, Brasilia; for Mexico the data refer to discharges from hospitals providing services to government employees as provided by Hilda Morales of ISSSTE; for the USA discharges and costs were broken down by 492 diagnosis related groups (DRGs) from Ernst & Young and Health Care Investment Analysts (1995).

EDUCATION

Brazil/USA comparison: for Brazil the number of students is from the *Ministerio da Educação* (1990). The gross value of output of public education was allocated over primary, secondary and tertiary education using the 1980 federal expenditure data by type of education as from Wilkie (1983, 1985). Expenditure data were available for 1978 and 1983 only. 1980 shares were estimated by using the annual average compound growth rate for 1978–83 period. USA: number of pupils from Department of Education, National Center for Education Statistics (1993, pp. 74, 227, 409–11). Expenditure and US shares from OECD (1992b, p. 102). The value of output in private education could not be allocated to the parts.

Mexico/USA comparison: for Mexico student enrolment is from the *Secretaria de Educación Publica* (1990); gross value of output from INEGI (1994a). The gross value of output of public education was allocated over primary, secondary and tertiary education using the 1988 federal expenditure data for Mexico by type of education is from Salinas de Gortari (1993, pp. 530–32). USA: student enrolment from Department of Education, National Center for Education Statistics (1993, p. 62). Gross value of output from Department of Commerce (January 1992 and May 1993), *Survey of Current Business.*

Appendix E: Reconciling Census and National Accounts Data

Production censuses were the main sources for our output and productivity comparisons, except for finance and real estate, education, health care and government. Censuses cover most establishments included in business registers. However, part of the production in each sector takes place in outlets excluded from these registers, such as unregistered outlets, streets and markets. Street vendors are particularly important in Brazil and Mexico. The national accounts use household surveys, international trade statistics, population censuses and tax records to impute the value added in unregistered activity.

The production censuses and national accounts of Brazil, Mexico and the USA provide sufficient detail for a sectoral reconciliation of value added and employment data. For 1975 the Mexican national accounts make much bigger adjustments for value added of unregistered units than the Brazilian accounts do, in particular in financial services and real estate, restaurants and hotels, wholesale and retail trade and other services.

To test the plausibility of the value added imputations of the national accounts, labour productivity of the registered sector was compared to that of the unregistered sector. Productivity in the former part of the economy should be higher than in the latter, because of the larger capital stock per worker, higher educational standards and a larger scale of production in the registered sector. This was the case for Brazil, but not for Mexico (Mulder, 1996). The value added of the national accounts was 2.5 times the value added of the census in Mexico, whereas national accounts employment was only twice the census figures, suggesting that labour productivity was higher in major parts of the Mexican unregistered economy than in the registered economy. This seems unrealistic and suggests that imputations made for unregistered activity by the Mexicans were too large.

In contrast, in Brazil the national accounts probably make too small imputations for informal activity. This is confirmed by Maddison and van Ark (1989) and Maddison and Associates (1992). In manufacturing in 1980 value added of census establishments accounted for 98.8 per cent of total value added. Only 1.2 per cent was produced by people outside these establishments. However, the industrial census reported 4.8 million persons engaged in manufacturing, compared to 6.9 million reported in the demographic census. This indicates that even after adjustment for misreporting and lower productivity in the informal sector, the national accounts underestimated manufacturing output. The national accounts estimate of the total unregistered sector was 10 per cent of GDP in 1980. The understatement of GDP in Brazil has also been stressed by Merrick and Graham (1979), Pfefferman and Webb (1979) and Melo Flores de Lima (1985).

ACCOUNTING FOR UNREGISTERED ACTIVITY

The above findings seriously point towards inadequate or exaggerated imputations for value added of the unregistered sector in Brazil and Mexico. A standardised approach has been used to impute value added in the unregistered sector to check the plausibility of the national accounts estimates of value added in the unregistered sector in Brazil and Mexico.

Workers excluded from the production censuses are considered as 'unregistered' here, even though some may be on payrolls, registered for social security or included in tax records. For those sectors included in the censuses, employment in the unregistered sector in Brazil was much less important than in Mexico in 1975 (8 per cent compared to 53 per cent). Most persons excluded from the production censuses are self-employed or work in small establishments. The labour productivity performance of unregistered persons was estimated using value added and employment information on establishments with less than five employees derived from production censuses (see Table E.1). Workers in small outlets performed worse than their colleagues working in larger registered establishments. Small establishments in services performed relatively better than those in the commodity-producing sector, except for construction.

Value added in the unregistered sector was imputed by using the labour productivity estimates of small establishments, as demonstrated in Tables E.2 and E.3. Employment in the unregistered sector equals the difference between the census and national accounts (see column 1). Value added of the unregistered sector was imputed by the number of unregistered workers times the labour productivity of small establishments (column 3). The sum of census value added and imputed value added of the unregistered sector yields the revised estimate of GDP by sector of the economy (see column 5).

Table E.1 *Labour Productivity in Small Establishments as a Percentage of that in Large Establishments, Brazil and Mexico, 1975*

	Brazil, 1975	Mexico, 1975
Mining	18.2	66.4
Manufacturing	19.6	43.3
Construction	236.1	n.a.
Transport	87.5	64.2
Distribution	29.2	23.0
Hotels and restaurants	55.5	41.5
Repair and maintenance	48.3	71.5
Amusement services	26.8	35.2
Professional services	72.7	106.4
Real estate	13.3	257.2
Total (all branches)	29.7	39.7

Note: Small establishments are those with less than five employees, while large ones have more than five.

Sources:Brazil: IBGE (1982), *Censos Economicos de 1975;* Mexico: INEGI (1993), *Censos Economicos 1976.*

The estimates of value added in Brazil for 1975 are not too different from the official GDP figures for most sectors, except for mining, construction, transport and 'other services' (see column 6). the total value added estimate was 12 per cent above the national accounts GDP, indicating that the alternative procedure to calculate total GDP yielded a higher result than the national accounts on the total economy level.

The same procedure was used to impute value added of the unregistered sector in Mexico. All the estimates of value added were below the official GDP figures for 1975, except for communications, mining, restaurants and hotels, and 'other services' (see Table E.3). Wholesale and retail trade showed the largest discrepancy between the value added estimate and official GDP. The estimate for value added of the total economy was 15 per cent below the national accounts GDP.

Table E.2 *Imputation of Value Added in Activity Omitted in Censuses and Adjusted Estimate of Total Value Added, Brazil, 1975*

	Employ-ment National Accounts Minus Census (000s) (1)	Labour Producti-vity in Small scale Establish-ments (Cruzeiros) (2)	Imputed Value Added Cols (1)*(2) (million Cruzeiros) (3)	Value Added from Census (million Cruzeiros) (4)	Total Value Added Cols (3)+(4) (Million Cruzeiros) (5)	Ratio Revised Value Added/ National Accounts (6)
Agriculture	160	4,069 [b]	652	82,785	83,438	0.75
Mining	120	22,235 [a]	2,674	7,520	10,194	1.44
Total primary	281		3,326	90,305	93,632	0.79
Manufacturing	–98	16,376 [a]	–1,608	257,012	255,404	0.86
Construction	1,510	43,473 [b]	65,663	34,247	99,910	1.95
Total secondary	1,412		64,055	291,259	355,314	1.02
Transport	750	38,088 [a]	28,557	20,630	49,187	1.34
Communications	1	74,250 [b]	38	11,358	11,396	1.19
Distribution	403	27,400 [a]	11,042	149,945	160,987	1.07
Other services	4,058 [d]	14,157 [a]	57,452	50,855	108,306	1.48
Total tertiary	4,760		84,708	232,788	317,496	1.15
Total	6,452		161,794	614,352	776,146	1.04
	Sectors Partly Covered by the National Accounts					
Health care	394 [e]	22,113	8,722	4,603	13,325	2.89
	Value Added Derived from the National Accounts					
Public utilities					20,345	1.00
Financial services					45,138	1.00
Real estate					66,814	1.00
Education					38,380	1.00
Government					74,918	1.00
Total					1,025,362	1.13

Notes:

[a] Establishments with less than five employees.
[b] All establishments.
[c] Estimated on basis of 1976 employment in mining from IBGE, *Pesquisa por Amostra a Domicilio 1976*, and imputation from 1960, 1970 and 1980 census.
[d] National accounts omits a large part of other services.
[e] National accounts employment refers to private health care only. Total employment equalled 603,000.

Sources: Census and national accounts employment from Appendix Table E.1, except for mining and health care, see Appendix A; labour productivity of small-scale establishments derived from production censuses as described in source in Table E.1. National accounts GDP from IBGE (1987), except for education and government. Education GDP was estimated by the extrapolation of the 1980 value added (from IBGE, 1989b) by the 1980 to 1975 volume and price changes. GDP in government from IBGE (1990).

Table E.3 Imputation of Value Added in Activity Omitted in Censuses and Adjusted Estimate of Total Value Added, Mexico, 1975

	Employment National Accounts Minus Census (000s) (1)	Labour Productivity in Small-Scale Establishments (Cruzeiros) (2)	Imputed Value Added Cols (1)*(2) (Million Cruzeiros) (3)	Value Added from Census (Million Cruzeiros) (4)	Total Value Added Cols (3)+(4) (Million Cruzeiros) (5)	Ratio Revised Value Added/ National Accounts (6)
Mining	111	85,400	9,485	24,271	33,755	1.06
Manufacturing	1,265	27,737	35,088	157,489	192,577	0.75
Transport	214	66,266	14,151	26,906	41,058	0.74
Communications	43	139,818	6,075	3,076	9,151	1.23
Distribution	880	34,829	30,641	77,988	108,629	0.46
Restaurants and hotels	44	21,563	957	9,548	10,505	1.10
Amusement services	−14	31,124	−431	4,692	4,262	0.45
Professional services	11	96,839	1,027	6,787	7,814	0.48
Other services	3,118	28,145	87,768	5,784	93,552	2.02
Total tertiary sector	4,296		140,189	134,781	274,970	0.72
	Value Added Derived from the National Accounts					
Agriculture					123,153	
Construction					68,425	
Public utilities					9,793	
Financial services					20,876	
Real estate					83,411	
Health care					28,929	
Education					39,708	
Government					40,432	
Total (all sectors)					916,028	0.85

Sources: Census and national accounts employment from Appendix Table E.2; labour productivity of small-scale establishments derived from production censuses as described in sources in Table E.2. National accounts value added from INEGI (1994a).

References

Abramovitz, M. (1989), *Thinking about Growth*, Cambridge: Cambridge University Press.

Academia Nacional de Medicina (1992), 'El Tratado de Libre Comercio y los Servicios Médicos: Elementos para el Análisis y la Negociación', mimeo, Mexico City: Academia Nacional de Medicina.

Adie, D.K. (1990), *The Mail Monopoly: Analysing Canadian Postal Performance*, Vancouver: The Fraser Institute.

Ahlroth, S. (1997), 'The Output of the Swedish Education Sector', *The Review of Income and Wealth*, **43** (1), 89–104.

Ark, B. van (1993), 'International Comparisons of Output and Productivity: Manufacturing Performance of Ten Countries from 1950 to 1990', *Monograph Series*, No. 1, Groningen: Groningen Growth and Development Centre.

Ark, B. van (1995), 'Sectoral Growth Accounting and Structural Change', *Research Memorandum*, No. GD-23, Groningen: Groningen Growth and Development Centre.

Ark, B. van and A. Maddison (1994), 'An International Comparison of Real Output, Purchasing Power and Labour Productivity in Manufacturing Industries: Brazil, Mexico and the USA in 1975', *Research Memorandum*, No. 567 (GD-6), Groningen: Groningen Growth and Development Centre.

Ark, B. van, E. Monnikhof and N. Mulder (1999), 'Productivity in Services: An International Comparative Perspective', *Canadian Journal of Economics*, **32** (2), 471–99.

Ark, B. van, and R.H. McGuckin (1999), 'International Comparisons of Labor Productivity and Per Capita Income', *Monthly Labor Review*, **122** (7), 33–41.

Ark, B. van and E.J. Monnikhof (2000), 'Productivity and Unit Labour Cost Comparisons: A Data Base', *Employment Paper* 2000/5, Geneva: International Labour Office.

Ark. B. van and M. Timmer (2001), 'PPPs and International Productivity Comparisons: Bottlenecks and New Directions', paper presented Joint World Bank/OECD seminar on purchasing power parities, 30 January – 2 February, Washington, DC.

Baer, W. (1995), *The Brazilian Economy*, New York: Praeger Publishers.

Baily, M.N. and R.J. Gordon (1988), 'The Productivity Slowdown, Measurement Issues, and the Explosion of Computer Power', *Brookings Papers on Economic Activity*, **19** (2), 347–431.

Balassa, B. (1964), 'The Purchasing Power Parity Doctrine: A Reappraisal', *Journal of Political Economy*, **72**, February, 584–96.

Banco Nacional de Desenvolvimento Econômico e Social (1996a), 'Comércio Varejista', *Comercio e Serviços*, Rio de Janeiro: BNDES.

Banco Nacional de Desenvolvimento Econômico e Social (1996b), 'Shopping Centers', *Comercio e Serviços*, Rio de Janeiro: BNDES.

Barger, H. (1951), *The Transportation Industries 1889–1946: A Study of Output, Employment and Productivity*, New York: NBER.

Barger, H. (1955), *Distribution's Place in the American Economy since 1869*, NBER, Princeton: Princeton University Press.

Barth, J.R. (1991), *The Great Savings and Loan Debacle*, Washington, DC: American Enterprise Institute Press.

Bartholomew, P.F. (1993), *Resolving the Thrift Crisis*, Washington, DC: Congressional Budget Office.

Batchelor, R.A., R.L Mayor and A.D Morgan (1980), *Industrialisation and the Basis for Trade*, Cambridge: Cambridge University Press.

Baumol, W.J. (1967), 'Macroeconomics of Unbalanced Growth: The Anatomy of Urban Crisis', *The American Economic Review*, **57** (3), 415–26.

Baumol, W.J., J. Blackman and E. Wolff (1991), *Productivity and American Leadership: The Long View*, Cambridge, MA: MIT Press.

Berg, S.A., F.R. Førsund, L. Hjalmarsson and M. Suominen (1993), 'Banking Efficiency in Nordic Countries', *Journal of Banking and Finance*, **17** (2/3), 371–88.

Berger, A.N. and D.B. Humphrey (1992), 'Measurement and Efficiency Issues in Commercial Banking', in Z. Griliches (ed.), *Output Measurement in the Service Sectors*, NBER, Chicago: University of Chicago Press, 245–79.

Bernard, A.B. and C.I. Jones (1996), 'Comparing Apples to Oranges: Productivity Convergence and Measurement Across Industries and Countries', *American Economic Review*. **86** (5), 1216–38.

Berry, A. (1978), 'A Positive Interpretation of the Expansion of Urban Services in Latin America', *Journal of Development Studies*, **14**, 210–31.

Betancourt, R.R. (1993), 'An Analysis of the U.S. Distribution System', *Economics Department Working Papers*, No. 135, Paris: OECD.

Bethell, L. (ed.) (1985), *The Cambridge History of Latin America, Volume III: From Independence to c. 1870*, Cambridge: Cambridge University Press.

Bhagwati, J.N. (1984), 'Why are Services Cheaper in the Poor Countries', *Economic Journal*, **94**, June, 279–86.

Blaug, M. (1976), *An Introduction to the Economics of Education*, London: Cox and Wyman.

Blendon, R.J. (1989), 'Three Systems: A Comparative Survey', *Health Management Quarterly*, **9** (1), 2–9.

Bobadilla, J.L., J. Frenk, R. Lozano, T. Frejka and C. Stern (1993), 'The Epidemiologic Transition and Health Priorities', in D.T. Jamison, W.T. Mosley, A.R. Measham and J.L. Bobadilla (eds), *Disease Control in Developing Countries*, New York: Oxford University Press, 51–63.

Boer, S. de (1999), 'A Volume Index for the Dutch Banking Industry Based on Quantity Indicators: A Pilot Study for the Period 1987–95', Voorburg: Statistics Netherlands.

Boerkamp, E. (1995), *Assessing Professional Services Quality: An Application in Health Care*, Ph.D. Thesis, University of Groningen, Ridderkerk: Labyrint Publications.

Bordo, M.D., H. Rockoff and A. Radish (1993), 'A Comparison of the United States and Canadian Banking Systems in the Twentieth Century: Stability vs. Efficiency', *NBER Working Paper*, No. 4546, Cambridge, MA: NBER.

Boyd, H.J. and G.M. Walton (1972), 'Social Savings from Nineteenth-century Rail Passenger Services', *Explorations in Economic History*, **9** (3), 233–54.

Briard, K. (2001), 'Productivités comparés des chemins de fer français et allemands', in N. Mulder and A. Remy (eds), *La productivité dans les transports*, Paris: Ministry of Transport, 43–73.

Brinkley, A., R.N. Current, F. Freidel and T.H. Williams (1991), *American History: A Survey*, New York: McGraw-Hill.

Broadberry, S.N. (1995), 'Micro-historical Foundations of the Convergence Debate', paper presented at EHES Summer School, 19–24 June, Groningen: University of Groningen.

Bruggink, A. (1989), *Performance Control in Banking: Theory and Application*, Ph.D. Thesis, Enschede: University of Twente.

Burns, E.B. (1993), *A History of Brazil*, Third Edition, New York: Columbia University Press.

Burt, S.L. and J.A. Dawson (1990), 'From Small Shops to Hypermarket: The Dynamics of Retailing', in D. Pinder (ed.), *Western Europe: Challenge and Change*, London: Belhaven Press, 142–61.

Cassedy, J.H. (1991), *Medicine in America: A Short History*, Baltimore: The Johns Hopkins University Press.

Castro, N. de (1988), 'Estrutura e Desempenho do Setor Transporte Rodoviário de Carga', *Pesquisa e Planejamento Economico*, **18** (1), 55–82.

Caves, R., L. Christensen and W.E. Diewert (1982), 'The Economic Theory of Index Numbers and the Measurement of Input, Output and Productivity', *Econometrica*, No. 50, 1393–414.

Cessti, R. (1989), *Water Resources: Problems and Issues for the Water Supply and Sanitation Sector*, Washington, DC: World Bank.

Chakraborty, A. and M. Kazarosian (1999), 'Product Differentiation and the Use of Information Technology: Evidence from the Trucking Industry', *Working Paper Series*, No. 7222, Cambridge, MA: NBER.

Chandler, A.D., Jr. (1990), *Scale and Scope: The Dynamics of Industrial Capitalism*, Cambridge, MA: Harvard University Press.

Chaves, M.R. de, M. Márquez and M.O. de Mendoza, *El Enfoque de la Salud, o Sector Social y Económico: Gasto y Financamiento para la Atención de la Salud en México*, Mexico City: Funsalud.

Chenery, H.B., S. Robinson and M. Syrquin (1986), *Industrialisation and Growth: A Comparative Study*, New York: Oxford University Press.

Chenery, H.B. and M. Syrquin (1975), *Patterns of Development, 1950–70*, London: Oxford University Press.

Chenery, H.B. and L. Taylor (1968), 'Development Patterns Among Countries and Over Time', *Review of Economics and Statistics*, **50** (4), 391–416.

Clark, C. (1940, 1957), *Conditions of Economic Progress*, First and Third Edition, London: McMillan.

Coatsworth, J.H. (1981), *Growth Against Development: The Economic Impact of Railroads in Porfirian Mexico*, DeKalb, IL: Northern Illinois University Press.

Comisión del Plan Hidraulico (1981), *Plan Nacional Hidraulico 1981*, Mexico City: CPH.

Contador, C. (1992), 'Nature of the Financial System, Capital Markets and Monetary Policy', background paper to A. Maddison, and Associates (1992), *The Political Economy of Poverty, Equity and Growth: Brazil and Mexico*, New York: Oxford University Press.

Cowen, R. and M. McLean (eds) (1985), *International Handbook of Education Systems, Volume III: Asia, Australasia and Latin America*, Chichester: John Wiley and Sons.

Cross, J.C. (1998), *Street Vendors and the State in Mexico City*, Stanford, CA: Stanford University Press.

Cutler, D.M., M.B. McClellan and J.P. Newhouse (1999), 'The Costs and Benefits of Intensive Treatment of Cardiovascular Disease', in J.E. Triplett (ed.), *Measuring the Prices of Medical Treatments*, Washington, DC: Brookings Institution Press, 34–71.

Davies, R.E.G. (1972), *Airlines of the United States Since 1914*, London: Putnam.

Davies, R.E.G. (1984), *Airlines of Latin America since 1919*, London: Putnam.

Davies, R.E.G. (1987), *Rebels and Reformers of the Airways*, Washington, DC: Smithsonian Institution Press.

Davies, R.L. (ed.) (1995), *Retail Planning Policies in Western Europe*, London: Routledge.

Davis, L.E., R.E. Easterlin and W.N. Parker (eds) (1972), *American Economic Growth: An Economist's History of the United States*, New York: Harper and Row.

Dawson, J.A. (1995), 'Retail Change in the European Community', in R.L. Davies (ed.), *Retail Planning Policies in Western Europe*, London: Routledge, 1–30.

Deakin, B.M. and T. Seward (1969), 'Productivity in Transport: A Study of Employment, Capital, Output Productivity and Technical Change', *Occasional Papers*, No. 17, Department of Applied Economics, Cambridge, UK: University of Cambridge.

Dean, E.R. and K. Kunze (1991), 'Productivity Measurement in the Service Industries', paper presented at the Conference on Output Measurement in the Service Sector, Charleston.

Den Hartog, P. and R. Bilderbeek (1999), 'Conceptualising Service Innovation and Service Innovation Patterns', mimeo, The Hague: Dutch Ministry of Economic Affairs.

Denison, E.F. (1967), *Why Growth Rates Differ*, Washington, DC: The Brookings Institution.

Döhrn, R. and U. Heilemann (1996), 'The Chenery Hypothesis and Structural Change in Eastern Europe', *Economics of Transition*, **4** (2), 411–25.

Drake, D.F. (1994), *Reforming the Health Care Market: An Interpretive Economic History*, Washington, DC: Georgetown University Press.

Dupuis, M. and R. de Maricourt (1989), 'Trois mondes, trois distributions', *Les cahiers de recherche*, No. 89/81, Paris: Ecole Supérieure de Commerce.

Durand, H. (1986), *Les systèmes monétaires et bancaires étrangers*, Paris: Editions Cujas.

Elfring, T. (1988), *Service Employment in Advanced Economies: A Comparative Analysis of its Implications for Economic Growth*, Aldershot: Avebury.

Emmet, B. and J.E. Jeuck (1950), *Catalogues and Counters: A History of Sears, Roebuck and Company*, Chicago, IL: University of Chicago Press.

Euromonitor (1995), *Retail Trade International 1995*, London.

Eurostat (2000), 'Price and Volume Measures for Financial Intermediation', Report of the Task Force, presented at Meeting for the Working Party on National Accounts, Luxembourg 5–6 June 2000.

Falvey, R.E. and N. Gemmell (1996), 'Are Services Income Elastic? Some New Evidence', *Review of Income and Wealth*, **42** (3), 257–69.

Fernandez, A. (1993), 'Trucking Deregulation in Mexico' in J.C. Carbajo (ed.), *Regulatory Reform in Transport: Some Recent Experiences*, Washington, DC: World Bank, 101–05.

Fisher, A.G.B. (1933), 'Capital and the Growth of Knowledge', *Economic Journal*, September.

Fisher, A.G.B. (1935), *The Clash of Progress and Security*, London: MacMillan.

Fisher, A.G.B. (1939), 'Production, Primary, Secondary and Tertiary', *The Economic Record*, June, 24–38.

Fishlow, A. (1965), *American Railroads and the Transformation of the Ante-Bellum Economy*, Boston: Harvard University Press.

Fitzgerald, J. and I. Knipper (1993), 'Distribution', in European Commission, 'Market Services and European Integration', *European Economy: Social Europe*, Reports and Studies, No. 3, Brussels.

Fixler, D. (1993), 'Measuring Financial Service Output of Commercial Banks', *Applied Economics*, **25**, 983–99.

Fixler, D. and K. Zieschang (1999), 'The Productivity of the Banking Sector: Integrating Financial and Production Approaches to Measuring Financial Service Output', *Canadian Journal of Economics*, **32**, (2), 547–69.

Fogel, R.W. (1964), *Railroads and American Economic Growth: Essays in Econometric History*, Baltimore: Johns Hopkins University Press.

Frank, R.G., E.R. Berndt and S.H. Busch (1999), 'Price Indexes for the Treatment of Depression', in J.E. Triplett, *Measuring the Prices of Medical Treatments*, Washington, DC: The Brookings Institution Press.

Friedman, M. and A.J. Schwartz (1963), *A Monetary History of the United States, 1867–1960*, NBER, Princeton: Princeton University Press.

Frischtak, C. (1992), 'Banking Automation and Productivity Change: The Brazilian Experience', *World Development*, **20** (12), 1769–84.

Froot, K. and K. Rogoff, (1995), 'Perspectives on PPP and Long Run Real Exchange Rates', in G. Grossman and K. Rogoff (eds), *The Handbook of International Economics*, Amsterdam: Elsevier, 1647–88.

Fundación Mexicana para la Salud (1994a), 'Demanda y Oferta de Servicios: Obstáculos a la Mejoría del Sistema de Salud en México', *Documentos para el Análisis y la Convergencia*, No. 6, Mexico City: FMS.

Fundación Mexicana para la Salud (1994b), 'Calidad y Eficiencia en las Organizaciones de Atención a la Salud', *Documentos para el Análisis y la Convergencia*, No. 8, Mexico City: FMS.

Gemert, H.G. van (1985), *Orde en beweging in de sectorstructuur*, Groningen: Wolters-Noordhoff.

Gemmell, N. (1982), *Structural Change and Economic Development: The Role of the Service Sector*, London: MacMillan Press.

Gil, F. (1992), 'The Mexican Financial Sector', in background paper to A. Maddison and Associates (1992), *The Political Economy of Poverty, Equity and Growth: Brazil and Mexico*, New York: Oxford University Press.

Gilbert, M. and I.B. Kravis (1954), *An International Comparison of National Product and Purchasing Power of Currencies*, Paris: OEEC.

Goldsmith, R.W. (1966), *The Financial Development of Mexico*, Paris: OECD Development Centre.

Goldsmith, R.W. (1983), *The Financial Development of India, Japan, and the United States: A Trilateral Institutional, Statistical, and Analytic Comparison*, New Haven: Yale University Press.

Goldsmith, R.W. (1986), *Desenvolvimento Financeiro sob um Século de Inflação*, São Paulo: Harper and Row do Brasil.

Gordon, R.J. (1990), *The Measurement of Durable Goods Prices*, Chicago: University of Chicago Press.

Gordon, R.J. (1996), 'Problems in the Measurement and Performance of Service Sector Productivity in the United States', *NBER Working Paper*, No. 5519, Cambridge, MA: NBER.

Gorman, J.A. (1969), 'Alternative Measures of Real Output and Productivity of Commercial Banks', in V.R. Fuchs (ed.), *Production and Productivity in the Service Industries*, NBER Studies in Income and Wealth, Vol. 34, New York: Columbia University Press, 155–89.

Gras, J.M. and W. Fraschetto (1993), 'Analysis of Retailing in Mexico', *International Trends in Retailing*, **10** (1), 5–19.

Gregory, R.G. and J.M. Griffin (1974), 'Secular and Cross-section Industrialization Patterns: Some Further Evidence on the Kuznets Chenery Controversy', *Review of Economics and Statistics*, **56** (3), 360–68.

Griliches, Z. (ed.) (1992), *Output Measurement in the Service Sectors*, NBER, Chicago: University of Chicago Press.

Guevara Niebla, G. (ed.) (1995), *El Catástrofe Silenciosa*, Mexico City: Fondo de Cultura Economica.

Gutierrez Junquera, P. (1993), *El Crecimiento de los Servicios: Causas, Repercusiones y Políticas*, Madrid: Alianza Editorial.

Haber, S. (1991), 'Industrial Concentration and the Capital Markets: A Comparative Study of Brazil, Mexico and the United States', *Journal of Economic History*, **51** (3), 559–80.

Haber, S. (ed.) (1997), *How Latin America Fell Behind: Essays on the Economic Histories of Brazil and Mexico*, Stanford, CA: Stanford University Press.

Haddad (1978), *Crecimento do Produto Real no Brasil 1900–1947*, Rio de Janeiro: Fundação Getulio Vargas.

Hall, M., J. Knapp and C. Winsten (1961), *Distribution in Great Britain and North America*, Oxford: Oxford University Press.

Harbison, R.W. and E. Hanushek (1992), *Educational Performance of the Poor: Lessons from Rural Northeast Brazil*, Oxford: Oxford University Press.

Hariton, G. and R. Roy (1979), 'Productivity Changes in Canadian Air and Rail Transport in the Last Two Decades', *Logistics and Transportation Review*, **15** (4), 507–16.

Hernandez Laos, E. (1973), *Evolución de la Productividad de los Factores en México, 1950–67*, Mexico City: Ediciones Productividad.

Hernandez Laos, E. (1994), 'Diferenciales de Productividad entre México, Canadá y Estados Unidos', *Cuadernos de Trabajo*, No. 5, Mexico City: Secretaría del Trabajo y Previsión Social.

Hill, P. (1999), 'Tangibles, Intangibles and Services: A New Taxonomy for the Classification of Output, *Canadian Journal of Economics*, **32** (2), 426–46.

Hofman, A.A. (1998), *The Economic Development of Latin American Development in the Twentieth Century*, Cheltenham, UK and Northhampton, MA, USA: Edward Elgar.

Hooper, P. (1996), 'Comparing Manufacturing Output Levels among the Major Industrial Countries', in OECD, *Productivity: International Comparison and Measurement Issues*, Paris: OECD.

Houben, A. (1990), 'An International Comparison of Real Output, Labour Productivity and Purchasing Power in the Mineral Industries of the United States, Brazil and Mexico for 1975', *Research Memorandum*, No. 368, Groningen: Institute of Economic Research.

Hughes, J. (1987), *American Economic History*, Glenview IL: Scott Foresman.

INEGI (1990), 'Medición del Sector Informal en México', paper presented at the X Inter-American Statistics Conference, Aguascalientes.

Inter-American Development Bank (1996), *Economic and Social Progress in Latin America: Making Social Services Work*, Washington, DC: IADB.

Inter-Secretariat Working Group on National Accounts (1993), *System of National Accounts 1993*, Brussels/Luxembourg, New York, Paris, Washington, DC.

Islas Rivera, V. (1992), *Estructura y Desarrollo del Sector Transporte en México*, Mexico City: El Colegio de México.

Jefferys, J.B. and D. Knee (1962), *Retailing in Europe*, London: MacMillan.

Jorgenson, D.W. and M. Kuroda (1990), 'Productivity and International Competitiveness in Japan and the United States, 1960–1985', in C.R. Hulten (ed.), *Productivity in the U.S. and Japan*, Studies in Income and Wealth, 51, Chicago, IL: University of Chicago Press.

Jorgenson, D.W. and B.M. Fraumeni (1992), 'Investment in Education and US Economic Growth', *Scandinavian Journal of Economics*, **94** (Supplement), S51–70.

Jorgenson, D.W. and B.M. Fraumeni (2000), 'The Output of the Education Sector as Determined by the Education's Effect on Lifetime Income', Workshop on Measuring Output and Productivity in the Service Sector, 7 April, Washington, DC: The Brookings Institution.

Karoly Kaznar, I. (1994), 'Description of Brazil's Financial and Banking Sectors', mimeo, Rio de Janeiro.

Katouzian, H. (1970), 'The Development of the Service Sector: A New Approach', *Oxford Economic Papers*, **22** (3), 362–77.

Kendrick, J.W. (1961), *Productivity Trends in the United States*, NBER, Princeton: Princeton University Press.

Kendrick, J.W. (1973), *Post-war Productivity Trends in the United States, 1948–1969*, NBER, New York: Columbia University Press.

Kendrick, J.W. and B.N. Vaccara (eds) (1980), *New Developments in Productivity Measurement and Analysis*, Studies in Income and Wealth, No. 44, NBER, Chicago: University of Chicago Press.

Kindleberger, C.P. (1967), *European Post-war Growth: The Role of Labour Supply*, Cambridge, MA: Harvard University Press.

Klodt, H., R. Maurer and A. Schimmelpfennig (1997), *Tertiarisiering in der Deutschen Wirtschaft*, Kieler studien 283, Tübingen: Mohr.

Kravis, I.B., A. Heston and R. Summers (1982), *World Product and Income: International Comparisons of Real Gross Product*, Baltimore: Johns Hopkins University Press.

Kravis, I.B., A. Heston and R. Summers (1983), 'The Share of Services in Economic Growth', in F.G. Adams and B.G. Hickman (eds), *Global Econometrics: Essays in Honour of Lawrence R. Klein*, Cambridge, MA: MIT Press, 188–218.

Kravis, I.B. and R.E. Lipsey (1983), 'Toward an Explanation of International Price Levels', *Princeton Studies in International Finance*, **52**, November, p; 21.

Kravis, I.B. and R.E. Lipsey (1988), 'National Price Levels and the Prices of Tradables and Nontradables', *American Economic Review*, **78** (2), 474–78.

Kuznets, S. (1957), 'Quantitative Aspects of the Economic Growth of Nations: II. Industrial Distribution of National Product and Labor Force', *Economic Development and Cultural Change*, **5** (4), Supplement, S3–61.

Kuznets, S. (1966), *Modern Economic Growth*, New Haven: Yale University Press.

Kuznets, S. (1971), *Economic Growth of Nations: Total Output and Production Structure*, Cambridge, MA: Harvard University Press.

Lahrèche-Révil, A. (1998), 'Taux de change réel et développement', Ph.D. Thesis, Paris: Sorbonne University.

Latapi, P. (1994), 'Asimetrías Educatives ante el TLC', *Comercio Exterior*, **44** (3), 199–205.

Lau, L.J., D.T. Jamison, S.C. Liu and S. Rivkin (1993), 'Education and Economic Growth: Some Cross-sectional Evidence from Brazil', *Journal of Development Economics*, **41** (1), 45–70.

Lee, F.C. and J. Tang (1999), 'Methodological Issues in Comparing Productivity Levels and International Competitiveness in Canada and the United States', paper presented at the meeting of the American Economic Association, 7–9 January 2000, Boston.

Loegering, L., R.C. Reiter and J.C. Gambone (1994), 'Measuring the Quality of Care', *Clinical Obstetrics and Gynecology*, **137** (1), 122–36.

Ludwig, A.K. (1985), *Brazil: A Handbook of Historical Statistics*, Boston: Hall and Company.

Maddison, A. (1974), 'What is Education For?', *Lloyds Bank Review*, No. 112, April, 19–30.

Maddison, A. (1980), 'Economic Growth and Structural Change in the Advanced Countries', in I. Leveson and J.W. Wheeler (eds), *Western Economies in Transition: Structural Change and Adjustment Policies in Industrial Countries*, Colorado: Westview Press, 41–60.

Maddison, A. (1992), 'A Long Run Perspective on Saving', *Scandinavian Journal of Economics*, **94** (2), 181–96.

Maddison, A. (1995a), *Explaining the Economic Performance of Nations: Essays in Time and Space*, Aldershot: Edward Elgar.

Maddison, A. (1995b), *Monitoring the World Economy, 1820–1992*, Paris: OECD Development Centre.

Maddison, A. and Associates (1992), *The Political Economy of Poverty, Equity and Growth: Brazil and Mexico*, New York: Oxford University Press.

Maddison, A. and B. van Ark (1988), 'Comparison of Real Output in Manufacturing,' *World Bank Working Papers*, WPS 5, Washington, DC: WB.

Maddison, A. and B. van Ark (1989), 'An International Comparison of Purchasing Power, Real Output and Labour Productivity: A Case Study for Brazilian, Mexican and US Manufacturing, 1975', *Review of Income and Wealth*, **53** (1), 31–55.

Maddison, A. and B. van Ark (1994), 'The International Comparison of Real Product and Productivity', Research Memorandum, No. 567 (GD-6), Groningen: Groningen Growth and Development Centre.

Maddison, A. and H. van Ooststroom (1993), 'The International Comparison of Value Added, Productivity and Purchasing Power Parities in Agriculture', *Research Memorandum*, No. 536 (GD-1), Groningen: Groningen Growth and Development Centre.

Maddison, A. and D.S. Prasada Rao (1996), 'A Generalised Approach to International Comparisons of Agricultural Output and Productivity', *Research Memorandum*, No. GD-27, Groningen: Groningen Growth and Development Centre.

Malmquist, S. (1953), 'Index Numbers and Indifference Surfaces', *Trabajos de Estadistica*, **4**, 209–42.

Marichal, C. (1997), 'Obstacles to the Development of Capital Markets in Nineteenth Century Mexico', in S. Haber (ed.), *How Latin America Fell Behind: Essays on Economic Histories of Brazil and Mexico, 1800–1914*, Stanford, CA: Stanford University Press, 118–46.

Mark, J.A. (1982), 'Measuring Productivity in Service Industries', *Monthly Labour Review*, June, 3–8.

Mazumdar, K (1995), 'Disproportional Growth of Service Sector in India', *Indian Economic Journal*, **43** (2), 103–9.

McKinsey and Company (1986), *Airline Personnel Productivity: A Comparative Study*, Amsterdam.

McKinsey Global Institute (1992), *Service Sector Productivity*, Washington, DC: MGI.

McKinsey Global Institute (1993), *Manufacturing Productivity*, Washington, DC: MGI.

McKinsey Global Institute (1994), *Latin American Productivity*, Washington, DC: MGI.

McKinsey Global Institute (1995), *Sweden's Economic Performance*, Washington, DC: MGI.

McKinsey Global Institute (1996), *Health Care Productivity*, Washington, DC: MGI.

McKinsey Global Institute (1997), *Boosting Dutch Economic Performance*, Washington, DC: MGI.

McKinsey Global Institute (1998), *Productivity – The Key to an Accelerated Development Path for Brazil*, Washington, DC: MGI.

Medici, A. (1991), 'Descentralização e Informação em Saúde', *Relatórios Tecnicos*, No. 05/91, Escola Nacional de Ciéncias Estatísticas (ENCE), Rio de Janeiro.

Melo Flores de Lima, B. (1985), *Criptoeconomia ou Economia Subterranea*, Rio de Janeiro: Vargas Foundation.

Merrick, T.W. and D.H Graham (1979), *Population and Economic Development in Brazil: 1800 to the Present*, Baltimore: Johns Hopkins University Press.

Meyer, J.R. and J.A. Gómez-Ibáñez (1980), 'Measurement and Analysis of Productivity in Transportation Industries', in J.W. Kendrick and B.N. Vaccara (eds), *New Developments in Productivity Measurement and Analysis*, Studies in Income and Wealth, No. 44, NBER, Chicago: University of Chicago Press,

Meyer, J.R. and A.L. Morton (1975), 'The US Railroad Industry in the Post-World War II Period: A Profile', *Explorations in Economic Research*, **2**, 449–501.

Meyer, J.W.F., O. Ramirez and Y.N. Soysal (1992), 'World Expansion of Mass Education, 1870–1980', *Sociology of Education*, **65**, April, 128–49.

Meyer, J.W., R. Rubinson, O. Ramirez and J. Boli-Bennett (1977), 'The World Educational Revolution', *Sociology of Education*, **50**, October, 242–58.

Mulder, N. (1991), 'An Assessment of Mexican Productivity Performance in Services: A Comparative View', mimeo, Groningen: University of Groningen.

Mulder, N. (1994a), 'Output and Productivity in Brazilian Distribution: A Comparative View', *Research Memorandum*, No. 578 (GD-17), Groningen: Groningen Growth and Development Centre.

Mulder, N. (1994b), 'Transport and Communications in Mexico and the United States: Value Added, Purchasing Power Parities and Labour Productivity, 1950–87', *Research Memorandum*, No. 579 (GD-18), Groningen: Groningen Growth and Development Centre.

Mulder, N. (1995), 'Transport and Communications Output and Productivity in Brazil and the USA, 1950–1990', *Research Memorandum*, No. 580 (GD-19), Groningen: Groningen Growth and Development Centre.

Mulder, N. (1996), 'Accounting for Informality: The Case of Brazil and Mexico', paper presented at the Conference of the International Association for the Research of Income and Wealth (IARIW), 18–24 August, Lillehammer.

Mulder, N. (1999), 'The Economic Performance of the Service Sector in Brazil, Mexico and the USA: A Comparative Historical Perspective', *Monograph Series*, No. 4, Groningen: Groningen Growth and Development Centre.

Mulder, N. and A. Maddison (1993), 'The International Comparison of Performance in Distribution: Value Added, Labour Productivity and Purchasing Power Parities in Mexican and US Wholesale and Retail Trade 1975/77', *Research Memorandum*, No. 537 (GD-2), Groningen: Groningen Growth and Development Centre.

Mulder, N., S. Montout and L. Peres Lopes (2002), 'Brazil and Mexico's Manufacturing Performance in International Perspective, 1970–99', *Working Paper*, No. 2002–5, Paris: CEPII.

Musgrove, P. and O. Galindo (1988), 'Do the Poor Pay More? Retail Food Prices in Northeast Brazil', *Economic Development and Cultural Change*, **37** (1), 91–111.

Nakamura, L.I. (1999), 'The Measurement of Retail Output and the Retail Revolution', *Canadian Journal of Economics*, **32** (2), 408–25.

Nordhaus, W.D. (1972), 'The Recent Productivity Slowdown', *Brookings Papers on Economic Activity*, **3**, 493–531.

OECD (1987), *The Measurement of Value Added at Constant Prices in Service Activities: Sources and Methods*, Paris: OECD.

OECD (1990), *Education in OECD Countries: A Compendium of Statistical Information*, Paris: OECD.

OECD (1992a), 'Structure and Change in Distribution Systems: An Analysis of Seven OECD Member Countries', Working Party 1 for the Economic Policy Committee, ECO/CPE/WP1(92)7, Paris: OECD.

OECD (1992b), 'US Health Care at the Cross-roads', *Health Policy Studies*, No. 1, Paris: OECD.

OECD (1994), *The Reform of Health Care Systems: A Review of Seventeen OECD Countries*, Paris: OECD.

OECD (1996), *Services: Measuring Real Annual Value Added*, Paris: OECD.

OECD (1997), *Economic Surveys: Mexico*, Paris: OECD.

Ohkawa, K. (1993), *Growth Mechanism of Developing Countries: Investment, Productivity, and Employment*, San Francisco: International Center for Economic Growth/Development Center of Japan.

Oi, W.Y. (1992), 'Productivity in the Distributive Trades: The Shopper and the Economies of Massed Reserves', in Z. Griliches (ed.), *Output Measurement in the Service Sectors*, NBER, Chicago: University of Chicago Press, 161–93.

Oi, W.Y. (1998), 'Adapting the Retail Format to a Changing Economy', paper presented at the Brooking Workshop on Measuring the Output of Retail Trade, 18 September, Washington, DC.

Oliveira and Mouro (1997), 'Regulation of Retail and Wholesale Trade in Brazil', mimeo, São Paulo: Fernand Braudel Institute.

Ornelas, C. (1995), *El Sistema Educativo Mexicano: La Transición de Fin de Siglo*, Mexico City: CIDE/Nacional Financiera/Fundo de Cultura Economica.

Osborn, T.N. (1976), *Higher Education in Mexico*, El Paso: Texas Western Press.

Oxley, H. and M. MacFarlan (1995), 'Health Care Reform Controlling Spending and Increasing Efficiency', *Economics Department Working Papers*, No. 149, Paris: OECD.

Paige, D. and G. Bombach (1959), *A Comparison of National Output and Productivity of the United Kingdom and the United States*, Paris: OEEC and the University of Cambridge.

Pandit, K. (1990), 'Changes in the Composition of the Service Sector with Economic Development and the Effect of Urban Size', *Regional Studies*, **25** (4), 315–25.

Peñazola Webb, T. (1985), 'La Productividad de la Banca en México', *Trimestre Economico*, **52**, 465–97.

Pfefferman, G.P. and R. Webb (1979), 'The Distribution of Income in Brazil', *World Bank Staff Working Paper*, No. 356, Washington, DC: World Bank.

Pereira de Melo, H., F. Rocha, G. Ferraz, R. Dweck and A. Di Sabbato (1999), 'Service Sector Growth in Brazil', paper presented at World Services Congress, 1–3 November, Atlanta, GA.

Petit, P. (1993), 'Les modalités de la croissance des services au Japon', mimeo, Paris: CEPREMAP.

Petty, W. (1690), *Political Arithmetic or Discourse*, reprinted in C.H. Hull (1963), *The Economic Writing of Sir William Petty*, New York: Augustus M. Kelly.

Pilat, D. (1994), *The Economics of Rapid Growth, The Experience of Japan and Korea*, Aldershot, UK and Brookfield, US: Edward Elgar.

Pilat, D. (1997), 'Regulation and Performance in the Distribution Sector', *Economics Department Working Papers*, No. 180, Paris: OECD.

Plank, D.N. (1996), *The Means of Our Salvation: Public Education in Brazil 1930–1995*, Boulder: Westview Press.

Pulliam, J.D. (1982), *History of Education in America*, Columbus: Merrill Publishing Company.

Ramos, L. (1991), 'Educação, Desigualdade de Renda e Ciclo Econômico no Brasil', *Pesquisa e Planejamento Econômico*, **21** (3), 423–48.

Rivkin, S.G. (2000), 'The Estimation of Productivity Change in Education', mimeo, Amherst, MA: Amherst College.

Rocha, F. (1997), 'Composição do Crecimento dos Serviços na Economia Brasileira: Uma Análise da Matriz Insumo–produto – 1985/92', *Textos para Discussão*, **522**, Rio de Janeiro: IPEA.

Rogoff, K. (1996), 'The Purchasing Power Parity Puzzle', *Journal of Economic Literature*, **34** (2), 647–68.

Romer, P.M. (1990), 'Human Capital and Growth: Theory and Evidence', *Carnegie-Rochester Conference Series on Public Policy*, **32**, 251–86.

Roos, P. (1997), 'Measurement of Productivity in Hospital Services Using Malmquist Index Approaches: A Discussion of Methods and Illustration to Eye Surgery', presented at Conference on Service Sector Productivity and Productivity Paradox, 11–12 April, Ottawa: Centre for the Study of Living Standards.

Rostas, L. (1948), *Comparative Productivity in British and American Industries*, NIESR, Occasional Papers, No. 13, Cambridge: Cambridge University Press.

Rostow, W.W. (1960), *The Stages of Economic Growth: A Non-communist Manifest*, Cambridge: Cambridge University Press.

Rostow, W.W. (1990), *Theorists of Economic Growth from David Hume to the Present*, New York: Oxford University Press.

Sabolo, Y. (1975), *The Service Industries*, Geneva: International Labour Office.

Scheppach, R.C. and L.C. Woehlke (1975), *Transportation Productivity: Measurement and Policy Implications*, Lexington: D.C. Heathn.

Schiefelbein, E. and L. Wolff (1993), 'Repetition and Inadequate Achievement in Latin America's Primary Schools: A Review of Magnitudes, Causes, Relationships and Strategies', *Estudos em Avaliação Educacional*, **7**, 45–89.

Schultz, T.W. (1961), 'Investment in Human Capital', *American Economic Review*, **51** (1), 1–17.

Schwartzman, D. (1971), *The Decline of Service in Retail Trade: An Analysis of Growth of Sales per Manhour, 1929–1963*, Bureau of Economic Research, Pullman: Washington State University.

Selvanathan, E.A. (1991), 'Standard Errors for Laspeyres and Paasche Index Numbers', *Economic Letters*, **35**, 35–38.

Shapiro, M.P. and D.W. Wilcox (1996), 'Mismeasurement in the Consumer Price Index: An Evaluation', *NBER Macroeconomics Annual*, **11**, 93–142.

Sherwood, M.K. (1994), 'Difficulties in the Measurement of Service Outputs', *Monthly Labor Review*, March, 11–19.

Sherwood, M.K. (1999), 'Output of the Property and Casualty Insurance Industry', *Canadian Journal of Economics*, **32** (2), 518–46.

Singer, P. (1978), 'Força de Trabalho e Emprego no Brasil: 1920–1969', *Cuadernos CEBRAP*, **3**, São Paulo: CEBRAP.

Smith, A.D., D.M.W.N. Hitchens and D.W. Davies (1982), *International Industrial Productivity: A Comparison of Britain, America and Germany*, Cambridge: Cambridge University Press.

Smith, A.D. and D.M.W.N. Hitchens (1985), *Productivity in the Distributive Trades: A Comparison of Britain, America and Germany*, National Institute of Economic and Social Research, London: Cambridge University Press.

Soto, H. de (1989), *The Other Path: The Invisible Revolution in the Third World*, New York: Harper and Row.

Speagle, E.S. and E. Kohn (1958), 'Employment and Output in Banking, 1919–55', *Review of Economics and Statistics*, 22–35.

Squire, L. and K. Deininger (1996), 'A New Data Set Measuring Income Inequality', *World Bank Economic Review*, **10** (3), 565–91.

Stralen, C. van (1996), *The Struggle Over a National Health Care System: The Movimento Sanitário and Health Policy Making in Brazil*, Ph.D. Thesis, Nijmegen: Mediagroep.

Summerhill, W. (1995), *Railroads and the Brazilian Economy Before 1914*, Ph.D. Thesis, Stanford, CA: University of Stanford.

Summerhill, W. (1997), 'Transport Improvements and Economic Growth in Brazil and Mexico', in S. Haber (ed.), *How Latin America Fell Behind: Essays on the Economic Histories of Brazil and Mexico, 1800–1914*, Stanford: Stanford University Press, 34–64.

Summers, R. (1985), 'Services in the International Economy', in R.P. Inman (ed.), *Managing the Service Economy: Prospects and Problems*, Cambridge, MA: Cambridge University Press.

Syrquin, M. (1984), 'Resource Reallocation and Productivity Growth', in M. Syrquin, L. Taylor and L.E. Westphal (eds), *Economic Structure and Performance: Essays in Honour of Hollis B. Chenery*, New York: Academic Press, 75–101.

Syrquin, M. (1986), 'Productivity Growth and Factor Reallocation', in H.B. Chenery, S. Robinson and M. Syrquin (eds), *Industrialisation and Growth: A Comparative Study*, New York: Oxford University Press.

Syrquin, M. (1988), 'Patterns of Structural Change', in H.B. Chenery and T.N. Srinivasan (eds), *Handbook of Development Economics*, Amsterdam: North-Holland, 203–73.

Szirmai, A. and D. Pilat (1990), 'The International Comparison of Real Output and Labour Productivity in Manufacturing: A Study for Japan, South Korea and the USA for 1975', *Research Memorandum*, No. 354, Institute of Economic Research, Groningen: University of Groningen.

Taylor, G.R. (1951), *The Transportation Revolution, 1850–1860*, New York: Rinehart.

The Economist (1998), 'No End to the Burden', London: *The Economist.*

Thomson, L. (1993), 'The Evolution of Railroad Regulation in the United States', in Carbajo, J.C. (ed.), *Regulatory Reform in Transport: Some Recent Experiences*, Washington, DC: World Bank.

Timmer, M.P. (2000), *The Dynamics of Asian Manufacturing. A Comparison in the late Twentieth Century*, Cheltenham, UK and Northhampton, MA, USA: Edward Elgar.

Timmer, M.P. and A. Szirmai (1997), 'Growth and Divergence in Manufacturing Performance in South and East Asia', *Research Memorandum*, No. GD-37, Groningen: Groningen Growth and Development Centre.

Timmer, M.P., B. van Ark,, N. Mulder, L. Nayman, and D. Ünal-Kesenci (2001), 'Formalization of the ICOP methodology for binary manufacturing comparisons', mimeo, Groningen and Paris: Groningen Growth and Development Centre and CEPII.

Torre Garcia, de la, R. (1991), 'Legislación y Regulación del Comercio Interno en México', in F. Gil and A.M. Fernandez (eds), *El Efecto de la Regulación en Algunos Sectores de la Economia Mexicana*, Mexico City: ITAM/Fundo de Cultura Económica/Centro Internacional para el Desarrollo Economico.

Tretheway, M.W., W.G. Waters and A.K. Fok (1994), 'Measuring Productivity and Financial Returns for Canadian National Railway and CP Rail, 1985–1991', *Monograph*, Center for Transportation Studies, Vancouver: University of British Colombia.

Triplett, J.E. and B.P. Bosworth (2000), 'Productivity in the Services Sector', paper presented at American Economic Association, 7–9 January, Boston.

Villela, A.V. and W. Suzigan (1977), 'Government Policy and the Economic Growth of Brazil, 1889–1945', *Brazilian Economic Studies*, **3**, Rio de Janeiro: IPEA/INPES.

Vogel, M.J. (1979), 'The Transformation of the American Hospital', in S. Reverby, and D. Rosner (eds), *Health Care in America: Essays in Social History*, Philadelphia: Temple University Press, 105–16.

Weisbrod, B.A. (1992), 'Productivity and Incentives in the Medical Care Sector', *Scandinavian Journal of Economics*, **94** (Supplement), S131–45.

Welch, J.H. (1992), *Capital Markets and the Development Process: The Case of Brazil*, London: MacMillan.

White, L.J. (1991), *The S&L Debacle: Public policy lessons for bank and thrift regulation*, New York: Oxford University Press.

White, L.J. (1992), 'Change and Turmoil in U.S. Banking: Causes, Consequences, and Lessons', Working Paper, S-92-23. New York: Salomon Center, New York University.

Wierenga, P. and A. Maddison (1985, 1990), 'International Comparison of Levels of Real Output in Mining and Quarrying in 1975', mimeo, Groningen: University of Groningen.

Williamson, J. (1974), *Late Nineteenth-century American Development: A General Equilibrium Approach*, New York: Cambridge University Press.

Winston, C. (1993), 'Economic Deregulation: Days of Reckoning for Microeconomists', *Journal of Economic Literature*; **31** (3), 1263–89.

Wood, R. and V. Keyser (1953), *United States Business Performance Abroad: The Case of Sears, Roebuck de Mexico, S.A.*, Washington, DC: National Planning Association.

World Bank (1993a), *World Development Report 1993: Investing in Health*, Washington, DC: WB.

Statistical References

American Hospital Association (1990), *Hospital Statistics 1988*, Chicago: AHA.

Association of American Railroads (various issues), *Railroad Facts*, Washington, DC: AAR.

Department of Commerce, Bureau of the Census (1975), *Historical Statistics of the United States*, Washington, DC: Government Printing Office (GPO).

Department of Commerce (various issues), *Statistical Abstract of the United States*, Washington, DC: GPO.

Department of Commerce, Bureau of Economic Analysis (various editions), *National Income and Product Accounts*, Washington, DC: GPO.

Department of Commerce, Bureau of Economic Analysis (January 1992; May 1993, May 1997), *Survey of Current Business*, Washington, DC: GPO.

Department of Commerce, Bureau of Economic Analysis (1979), 'Dollar Values for the 1972 Input Output Study', *Survey of Current Business*, April.

Department of Commerce, Bureau of Economic Analysis (1986), *The National Income and Product Accounts of the United States, 1929–82*, Washington, DC: GPO.

Department of Commerce, Bureau of Economic Analysis (1992), *The National Income and Product Accounts of the United States, 1929–1988*, Washington, DC: GPO.

Department of Commerce, Bureau of Economic Analysis (1997), 'Benchmark Input-output Accounts for the US Economy, 1992', *Survey of Current Business*, November, Washington, DC: GPO.

Department of Commerce, Bureau of Economic Analysis (various issues), *Survey of Current Business*, Washington, DC: GPO.

Department of Commerce, Bureau of the Census (1981a), *1977 Census of Wholesale Trade*, Washington, DC: GPO.

Department of Commerce, Bureau of the Census (1981b), '1977 Merchant Wholesalers', *1977 Census of Wholesale Trade*, Washington, DC: GPO.

Department of Commerce, Bureau of the Census (1981c), *1977 Census of Retail Trade*, Washington, DC: GPO.

Department of Commerce, Bureau of the Census (1981d), 'Characteristics of Retail Trade', *1977 Census of Retail Trade*, Washington, DC: GPO.

Department of Commerce, Bureau of the Census (1981e), *1977 Census of Construction Industries*, Washington, DC: GPO.

Department of Commerce, Bureau of the Census (1991), *1987 Census of Service Industries*, Washington, DC: GPO.

Department of Commerce, Bureau of the Census (1998), *International Data Base*, Washington, DC: GPO.

Department of Education, Educational Testing Service (1992a), *Learning Mathematics*, Princeton, NJ: ETS.

Department of Education, Educational Testing Service (1992b), *Learning Science*, Princeton, NJ: ETS.

Department of Education, National Center for Education Statistics (1993), *Digest of Education Statistics*, Washington, DC: GPO.

Department of Housing and Urban Development, Bureau of the Census and Department of Housing and Urban Development (1983), *Annual Housing Survey 1980 – Part E: Urban and Rural Housing Characteristics*, Washington, DC: GPO.

Department of Labor, Bureau of Labor Statisticis (1978a), *Producer Prices and Price Indexes*, Supplement 1978, Data for 1977, Washington, DC: GPO.

Department of Labor, Bureau of Labor Statistics (1978b), *Consumer Prices and Price Indexes*, Supplement 1976, Data for 1975, Washington, DC: GPO.

Department of Labor, Bureau of Labor Statistics (1999), 'Major Sector Productivity and Costs Index', mimeo, Washington, DC: GPO.

Department of Transportation (1975, 1977, 1981), *National Transportation Statistics*, Washington, DC: GPO.

Department of Transportation (1994), *North American Transportation: Statistics on Canadian, Mexican and US Transportation*, Washington, DC: GPO.

Economic Commission for Latin America and the Caribbean (ECLAC) (various issues), *Statistical Abstract of Latin America and the Caribbean*, Santiago de Chile: ECLAC.

ECLAC/UNIDO (1994), Unpublished Worksheets of Quality Indicators in Telecommunications, Santiago: ECLAC.

Ernst & Young and Health Care Investment Analysts (1995), *The Medicare Diagnosis Related Groups (DRG) Handbook: Comparative Clinical and Financial Standards 1993*, Cleveland.

Federal Reserve Bank (1977), *Functional Cost Analysis 1975*, Washington, DC: Federal Reserve.

Government of Mexico (1979), *Plan Nacional de Desarrollo Industrial*, Mexico City.

Gusmão Veloso, M.A. (1987), 'Brazilian National Accounts', paper presented at 20th conference of the International Association for the Research in Income and Wealth, 23–29 August, Roca di Papa.

Instituto Brasileiro de Estatísticas e Geografia (IBGE) (various issues), *Anuario Estatístico do Brasil*, Rio de Janeiro: IBGE.

IBGE (various issues), *Censo Comercial*, Rio de Janeiro: IBGE.

IBGE (various issues), *Censos Economicos*, Rio de Janeiro: IBGE.

IBGE (various issues), *Contas Nacionais*, Rio de Janeiro: IBGE.

IBGE (various issues), *Matriz de Insumo-Produto*, Rio de Janeiro: IBGE.

IBGE (various years), *Pesquisa de Assistencia Medico Sanitaria*, Rio de Janeiro: IBGE.

IBGE (various issues), *Pesquisa Nacional por Amostra de Domicilios*, PNAD, Rio de Janeiro: IBGE.

IBGE (1979), *Matriz de Relações Intersetoriais – Brasil 1970*, Rio de Janeiro: IBGE.

IBGE (1981a), *Censo Comercial*, Rio de Janeiro: IBGE.

IBGE (1981b), 'Inquérito Especial Transporte', *Censos Economicas de 1975*, Rio de Janeiro: IBGE.

IBGE (1982), 'Inquérito Especial Industria da Construção Brasil', *Censos Econômicos de 1975*, Rio de Janeiro: IBGE.

IBGE (1984), *Censo Demografico 1980*, Rio de Janeiro: IBGE.

IBGE (1987), *Matriz de Relações Intersetoriais Brasil 1975*, Rio de Janeiro: IBGE.

IBGE (1989a), 'Sistema de Contas Nacionais Consolidadas', Rio de Janeiro: IBGE.

IBGE (1989b), *Matriz de Insumo Produto do Brasil 1980*, Rio de Janeiro: IBGE.

IBGE (1990), *Estatísticas Históricas do Brasil*, Rio de Janeiro: IBGE.

IBGE (1992), 'Contas Consolidadas para a Nação, 1980–1991', Rio de Janeiro: IBGE.

IBGE (1995a), 'Contas Consolidadas para a Nação, 1990–1994', Rio de Janeiro: IBGE.

IBGE (1995b), *Matriz de Insumo Produto do Brasil 1985*, Rio de Janeiro: IBGE.

IBGE (1998), 'Contas Consolidadas para a Nação, 1990–1996', Rio de Janeiro: IBGE.

Instituto Nacional de Estadísticas, Geografía e Informatica (INEGI) (various issues), *Anuario Estadístico de los Estados Unidos Mexicanos* Mexico City: INEGI.

INEGI, (various editions), *Sistema de Cuentas Nacionales*, Mexico City: INEGI.

INEGI (1982), *El Sector Electrico en México*, Mexico City: INEGI.

INEGI (1984), 'Resumen General Abreviado', *X Censo General de Poblacion y Vivienda, 1980*, Mexico City: INEGI.

INEGI (1993), 'XI Censo de Servicios', *Censos Económicos 1994*, Aguascalientes: INEGI.
INEGI (1994a), *Cuentas Nacionales de México*, CD-ROM, Mexico City: INEGI.
INEGI (1994b), *Estadísticas Históricas de México*, CD-ROM, Mexico City: INEGI.
INEGI (1998), 'Cuentas nacionales de México', mimeo, Mexico City: INEGI.
International Monetary Fund (IMF) (various issues), *International Financial Statistics*, Washington, DC: IMF
Ministerio da Educação (1990), *A Educação no Brasil na Decada de 80*, Brasilia: Ministerio da Educação.
Ministerio dos Transportes (1982), *Anuário Estatístico do Transportes*, Brasilia: Ministerio do Transportes.
Mitchell, B.R. (1998) *International Historical Statistics: the Americas, 1750–1993*, London: MacMillan Reference.
Nacional Financiera (1978), *La Economia Mexicana en Cifras*, Mexico City: Nacional Financiera.
Organisation for Economic Cooperation and Development (OECD) (1992), *Public Expenditure and Financing: An Analysis of Trends 1970–88*, Paris: OECD.
OECD (1993), *Education at a Glance: OECD Indicators*, Paris: OECD.
Office of Management and the Budget (1972), *Standard Industrial Classification*, Washington, DC: GPO.
Pan-American Health Organisation (1994, 1995), *Health Conditions in the Americas*, Washington, DC: Pan-American Health Organisation.
Salinas de Gortari (1993), *Quinto Informe del Gobierno*, Mexico City.
Secretaria de Educación Publica (SEP) (1990), *Estadistica Basica del Sistema Educativo Nacional*, Mexico City: SEP.
Secretaría de Programación y Presupuesto (SPP) (1979), *VII Censo de Transportes y de Comunicaciones*, Mexico City: SPP.
SPP (1977, 1980), *Anuario Estadístico de los Estados Unidos Mexicanos*, Mexico City: SPP.
SPP (1981a), *VII Censo Comercial 1976, Datos de 1975*, Mexico City: SPP.
SPP (1981b), *Manual de Estadísticas del Sector Comunicaciones y Transportes*, Mexico City: SPP.
SPP (1981c), *Matriz de Insumo-producto 1970*, Mexico City: SPP.
SPP and Cámara Nacional de la Industria de la Construcción (1980), *La Actividad de la Construcción en México*, Mexico City: SPP.
SPP/INEGI (various issues), *Censo Comercial*, Aguascalientes and Mexico City: SPP and INEGI.
Secretaria de Salud (SSA) (1989), *Anuario Estadístico 1988*, Mexico City: SSA.
SSA (1994), *Brevario Estadístico Sectorial 1980–1990*, Mexico City: SSA.

United Nations (1965), *Demographic Yearbook*, New York: UN.

UN (1993), *Statistical Yearbook*, New York: UN.

Wilkie, J.W. (various issues), *Statistical Abstract of Latin America*, Los Angeles: UCLA.

World Bank (various issues), *World Development Indicators*, Washington, DC: WB.

World Bank (1993b), *World Tables*, Washington, DC: WB.

World Bank (2001), Unpublished worksheets of the 1993 Benchmark Study of the International Comparisons Programme, Washington, DC: WB.

World Health Organisation (WHO) (1979, 1992), *World Health Statistics Annual*, Geneva: WHO.

Name Index

Adie, D.K. 73
Ahlroth, S. 204
Ark, B. van 1, 2, 3, 32, 33, 63, 67, 68, 74, 112, 113, 215, 225, 227, 228, 234, 236, 243, 254, 274, 277

Baer, W. 271
Baily, M.N. 140, 141
Balassa, B. 251
Barger, H. 52, 83, 86, 103
Barth, J.R. 135
Bartholomew, P.F. 135
Batchelor, R.A. 13
Baumol, W.J. 23, 26
Berger, A.N. 143, 145
Bernard, A.B. 260
Berry, A. 10
Betancourt, R.R. 96, 98
Bethell, L. 44, 50
Bhagwati, J.N. 24
Bilderbeek, R. 31
Blaug, M. 205, 206
Bobadilla, J.L. 155
Boer, S. de 143, 144
Boerkamp, E. 180
Bombach, G. 3, 73
Bordo, M.D. 129
Bosworth, B.P. 34, 104, 147
Briard, K. 59
Brinkley, A. 56
Broadberry, S.N. 246
Bruggink, A. 146
Burns, E.B. 50, 55
Burt, S.L. 92

Cassedy, J.H. 157, 158, 163, 169
Castro, N. de 52
Caves, R. 145
Cessti, R. 273
Chakraborty, A. 59
Chandler, A.D. 98, 100, 101
Chaves, M.R. de 275
Chenery, H.B. 12, 14, 246
Clark, C. 2, 11, 14
Coatsworth, J.H. 46
Contador, C. 132, 140
Cross, J.C. 90
Cutler, D.M. 178

Davies, R.L. 101
Davis, L.E. 44, 51
Dawson, J.A. 88, 92
Dean, E.R. 145
Den Hartog, P. 31
Denison, E.F. 246
Döhrn, R. 13
Drake, D.F. 163
Dupuis, M. 96
Durand, H. 131

Elfring, T. 33

Falvey, R.E. 15
Fisher, A.G.B. 11, 14
Fishlow, A. 45
Fitzgerald, J. 83
Fixler, D. 143, 144, 145
Fogel, R.W. 45
Frank, R.G. 178
Fraschetto, W. 87, 91
Fraumeni, B.M. 204
Friedman, M. 133
Frischtak, C. 140, 141, 145
Froot, K. 251

Gemmell, N. 13, 15
Gil, F. 131, 139
Gilbert, M. 2, 31
Goldsmith, R.W. 123, 124, 145, 268, 271, 272
Gómez-Ibáñez, J.A. 58, 59, 70
Gordon, R.J. 23, 33, 140, 141

Gorman, J.A. 145
Graham, D.H. 278
Gras, J.M. 87, 91
Gregory, R.G. 13
Griffin, J.M. 13
Griliches, Z. 33
Guevara Niebla, G. 200, 201, 202
Gulindo, O. 90
Gusmão Veloso, M.A. 268, 272
Gutierrez Junquera, P. 15

Haber, S. 125, 129
Haddad 268, 272
Hall, M. 95, 103, 109
Hanushek, E. 190, 200
Harbison, R.W. 190, 200
Heilemann, U. 13
Hernandez Laos, E. 2
Heston, A. 2
Hill, P. 31
Hitchens, D.M.W.N. 103, 109
Hofman, A.A. 19, 92, 247
Hooper, P. 3
Houben, A. 274
Hughes, J. 44
Humphrey, D.B. 143, 145

Jeffreys, J.B. 103
Jones, C.I. 260
Jorgenson, D.W. 3, 204

Karoly Kaznar, I. 131
Katouzian, H. 16
Kazarosian, M. 59
Kendrick, J.W. 33, 58, 265, 269
Keyser, V. 89
Kindleberger, C.P. 246
Klodt, H. 21
Knee, D. 103
Knipper, I. 83
Kohn, E. 145
Kravis, I.B. 2, 3, 15, 31, 32, 164, 179, 180, 205, 248, 249, 251, 274
Kunze, K. 145
Kuroda, M. 3
Kuznets, S. 14

Lahrèche-Révil, A. 251
Lee, F.C. 3
Lipsey, R.E. 251
Loegering, L. 180
Ludwig, A.K. 157, 195, 263

McGuckin, R.H. 3
Maddison, A. 2, 13, 14, 90, 104, 110, 112, 172, 187, 197, 205, 213, 214, 215, 225, 227, 228, 234, 236, 242, 246, 247, 253, 254, 263, 267, 271, 274, 277
Malmquist, S. 145
Marichal, C. 125
Maricourt, R. de 96
Mark, J.A. 145
Mazumdar, K. 10
Melo Flores de Lima, B. 278
Merrick, T.W. 278
Meyer, J.R. 58, 59, 70
Meyer, J.W.F. 203
Monnikhof, E.J. 1, 33, 63, 68, 74, 113
Morton, A.L. 59
Mouro 96
Mulder, N. 33, 104, 110, 112, 215, 227, 273, 277
Musgrove, P. 90

Nordhaus, W.D. 243

Ohkawa, K. 242
Oi, W.Y. 104
Oliveira 96
Ooststroom, H. van 213, 214, 274
Ornelas, C. 202
Osborn, T.N. 195, 196, 197

Paige, D. 3, 73
Pandit, K. 19
Peñazola Webb, T. 145
Pereira de Melo, H. 10, 24, 26
Petit, P. 26
Petty, Sir William 11
Pfefferman, G.P. 278
Pilat, D. 1, 33, 87, 93, 103, 109, 115, 205, 236
Plank, D.N. 195, 200, 201, 202
Pulliam, J.D. 200

Ramos, L. 205
Rao, D.S.P. 213
Rivkin, S.G. 205

Rocha, F. 10
Rogoff, K. 251
Roos, P. 178
Rostas, L. 3
Rostow, W.W. 11, 45

Sabolo, Y. 16
Salinas de Gortari 275, 276
Schiefelbein, E. 188
Schwartzman, D. 103
Schwarz, A.J. 133
Selvanathan, E.A. 222
Shapiro, M.P. 178
Sherwood, M.K. 31, 147, 148
Smith, A.D. 70, 73, 103, 109
Soto, H. de 97
Speagle, E.S. 145
Stralen, C. van 157, 160, 171, 172, 173, 175, 176
Summerhill, W. 45, 47, 50
Summers, R. 2, 15
Syrquin, M. 12, 242
Szirmai, A. 115, 243

Tang, J. 3
Taylor, G.R. 50, 54
Taylor, L. 12, 14
Thomson, L. 49, 52
Timmer, M.P. 3, 221, 243
Torre Garcia, R. de la 97
Tretheway, M.W. 59
Triplett, J.E. 34, 104, 147

Vogel, M.J. 169

Webb, R. 278
Weisbrod, B.A. 178
Welch, J.H. 139, 140, 143, 145
White, L.J. 134, 135
Wieringa, P. 214
Wilcox, D.W. 178
Williamson, J. 46
Winston, C. 49, 57
Wolff, L. 188
Wood, R. 89

Zieschang, K. 143, 145

Subject Index

advertising 101
agricultural output measures 213
agriculture 213-14, 253, 257
  Brazil 213, 214, 253
  employment shift from 243
  labour productivity 243
  Mexico 213, 214, 253
air transport 53, 58
  Brazil 53, 72
  Mexico 53, 72
  USA 53, 72
American Hospital Association 275
asset approach 145

'Balassa-effect' 251
banking 25
  Brazil 130-32, 140, 141, 260
  Mexico 129, 130-31, 133, 141
  output and productivity levels 143-7
  real output measures 38
  USA 125-34, 142
branding 101
Brazil
  agriculture 213, 214, 253
  banking 140, 141, 260
    central bank 130, 139
    development banks 130
    regulation 130-32
  capital formation 132
  communications 72
  CONASP plan 170
  construction 236-7
  Cruzado plan 150
  education 187-8, 276
    enrolment 188-90
    expenditure 192
    political obstacles to 201-2
    quality 190-91
    quality of schools 200-201
    teaching quality 200
  education system, history 194-5

Eloy Chaves Law (1923) 158-9
employment 7, 8, 263-4
  in distributive services 107-8
  in education 203
exchange rates 271
financial services 123-4, 126-9, 256-7, 274
financing budget deficits 139-40
FOBAPROA scheme 151-2
foreign direct investment (FDI) 25
FUNRURAL programme 171
GDP 2, 7, 9, 10, 268-9
  understatement of 278
health care 157, 158-60, 176, 275-6
  Decentralised Unified Care System (SUDS) 170, 174
  private health care 173-4
  problems 174-5
  provision 166
  public health schemes 171
  reform 175-6
health outcomes 156-7
illiteracy 191-2
income distribution 16
indexation mechanism 132
inflation 21-2
inflation rates 135, 136-7, 139
inflation tax (seignorage) 139-40
informal activity 236, 278-81
informal work-force 24
Institute of Social Security (INPS) 170
international trade 25
Jesuits 194
labour productivity 77, 241
  growth 243
  and manufacturing 228-30
manufacturing 216, 217
  international comparisons 215, 227-8
  and labour productivity growth 216

relative prices and productivity 230-33
mining 214-15
Ministerio de Educação 276
national accounts 267, 268
per capita income 16, 93
post offices 54
price deflators, by sector 271-2
productivity, in financial services 150
productivity growth, factors constraining 24-5
public utilities 273
real estate 274-5
Secretaria de Salud 275
service sector 5
services, demand for 14
social security schemes 169-71
source notes 268-9
telecommunications 55-7
transport 79, 273
air transport 53, 72
rail transport 66-70
railways 44, 47, 49
road passenger transport 70
road transport 49, 50-51
unit labour costs, manufacturing 233-4
urbanisation 19
value added, per person engaged 255
Vargas administration (1930-45) 159, 160
vehicle stock 51-2
wholesale and retail trade 83-4, 86, 88-9, 96-7, 100, 274
Brazilian Education Association 195
Brookings Institution 34
Bureau of Labor Statistics 33, 103

Canadian Journal of Economics 33
census data
and national accounts data, reconciliation 115, 277-81
transport and communications 75-6
censuses of production 220
Centre for the Study of Living Standards 33
Clayton Act (1914), US 96
commodity sector 1, 5-6, 241-62
and service sector, comparative performance 241-62
communications 53-7, 72-4
Brazil 72
Mexico 72
output and productivity levels in 1975 64-5
real output measures 35, 37
USA 72
Communications Act (1934), USA 56
consortium system 91
construction 236-7, 257
PPPs for 236
consumer demand 92-102
consumer mobility, and distributive services 94-5
consumer preferences hierarchy 14
consumer price index 37, 103
consumption abroad 91
cost disease 26
CPD (country product dummy) method 213
cross-section analysis 12
currency conversion method 3

debt crisis 215
demand elasticity, and income 14-16
Department of Commerce, USA 105, 165, 172, 263, 265, 269, 272, 273, 274, 275, 276
Department of Education
USA 276
Educational Testing Service 190, 205
Department of Housing and Urban Development, USA 275
Department of Labor, USA 33, 274
developing countries, service sector 10
disability-adjusted life years (DALYs) 156
diseases 155-6, 157
distributive services
demand for 92-102
demographic and socio-economic changes 92-3
and the legal environment 96-8
employment in 1975/77 107-8
measurement of output and productivity 103-7
technological progress 98
value added in 1975/77 107-8
see also wholesale and retail trade

e-commerce 104
ECLAC (Economic Commission for Latin America and the Caribbean) 273
economic growth, contribution of labour reallocation 247-8
The Economist 152
education 18, 187-211, 254, 276
  and economic growth 187
  employment in 193-4, 203, 204
  enrolments 188-90, 205
  expenditure 192-4
  inequality in 200-201
  as an investment good 204
  and labour productivity 207-9
  outcomes 191-2
  output
    measurement 203-6
    real measures 40-41
  output and productivity levels 203-9
  and political obstacles 201-2
  quality 190-91, 206
  quality control 201
  test scores 205
  unit value ratios 206-7
  value added 192-4, 204
employment 263-5
  Brazil 7, 8, 107-8, 203, 263-4
  distributive services, 1975/77 107-8
  education 193-4, 203, 204
  Mexico 7, 8, 107-8, 203, 264-5
  primary sector 241
  retail trade 83
  service sector 22-6
  USA 7, 8
  wholesale trade 83, 107-8
Engel's law 14, 15, 93
Ernst & Young and Health Care Investment Analysts 276
Euromonitor 84, 87, 89, 91, 93, 94, 102
European System of Accounts (ESA) 34
Eurostat 2, 34, 267
Eurostat Task Force 144, 148, 179
exchange rates 2, 108-9, 271
expenditure
  purchasing power parities (PPPs) 3
  and services 15-16

Federal Reserve Bank 274
Federal Trade Commission Act (1914), USA 96
final expenditure, international comparison 2
finance 274
financial services 253, 254
  1800-1950 123-5
  1950-96 126-8
  government intervention 129-35
  labour productivity in 150-51
  long-term development 123-8
    determinants 128-43
  technological developments 140-41
  unit value ratios (UVRs) for 149
financial services indirectly measured (FISIM) 38, 143, 145
Fisher index 224
five stages of economic growth theory 11, 12
Food and Agriculture Organisation (FAO) 213
foreign direct investment 25, 98
  Brazil 25
  Mexico 25
foreign trade, liberalisation 215-16
franchising 89

GDP
  Brazil 2, 7, 9, 10, 268-9, 278
  indices and levels of 267-8
  Latin America 10
  Mexico 2, 7, 9, 10, 269
  service sector 22-6
  USA 7, 9, 10, 269
  wholesale and retail trade 83
GDP growth, sources 247
Geary-Khamis agricultural output measures 213
Gini coefficients 17, 94
government, expanding role 19-20
government intervention, in financial services 129-35
Government of Mexico 265
Gronigen University 1

health care 18, 155-8, 253, 254, 275-6
  demand 167
  developments after 1950 163-6
  developments before 1950 157-63
  employment in 165-6

labour productivity 1950–96 181–4
long-term development 166–76
output
measurement 178–81
real measures 39–40
output and productivity levels 176–84
international comparison 179
and poverty 175
quality evaluation 180–81
scientific improvements 167, 169
unit value ratios 1950–96 181, 182
hedonic approach 33
high-income inequality 17
home shopping 91
housing 18
human capital formation 203

IADB (Inter-American Development Bank) 156, 174, 188, 201
IBGE (Instituto Brasileiro de Estasticas e Geografia) 24, 263, 264, 268, 272, 273, 274, 275
ICOP (International Comparison of Output and Productivity) project 1, 33, 112, 213
IMF 267, 271
import substitution policy (ISI) 98
income
and demand elasticity 14–16
and education 206
and the retail sector 93–4
income distribution
Brazil 16
Mexico 16
and per capita incomes 16–17
India, service sector 10
industrial census data, reconciliation with national accounts 226–8
industry of origin approach 3
and productivity performance 4
INEGI (Instituto Nacional de Estadisticas, Geografia e Informatica) 24, 265, 267, 269, 271, 272, 273, 274, 275, 276
inequality, in education 200–201
infant mortality rate 94, 155, 180
inflation 101–2
Brazil 21–2, 135–7, 139–40
Mexico 22, 135–6
inflation rates 135
informal activity 24, 26
Brazil 236, 278–81
Mexico 24, 236
see also unregistered activity
informal retailing 89–91
Mexico 90–91
innovation 21
insurance
output and productivity levels 147–52
real output measures 38–9
interest margin approach *see* financial services indirectly measured (FISIM)
interest rates 25, 135–9
intermediate demand, share of services in 20–21
international comparisons, manufacturing 215
International Comparisons Project (ICP) 2–3, 205
International Financial Statistics 271
International Standard Industrial Classification (ISIC) 60
international trade, Brazil 25
investment, as a percentage of GDP 142
investment rates 142–3

labour force
comparisons of changes in composition 11
women in 18–19, 92–3
labour productivity 2, 241, 259
1975 levels 116, 251–4
agriculture 243
Brazil 77, 228–30, 241, 243
comparative performance 1950–96 254–7
education 207–9
financial services 150–51
growth 245–6
health care, 1950–96 181–4
impact of sectoral change 242–6
long term trends 116–18
manufacturing 228–30
Mexico 77, 151, 228–30, 241, 243
USA 77, 228–30, 241
labour productivity growth 22–4
and manufacturing 216
labour reallocation, contribution to economic growth 247–8

labour-force participation, and changes in demographics 18–19
Laspeyres agricultural output measures 213
Laspeyres index 224
Laspeyres PPPs 109
Laspeyres UVRs 112
Laspeyres variance 222
Latin America, GDP 10
Learning Mathematics and Learning Science 190
life expectancy 155
liquidity approach 145
longitudinal analysis 12

M2 to GDP ratio 145
McKinsey Global Institute (MGI) 33–4, 58, 73, 74, 84, 88, 109, 140, 145, 146, 150, 179
manufacturing 215–36, 257
  international comparisons 215
    methodology 220–26
  and labour productivity 228–30
    growth 216
  relative prices and productivity 230–33
  unit labour costs 233–4
  unit value ratios (UVRs) 220–26
Mercosur 216
Mexico
  agriculture 213, 214, 253
  Aztecs 195
  banking 141
    central bank 130
    development banks 130
    regulation 129, 130–32, 133
  capital formation 132
  communications 72
  construction 236–7
  education 187–8, 193, 276
    enrolments 188–90
    expenditure 192
    political obstacles to 201–2
    quality 190–91
    quality of schools 200–201
    teaching quality 200
  education system, history 195–7
  employment 7, 8, 264–5
    in distributive services 107–8
    in education 203
  exchange rates 271
  financial services 124–5, 126–9, 274
  financing budget deficits 139–40
  foreign direct invesment (FDI) 25
  GDP 2, 7, 9, 10, 269
  General Law of Credit Institutions and Auxiliary Organisations (1941) 130
  health care 157, 158, 160–61, 174–5, 275–6
    private 173–4
    problems 174–5
    provision 166
    public health schemes 172
    reform 176
  health outcomes 156
  illiteracy 191–2
  income distribution 16
  inflation 22
  inflation rates 135–6
  informal activity 24, 236
  informal retailing 90–91
  international trade 25
  Jesuits 196
  labour productivity 77, 151, 241
    growth 243
    and manufacturing 228–30
  manufacturing 216, 218
    international comparisons 215, 228
    and labour productivity growth 216
    relative prices and productivity 230–33
    unit labour costs 233–4
  mining 214–15
  Nacional Financiera 264, 269, 272
  national accounts 267, 268
  per capita income 16, 93
  post offices 54
  price deflators, by sector 272
  public utilities 273
  real estate 274–5
  Revolution 128
  Secretaria de Educación Publica 276
  service sector 5, 256
  services, demand for 14
  social security schemes 171
  source notes 269
  SPP (Secretaria de Programación y Resupuesto) 273, 274
  telecommunications 55–7

transport 79, 273
air transport 53, 72
rail transport 66–70
railways 43, 45, 46, 47, 49
road transport 49, 51, 52
freight 70–71
passenger 70
transport firms 52–3
unregistered activity 278–81
urbanisation 19
value added, per person engaged 256
vehicles, stock of 51–2
wholesale and retail trade 83–4, 86–7, 88–9, 97–8, 100, 274
mining 214–15
money supply, role of silver 124

Nacional Financiera, Mexico 264, 269, 272
NAFTA 216
Nakamura, L.I. 103
national accounts
Brazil 267, 268
Mexico 267, 268
national accounts data
and census data, reconciliation 115, 277–81
reconciliation with industrial census data 226–8
transport and communications 75–6
National Bureau of Economic Research 33
Netherlands, national accounts 144, 178

OECD 1, 3, 34, 39, 58, 73, 86, 100, 103, 144, 148, 161, 172, 174, 175, 176, 203, 267, 276
Opera Medicinales 157
opportunity cost of education 40, 205
The Other Path 97
output and productivity levels
banking 143–7
education 203–9
health care 176–84
insurance 147–52
outsourcing 21

Paasche agricultural output measures 213
Paasche index 224
Paasche PPPs 109
Paasche UVRs 112
Paasche variance 222
packaging 101
Pactman Act (1936), US 96
per capita income
Brazil 16, 93
and income distribution 16–17
Mexico 16, 93
PNAD (Pesquisa Nacional por Amostra de Domicilios) 263, 264
population 92, 263
population structure 18
post offices
Brazil 54
Mexico 54
postal companies, output 35, 37
postal services 73
poverty 5
PPPs *see* purchasing power parities
price deflators, by sector 271–2
price indices
financial services 144–5
for medical treatment 178–9
price levels, comparison 250–51
private health care
Brazil 173–4
Mexico 173–4
USA 173–4
productivity, impact of differences in production structure 258–9
productivity growth 2, 259–60
constraining factors, Brazil 24–5
productivity performance 6
and industry of origin approach 4
public health schemes
Brazil 171
Mexico 172
USA 172
public utiltiies 273
purchasing power parities (PPPs) 2, 3, 15, 37
for construction 236
for sales 111

quality-adjusted life years (QUALYs) 39, 178, 179

rail transport
Brazil 66–70

Mexico 66-70
railways 43-49
Brazil 44, 47, 49
impact on transport costs 45
Mexico 43, 45, 46, 47, 49
output measurement 59
transport 57-8
USA 43, 44, 45-6, 47, 49
real estate 274-5
real output measures 39
regulatory environment 24-5
retail sector, and income 93-4
retail services 18
retail trade *see* wholesale and retail trade
risk-assumption model 147-8
risk-pooling model 147-8
road transport 49-53
Brazil 49, 50-51, 70
freight 70-71
Mexico 49, 51, 52, 70-71
passenger 31-2, 70
USA 49-50, 52, 70

Savings and Loans Crisis 25, 133, 134-5
Scandinavian Journal of Economics 33
sectoral change, impact on labour productivity 242-6
sectoral composition changes, and development 11-13
service output
difficulties in defining basic units 31-3
measurement 31-3
quality changes 32-3
research on measurement 33-4
service sector 1, 4, 253, 273-6
Brazil 5
and commodity sector, comparative performance 241-62
developing countries 10
Mexico 5, 256
as a refuge for labour 24
share in employment 22-6
share in final and intermediate demand 14-22
share in GDP 22-6
and urbanisation 19
USA 5
service sectors, comparative performance 241-62
Sherman Antitrust Act (1890), US 96
silver, role in money supply 124
SNA (System of National Accounts) 34, 35, 143, 144, 146, 147, 148, 203
social security schemes
Brazil 169-71
Mexico 171
Stages of Economic Growth 45
Statistical Abstract of the United States
1977 274
1979 273
1991 276
1993 275
Survey of Current Business 265, 269, 272, 276

teacher-based quality index 205
teaching quality 200
telecommunications 251
Brazil 55-7
Mexico 55-7
output 37, 73-4
USA 56-7
Törnqvist index formulae 178
transactions approach 145, 146
transport 251, 273
air 53, 58, 72
international comparisons 59-63
long-term trends 57-8
output and productivity levels in 1975 64-5
rail 66-70
railways 43-9, 57-8, 59
real output measurement 35, 58-63
road 49-53
freight 70-71
passenger 31-2
UVR for 60, 61, 62-3
water 72
transport and communications
census data 75-6
national accounts data 75-6
transport firms, Brazil 52-3
trucking industry 52
tuberculosis (TB) 155

unit labour costs, manufacturing 233-4
unit value ratios (UVRs) 112-14, 248-51
for communications 74-5

for financial services 149
for health care, 1950-96 181–4
for manufacturing 220–26
for transport 60, 61, 62–3, 74–5
United Nations 267
unregistered activity 115, 277
accounting for 278–81
urbanisation
Brazil 19
and demand for distributive services 95
Mexico 19
and the service sector 19
USA 19
USA
agriculture 214
bank failures 133–4
banking
central bank 130
regulation 129–32
supervision 142
system 125, 126–9
Bureau of Labor Statistics 103
Clayton Act (1914) 96
communications 72
Communications Act (1934) 56
construction 236–7
cost disease 26
Deposit Insurance Act 134
Depository Institutions Deregulation and Monetary Control Act (1980) 133
education 187–8, 276
enrolment 188–90
expenditure 192
quality 190
education system, history 197–200
employment 7, 8, 265
Federal Deposit Insurance Corporation (FDIC) 133
Federal Deposit Insurance Corporation Improvement Act (1991) 134
Federal Reserve Act (1913) 131
Federal Savings and Loan Insurance Corporation (FSLIC) 134
Federal Trade Commission Act (1914) 96
finance 274
GDP 7, 9, 269
health care 158, 161–3, 176, 275–6
private health care 173–4
provision 166
public health schemes 172–3
high schools 198–9
higher education 199
Hill-Burton Act (1946) 163
illiteracy 191–2
inflation rates 135, 139
labour productivity 77, 241
and manufacturing 228–30
McFadden Act (1927) 132
manufacturing 216, 219
international comparisons 215, 228
relative prices and productivity 230–33
unit labour costs 233–4
Medicaid 172–3
Medicare 172–3
mining 214–15
Money Market Mutual Funds (MMMFs) 134
Motor Carrier Act 52
National Banking Act (1863) 125, 130
Pactman Act (1936) 96
price deflators, by sector 272
public utilities 273
real estate 274–5
Regulation Q 134, 139
retail 103
Savings and Loan Associations 134–5
service sector 5
services, demand for 14
Sheppard-Towner Act 162
Sherman Antitrust Act (1890) 96
source notes 269
telecommunications 56–7
transport 273
air transport 53, 72
railways 43, 44, 45–6, 47, 49
road 49–50, 52
passenger 70
urbanisation 19
vehicles, stock of 51–2
wholesale and retail trade 83–4, 86, 88, 92, 98–100, 274
user cost approach *see* financial services indirectly measured (FISIM)

value added
per person engaged

Brazil/USA 255
Mexico/USA 256
vehicle stock 51-2
Voorburg Group 34

warehouses 91-2
water transport 72
wholesale and retail trade 251, 253, 274
Brazil 83-4, 86, 88-9, 96-7, 100, 274
comparative output and productivity levels 108-18
comparison of single and double deflation 114-15
double deflation 11-14
single deflation 108-11
employment 83
establishments 83-4, 105
GDP 83
informal retailing 89-91
internationalisation 88-9
long-term trends 83-92
margins 105, 107
Mexico 83-4, 86-7, 88-9, 97-8, 100
retail trade 254
real output measures 37-8
USA 103
scale and scope 98-100
store types 84-8
USA 83-4, 86, 88, 92
vertical integration 88
wholesale trade
employment 107-8
real output measures 37-8
USA 98-100
and value added 107
women, in labour force 18-19, 92-3
working hours 19
World Bank 10, 16, 156, 164
World Economic Indicators 164